DC THROUGH THE '80s

VOLUME ONE

THE END OF ERAS

Edited by **PAUL LEVITZ**

Additional essays by **J.M. DeMATTEIS**
JACK C. HARRIS
ANDY KUBERT
PAUL KUPPERBERG
ELLIOT S! MAGGIN

Collection cover art by **CURT SWAN**
and **MURPHY ANDERSON**

SUPERMAN created by **JERRY SIEGEL** and **JOE SHUSTER**
By special arrangement with the Jerry Siegel family

BATMAN created by **BOB KANE** with **BILL FINGER**

WONDER WOMAN created by **WILLIAM MOULTON MARSTON**

Editors – Original Series	**ROSS ANDRU** **KAREN BERGER** **MURRAY BOLTINOFF** **ALAN GOLD** **JACK C. HARRIS** **JOE KUBERT** **PAUL LEVITZ** **DAVE MANAK** **JOE ORLANDO** **JULIUS SCHWARTZ** **LEN WEIN** **MARV WOLFMAN**
Associate Editor – Original Series	**E. NELSON BRIDWELL**
Group Editor – Collected Editions	**JEB WOODARD**
Editors – Collected Edition	**PAUL LEVITZ** **SCOTT NYBAKKEN**
Design Director – Books	**STEVE COOK**
Publication Design	**CURTIS KING JR.**
Publication Production	**ERIN VANOVER**
Senior VP – Editor-in-Chief, DC Comics	**BOB HARRAS**
Publisher & Chief Creative Officer	**JIM LEE**
VP – Global Publishing Initiatives & Digital Strategy	**BOBBIE CHASE**
VP – Manufacturing Operations & Workflow Management	**DON FALLETTI**
VP – Talent Services	**LAWRENCE GANEM**
Senior VP – Manufacturing & Operations	**ALISON GILL**
Senior VP – Publishing Strategy & Support Services	**HANK KANALZ**
VP – Publishing Operations	**DAN MIRON**
VP – Manufacturing Administration & Design	**NICK J. NAPOLITANO**
VP – Sales	**NANCY SPEARS**
VP – Marketing & Creative Services	**JONAH WEILAND**
VP & Executive Editor, Young Reader	**MICHELE R. WELLS**

Interior color reconstruction by
MICHAEL KELLEHER and **GABRIELA DOWNIE**

DC THROUGH THE '80S: THE END OF ERAS

DC COMICS
2900 West Alameda Ave., Burbank, CA 91505
Printed by LSC Communications, Willard, OH, USA. 11/6/20.
First Printing. ISBN: 978-1-77950-087-8

Library of Congress Cataloging-in-Publication Data is available.

PEFC Certified
This product is from sustainably managed forests and controlled sources
PEFC
PEFC/29-31-337
www.pefc.org

CONTENTS

IN
MEMORIAM

THE END OF AN ERA

Comics were dying—at least, comic books as we had known them for the 50 years since the first magazine-format comics were published during the Great Depression were dying. The newsstands of America, which had been comics' home for so long, were fading away as an effective place to sell comics. (In fact, newsstand sales on *all* magazines were declining, but comics—a traditionally weaker member of the periodical family—were fading faster.)

There were arguments about the causes. The kids who had been the primary audience for comics were watching more television (original cartoons and syndicated reruns were starting to run during after-school hours, so Saturday morning was no longer the only time TV time aimed at children). The country's population was becoming more suburban, and walks past a newsstand en route to shopping or school were being replaced by car-oriented trips. The mom-and-pop retailers who used to be hospitable to comics racks were being replaced by chain stores whose employees were annoyed by kids and messy racks and whose financial people calculated sales per square foot and found comics to be lacking. They were getting too expensive (50 cents an issue!). Maybe the stories just weren't as good as they used to be.

What was inarguable was that the field as generations had known it was going away. Western Publishing, whose titles featuring Disney and Warner Bros. cartoon characters had dominated the industry in the 1950s and early 1960s, gave up on comics and retreated to coloring books. Harvey Comics, whose mainstay *Richie Rich* had lived up to his name in the 1970s and had over 20 different titles published regularly, ran out of cash and closed, ending a family legacy that stretched back to the medium's earliest days. Archie Comics was sustained by reprint digests, racked at the checkout counters of supermarkets for mothers to buy with their latest *National Enquirer*. Marvel and DC were still putting out full lines, but staffers saw that the future of the newsstand was grim.

And that other habitat of print cartooning in America, the newspaper strip, wasn't thriving either. Cities with multiple daily papers were beginning to consolidate down to a single paper per city, and a new national paper, *USA Today*, contained no comics at all and took a very different approach to what a paper should be. The last adventure strips were being launched, and, except for *Spider-Man*, none of them would endure for long.

There was a glimmer of hope in the small number of comic book specialty shops that had opened, at least for the superhero titans. The audience that these shops were attracting and holding was small, but it was made up of older individuals who could travel to the stores without their parents and who were passionate about the material. They knew who the writers and artists were and what was coming out, and they could endlessly debate their preferences. They also seemed to be willing to spend a lot more on comics than the younger kids who had been the primary audience for so long.

In response, publishers began to create comics that better served this new audience: a strategic shift that was both a retreat and an advance at the same time. The industry would no longer aim to reach the whole American kid population but would instead selectively concentrate on their new primary market: young men aged 16-24 who loved comics and would keep the medium alive. Comic books could become more sophisticated and better produced, creative talent could be better paid and treated, and the readers (with any luck) would happily pay for it all. But to achieve these goals, something had to go. There were only so many working comics creators, and only so many titles that the publishers could produce.

And so we come to the theme of this collection: a look at the end days of comics as they were. There'll be two further volumes of *DC Through the '80s* in this series—one devoted to the experiments that resulted from the search for future directions and one focusing on *Crisis on Infinite Earths* and the new DC Universe that emerged in its aftermath. But first, we have to wrap up the past. The six sections presented here look back at the early 1980s through several lenses: the last of the pre-*Crisis* heroes; the mystery anthologies facing their own doom after seeing off so many of their unlucky characters; the war titles finally allowing World War II to end; the less dominant genres like sword and sorcery, science fiction, and westerns closing up shop; a selection of several other unique moments in comics history; and, in the end, a last word (or three) by the best of the emerging writers from the time to usher the old eras into their twilight.

If you were with us at the time, enjoy visiting with some of your old friends. If you weren't around for the early '80s, thanks for taking a moment to join this nostalgia trip. Either way, we appreciate you taking part in the happy ending of comics finding their way to the second Golden Age that is the 21st century.

Paul Levitz
March 2020

Paul Levitz was managing DC's business activities in the early 1980s in addition to writing comics. Over the course of his career he served on the editorial side of the company as well, and he ended his time on staff as DC's president and publisher. For his efforts, he was inducted into the Will Eisner Hall of Fame in 2019.

SUPPLY ROOM
THAT'S JIMMY'S SUPERSONIC SIGNAL! HE'S LANDED IN TROUBLE... AGAIN!
ZEE ZEE
DAILY PLANET EDITORIAL OFFICES
LEVITZ
TUSKA
Colletta

HEROES

By the beginning of the 1980s, the cadre of creators who had filled the pages of DC's superhero comics since the Man of Steel first leaped over a tall building had mostly aged out of the action. On the writing side of the credits, it was all young men in their 20s and 30s taking over; on the art side, a few of the titans of the Silver Age still contributed, but less and less frequently. The themes and story structures that had sustained Earth's protectors were changing, too. Thicker anniversary issues and annuals allowed for longer tales, and even the regular monthly periodicals began to run multi-issue stories as the assumption that readers bought their comics randomly based on the cover art shifted to a conviction that we had regular followers.

The editorial offices were populated by a new breed: comics fans who had grown up to be lords of the universes they loved. Of the old guard who had steered DC from its earliest days, only Julie Schwartz hung in. Most of new editors also doubled as writers, and all were actively encouraging new voices while at the same time delighting in every opportunity to work with

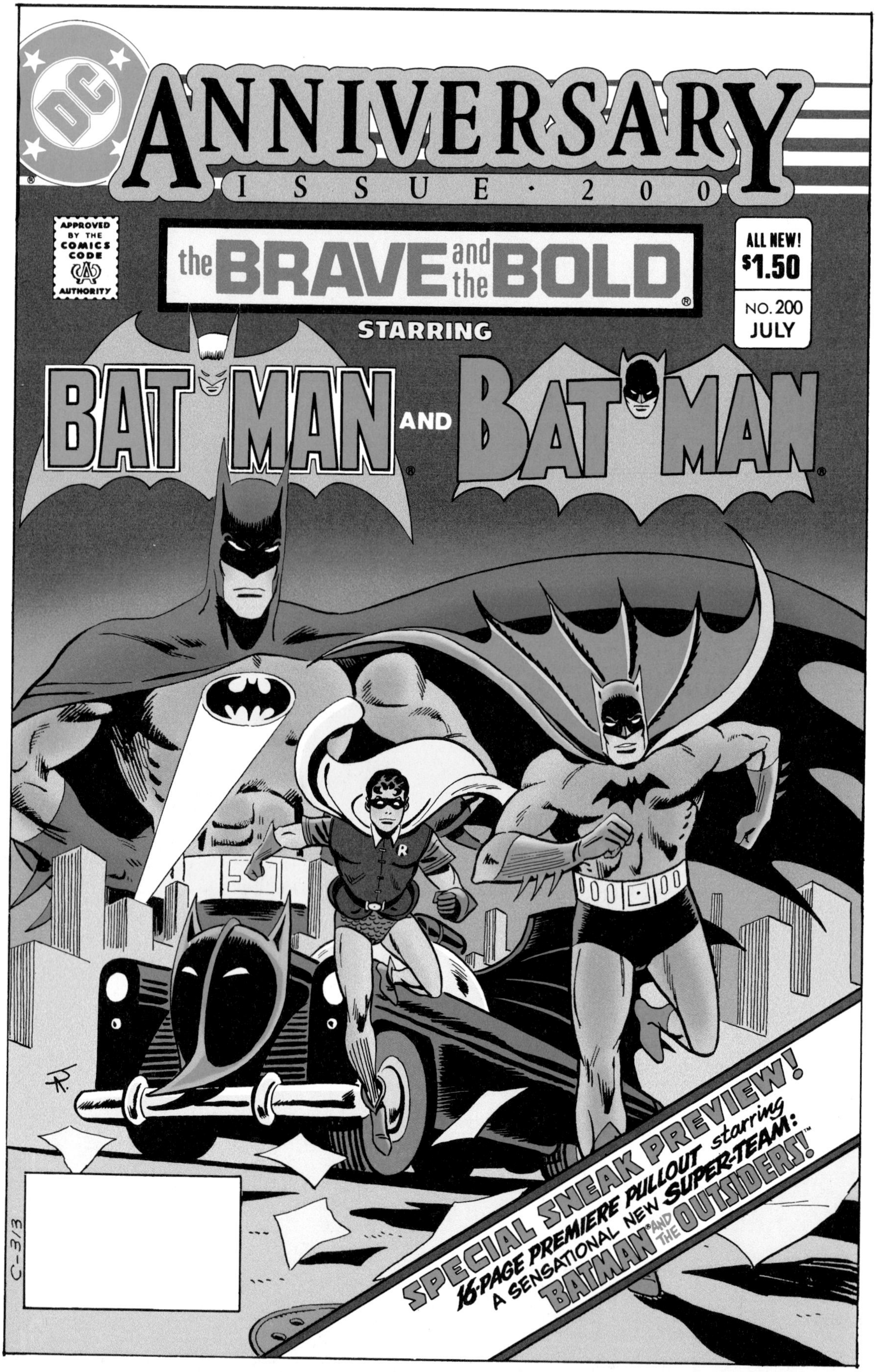
DC
ANNIVERSARY
ISSUE · 200
APPROVED BY THE COMICS CODE AUTHORITY
the BRAVE and the BOLD
ALL NEW! $1.50
NO. 200 JULY
STARRING
BATMAN AND BATMAN
SPECIAL SNEAK PREVIEW!
16-PAGE PREMIERE PULLOUT starring
A SENSATIONAL NEW SUPER-TEAM:
BATMAN AND THE OUTSIDERS!
C-3/3

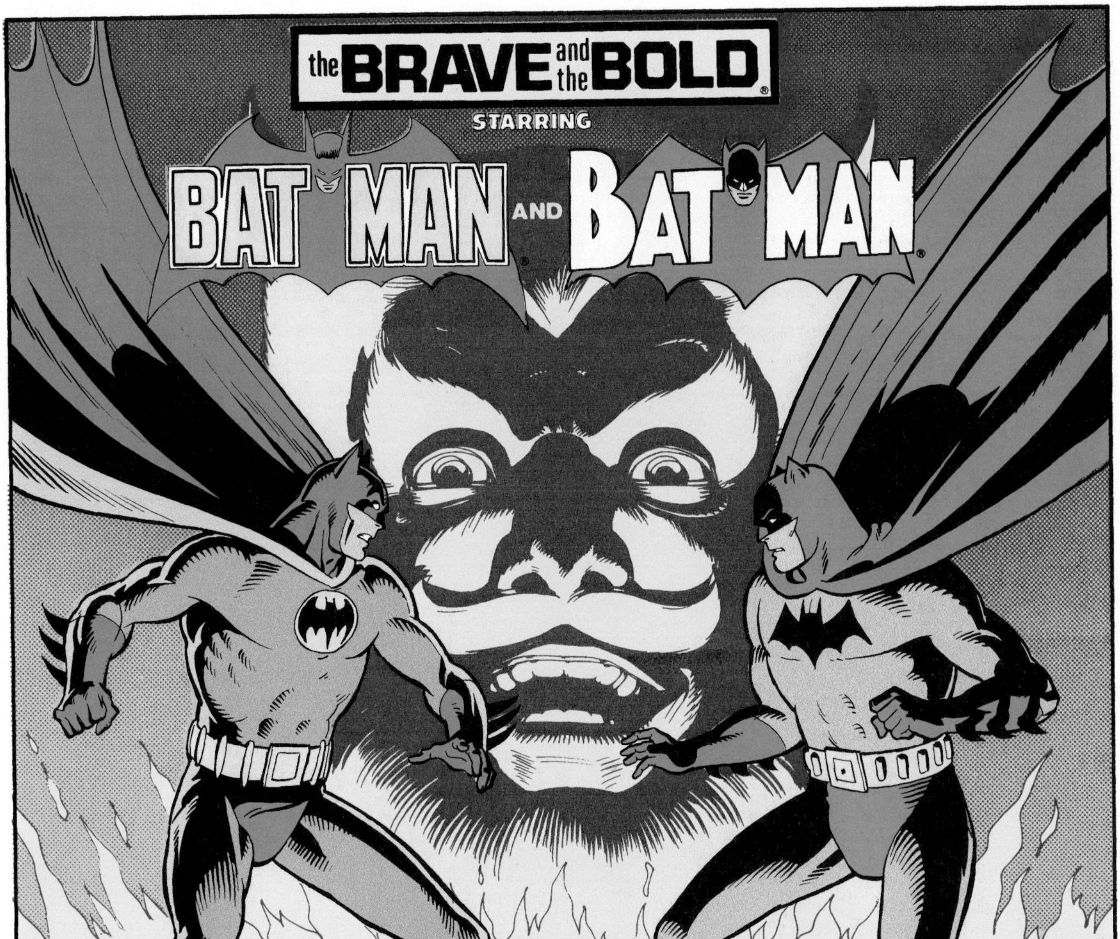
the BRAVE and the BOLD
STARRING
BATMAN AND BATMAN
SMELL OF BRIMSTONE, STENCH OF DEATH!
** An ** ANNIVERSARY CELEBRATION by
MIKE W. BARR Writer
DAVE GIBBONS Artist
GARY MARTIN (PGS. 4-19) Inker
GIBBONS + GASPAR Letterers
ADRIENNE ROY Colorist
LEN WEIN Editor

PROLOGUE
ONLY THE TRULY WISE CAN KNOW WHERE A STORY TRULY BEGINS. THIS STORY, FOR EXAMPLE ...
... DID IT BEGIN AEONS AGO, WHEN PARALLEL EARTHS WERE FUSED FROM STAR-DUST, EACH SEPARATED FROM THE OTHER BY A DIMENSIONAL BARRIER...
...OR DID IT BEGIN AT 5:26 A.M. ON MAY 21, 1933? FOR AT THAT MOMENT, ON EACH EARTH, A CHILD WAS BORN...
...A CHILD WHO KNEW, DEEP IN HIS HEART OF HEARTS, THAT HE WAS NOT ALONE IN THE UNIVERSE...
...FOR SOMEWHERE, ANOTHER OF HIM EXISTED, A COSMIC TWIN WHOSE PHYSICAL FACE WAS INDISCERNABLE FROM HIS OWN...

ONE GLOOMY NIGHT, OUTSIDE AN ABA
MEAT-PACKING PLANT IN GOTHAM
DIS IS DA PLACE, PINSTRIPE! THINK DAT NOTE YOU GOT WAS ON DA LEVEL?
GOTHAM MEAT PACK
DUNNO, JOJO--BUT THERE'S ONLY ONE WAY TO FIND OUT!
SUDDENLY...
YOW! DAT GLOW..!
ALL RIGHT, FREEZE, OR I'LL--
FAMILIAR? SIR, YOU ARE IN THE PRESENCE OF THE MIGHTY BRIMSTONE!
B-BRIMSTONE?
...EACH SIMILAR TO THE OTHER, YET EACH POSSESSING A UNIQUE GROUP OF SUPER-HEROES..?
...THOUGH THE FACES OF THEIR SOULS DIFFERED LIKE NIGHT AND DAY.
FOR ONE NICHOLAS LUCIEN TURNED DOWN THE CRIMSON ROAD OF CRIME...
...WHILE THE OTHER CHANNELLED HIS AGGRESSIONS TOWARD A MORE SOCIALLY ACCEPTABLE PATH.
AND--BECAUSE WE ARE BUT MEN, AFTER ALL--IT IS HERE THAT WE HAVE DECIDED THIS STORY WILL BEGIN.

HE'S BACK! THAT PLUTONIC PL
THAT MODERN MEPHISTOPH
RETURNS TO BEDEVIL GOTHAM
AND TO TAKE REVENGE AGAINST
DYNAMIC DUO! BUT BEFORE
AND ROBIN CAN MAKE THINGS
THEIR OLD FOE, THEY'LL HAVE TO
FIRE and

YOU DARE MOCK ME? MY NAME IS BRIMSTONE, AND--
YER NAME IS MUD IN DIS TOWN, BRIMMY...
"...EVER SINCE BATMAN AND ROBIN PUT YOU AWAY! LOOKS LIKE YER TRYIN' TA PUT A NEW GANG TOGETHER..."
...BUT INCLUDE US OUT! PIN-STRIPE AND ME GOT PLANS'A OUR OWN!
YEAH! BUT IF WE NEED A CAMP-FIRE LIT, WE'LL GIVE YOU A CALL!
FOOLS! CONSIDER THIS AN ACT OF MERCY...
...THAT I DEIGNED TO GIVE YOU A SECOND CHANCE!
HEY!
MY WHITE PHOSPHOROUS PELLETS EXPLODE INTO FLAME ON CONTACT! JUST ONE OF THE MANY IMPROVE-MENTS I'VE MADE IN MY ARSENAL OF CRIME! JUST AS SATAN RULES THE UNDERWORLD, SO SHALL I RULE...
...THE UNDER-WORLD OF GOTHAM CITY!
I SHALL CRUSH ALL WHO OPPOSE ME... BEGINNING WITH BATMAN AND ROBIN!
6

THE FOLLOWING NIGHT, IN THE HOME OF SOCIALITE BRUCE WAYNE, AND HIS WARD, DICK GRAYSON...
THAT'S CHECK AND--UH-OH, THE BAT-SIGNAL! COMMISSIONER GORDON NEEDS US!
THAT'S OKAY WITH ME!
AND AFTER DONNING THEIR FAMED CRIME-FIGHTING GARB, THE DYNAMIC DUO ROARS OFF IN THE MIGHTY BATMOBILE!
WONDER WHAT'S UP, BATMAN?
WE'LL KNOW SOON, ROBIN!
SOON, IN COMMISSIONER GORDON'S OFFICE...
BAD NEWS, BATMAN! BRIMSTONE'S BACK!
I WAS AFRAID WE'D HEAR FROM HIM WHEN HE BROKE OUT OF PRISON! WHAT'S HE UP TO, COMMISSIONER?
HE SENT THIS NOTE, CHALLENGING YOU TO STOP HIS SERIES OF DARING ROBBERIES!
AND THE PACKAGE?
IT'S A BUNCH OF RINGS, BATMAN!
AND THIS SECOND NOTE WAS IN WITH THEM! Hmmm...
Here's a clue to my first crime, BATMAN! It has nine rings, just like Dante's Inferno!
7

YOU'VE GOT TO STOP HIM, BATMAN!
WE'LL DO OUR BEST, eh, ROBIN?
AND SOON...
I'LL BET HE'S ROBBING A JEWELRY STORE, BATMAN! WHAT ELSE COULD A CLUE OF RINGS MEAN?
PERHAPS, ROBIN, BUT THERE'S ANOTHER INTERPRETATION!
YOU SEE? EACH RING IS SMALLER THAN THE OTHER! WHEN ASSEMBLED, THEY FORM A BULLSEYE PATTERN!
GOLLY!
THEN THERE'S ONLY ONE PLACE THEY COULD BE!
WE'RE ON OUR WAY, CHUM!
ACROSS TOWN, AT THE PALATIAL NEW GOTHAM ARENA...
AM ARENA
1955 ARCHERY COMPETITION TONITE!! $50,000 PRIZE
ARCHERY TONITE
AND INSIDE, AT THE ARCHERY COMPETITION...
YOU AIM AT THE TARGET...I AIM AT THE PRIZE!
8

SUDDENLY, LOOMING OVER THE ARENA...
BATMAN AND ROBIN! YOU FIGURED OUT MY CLUE OF RINGS?
SURE WE DID, BRIMSTONE! AND NOW WE'RE GOING TO "RING" THE CURTAIN DOWN-- ON YOU!
NO FAIR SHOOTING AT ME, BRIMSTONE...
...YOU HAVE TO USE A TARGET, LIKE EVERYONE ELSE!
ROBIN HOOD STOPS ROBBING HOODS!
STAND STILL, OR-- URKKKK!
CHIN UP, BRIMSTONE!
BUT THE FIERY BLAST FROM THE HADEAN HIGHWAYMAN'S TRIDENT TRAVELS UPWARD, ACTIVATING THE ARENA'S SPRINKLER SYSTEM!
9

HOW IRONIC! THE MASTER OF FIRE, AIDED BY WATER!
CAN'T STOP FROM SLIPPING..!
BATMAN? UNNNGHHH
DAT'LL KEEP DA BRAT! LET'S MAKE TRACKS, PINSTRIPE!
WAK!
AND LATER...
WE SAVED THE MONEY, BATMAN, BUT WE LOST BRIMSTONE!
WE'LL HAVE ANOTHER CRACK AT BRIMSTONE, ROBIN! HIS NOTE CHALLENGED US TO STOP HIS "SERIES" OF ROBBERIES, REMEMBER?
SURE ENOUGH, THE NEXT NIGHT...
THIS WAS JUST DELIVERED BY MESSENGER!
WHAT IS IT, BATMAN?
LOOKS LIKE A CHARRED PIECE OF PAPER, ROBIN! LET'S RUN A SERIES OF TESTS ON IT IN THE BATCAVE!
SOON, IN THE SUBTERRANEAN BATCAVE...
ANYTHING YET, BATMAN?
E PLURIBUS
ONE CENT
MICROSCOPIC ANALYSIS REVEALS NOTHING, ROBIN! LET'S GO ON...
MINUTES BLEND INTO HOURS, BUT...
CHEMICAL TESTS PROVE NOTHING! I DON'T UNDERSTAND IT!
MAYBE IT'S JUST AN ORDINARY PIECE OF PAPER, BATMAN... LIKE FROM A WASTEBASKET!
ROBIN! THAT'S IT!
10

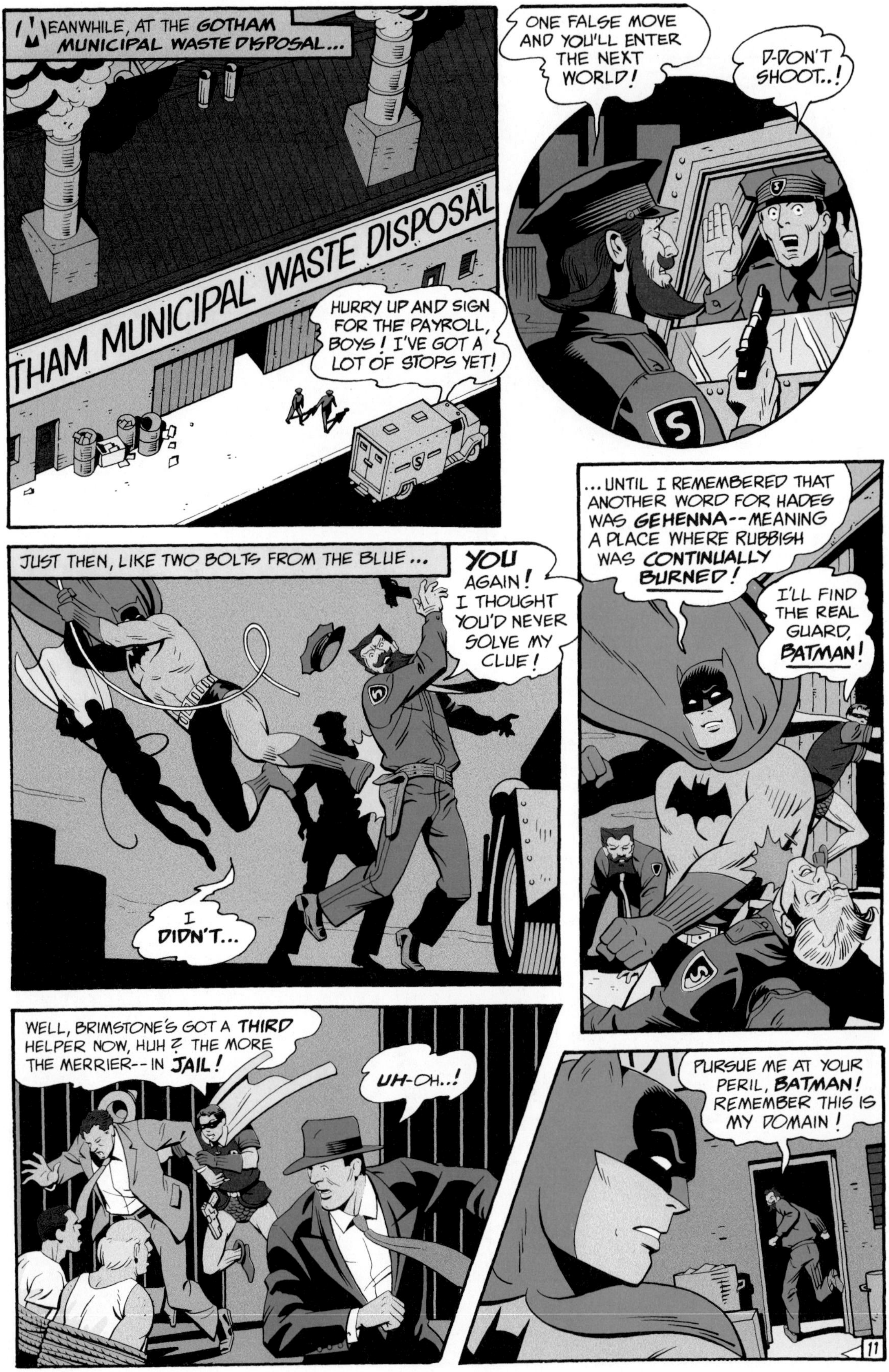
MEANWHILE, AT THE GOTHAM MUNICIPAL WASTE DISPOSAL...
THAM MUNICIPAL WASTE DISPOSAL
HURRY UP AND SIGN FOR THE PAYROLL, BOYS! I'VE GOT A LOT OF STOPS YET!
ONE FALSE MOVE AND YOU'LL ENTER THE NEXT WORLD!
D-DON'T SHOOT..!
JUST THEN, LIKE TWO BOLTS FROM THE BLUE...
YOU AGAIN! I THOUGHT YOU'D NEVER SOLVE MY CLUE!
I DIDN'T...
...UNTIL I REMEMBERED THAT ANOTHER WORD FOR HADES WAS GEHENNA--MEANING A PLACE WHERE RUBBISH WAS CONTINUALLY BURNED!
I'LL FIND THE REAL GUARD, BATMAN!
WELL, BRIMSTONE'S GOT A THIRD HELPER NOW, HUH? THE MORE THE MERRIER--IN JAIL!
UH-OH..!
PURSUE ME AT YOUR PERIL, BATMAN! REMEMBER THIS IS MY DOMAIN!
11

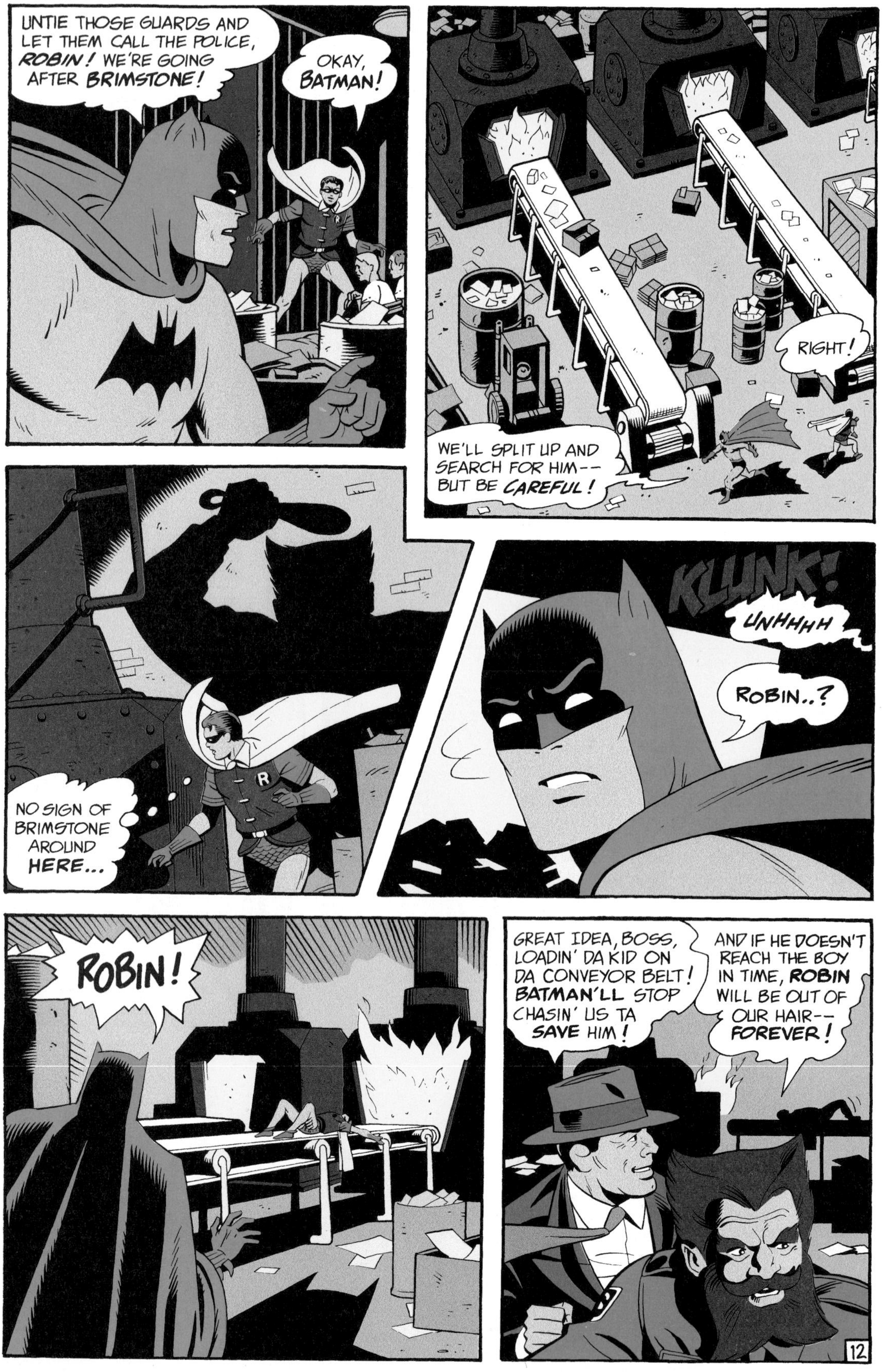
UNTIE THOSE GUARDS AND LET THEM CALL THE POLICE, ROBIN! WE'RE GOING AFTER BRIMSTONE!
OKAY, BATMAN!
RIGHT!
WE'LL SPLIT UP AND SEARCH FOR HIM-- BUT BE CAREFUL!
NO SIGN OF BRIMSTONE AROUND HERE...
KLUNK!
UNHHHH
ROBIN..?
ROBIN!
GREAT IDEA, BOSS, LOADIN' DA KID ON DA CONVEYOR BELT! BATMAN'LL STOP CHASIN' US TA SAVE HIM!
AND IF HE DOESN'T REACH THE BOY IN TIME, ROBIN WILL BE OUT OF OUR HAIR-- FOREVER!
12

UNLEASHING HIS SILKEN BAT-ROPE, THE CAPED CRUSADER LEAPS, SWINGS, AND...
GOT YOU!
B-BATMAN..? OOOOHHH...
ARE YOU ALL RIGHT, CHUM? IF ANYTHING HAPPENED TO YOU--
I-I'LL BE OKAY, BATMAN -KAFF- AS SOON AS I GET INTO A NEW COSTUME! -KAFF- THE SMELL OF THIS ONE'S ABOUT TO KILL ME!
AND AT THE MEAT-PACKING PLANT...
AGAIN HE'S THWARTED ME! I'M AS CUNNING AS SATAN HIMSELF, YET AGAIN HE'S THWARTED ME!
FOOOOSH
T-TAKE IT EASY, BOSS!
IT IS NO LONGER ENOUGH TO CONFOUND AND DEFEAT BATMAN! NO, THERE IS ONLY ONE WAY FOR ME TO REGAIN MY LOST STATUS...
...BATMAN MUST DIE!
AND SO, THE NEXT EVENING...
DID A PACKAGE ARRIVE, COMMISSIONER?
YES, BATMAN, THOUGH I DON'T KNOW HOW YOU CAN MAKE ANY SENSE OUT OF IT!
13

WHY, IT'S JUST AN ORDINARY FISHING LURE... BAIT!
BUT THERE MUST BE HUNDREDS OF BAIT STORES IN GOTHAM CITY, BATMAN! HOW WILL WE FIND THE RIGHT ONE?
THERE ARE MANY BAIT STORES IN THE CITY, ROBIN...
...BUT ONLY ONE THAT SELLS THE AMERICAN INSECT LARVA KNOW AS THE HELLGRAMMITE!
AMAZING!
AND WAITING ATOP THE ROOF OF THE GOTHAM BAIT COMPANY...
DO YA BELIEVE THE PRESIDENT O' THIS COMPANY? HE LIKED FISHIN' SO MUCH HE HAD DIS GIANT FISHIN' ROD INSTALLED HERE!
I JUST HOPE IT'S US WHO ARE BAITIN' A TRAP FOR BATMAN...
GOTHAM BAIT COMPAN
...AND NOT THE OTHER WAY AROUND! ARE YOU SURE HE'LL BE HERE, BOSS?
HE'LL BE HERE.
14

THERE THEY ARE, BATMAN! LET'S GET 'EM!
WAIT, ROBIN--!
I'VE TAKEN A POLE, FELLAS--AND EVERY-ONE'S CARPING ABOUT YOU!
UNNGH!
FOOOSH!
HOW OBLIGING OF YOU TO DROP IN, ROBIN...
THE CABLE, SEVERED BY BRIMSTONE'S FLAME, WINDS GREEDILY AROUND THE BOY WONDER!
CAN'T MOVE..!
...PLEASE DO STAY FOR A WHILE!
GOOD EVENING, BATMAN! I TRUST YOU'LL SURRENDER?
I'LL DO ANYTHING YOU WANT, BRIM-STONE--JUST DON'T HURT THE BOY!
I'VE GOT HIS UTILITY BELT...
AN' I'VE TIED HIS HANDS! WE GONNA VENTILATE 'IM NOW, BOSS?
THAT WOULD BE FAR TOO PROSAIC, JOJO! I HAVE SOMETHING MUCH MORE FITTING IN MIND!
AND BACK AT BRIMSTONE'S HIDEOUT...
AS I'VE TOLD MY MINIONS, BATMAN, THERE'S ONLY ONE WAY FOR ME TO BECOME RULER OF GOTHAM'S UNDERWORLD...
AM MEAT PACKING CO.
CLOSED
15

...BY REMOVING THE GREATEST FORCE ON THE SIDE OF THE ANGELS--YOU!
THIS WAY, BATMAN! I'VE PREPARED A RATHER WARM RECEPTION FOR YOU!
I'M SURE YOU HAVE!
THROUGH THIS DOOR IS YOUR TEST, BATMAN! IF YOU ESCAPE, IT WILL PROVE GOOD IS SUPERIOR TO EVIL!
IF YOU FAIL... WELL...
UNHAPPY LANDIN', BATMAN! HAHAHA
LIKE A STONE, THE CAPED CRUSADER DROPS THROUGH UTTER DARKNESS! AND THEN...
OOF!
FEELS LIKE THE LAST STOP! BETTER GET OUT OF THESE ROPES, AND--
THAT RED GLOW...! AT LEAST I CAN SEE WHERE I AM...
16

...AT THE BOTTOM OF SOME KIND OF PIT! WHATEVER BRIM-STONE'S GOT PLANNED, IT'S NOTHING GOOD!
AND ABOVE...
WE MAY OBSERVE BATMAN'S DEMISE BY THIS MIRROR, ANGLED TO LET US SEE INTO MY DEATH-PIT!
HOLY SMOKE!
"AND HIS DEMISE BEGINS WITH MOLTEN LAVA, HOT AS HADES ITSELF!"
AAAGGGH!
"THERE'S NOWHERE HE CAN GO, BOY! THE WALLS ARE TOO ROUGH TO CLIMB, AND--WHAT'S HE DOING? PULLING OUT THAT NOZ-ZLE WILL ONLY INCREASE THE LAVA FLOW!"
"HE HIDES HIMSELF FROM ME, I WONDER--? BUT NO MATTER. HIS ARE THE LAST ACTS OF A DESPERATE MAN..."
...AND SOON HE SHALL BE A DEAD MAN! HAHAHAHA
NO--NO! BATMAN!
R
17

SUDDENLY...
AN EXPLOSION? BUT HOW..?
I'LL TELL YOU IN A MINUTE, BRIMSTONE-- WHEN YOU'RE THE CAPTIVE AUDIENCE!
BATMAN!
WAK!
"...SO I SNEAKED SOME POTTASIUM NITRATE FROM THOSE ABANDONED SACKS IN THE OUTER ROOM! IT'S USED FOR PRESERVING MEAT... BUT IT'S ALSO ONE OF THE INGREDIENTS OF GUNPOWDER! UNDER COVER OF MY CAPE..."
YOU COULDN'T HAVE ESCAPED! IT WAS IMPOSSIBLE, IT--
IT WAS YOUR OWN VANITY THAT HELPED ME TO ESCAPE, BRIMSTONE! I REASONED ANY DEATH-TRAP YOU'D PREPARE WOULD HAVE A SATANIC THEME...
"...I PICKED THE TWO OTHER INGREDIENTS-- CHARCOAL AND SULPHUR-- FROM THE WALL OF YOUR PIT..."
"...AND DUMPED THEM ALL IN THE CRIMPED NOZZLE I TORE FROM THE PIT! A STRIP TORN FROM MY COSTUME PROVIDED THE FUSE..."
"...AND I HAD A CRUDE BOMB! CRUDE... BUT IT WORKED!
18

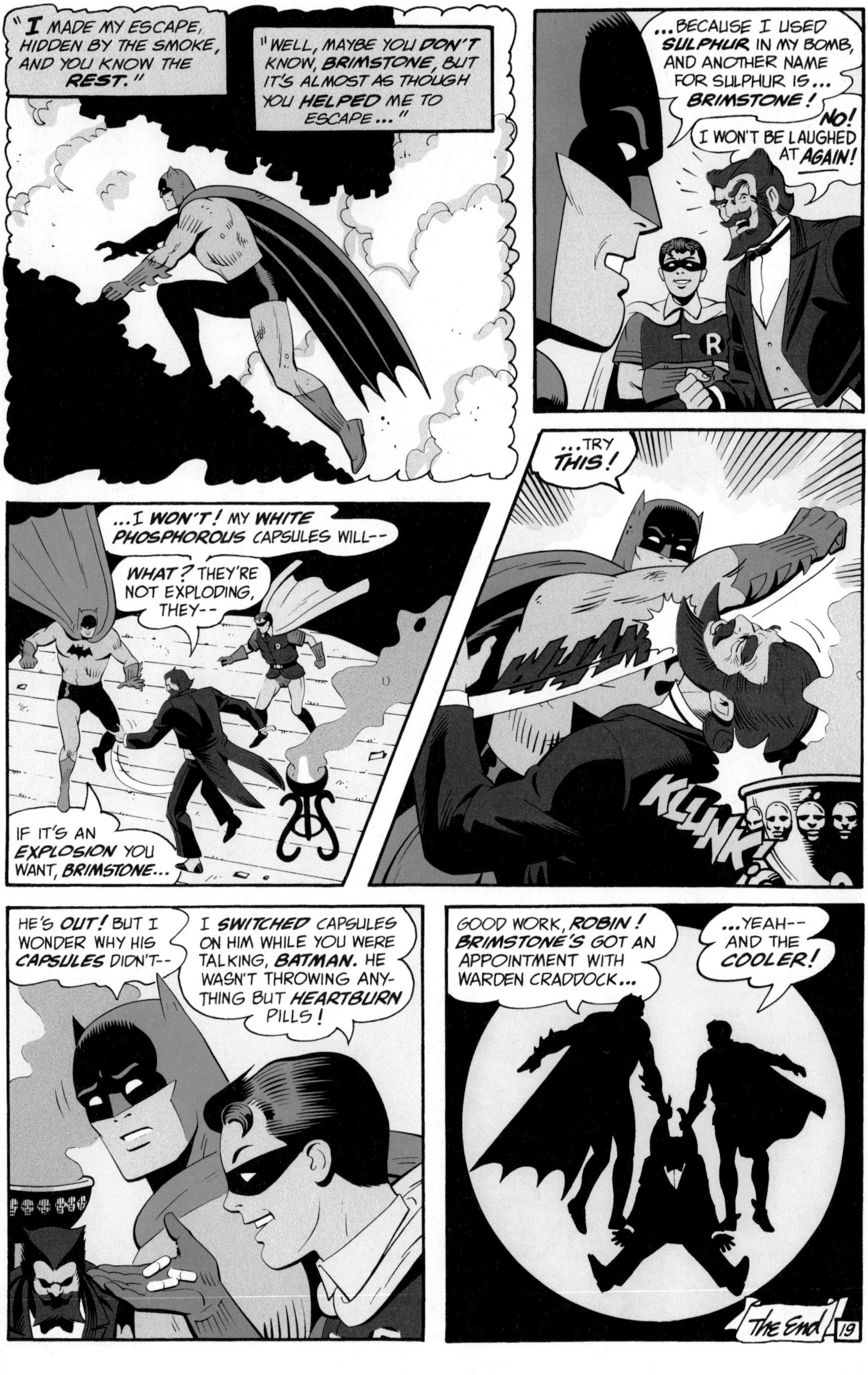
"I MADE MY ESCAPE, HIDDEN BY THE SMOKE, AND YOU KNOW THE REST."
"WELL, MAYBE YOU DON'T KNOW, BRIMSTONE, BUT IT'S ALMOST AS THOUGH YOU HELPED ME TO ESCAPE..."
...BECAUSE I USED SULPHUR IN MY BOMB, AND ANOTHER NAME FOR SULPHUR IS... BRIMSTONE!
NO! I WON'T BE LAUGHED AT AGAIN!
...I WON'T! MY WHITE PHOSPHOROUS CAPSULES WILL--
WHAT? THEY'RE NOT EXPLODING, THEY--
IF IT'S AN EXPLOSION YOU WANT, BRIMSTONE...
...TRY THIS!
WHAK
KLONK!
HE'S OUT! BUT I WONDER WHY HIS CAPSULES DIDN'T--
I SWITCHED CAPSULES ON HIM WHILE YOU WERE TALKING, BATMAN. HE WASN'T THROWING ANY-THING BUT HEARTBURN PILLS!
GOOD WORK, ROBIN! BRIMSTONE'S GOT AN APPOINTMENT WITH WARDEN CRADDOCK...
...YEAH-- AND THE COOLER!
The End
19

INTERLUDE
1983
OKAY, I'M COMIN'!
GOTHAM STATE PRISON
STOP AT GATE
STOP
HONK HONK
ALL RIGHT, I'LL NEED TO SEE SOME I.D., AND --
GOOD EVENING, SAM.
SORRY, DR. LINCOLN, DIDN'T RECOGNIZE THE CAR. MEAN NIGHT, HUH?
FOR SOME OF US, SAM... FOR OTHERS, IT MAY BE A VERY GOOD NIGHT!
...AND YOU THINK THIS SERUM OF YOURS WILL CURE NICHOLAS LUCIEN, DOCTOR?
'CURE' ISN'T QUITE THE PROPER TERM, WARDEN CRADDOCK...
...WHAT I HOPE TO DO IS STIMULATE THAT PORTION OF HIS BRAIN THAT'S BEEN IN A COMA FOR 28 YEARS...
WHEN HE STRUCK HIS HEAD FIGHTING BATMAN. I REMEMBER.
LUCIEN 3047
POOR FELLOW'S BEEN LIKE THAT FOR A QUARTER-CENTURY, DOCTOR -- ISN'T IT CRUEL TO BRING HIM OUT?
SOCIETY HAS THE RIGHT TO IMPRISON HIS BODY, WARDEN...
...BUT EVERY MIND HAS THE RIGHT TO BE FREE!
W-WHAT...
20

DON'T TRY TO TALK, MR. LUCIEN. JUST REST.
WELCOME BACK, LUCIEN.
F-FEEL SO... STRANGE... WHAT'S HAPPENED TO ME?
MY HANDS? WHAT...
WHAT'S HAPPENED TO ME?
PUT SIMPLY, NICHOLAS LUCIEN'S BODY HAS ALMOST TOTALLY ATROPHIED, 'SHUT DOWN' FROM YEARS OF DISUSE...
HE COULDN'T GO TO THE BATHROOM BY HIMSELF. BUT HE COULD STILL THINK...
...AND HOW HE COULD HATE!
I WAS A YOUNG MAN WHEN BATMAN DID THIS TO ME... BUT HE'LL PAY...
I WOULDN'T COUNT ON THAT, PRUNE-FACE...
...UNLESS YOU'VE GOT A TERRIFIC COLLECTION AGENCY!
HA HA HA
HERE, HAVE A READ. IT'S COLD OFF THE PRESS...
BUT LIKE THEY SAY, ANY BOOK YOU HAVEN'T READ IS A NEW BOOK!
HA HA HA
GOTHAM GLOBE
BATMAN DEAD!
21

ALONE NOW, IN THE SILENCE, HE CAN FEEL HIMSELF WITHERING, DYING.
HIS HATE IS ALL THAT HAS KEPT HIM ALIVE THESE PAST DAYS, PERHAPS THESE PAST THREE DECADES.
BUT NOW EVEN THAT BEGINS TO PALE.
HOW LONG CAN HATE SURVIVE, WHEN THE HATED ONE IS DEAD?
THEN HE REMEMBERS...
...UNEARTHS LONG-BURIED MEMORIES OF ANOTHER NICHOLAS, SOMEWHERE...
...AND IF THERE IS ANOTHER NICHOLAS, MAY THERE NOT BE ANOTHER HATED ONE?
YES.
YOU OKAY, LUCIEN? IF YOU WANNA GLASS 'A WATER OR SOMETHIN', I'LL --
LUCIEN?
I DON'T UNDERSTAND THIS.
IS IT THE COMA AGAIN, DOCTOR?
NO, WARDEN, IT'S ALMOST AS THOUGH HIS MIND IS...
...GONE.
22

APRIL 24, 1983. NOON
JESUS, RISEN FROM THY TOMB...
SAVE US FROM PAIN AND SIN--
AND DOOM.
2:00 P.M.
YOU HEAR ABOUT THAT CHURCH UPTOWN?
SÍ, A GREAT TRAGEDY. WHO WOULD BE EVIL ENOUGH TO--
SOCIETÁ HISPÁNICA
WHOOOM
6:00 P.M.
THEN WE ARE AGREED, GENTLEMEN..?
WE MUST SHOW THE COMMUNITY THAT WE STAND TOGETHER, AND...
AND DIE TOGETHER.
23

6:30 P.M.
JOAN LINCOLN, BEFORE GOTHAM POLICE HEAD-QUARTERS, WHERE AN ANGRY CROWD HAS GATHERED TO DEMAND THE BOMBER'S CAPTURE.
HEADQUARTERS
POLICE
BUT RIOTERS AND LOOTERS MAY DO MORE DAMAGE THAN THE BOMBER HIMSELF. TO THIS END, THE CITY COUNCIL HAS SUMMONED THREE NATIONALLY-KNOWN FIGURES TO REQUEST AN END TO THE VIOLENCE...
GT
...THE REVEREND SAMUEL BRIDGEMAN KNIGHT, CIVIL RIGHTS LEADER AND PACIFIST...
CARLOTTA HERNANDEZ, WIDOW OF SLAIN LABOR LEADER FRANCISCO HERNANDEZ...
AND RABBI DAVID KLINE, FORMER WAR RESISTER AND CIVIL DISOBEDIENT. THEY'LL MAKE A SPECIAL BROADCAST TO ALL GOTHAM CITY AT MIDNIGHT.
LIBERT
COMMISSIONER GORDON... MIDNIGHT IS A LONG WAY OFF-- WHAT ARE YOU DOING TO STOP THE RIOTS, AND THE BOMBING?
MY MEN ARE WELL-INSTRUCTED IN RIOT-TECHNIQUE, MISS LINCOLN, AND WILL CALM THE VIOLENCE WITHOUT ADDING TO IT. AS FOR THE BOMBER...
...I'VE PUT THE BEST MAN I KNOW ON IT.
24

SO, BRUCE, AFTER MONTHS OF WAITING, I'VE FINALLY GOT YOU ALL TO MYSELF..!
THAT YOU HAVE, CLARISSE.
WE'LL WIND UP AT MY PLACE, OF COURSE, BUT WE'VE GOT THE WHOLE EVENING AHEAD OF US TO-- BRUCE ?
I'M SORRY, CLARISSE...
...BUT I HAVE TO LEAVE. SOME OTHER TIME, PERHAPS ?
BUT...
NOW WHAT GOT INTO HIM ?
BRUCE WAYNE IS GONE --AND ARCING THROUGH THE NIGHT IN HIS PLACE IS THE DREAD...
BATMAN®
...IN A CONTEST WITH PERHAPS THE ULTIMATE EVIL, TO PREVENT GOTHAM CITY FROM BECOMING...
HELL ON EARTH!
25

COMMISSIONER?
BATMAN! I DIDN'T HEAR--
--BUT THEN, I NEVER DO!
THE BOMBER SENT THIS NOTE...
DON'T WANT MONEY, ONLY GOTHAM'S DEATH. JUST WANTED YOU TO KNOW
...FOR ALL THE GOOD IT DOES US. IS THE WORLD GOING MAD, BATMAN?
DON'T WANT MONEY, ONLY GOTHAM'S DEATH. JUST WANTED YOU TO KNOW
NOT THE WORLD, COMMISSIONER-- JUST THE PEOPLE IN IT.
I'LL BE IN TOUCH.
THANK YOU, BATMAN...
...I KNOW YOU'LL DO YOUR BEST...
...BUT THIS TIME, I WONDER IF EVEN THAT WILL BE ENOUGH.
26

9:30 P.M.
...REPORT OVER 200 DEAD IN RIOTS ACROSS THE CITY...
...WITH NO END IN SIGHT.
MY WORD.
MASTER BRUCE? I'VE PREPARED SOME NOURISHMENT FOR YOU, SIR...
...HAS YOUR RESEARCH BORNE ANY FRUIT, SIR?
I THINK SO, ALFRED-- IN MORE WAYS THAN ONE. THIS NOTE HAS SPECKS OF A POWDER GROUND FROM THE HELLEBORE FLOWER ON IT...
...AND ONCE I'VE ENTERED THAT INFORMATION INTO THE COMPUTER...,
...I'LL KNOW EXACTLY HOW MANY LABORATORIES IN GOTHAM CITY PROCESS THAT POWDER.
NOT MANY. EXCELLENT.
SEE YOU LATER, ALFRED. DON'T WAIT UP.
GODSPEED, MASTER BRUCE! I--
MASTER BRUCE! YOUR NOURISHMENT..!
27

9:45 P.M.
"...AND THERE SHALL BE WEEPING, AND WAILING, AND GNASHING OF TEETH..." THE BIBLICAL DESCRIPTION OF HELL APPLIES TO GOTHAM TONIGHT, TOO!
GORDON'S MEN ARE HOLDING THEIR OWN, BUT THEY COULD USE SOME HELP...
...HELP I DON'T HAVE TIME TO GIVE RIGHT NOW!
THE RIOTING...THE DESTRUCTION...AND THE MAN BEHIND IT DOESN'T EVEN WANT MONEY-- OR NOTORIETY!
I'VE NEVER MET AN ENEMY WHO'S COME AS CLOSE TO MY DEFINITION OF PURE EVIL. OF COURSE, THIS WHOLE CHARADE WITH THE NOTE IS A TRAP...
...AND OF COURSE, I'M GOING TO SPRING IT!
THERE'S THE FIRST NAME ON MY LIST... BUT NICHOLAS LUCIEN IS AN OUTSTANDING CIVIC LEADER--IS HE MIXED UP IN THIS?
LUCIEN CHEMICAL CO
I'M NOT CERTAIN I COULD DE-ACTIVATE HIS BURGLAR ALARM WITH MY EYES CLOSED...
...BUT IF THERE WEREN'T SO MUCH AT STAKE, I WOULDN'T MIND TRYING!
LOOKS NORMAL ENOUGH ...BUT IF THIS WAS A TRAP, I'D SNAP IT SHUT RIGHT ABOUT--
UH HUH.
28

AT FIRST, THE SOUNDS COME SOFTLY, LIKE THE MEREST WHISPER OF WIND ON CREPE. THEN THE SOUNDS BECOME FORMS, GIVEN SUBSTANCE BY THE LIGHT...
...AND THE BATMAN KNOWS HE IS NOT ALONE.
CAN'T TELL HOW MANY OF THEM THERE ARE WITH THAT LIGHT IN MY EYES...
...SO I'LL JUST HAVE TO PULL ITS PLUG.
KRASSSSH
GOOD EVENING, BATMAN. MY NAME IS...IS...BRIMSTONE, AND I AM YOUR HOST.
YOUR FIRST TASK IN OUR REMATCH IS TO FIGHT YOUR WAY PAST THESE GENTLEMEN...AND...AND FIND ME!
REMATCH? BUT WE'VE NEVER--
SHOULD YOU...FAIL TO FIND ME...
...MY FINAL STROKE WILL FAN THE FLAMES OF VIOLENCE THAT SEAR THIS TOWN...
29

...AND NOTHING WILL SAVE GOTHAM!
VOICE DOESN'T SOUND LIKE ANY OF MY OLD ENEMIES...
GET 'IM!
...AND THAT ODD HESITATION--ALMOST AS IF HE'S BEING MADE TO SPEAK AGAINST HIS WILL!
SHAKKKT
HEY, LEGGO MY--
--CHAIN! UNNNGG
THESE SELF-STYLED 'DEMONS' ARE TOUGH, BUT I'VE GOT AN EDGE THEY NEVER THOUGHT OF!
THEY'RE USED TO 'RUMBLING' WITH OTHER GANGS, SO WHEN THEY TRY TO TAKE ONE MAN...
...THEY MAY DO MORE DAMAGE TO EACH OTHER...
LOOK OUT--!
YOU FREAKIN' DOPE..!
BANG
SORRY, MAN--!
SORRY? YUH SHOOT ONE'A YER GANG BROTHERS, AN' YUH SAY YER SORRY?
GAKKK
...THAN THEY DO TO ME.
30

THESE GOONS ARE NO MATCH FOR ME, BRIMSTONE--
--WE BOTH KNOW THAT!
PER-PERHAPS, BATMAN--BUT MY DEMONS ARE WASTING YOUR PRECIOUS TIME...
DON'T KNOW WHAT THAT LAST PART MEANS...
...AND THAT, YOU CANNOT REPLACE--AS I WELL KNOW!
...BUT HE'S RIGHT ABOUT WASTING TIME! ONLY A FEW OF THESE LICE LEFT...
...SO I'LL END THIS...
...WITH A LITTLE BOXING --OF MY OWN DESIGN!
AGGGH--!
KRAAASH
31

WHAT NEXT, BRIMSTONE?
NEXT, MY OLD FOE, YOU MUST FIND ME.
TO THAT END, I HAVE PLANTED A CLUE TO MY WHEREABOUTS ON ONE OF THESE GENTLEMEN...
...YOU NEED ONLY FIND IT... TO FIND ME.
BRIMSTONE, THIS ISN'T A GAME! IF YOU WANT ME, JUST--
KLIK
DEAD. HAVE TO PLAY THIS HIS WAY.
A CLUE, HE SAID...
...NO TIME FOR THOROUGH ANALYSIS--IT WOULD HAVE TO BE SOMETHING READILY APPARENT, WITHOUT BEING OBVIOUS...
...A BOOK..?
ONE OF THESE CAVE-MEN IS CARRYING A BOOK?
NOTHING HIDDEN IN THE PAGES... AGAIN, THE CLUE MUST BE APPARENT WITHOUT--
32

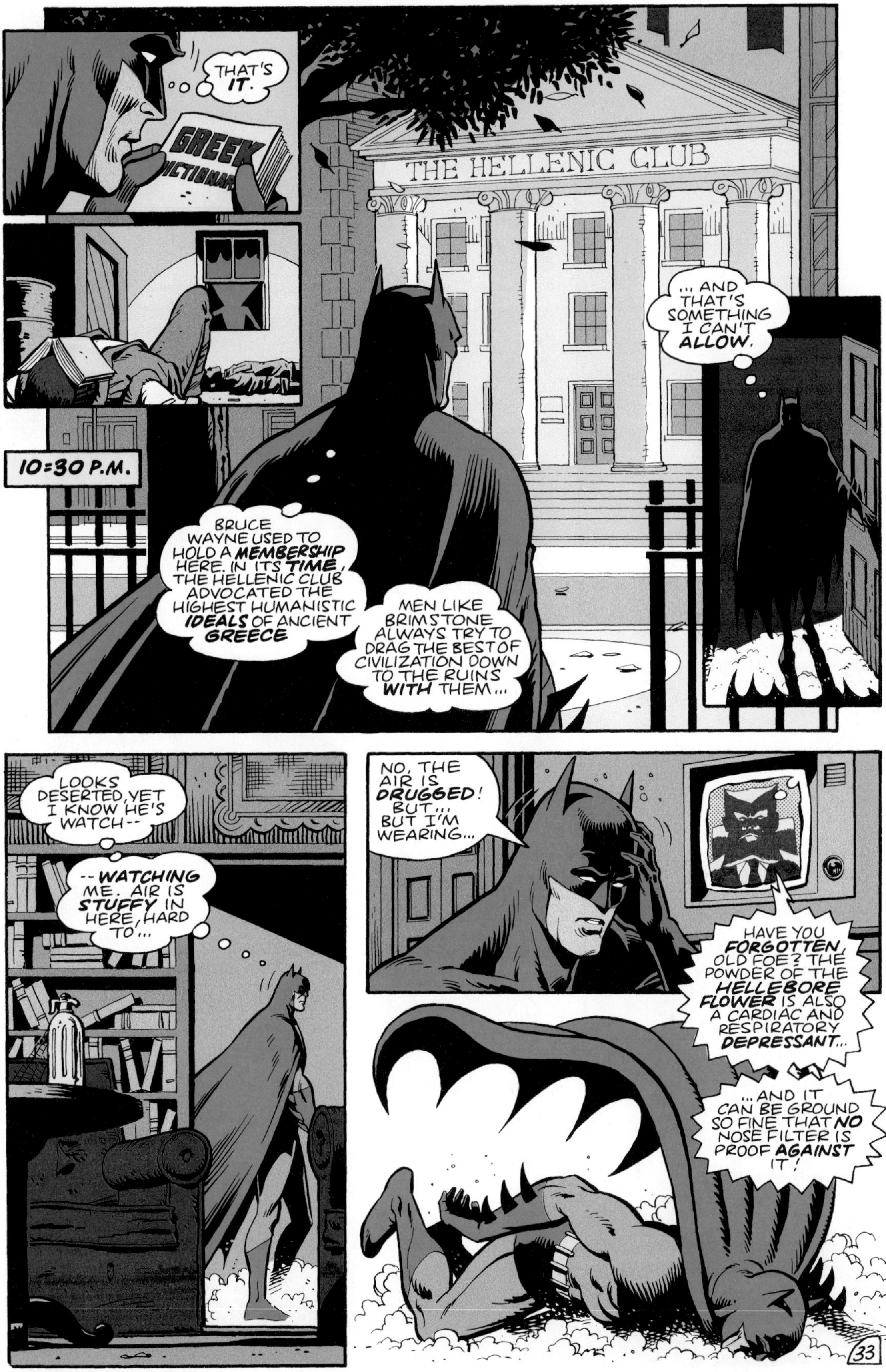
THAT'S IT.
GREEK DICTIONARY
THE HELLENIC CLUB
10:30 P.M.
BRUCE WAYNE USED TO HOLD A MEMBERSHIP HERE. IN ITS TIME, THE HELLENIC CLUB ADVOCATED THE HIGHEST HUMANISTIC IDEALS OF ANCIENT GREECE
MEN LIKE BRIMSTONE ALWAYS TRY TO DRAG THE BEST OF CIVILIZATION DOWN TO THE RUINS WITH THEM...
...AND THAT'S SOMETHING I CAN'T ALLOW.
LOOKS DESERTED, YET I KNOW HE'S WATCH--
--WATCHING ME. AIR IS STUFFY IN HERE, HARD TO...
NO, THE AIR IS DRUGGED! BUT... BUT I'M WEARING...
HAVE YOU FORGOTTEN, OLD FOE? THE POWDER OF THE HELLEBORE FLOWER IS ALSO A CARDIAC AND RESPIRATORY DEPRESSANT...
...AND IT CAN BE GROUND SO FINE THAT NO NOSE FILTER IS PROOF AGAINST IT!
33

11:45 P.M.
WELCOME BACK, OLD FOE. IN 15 MINUTES IT WILL PLEASE ME TO BLOW UP MIDNIGHT'S 'RACIAL UNITY BROADCAST'...
...THUS PLUNGING GOTHAM CITY INTO AN INFERNO OF VIOLENCE THAT WILL IMMOLATE IT! YOU'LL TRY TO STOP ME, BUT YOU WON'T...
...FOR I'VE IMPROVED MY HELLPIT. YOU'LL NOT ESCAPE THIS TIME, BATMAN. YOU'LL LOSE YOUR LIFE...
...AND GOTHAM WILL LOSE HERS.
'THIS TIME?' WHAT DOES HE--
THEN THE ORDEAL BEGINS ANEW...
SSSSS
? LAVA, AND SOME SORT OF NOXIOUS GAS. ALREADY GETTING HARD TO BREATHE.
LOOK EVERYWHERE FOR AN ESCAPE, BATMAN ...BUT YOU'LL FIND NONE...
...FOR THIS HELLPIT IS WITHOUT THE MINERALS USED TO MAKE GUNPOWDER. HOWEVER, IT WILL MAKE A MOST SUITABLE TOMB.
TEN MINUTES TO MIDNIGHT, PEOPLE--EVERYONE READY?
WE ARE, SIR.
IT--IT'S TAKEN TWENTY-EIGHT YEARS, BATMAN--
--AND IT'S WORTH EVERY DAY OF IT!
34

GOT TO FORGET BRIMSTONE AND HIS RAVINGS... CONCENTRATE ON SAVING MYSELF -- AND GOTHAM!
RRRRP
GAS IS GETTING TO ME, BUT LAVA IS THE IMMEDIATE DANGER...
... BUT IF THIS WORKS, I'LL HAVE AT LEAST A CHANCE OF ESCAPING!
LAVA CAN'T PENETRATE THE PIT'S INSULATION, SO THIS LITTLE RAFT WILL KEEP ME ON TOP OF IT FOR A WHILE...
...BUT IT'S ALREADY BUCKLING! IF I CAN JUST KEEP MY WEIGHT SHIFTED..!
INGENIOUS, BATMAN, BUT FUTILE, UTTERLY--
LEAVE ME, USURPER! THIS IS MY LIFE!
YOU'VE NO RIGHT...
NO! I'LL NOT LEAVE! THIS DAY, I'LL SEE THE DEATH OF MY TWO DEADLIEST ENEMIES...
...THE BATMAN AND MY OTHER SELF!
35

YOU MAY ACHIEVE THE TOP OF MY PIT, BATMAN--BUT THERE IS NO EXIT! YOU ARE DOOMED, YOU--
? WHAT IS HE DOING, HE--
THE CAMERA ...IT'S GONE DEAD! BUT--
WHOOOM
NO! NOT AGAIN!
ONCE HAS BEEN QUITE ENOUGH, BRIMSTONE!
IT'S NOT OVER YET..!
WHEN I PRESS THAT BUTTON, THE TV STUDIO WILL EXPLODE...
...AND WITH IT--GOTHAM CITY!
36

DON'T EVEN TRY, BRIMSTONE --OR LUCIEN-- OR WHATEVER YOU CALL YOURSELF!
UNNNGH!
YOU'RE ON!
BROTHERS AND SISTERS OF GOTHAM, DO AS OUR SAVIOR WOULD HAVE YOU DO.
THROW DOWN THE TOOLS OF VIOLENCE...
...INSTEAD, RECEIVE THE DOVE OF PEACE.
YOU'RE MY EQUAL IN BRAINS--MY SUPERIOR IN CUNNING...
...BUT WHEN IT COMES TO SHEER FORCE--
--THERE'S NO CONTEST!
KRAK
DON'T THINK GOTHAM HAS EVER HAD A CLOSER CALL...
...I KNOW I NEVER HAVE...
37

COULDN'T SEE ANY WAY OUT OF HIS PIT -- UNTIL HE MENTIONED GUNPOWDER. THAT BROUGHT TO MIND EXPLOSIONS...
"... AND I REALIZED THAT THE GAS PRODUCED BY THE LAVA MIGHT BE EXPLOSIVE. BUT I NEEDED A SPARK...
"... AND BY REACHING THE TV CAMERA, AND TOUCHING TWO STRIPPED WIRES TOGETHER, I HAD ONE!"
THE EXPLOSION BLEW THE PIT OPEN, AND --
WHERE AM I?
BATMAN? WHAT ARE YOU DOING HERE?
I REMEMBER A FEELING OF BEING CAGED... A PRISONER IN MY OWN MIND... BUT NOW I'M FREE.
I'LL TAKE YOU TO SOME PEOPLE WHO CAN HELP YOU, MR. LUCIEN.
HIS TONE IS TOTALLY SINCERE. I'D BET MY LIFE HE'S NOT FAKING.
BATMAN, DO YOU BELIEVE ME?
I DON'T KNOW, MR. LUCIEN. BUT I NEVER USED TO BELIEVE IN POSSESSION, EITHER.
NOW I'M NOT SO SURE.
END
38

EPILOGUE
DO YOU THINK THIS IS SOME SORT OF SIDE-EFFECT OF THE COMA, DR. LINCOLN?
I DON'T KNOW, WARDEN. HIS BRAIN READINGS ARE PERFECTLY NORMAL AGAIN...
...BUT NOW HE'S TOTALLY PARALYZED.
CAN YOU KEEP HIM ALIVE, DOCTOR?
FOR YEARS, WARDEN. THERE'S NO REASON WHY HE SHOULDN'T LIVE OUT HIS NATURAL LIFE-SPAN.
POOR FELLOW. I'D RATHER DIE THAN LIVE THROUGH THE HELL HE'S GOING THROUGH NOW.
THE RIOTS HAVE STOPPED, THE CITY IS RELATIVELY QUIET...
LUCIEN'S ORDEAL SEEMS TO BE OVER, TOO.
AT LEAST, HE PASSED THE MOST SOPHISTICATED LIE-DETECTOR TESTS. I KNOW I BELIEVE HIM--
--IT'S ALMOST AS THOUGH HIS BODY REALLY WAS BEING USED BY... BY ANOTHER FORCE.
CE
I DON'T SUPPOSE I'LL EVER REALLY KNOW WHAT WENT ON...
39

...I ONLY KNOW THAT I FEEL LIKE I'VE FACED MY GREATEST CHALLENGE...
...AND I WON.
In Memoriam: The BRAVE and the BOLD 1955-1983
40

WONDER WOMAN
75¢
311
JAN. 84
APPROVED BY THE COMICS CODE AUTHORITY
GREAT HERA! GREMLINS?
ANDRU + GIORDANO

CALLING ROBOT PLANE... ROBOT PLANE, COME TO ME!
IN ATHENA'S NAME, WHERE ARE YOU?!
Y'HEAR THAT WHOOSHING, WENDELL? IT MUST BE WONDER WOMAN'S INVISIBLE JET!
OH, HAROLD, TAKE A SNAPSHOT OF IT!
MILDRED, IT'S INVISIBLE!
HOW AM I SUPPOSED TO TAKE ITS PICTURE?!
SOMETHING'S WRONG HERE! I'M NOT IN CONTROL OF ITS FLIGHT PATH!
AND IT LOOKS LIKE IT'S ON--
... A STRAFING RUN!
ALL YOU PEOPLE, HIT THE DIRT!
MY PLANE'S GONE WILD!

SHE WAS BORN A PRINCESS-- DAUGHTER OF HIPPOLYTA, QUEEN OF THE AMAZONS-- BUT SHE LEFT THE TRANQUIL GROVES OF PARADISE ISLAND TO BATTLE EVIL IN A WORLD SHE NEVER MADE! SHE IS BEAUTIFUL AS APHRODITE... WISE AS ATHENA... STRONGER THAN HERCULES... SWIFTER THAN MERCURY!
SHE IS...
WONDER WOMAN®
MERCIFUL MINERVA! SOMEBODY'S CONTROLLING THE PLANE ALL RIGHT!
SOMEBODY OR SOME THING!
GREMLINS!
DAN MISHKIN WRITER
DON HECK ARTIST
BEN ODA LETTERER
NANSI HOOLAHAN COLORIST
ALAN GOLD EDITOR
2

WHATEVER THAT CREATURE IS, IT'S NOT GETTING AWAY WITH THIS!
I WON'T HAVE MY OWN PLANE NEARLY TAKING MY HEAD OFF!
...OR ENDANGER-ING INNOCENT PEDESTRIANS!
I SEE IT! I SEE IT, ALICE!
THANK ARTEMIS MY AIM IS TRUE!
I'VE GOT HOLD OF IT NOW AND I'M NOT LETTING GO!
IT WILL ONLY TAKE A FEW MOMENTS TO CLIMB MY MAGIC LASSO AND THEN I'LL--
GREAT HERA! WHAT'S THAT IMP UP TO NOW?!
WALKING ON THE OUTSIDE OF THE JET--? THAT'S MY ROUTINE!
IBIDDY-HIP B'DEE!
HIH HIH HIH HIH
OH NO!
3

HE SET ME LOOSE JUST WHEN I ALMOST HAD HIM!
AND HE SEEMS TO THINK IT'S FUNNY!
WELL AS FAR AS I'M CONCERNED, AIR PIRACY IS NO JOKING MATTER!
ROBOT PLANE... OBEY YOUR MISTRESS!
NO GOOD! MY MENTAL COMMANDS ARE BEING OVERRIDDEN AND I--
WHAT NOW?
U.S. AIR
THE SIGHT OF WONDER WOMAN RACING THROUGH THE SKY ANSWERED ONE OF MY QUESTIONS...
AND I BREATHED EASIER KNOWING THAT SHE WASN'T THE ONE WHO'D GONE BERSERK IN HER PLANE...!
U.S. AIR FORCE
CHASE LEADER TO CHASE ONE... KEEP AFTER IT, MITCH! I'VE GOT A DATE WITH AN ANGEL!
WE'LL CATCH UP WITH YOU SOON!
4

HEY, LADY-- YOU THE ONE WHO CALLED FOR A CAB?
STEVE!
TREVOR'S TAXI-- AT YOUR SERVICE!
HOP ON BOARD AND I'LL GIVE YOU A LIFT!
USAF
I GUESS IT'S NEWS TO YOU THAT YOUR ROBOT PLANE BUZZED A SECRET AIR FORCE INSTALLATION A LITTLE WHILE AGO!
U.S. AIR FORCE
GREAT GODDESSES!
THAT'S WHAT I FIGURED... ANYHOW, I'VE SPENT THE LAST HALF HOUR OR SO ON A WILD GOOSE CHASE--
--LOOKING FOR A PLANE THAT I CAN HARDLY SEE THAT GOES FASTER THAN OUR NEWEST FIGHTERS!
WHO'S FLYING THAT THING ANYWAY?
A LITTLE MAN... A VERY HAPPY, MISCHIEVOUS LITTLE MAN...!
BUT NOT A MAN EXACTLY... MORE LIKE--
--A GREMLIN! HOLY COW!
A GREMLIN?...
DO SUCH THINGS REALLY EXIST?
5

YOU EXIST, DON'T YOU? WHY NOT GREMLINS?
CHASE ONE TO CHASE LEADER...! I THINK WE'VE LOST HER, COLONEL!
RATS! OUR GREMLIN'S PROBABLY LONG GONE BY NOW... AND YOUR PLANE WITH HIM!
NO, STEVE! I SEE IT--AT TEN O'CLOCK HIGH!
IF YOU SAY SO, ANGEL... JUST POINT ME IN THE RIGHT DIRECTION AND--
YEAH! I CAN SEE THE SUN GLINTING OFF ITS TAIL!
HURRY, STEVE, OR HE'LL ESCAPE THROUGH THOSE CLOUDS!
ALWAYS THE BACK SEAT DRIVER!
DON'T WORRY, WE'RE RIGHT BEHIND HIM! ONCE WE PIERCE THIS CLOUD LAYER, WE'LL--
HOLY HANNAH! WE ALMOST HIT THAT DIRIGIBLE!
...!
DIRIGIBLE?!
6

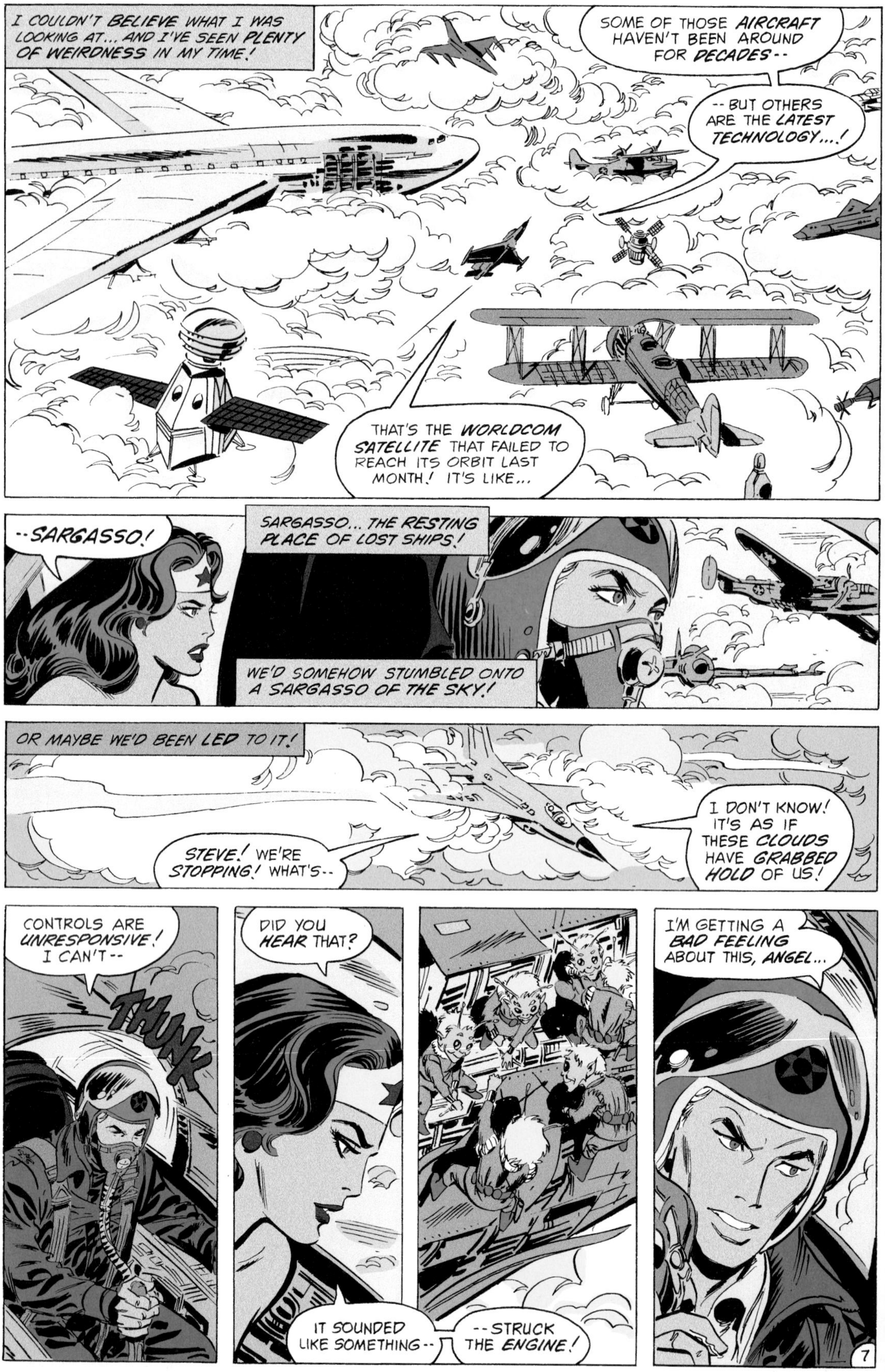

I COULDN'T BELIEVE WHAT I WAS LOOKING AT... AND I'VE SEEN PLENTY OF WEIRDNESS IN MY TIME!
SOME OF THOSE AIRCRAFT HAVEN'T BEEN AROUND FOR DECADES--
--BUT OTHERS ARE THE LATEST TECHNOLOGY...!
THAT'S THE WORLDCOM SATELLITE THAT FAILED TO REACH ITS ORBIT LAST MONTH! IT'S LIKE...
--SARGASSO!
SARGASSO... THE RESTING PLACE OF LOST SHIPS!
WE'D SOMEHOW STUMBLED ONTO A SARGASSO OF THE SKY!
OR MAYBE WE'D BEEN LED TO IT!
STEVE! WE'RE STOPPING! WHAT'S--
I DON'T KNOW! IT'S AS IF THESE CLOUDS HAVE GRABBED HOLD OF US!
CONTROLS ARE UNRESPONSIVE! I CAN'T--
THUNK
DID YOU HEAR THAT?
IT SOUNDED LIKE SOMETHING--
--STRUCK THE ENGINE!
I'M GETTING A BAD FEELING ABOUT THIS, ANGEL...
7

HEY! HEY, YOU LITTLE CREEPS-- STOP!
COME BACK HERE WITH MY ENGINE!
GUESS WHAT! THEY DIDN'T LISTEN TO ME...
AND AS I WATCHED THEM SOAR AWAY, I LOOKED UP HIGHER AND...
HOT ROCKETS!
WHAT IN THE NAME OF GEORGE LUCAS IS THAT!?
US AIR FORCE
BUT THIS WAS NO "STAR WARS" FANTASY... AND IT WASN'T HAPPENING IN SOME FARAWAY GALAXY!
THIS WAS AMERICA IN 1983... AND UP ABOVE US WAS AN ALIEN SPACESHIP THAT COULD HOUSE THE PENTAGON SEVEN TIMES OVER!
8

WHOEVER'S BEHIND THIS HAS GOT TO BE UP IN THAT SHIP, ANGEL!
HOW ABOUT A BOOST?
SOMETIMES...
ALLEZ-OOP!
... I MAKE THE MOST RASH SUGGESTIONS!
ONE THING ABOUT WONDER WOMAN, THOUGH-- I'D ALWAYS TRUST HER AS FAR AS SHE COULD THROW ME.
I TOUCHED DOWN NEATLY AT THAT SPACESHIP'S FRONT DOOR!
I'D BETTER POKE AROUND HERE SOME BEFORE I--
YIKES!
LIKE I SAID, RASH... YOU KNOW, RECK-LESS, FOOLHARDY, HAREBRAINED!
BUT LUCKY!
MY TURN TO OFFER A LIFT, STEVE!
YOU'LL GET NO ARGUMENT FROM ME!
THEY MUST ONLY HARDEN THE CLOUDS IN CERTAIN SPOTS! WEIRD SCENE...!
WHAT'S THE PHRASE FROM ARISTOPHANES?
"CLOUD CUCKOO LAND," YOU'VE BEEN READING!
IT'S A DIRTY LITTLE HABIT, BUT WHAT CAN I DO?
9

CAUTIOUSLY, WE MADE OUR WAY INSIDE THE HUGE AND STRANGELY SILENT SPACECRAFT--AND I WAS PRETTY WELL CONVINCED WE WERE ALONE WHEN...
HOLD IT, STEVE-- I THINK WE'VE FOUND THE OWNERS!
IT'S FUNNY THOUGH...
THEY DON'T SEEM TO BE MOVING!
WHAT?
PERHAPS THEY HAVE A SLOW METABOLISM AND LET THE GREMLINS DO THEIR RUNNING FOR THEM!
I'M GOING TO TRY TO COMMUNICATE WITH THEM!
THAT WOULDN'T HAVE BEEN MY APPROACH-- BUT I'M NOT THE IDOL OF MILLIONS IN THE SKIN-TIGHT COSTUME...
HOLA!
WE COME IN PEACE!
INTRUDERS! LAY DOWN YOUR WEAPONS AND SURRENDER!
PLEASE UNDERSTAND-- WE HAVE NO WISH TO BATTLE WITH YOU!
BUT I BELIEVE YOU HAVE MY AIRPLANE!
10

CHIGGA CHIGGA CHIGGA!
IBBIHIP-HIP! HEE HEE HEE!
RESISTANCE IS FUTILE! YOU ARE OUR PRISONERS!
I'M ALL FOR PEACE AND FRIENDSHIP, ANGEL! BUT THESE GUYS AREN'T BUYING!
LAY DOWN YOUR ARMS!
PUT AWAY YOUR GUN, STEVE! IT LOOKS LIKE A THREAT...
YOU HAVE NO CHOICE!
...AND IT PROBABLY WOULDN'T HURT THEM ANYWAY!
PLAN B, ANGEL?
I PROMISE YOU WE MEAN NO HARM!
THE PROBLEM WITH UNILATERAL DISARMAMENT, OF COURSE --
--IS THAT IT COULD BE JUST WHAT THE OTHER FELLA'S WAITING FOR!
I'M AFRAID SO!
IT'S TIME THESE ALIENS LEARNED--
PANK
--JUST WHOM THEY'RE DEALING WITH!
11

KER-RASH!
I'VE SEEN WONDER WOMAN KICK OVER TANKS AND LIFT UP AIRPLANES!
--SO I WASN'T SURPRISED WHEN SHE SENT THE DRONE HURTLING INTO A WALL...
BUT WHEN IT GOT UP AGAIN--
BRZZAT
THEN I STARTED TO WORRY!
PZINGG!
AND WHILE WONDER WOMAN HELD HER OWN WITH HER AMAZONIUM BRACELETS...
...ALL I COULD DO WAS WISH FOR A PAIR OF LASER-PROOF CUFFLINKS--
--AND DIVE!
SAY-- THE RAY BLAST PUT A HOLE IN THE HULL!
IF I CAN WIDEN IT A BIT...
I THINK IT'S TIME WE BEAT A HASTY RETREAT AND REGROUP OUTSIDE!
I'M RIGHT BEHIND YOU, STEVE!
12

THAT THING'S STILL BLASTING... I'VE GOTTA MOVE IT! WONDER WHERE THIS TAKES--
--MEEEEEEEE...
THE LAST SOUND I HEARD WAS OF CRASHING METAL...
...AND THE WORLD WENT ON WITHOUT ME...
HAVE YOU ANY CLOSING COMMENTS?
ONLY TO SAY THAT I APPRECIATE THE COMMITTEE'S VALUABLE TIME, SENATOR--
THANK YOU, GENERAL DARNELL...
--AND TO REITERATE MY SUPPORT FOR CONTINUED DIVERSIFICATION AMONG THE INTELLIGENCE BRANCHES!
LISA ABERNATHY OF GBS NEWS, GENERAL...
CAN YOU SHED SOME LIGHT ON THE NATURE OF THESE CLOSED HEARINGS?
I CAN SAY THIS, MS. ABERNATHY... WE -- WHAT?!
EMERGENCY, SIR... NEED YOU AT ONCE...
EXCUSE ME, LADIES AND GENTLEMEN... THIS WILL HAVE TO WAIT! CONTACT MY OFFICE IF YOU HAVE FURTHER QUESTIONS!
BUT, GENERAL...!
13

IT TOOK ME A MOMENT TO GRASP THAT I WAS CONSCIOUS IN THE DARKNESS...
THEN I REALIZED I WAS ON TOP OF A GIANT JUNK HEAP --A MOUNTAIN OF USED AND USELESS AIRCRAFT PARTS!
CRASH CLATTER
WHAT THE--?
AND THE PILE WAS GETTING BIGGER AND MORE JUNK KEPT DROPPING IN FROM ABOVE!
STEVE!
IS THAT YOU, PRINCESS? MY EYES ARE STILL ADJUSTING TO THIS PLACE!
YES, I'M OVER--
HERA!
WONDER WOMAN! ARE YOU OKAY?!
I'M ALL RIGHT... THAT LAST LOAD OF SCRAP UNSETTLED THE HEAP!
HERE--YOUR LEG'S STUCK! LET ME GIVE YOU A HAN--
14

SUFFERING SAPPHO! IT'S GOT ME!
THERE'S SOME WORKING MACHINERY DOWN THERE--CHURNING AT MY LEG!
HOLD ON! MAYBE I CAN CLEAR THIS JUNK AWAY AND--
RGWHIRRRRGWHIRRRRGWHIRRRRGWHIR-K-K
I SEE IT! TRY TO SEPARATE THE PIECES THAT ARE CLAMPED AROUND YOUR CALF!
I'M DOING IT! BUT I DON'T KNOW IF--
JUST ANOTHER SECOND...
THERE! I'VE GOT IT WEDGED OPEN NOW!
THANK YOU!
NO SWEAT...IT LOOKED LIKE YOU'D ALREADY KILLED THE ENGINE ANYHOW!
HERE YOU GO!
YOU DON'T GIVE YOURSELF ENOUGH CREDIT, STEVE!
MAYBE I DON'T EITHER...
15

STEVE, THERE'S SOMETHING I WANT TO TELL YOU... SOMETHING I SHOULD HAVE TOLD YOU LONG AGO!
AND JUST IN CASE WE DON'T GET OUT OF HERE...
HEY NOW-- SURE, WE'LL GET OUT!
LET ME FINISH... I WANT TO TELL YOU MY SECRET IDENTITY!
I'M REALLY--
CLANG CLANG CLANG CLANG CLANG
WHAT THE HECK WAS THAT?
I'M NOT CERTAIN! IT FEELS LIKE...
OH NO!
SUDDENLY OUR WORLD WENT COCKEYED! THE JUMBLE OF JUNK AND SCRAP BENEATH US SLID AWAY AS THE WHOLE ROOM TILTED OVER...
...AND WE WENT SLIDING WITH IT!
ROLL WITH THE FALL, STEVE!
I'LL SHIELD YOU FROM THE FALLING PIECES!
I DON'T THINK THAT'LL DO MUCH GOOD, ANGEL...
...NOT MUCH GOOD AT ALL!
NEXT: INTO THE INCINERATOR!

DC
75¢
312
FEB. 84
APPROVED BY THE COMICS CODE AUTHORITY
WONDER WOMAN
ESCAPE FROM CLOUD-CUCKOO LAND...
...IT WON'T BE EASY!
C-604

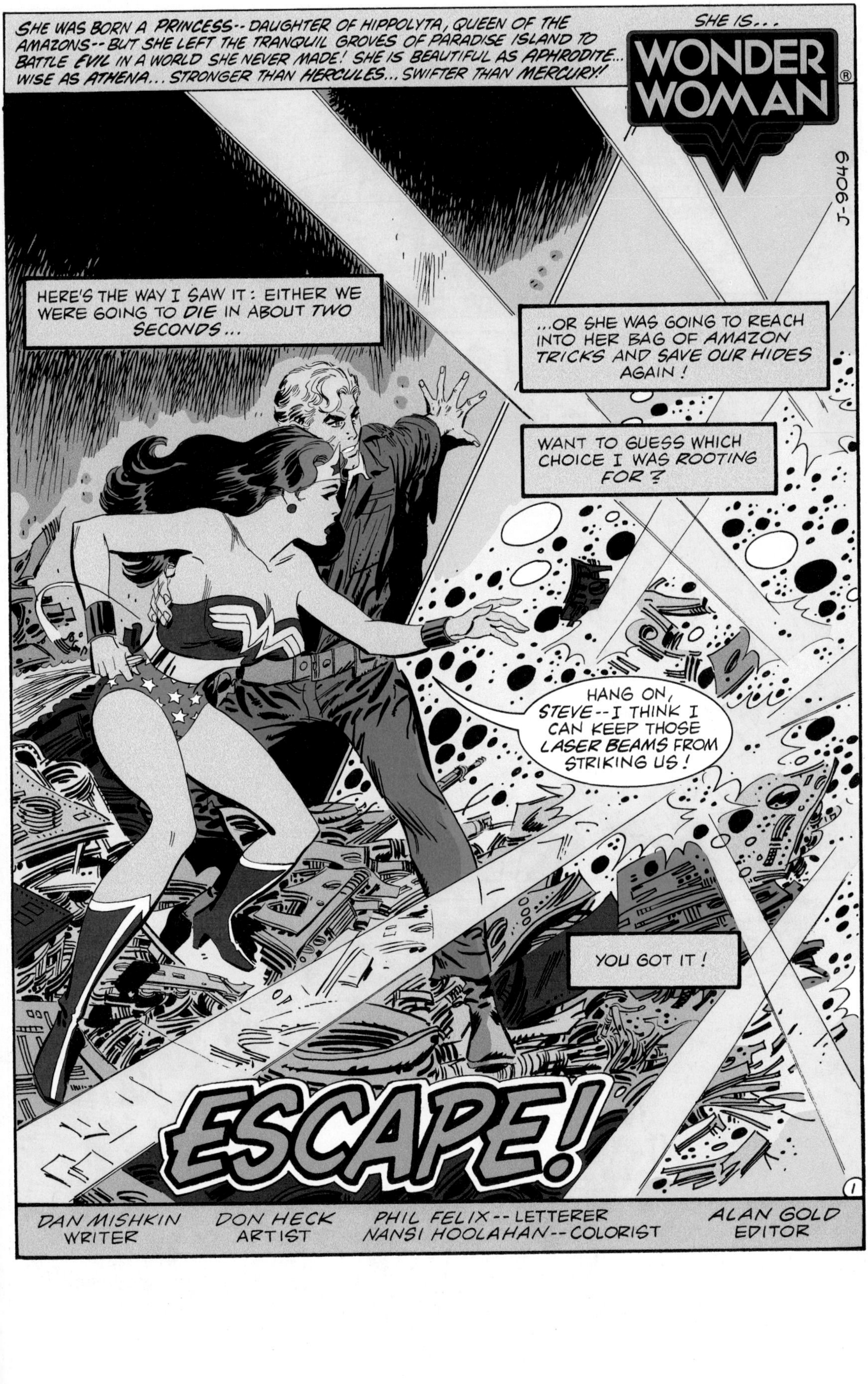
SHE WAS BORN A PRINCESS-- DAUGHTER OF HIPPOLYTA, QUEEN OF THE AMAZONS-- BUT SHE LEFT THE TRANQUIL GROVES OF PARADISE ISLAND TO BATTLE EVIL IN A WORLD SHE NEVER MADE! SHE IS BEAUTIFUL AS APHRODITE... WISE AS ATHENA... STRONGER THAN HERCULES... SWIFTER THAN MERCURY!
SHE IS...
WONDER WOMAN®
J-9049
HERE'S THE WAY I SAW IT: EITHER WE WERE GOING TO DIE IN ABOUT TWO SECONDS...
...OR SHE WAS GOING TO REACH INTO HER BAG OF AMAZON TRICKS AND SAVE OUR HIDES AGAIN!
WANT TO GUESS WHICH CHOICE I WAS ROOTING FOR?
HANG ON, STEVE--I THINK I CAN KEEP THOSE LASER BEAMS FROM STRIKING US!
YOU GOT IT!
ESCAPE!
1
DAN MISHKIN WRITER
DON HECK ARTIST
PHIL FELIX--LETTERER
NANSI HOOLAHAN--COLORIST
ALAN GOLD EDITOR

THERE ARE TOO MANY BEAMS IN THIS ALIEN INCINERATOR--
-- FOR MY BRACELETS ALONE TO DEFLECT THEM ALL !
BUT BY TWIRLING MY MAGIC LASSO WITH THE SPEED OF HERMES, I CAN FORM A PROTECTIVE SHIELD !
STILL, IT'S JUST A HOLDING ACTION ! AS LONG AS THESE DESTRUCTIVE RAYS KEEP COMING ...
HEY, LOOK !
THAT COULD BE OUR ANSWER, I THOUGHT. SOME SORT OF CONTROL PANEL ...
IF WE HAD A WAY TO KNOCK IT OUT ... !
I COULD USE MY TIARA, STEVE, BUT I NEED BOTH HANDS TO KEEP THOSE DEADLY BLASTS AWAY !
THEN LET ME GIVE IT A TRY !
I'VE ONLY GOT ONE QUESTION FIRST ...
YES ?
WOULD IT HELP IF I SAID, "ARTEMIS GUIDE MY AIM" ?
GREAT GODDESSES ! JUST DO IT !
2
I DID ...

IT WAS A LOT LIKE PITCHING HORSE-SHOES AS A KID--
--ONLY "ALMOST" DIDN'T COUNT IN THIS GAME!
BUT WITH OR WITHOUT DIVINE ASSISTANCE--
--MY TOSS DID THE TRICK...
HOW'S THAT FOR TEAM-WORK, ANGEL?
LET'S PICK UP YOUR JEWELRY AND GET OUT OF HERE!
WE WEREN'T OUT OF THE FIRE YET, OF COURSE: WE WERE STILL ON BOARD AN ALIEN SPACECRAFT...
...AND STILL MISSING ONE ROBOT PLANE...
...BUT THEN...
GREMLINS AGAIN! THEY'RE DISASSEMBLING AN OLD RUSSIAN SPACE LAB!
IN FACT, THIS ROOM IS FILLED WITH AEROSPACE PARTS OF EVERY KIND! PERHAPS MY PLANE IS AROUND HERE TOO!
ONE WAY TO FIND OUT...
...AND THAT'S TO GET MY HANDS ON ONE OF THOSE SUCKERS!
ALL RIGHT, YOU LITTLE CREEPS! HOLD STILL!
I SOON DISCOVERED THEY WERE AWFULLY FAST FOR HAVING SUCH SHORT LEGS!
BUT ONE OF 'EM--
3

--WASN'T FAST ENOUGH!
GOTCHA!
Yeow! Okay, Okay!
It's all IHIP MY FAULT! I admit it! But I didn't know the GLASS PLANE had an owner! Ooh, she's such a BEAUTY!
I just HAD to HAVE her! IHIP IHIP
Then I buzzed that AIRSTRIP--thought I'd have a little FUN, y'know--but you guys started CHASING me--
--and you were so DUMB you went and got CAUGHT and now we'll be EXPOSED, and gosh, I'm gonna GET it and--
WHOA! SLOW DOWN!
TAKE A BREATH BEFORE YOU--
TROUBLE, STEVE!
THE OTHER IMPS MUST HAVE SOUNDED AN ALERT...
THEIR GIANT MASTERS ARE BACK!
WHEN WE'D RUN INTO THESE GORILLAS BEFORE, THEY'D BEEN ABOUT AS SPEEDY AS A BUNCH OF WOODEN INDIANS...! THIS ONE, HOWEVER, WAS CLOSING IN FAST!
4

BUT WONDER WOMAN'S GOLDEN LASSO...
HERA GRANT ME STRENGTH!
...WAS FASTER!
THUD
WAIT! WHAT IS THIS?
WHEELS?
COME BACK!
Eeba jeeba!
WHAT'S GOING ON HERE? THAT ALIEN'S NOT EVEN REAL! HE'S JUST A BIG...STUFFED TOY!
Oh, he's real! He's just been-- =IHIP= --minus LIFE SUPPORT for several of your decades...
...so we put him to GOOD USE...
...what you might call a... "SCARECROW"!
Sigh! I suppose I should explain...
...long as anyone remembers, we've been working for the YTIRFLIRKS! =IHIP= But it's not like we SIGNED UP for it or anything! It's just that they're so BIG and DUMB and CLUMSY that they're always BUSTING things that they can't put back =IHIP= TOGETHER!
So that's why they've got US!
We're the ones who keep their =IHIP= SHIPS in TOP CONDITION so they can go on CONQUERING PLANETS and making every-one their SLAVES!
5

THE GREMLINS TOLD US HOW THEIR MASTERS DROVE THEM MERCILESSLY...
...AND SO THEY'D SKIP OUT AWOL EVERY CHANCE THEY GOT!
THREE QUARTERS OF A CENTURY AGO, THEY GOT A CHANCE NEAR EARTH AND STOLE THE MOTHER SHIP--
--WHILE THE YTIRFLIRKS PURSUED IN SMALL SURVEILLANCE CRAFT!
BUT THE BEST MECHANIC'S NOT ALWAYS THE GREATEST DRIVER--
--A LESSON I'D LEARNED MY-SELF IN A '63 CORVETTE...
THE GREMLINS FOUND THAT OUT IN A NOT-TOO-PERFECT LANDING IN SIBERIA'S FROZEN WASTES!
HROOM
But we never meant any IHIP harm! We just kept gathering up old aircraft parts and trying to re-pair the ship!
THE STORIES I'VE HEARD HAVE GOT YOU GUYS TAKING PLANES APART IN MID-FLIGHT!
WHICH REMINDS ME...
...WHERE EXACTLY IS MY ROBOT PLANE?
Er, well, IHIP
Part of it is over there...
MERCIFUL MINERVA!
AS I FOUND OUT LATER, SHOCKING EVENTS I HAD AN INTEREST IN WERE TRANS-PIRING NOT ONLY HIGH IN THE ATMOSPHERE--
6

---BUT ALSO IN WASHINGTON, D.C., ON THE STEPS OF THE U.S. CAPITOL...
GENERAL DARNELL!
I'M SORRY, MS. ABERNATHY...
U.S.
U.S.
BUT I CAN'T MAKE ANY COMMENT--NOT EVEN TO TELL YOU IF THERE'S ANYTHING TO COMMENT ABOUT!
BUT...
U.S
MARTY, HOW ABOUT TAKING THAT MINICAM FOR A WALK AROUND THE BLOCK?
WHATEVER YOU SAY, LISA.
ALL RIGHT NOW, GENERAL, OFF THE RECORD...
...I HEARD YOUR AIDE MENTION KEITH GRIGGS--A MAN WHO HELPED SAVE MY FATHER'S LIFE! *
IS HE IN SOME KIND OF DANGER?
OFF THE RECORD, YOUNG LADY--
* IN WW #307--ALAN.
--THE DANGER MAY ALREADY BE OVER...
"...BECAUSE MAJOR GRIGGS MAY ALREADY BE DEAD!"
WE'VE GOT NO CHOICE! THOSE WOLVES KEEP GAINING ON US--LIKE BEASTS OUT OF HELL!
IT'S NO USE, GRIGGS... WE CAN'T KEEP RUNNING!
7

THEY DON'T SEEM TO BE TIRING!
PUFF
THEY DON'T BELONG IN THE CARIBBEAN! WHAT COULD IT-- ?!
AND THESE OTHER ANIMALS...
GREAT GUNS! THAT SCORPIAN'S GOT A -- HUMAN FACE!
McCURTIN, LOOK! THAT TEMPLE...!
MAYBE WE'LL GET OUR ANSWERS DOWN THERE!
NO, MAJOR...
...YOU'LL GET YOUR ANSWER--
--NOW!
VERY GOOD, MY PET...
YOU'VE ADDED ANOTHER PIECE TO MY COLLECTION...
ANOTHER MAN WHO'LL HAVE THE ANIMAL IN HIS SOUL BROUGHT FORTH BY THE MAGIC MINISTRATIONS...
...OF CIRCE!
8

IN THE MEANTIME, MY PROBLEMS WEREN'T OVER BY A LONG SHOT...
HOW DO WE KNOW THIS ISN'T A TRAP?
sheesh! I said I was ≡IHIP≡ SORRY!
I THINK HE'S PLAYING IT STRAIGHT, ANGEL...
...AS STRAIGHT AS HE CAN, ANYWAY!
Yeah ≡IHIP≡ as straight as I--
HEY! what's THAT supposed to mean?!
I FIGURED HIS INTENTIONS WERE OKAY, BUT I WORRIED ABOUT HIS FOLLOW-THROUGH...
STILL, HE GOT US TO THE ENGINE ROOM WITHOUT ANY PROBLEMS ...AND THERE WE FOUND IT --
MY ROBOT PLANE!
BUT WHY IS IT RIGGED UP THAT WAY?
It's the ≡IHIP≡ PROPULSION SYSTEM! We're pretty sure it'll boost the PRIMARY THRUSTERS enough--
--to break us free ≡IHIP≡ of your planet's GRAVITY!
IF IT'S ALL THE SAME TO YOU, I'D LIKE TO KEEP MY PLANE EARTH-BOUND FOR--
WHAT!?
INTRUDER ALERT! INTRUDER ALERT!
9

Ooops! IHIP sorry about that.
BY MY MOTHER'S CROWN! WHAT'S THE MEANING OF THIS?
MY APOLOGIES, MISTRESS... I'VE BEEN ALTERED!
HUH? SINCE WHEN DOES--
HUSH, STEVE --LISTEN!
BUT I DON'T HEAR--
THEN I DID HEAR THE PITTER PATTER OF THEIR TINY GREMLIN FEET ABOVE...
ROBOT PLANE... OBEY ME NOW AND FLY AWAY FROM HERE!
I CANNOT, MISTRESS... THE LAUNCH SEQUENCE HAS ALREADY BEEN ACTIVATED!
WHAT ABOUT YOU, GREMLIN...
COULD YOU REMOVE THOSE THRUSTERS FROM ITS TAIL?
ME? IHIP
You bet!
OBEY COLONEL TREVOR FROM NOW ON, ROBOT PLANE...
SAY WHAT!?
YOU'RE GOING TO FLY IT OUT OF HERE WHEN THE TIME COMES, STEVE, WHILE I DIVERT THE GREMLINS!
WISH ME LUCK!
10

BUT I HARDLY HAD A CHANCE TO DO EVEN THAT AS--
COME AND GET ME, YOU BUG-FACED BABIES!
THAT'S RIGHT --RUN!
OH-OH! TRYING TO SURROUND ME, ARE YOU? BUT THAT WOULD NEVER STOP SOMEONE WITH AMAZON TRAINING--
--SEE?
BYE BYE, GREMLINS...
...CATCH ME IF YOU CAN!
Ibbihip-jeep!
I DON'T MEAN TO SOUND PUSHY, BUT CAN'T YOU WORK ANY FASTER?
I'm HURRYING IHIP as it IS! Some things just IHIP take TIME!
BUT TIME WAS SOMETHING WE HAD PRECIOUS LITTLE OF!
HOW MUCH LONGER, ROBOT PLANE?
TWO MINUTES TO MAIN ENGINE START-UP, COLONEL...
Yikes! IHIP
11

2:00:00
Any HIBIHIP sign of her?
Negative IJIP she's--
YOO HOO! OVER HERE!
Eep!
1:32:04
SEE YOU, BOYS!
Everybody follow ME!
YIP HIP
MERGING TRAFFIC, FELLOWS!
0:57:31
LOOK OUT!
Heek!
Don't let her get away!
AFTER HER!
0:09:26
Uh oh.
"Uh oh"? Who said "uh oh"?
0:02:00
BOARRR
THE ENGINES ARE STARTING! I PRAY THAT STEVE IS READY!
12

HEY! WE'RE TAKING OFF!
I Know! ≡IHIP≡ I KNOW!
THERE! ≡IHIP≡ It's DISCONNECTED!
BUT THE TAIL'S STILL NOT ON!
D-don't w-worry! ≡IHIP IHIP≡ You just c-climb aboard!
I can get it done... I ≡IHIP≡ think!
THE OTHER GREMLINS HAVE MADE IT BACK ON...
BUT THERE'S STILL NO SIGN OF STEVE!
ATHENA! WHAT DO I DO NOW?!
HRRRRR
YA-HOO! WE DID IT, PAL! HEY, YOU STILL WITH ME?
S-still here... but the TAIL'S--
YEAH, I CAN TELL! YOU'D BETTER FINISH CONNECTING IT ANY WAY YOU CAN...
...'CAUSE THE GROUND IS COMING UP FAST!
≡Gulp≡
Okay, STEVE! I think ≡IHIP≡
13

--I've GOT it!
CONTROLS ARE RESPONDING!
WE'RE GONNA MAKE IT, LITTLE BUDDY!
Yiiee! Not ≡IHIP≡ ALL of us!
CAREFUL, SMALL ONE...WE DON'T WANT TO LOSE YOU NOW!
Hoosh!
AND AFTER WE HAD REACHED THE GROUND AGAIN -- HORIZONTALLY THIS TIME...
YOU KNOW, BY HELPING US, HE MISSED HIS CHANCE TO RETURN TO THE STARS...
ZOOM!
Jeeba heep!
I GUESS THAT MAKES US RESPONSIBLE FOR HIM NOW!
ACTUALLY, I'M GROWING RATHER FOND OF HIM!
I KNOW WHAT YOU MEAN, STEVE.
HAH! I'D BETTER TELL HIM TO COME DOWN BEFORE HE SCARES THE DAY-LIGHTS OUT OF--
WAIT, STEVE...
WHAT IS IT, ANGEL?
ONE PIECE OF UNFINISHED BUSINESS.
BEFORE THINGS GOT SO OUT OF HAND ON THE SPACESHIP--
--I WAS GOING TO TELL YOU MY SECRET IDENTITY!
14

WHOA,... STOP! HOLD IT RIGHT THERE!
WHAT'S THE MATTER, STEVE?
LOOK, I'M REALLY HAPPY THAT YOU WANT TO SHARE YOUR SECRET WITH ME... HONESTLY!
I KNOW WHAT THAT MUST TAKE --AND ALL THE LOVE AND TRUST IT REPRESENTS...
...BUT I DON'T WANT TO KNOW YOUR SECRET IDENTITY!
WHAT...?
BUT WHY NOT?
YOU'RE MY ANGEL, ANGEL, AND THAT'S WHAT I WANT YOU TO STAY...
...NOT TURN OUT TO BE SOMEONE WHO SWEEPS UP AT THE PENTAGON AT NIGHT!
OH, STEVE, IT'S HARDLY--
NO--DON'T SAY ANOTHER WORD ABOUT IT!
ALL I WANT IS FOR YOU TO BE MY ANGEL... MY FRIEND... MY LOVE...
...ALWAYS.
15

PARADISE ISLAND...
NOW IS MY OPPORTUNITY...
I'VE BEEN WAITING FOR THIS CHANCE--
--EVER SINCE I OVER-HEARD QUEEN HIPPOLYTA TALKING TO THE GODDESSES ATHENA AND APHRODITE... *
* SEE ISSUE #308--ALAN.
...AND LEARNED THAT THEY'VE ROBBED WONDER WOMAN OF HER MEMORIES!
THEN I FOUND OUT THAT THOSE MEMORIES HAVE BEEN PUT IN STORAGE...
...HERE!
NOW I'LL--EH?
...BUT STILL I HAVE A VAGUE SENSE OF UNEASE, ANTIOPE.
I CANNOT PLACE IT, YET I FEAR MY --HOLD!
MY QUEEN...?
I THOUGHT I HEARD SOMETHING--
--BUT THERE IS NO ONE HERE BESIDE US TWO.
MY MIND PLAYS TRICKS ON ME NOW...
...OR A TROUBLED CONSCIENCE PERHAPS!
AND SOON I WILL KNOW THE SECRET REASONS WHY!
MEMORY TAPE OF PRINCESS DIANA
NEXT
AT THE MERCY OF CIRCE!
(AND SHE HAS NONE, BELIEVE US!)

DC
EXTRA! FIRESTORM STRIKES AGAIN!
50¢ ALL NEW!
NO. 296 APR.
The FLASH
APPROVED BY THE COMICS CODE AUTHORITY
FASTEST MAN ALIVE!
THE CRIMSON COMET BATTLES THE Elongated Man!
ALL-OUT ACTION THAT WILL MAKE YOUR HEAD SPIN!
INFANTINO & GIORDANO
C-536

The FLASH GUEST-STARRING The ELONGATED Man
PRESENTING: ONE OF THE STRANGEST CRIMINAL GANGS IN THE HISTORY OF CENTRAL CITY'S POLICE FILES!
A TRIO OF THIEVES WHO NEVER STEAL MONEY... THOUGH THE "LOOT" THEY STOCKPILE IS INFINITELY MORE VALUABLE!
THREE PLUNDERERS SO INDESCRIBABLE... SO SPELL-BINDING... THEY BRING ABOUT A DEADLY RIFT BETWEEN THE FLASH AND THE ELONGATED MAN-- AND INSTIGATE A BATTLE ONLY ONE HERO CAN POSSIBLY WIN!
J-6971
1
THE Man who was CURSED TO THE BONE!
CARY BATES writer
CARMINE INFANTINO penciller
BOB SMITH inker
JOHN COSTANZA letterer
GENE D'ANGELO colorist
LEN WEIN editor

RALPH!
WHAT SORT OF FINE MESS HAVE YOU AND YOUR TWITCHING MYSTERY-SNIFFING NOSE GOTTEN YOU INTO THIS TIME?
AND HOW THE BLAZES AM I SUPPOSED TO TRACK YOU DOWN WITHOUT THE SLIGHTEST HINT OF A CLUE TO GO ON?
THE BLURRED STREAK OF CRIMSON WITH ALL THE QUESTIONS IS SECRETLY A POLICE SCIEN-TIST NAMED BARRY ALLEN...
...BUT BETTER KNOWN TO THE WORLD AT LARGE AS... THE FLASH!
WHILE THE MISSING RALPH ON HIS MIND IS NONE OTHER THAN ONE RALPH DIBNY--
--WELL-KNOWN THROUGHOUT THE WORLD AS THE CELEBRATED DUCTILE DETECTIVE WHO CALLS HIMSELF THE ELONGATED MAN!
AFTER ALL THESE YEARS, SUE HAS BEEN A SUPER-HERO'S SPOUSE LONG ENOUGH TO BE ACCUSTOMED TO THE LONG AND ODD HOURS THAT GO WITH THE JOB...
...WHICH IS WHY I FIGURED SHE PROBABLY HAD A GOOD REASON TO BE WORRIED WHEN SHE CONFIDED IN ME YESTERDAY DURING OUR LUNCH DATE!
...AND CHICAGO WAS OUR FIRST STATESIDE STOP AFTER RETURNING FROM A SIX WEEK VACATION TOUR ACROSS EUROPE!
BUT WITHIN HOURS AFTER WE ARRIVED... RALPH DISAPPEARED! THAT WAS THREE DAYS AGO!
I FILED A MISSING PERSONS REPORT WITH THE CHICAGO POLICE... BUT SO FAR THEY HAVEN'T FOUND A TRACE OF HIM!
TELL YOU WHAT, SUE! FLASH IS SUPPOSED TO STOP BY THE STATION TODAY! SUPPOSE I ASK HIM TO SET OUT ON A SUPER-SPEED SEARCH ACROSS CHICAGO?
OH, THANK YOU, BARRY! I WAS HOPING YOU'D SUGGEST SOMETHING LIKE THAT! IF ANYONE CAN FIND THAT NOSE-TWITCHING HUSBAND OF MINE, IT'S THE FLASH!
"CONSIDERING THE OVERWHELMING FAITH POOR SUE PUT IN ME YESTERDAY..."
...HOW WILL I BE ABLE TO FACE HER AND TELL HER THE FLASH CAME UP EMPTY?
HUH? SOMETHING VERY ODD GOING ON INSIDE THAT PATROL CAR COMING MY WAY--
2

--IN FACT, "ODD" DOESN'T EVEN BEGIN TO COVER IT!
THOSE TWO COPPERS WILL BE PUTTIN' OUT THE WORD ON THEIR MISSIN' AUTOMOBILE ANY MINUTE NOW! YOU SHOULDA ZAPPED 'EM AGAIN, HOKUS!
NOT TO WORRY, SCRUNCH! WE'LL BE DISCARDING THE SQUAD CAR IN OUR PRE-SELECTED PLACE OF CONCEALMENT JUST A FEW MILES UP AHEAD!
CAN'T YOU DRIVE THIS RIG ANY FASTER, BLUBBA?
WHADDYA SO HYPER ABOUT, RUNT? YOU DON'T SEE ANYTHING ON OUR TAIL, DO YOU?
BUT THE NEXT INSTANT, AS THE FASTEST MAN ALIVE BOLTS INTO ACTION STILL FAR TOO SWIFT TO BE SEEN...
AIEEE! IF THIS IS ONE OF YOUR TRICKS, HOKUS--
I ASSURE YOU, BLUBBA--I'M JUST AS MYSTIFIED AS YOU ARE! MOST EXTRAORDINARY!
MONKEY FUZZ! WE'RE TURNIN' 180 DEGREES... IN MID-AIR!
THANKS TO MY CLOCKWISE SUPER-SPEED WHIRLWIND!
EVEN THOUGH THE CAR'S MOMENTUM IS STILL CARRYING IT FORWARD--
3

--ITS TIRES WILL BRING IT TO A QUICK STOP WHEN THEY HIT THE GROUND SPINNING IN THE OPPOSITE DIRECTION!
GADZOOKS! ISN'T THAT THE FAMOUS FLASH ON OUR FLANK?
MMMFFFF! W-WE'RE IN B-I-G TROUBLE NOW!
OWWWW!
A MOMENT LATER...
YOU HEARD ME--OUT OF THE CAR! I'D SAY YOU THREE HAVE A LOT OF QUESTIONS TO ANSWER!
LIKE WHERE ARE THE POLICE OFFICERS WHO BELONG TO THIS CAR?
OOOFF! PUFF!
I ASSURE YOU, MY DEAR FLASH, THE TWO YOUNG PATROLMEN ARE IN SOMEWHAT DIS-ORIENTED BUT OTHERWISE EXCEL-LENT CONDITION!
I REALIZE YOU FEEL IT'S YOUR DUTY TO TURN US IN, SPEEDSTER--BUT I'M AFRAID WE MUST PROTEST!
I DON'T KNOW WHAT'S IN YOUR POCKET--BUT I WOULDN'T GO FOR IT IF I WERE YOU!
UHFFF!
NOT SMART! WHATEVER YOUR WEAPON, THESE VIBRATION-WAVES WILL FORCE YOU TO DROP IT!
IT'S MERELY A BOUQUET OF FLOWERS, MY GOOD MAN--NOTHING MORE!
FLOWERS?!?
UHHH... WHAT'S HAPPENING?!? MY MIND FEELS LIKE IT'S SUDDENLY BEEN LOCKED IN A TELEPATHIC VISE!
NOT EVEN SUPER-SPEED MAKES YOU IMMUNE TO THE MAGICIAN'S CLASSIC ART OF MISDIRECTION, FLASH!
WHILE YOUR ATTENTION WAS FOCUSED ON ME, YOU DID NOT NOTICE SCRUNCH SUBJECTING YOU TO MY HYPNO-BEEPER...
4

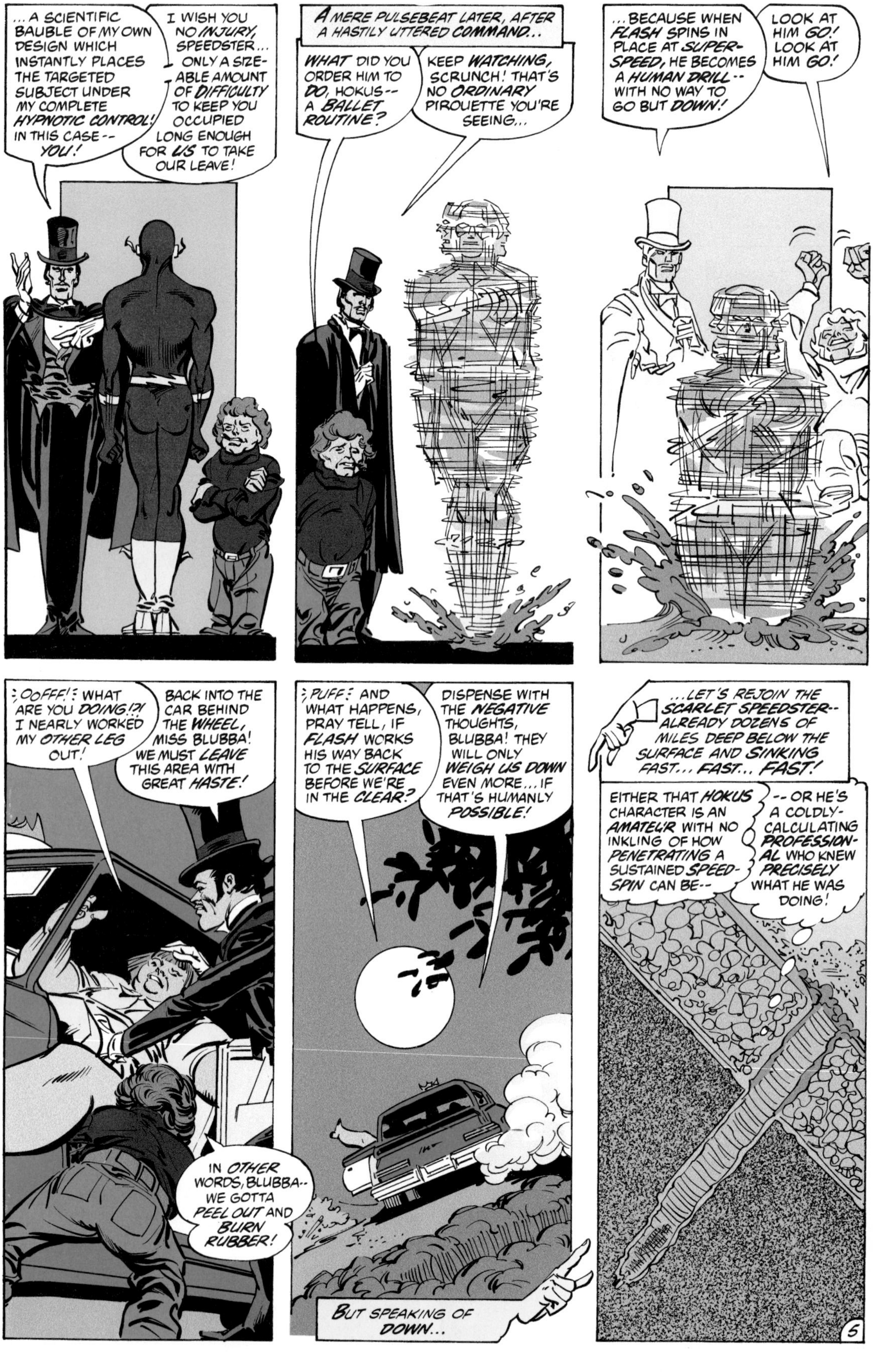
...A SCIENTIFIC BAUBLE OF MY OWN DESIGN WHICH INSTANTLY PLACES THE TARGETED SUBJECT UNDER MY COMPLETE HYPNOTIC CONTROL! IN THIS CASE -- YOU!
I WISH YOU NO INJURY, SPEEDSTER... ONLY A SIZE-ABLE AMOUNT OF DIFFICULTY TO KEEP YOU OCCUPIED LONG ENOUGH FOR US TO TAKE OUR LEAVE!
A MERE PULSEBEAT LATER, AFTER A HASTILY UTTERED COMMAND...
WHAT DID YOU ORDER HIM TO DO, HOKUS-- A BALLET ROUTINE?
KEEP WATCHING, SCRUNCH! THAT'S NO ORDINARY PIROUETTE YOU'RE SEEING...
...BECAUSE WHEN FLASH SPINS IN PLACE AT SUPER-SPEED, HE BECOMES A HUMAN DRILL-- WITH NO WAY TO GO BUT DOWN!
LOOK AT HIM GO! LOOK AT HIM GO!
OOFFF! WHAT ARE YOU DOING!?! I NEARLY WORKED MY OTHER LEG OUT!
BACK INTO THE CAR BEHIND THE WHEEL, MISS BLUBBA! WE MUST LEAVE THIS AREA WITH GREAT HASTE!
IN OTHER WORDS, BLUBBA-- WE GOTTA PEEL OUT AND BURN RUBBER!
PUFF! AND WHAT HAPPENS, PRAY TELL, IF FLASH WORKS HIS WAY BACK TO THE SURFACE BEFORE WE'RE IN THE CLEAR?
DISPENSE WITH THE NEGATIVE THOUGHTS, BLUBBA! THEY WILL ONLY WEIGH US DOWN EVEN MORE... IF THAT'S HUMANLY POSSIBLE!
BUT SPEAKING OF DOWN...
...LET'S REJOIN THE SCARLET SPEEDSTER-- ALREADY DOZENS OF MILES DEEP BELOW THE SURFACE AND SINKING FAST... FAST... FAST!
EITHER THAT HOKUS CHARACTER IS AN AMATEUR WITH NO INKLING OF HOW PENETRATING A SUSTAINED SPEED-SPIN CAN BE--
-- OR HE'S A COLDLY-CALCULATING PROFESSION-AL WHO KNEW PRECISELY WHAT HE WAS DOING!
5

WHAT HE DOESN'T KNOW IS THAT I'VE JUST INSTANTANEOUSLY REVERSED MY SPEED-SPIN--
--SWIFTLY PUTTING A STOP TO MY DESCENT--
--BY WHIPPING UP A CUSHION OF COMPRESSED AIR UNDERNEATH MY FEET!
NOW I'VE GOT NOWHERE TO GO BUT UP!
AND THIS TIME I'LL BE MORE THAN READY--
--IF HOKUS TRIES TO ZAP ME... WITH ANOTHER SAMPLE... OF HIS HYPNOTIC... "POCUS"...
WHAT'S WRONG... MY... THINKING PROCESS... SO SLUGGISH...
ONLY... ONE... EXPLANATION...
THAT... HOLLOW PATCH... I PASSED THROUGH...
...MUST'VE BEEN... A NATURAL GAS POCKET...
BREATHED IN... TOO MANY FUMES...
EVERYTHING'S FADING... BUT I CAN'T GIVE IN...
GOT TO GET BACK... ON MY FEET...
... ON MY FEET...
6

TWENTY MINUTES LATER, ELSEWHERE IN THE GREATER CHICAGO AREA-- A BIZARRE TRIO OF THIEVES REPORT TO A MOST MYSTERIOUS LEADER...
SPLENDID, HOKUS! I SEE YOUR "EXCURSION" TO THE GLAZER RESEARCH CENTER TURNED OUT TO BE WORTHWHILE!
SEE FOR YOURSELF, MASTER JERO-- A FULL FIVE MILLIGRAMS OF INTERFERON!
THAT'S TWO C.C.'S MORE THAN OUR INFORMANT TOLD US TO EXPECT!
THEN WE ARE JUST THAT MUCH CLOSER TO MEETING OUR LONG-PROJECTED QUOTA, KINDRED ONES!
WHICH MEANS, WITH ANY LUCK, THE NEXT STOP ON OUR TARGET LIST WILL DEFINITELY BE OUR LAST!
LET'S DRINK TO THAT, SHALL WE?
TO CENTRAL CITY-- MAY IT BRING AN END TO OUR DANGER-FROUGHT QUEST!
AND PROVIDE A NEW BEGINNING FOR MASTER JERO!
AND MOST OF ALL-- KEEP THE FLIPPIN' FLASH TOO BUSY TO MESS WITH US!
LET'S JUMP AHEAD THREE DAYS AND ACROSS SEVERAL STATES-- TO A SKYLINE FAMILIAR TO ALL RESIDENTS OF CENTRAL CITY...
BARRY--? IT'S SUE DIBNY!
HI, SUE! I WISH I COULD TELL YOU I'M CLOSER TO FINDING RALPH... BUT EVEN THE FLASH HASN'T HIT ON ANY CLUES YET!
WELL MAYBE I HAVE! I FINALLY GOT AROUND TO UNPACKING THE REST OF OUR LUGGAGE TODAY...
...ONLY TO FIND A SERIES OF NEWSPAPER CLIPPINGS IN RALPH'S SUITCASE... EACH ONE FROM A DIFFERENT EUROPEAN CITY:
NAPLES... LUXEMBOURG ...GENEVA... MADRID... AND SO ON!
WE VISITED EACH OF THESE CITIES, BARRY...
...AND ACCORDING TO THESE CLIPPINGS, OUR VISITS ALWAYS COINCIDED WITH THE ITINERARY OF A TRAVELING CIRCUS THAT WAS TOURING EUROPE AT THE TIME!
SUE-- WOULD YOU BY ANY CHANCE BE TALKING ABOUT THE BAXXUM BROTHERS?
BAXXUM BROTHERS CIRCUS TO PERFORM HERE THROUGH THE 28TH

W-WHY YES, BARRY... BUT HOW DID YOU KNOW?
WOULD YOU BELIEVE THE BAXXUM BROTHERS CIRCUS PITCHED ITS TENTS OUTSIDE CENTRAL CITY THIS MORNING FOR A FIVE-DAY ENGAGEMENT?
BARRY'S RING EJECTING THE COMPRESSED SCARLET UNIFORM WHICH INSTANTLY EXPANDS ON CONTACT WITH THE AIR!
OH, BARRY! DO YOU THINK THERE'S SOME CONNECTION BETWEEN THIS CIRCUS AND RALPH?
ASK ME AGAIN IN A COUPLE OF HOURS! I'M GOING TO TAKE A RUN OVER THERE MYSELF AND SEE WHAT I CAN FIND OUT!
BARRY SWITCHING CLOTHES SO INCREDIBLY SWIFTLY THERE ISN'T ENOUGH TIME FOR THE PHONE TO DROP!
ONE THING'S FOR CERTAIN: TWITCHING NOSE OR NOT, RALPH WAS OBVIOUSLY WORKING ON A SECRET CASE THROUGHOUT HIS EUROPEAN "VACATION"--
--AND SOMEHOW THE BAXXUM CIRCUS MUST BE INVOLVED... ALL THE WAY UP TO ITS TENT-POLES!
SCARCELY AN EYE-BLINK LATER, SEVERAL MILES OUTSIDE THE TOWN LIMITS...
THE CIRCUS MUST'VE CLOSED DOWN FOR THE NIGHT SEVERAL HOURS AGO!
GOOD-- THAT MEANS I WON'T HAVE TO CONTEND WITH HOARDS OF PEOPLE--
--WHILE I CONDUCT MY SUPER-SPEED--
--TENT-TO-TENT SEARCH FOR ANY TELL-TALE CLUES--
--THAT MIGHT PUT ME CLOSER TO FINDING--
--RALPH???
8

RALPH! WHAT THE BLAZES ARE YOU DOING IN THAT CAGE-- UNDER A PHONEY MOUSTACHE AND GOATEE? AND THAT CORNY COSTUME IS REALLY THE PITS!
NOW WOULD YOU MIND DROPPING THE AMATEUR HUMAN PRETZEL ROUTINE AND START FILLING ME IN?
GONZO
THE ASTOUNDING TRIPLE-JOINTED MAN
BUT WHEN A BAFFLED SCARLET SPEEDSTER HEARS ONLY SILENCE...
INCREDIBLE! APPARENTLY RALPH DOESN'T EVEN KNOW I'M HERE! AND THAT BLANK LOOK ON HIS FACE... IT'S AS IF HE'S BEEN PUT INTO SOME SORT OF TRANCE!
WAITAMINNIT! IF THIS IS A TRANCE--
--IT COULD BE A LONG-TERM VERSION OF WHAT THAT HOKUS CHARACTER DID TO ME IN CHICAGO!
I NEVER DID TRACK DOWN THOSE THREE WEIRDOS...BUT IT NEVER OCCURRED TO ME TO LOOK FOR THEM IN A CIRCUS!
HMMM... PIECES OF THIS PUZZLE ARE STARTING TO FIT!
ASSUMING RALPH BECAME A THREAT TO THEM... WHAT AN INGENIOUS WAY TO KEEP THE FAMOUS ELONGATED MAN THEIR PRISONER--
--PUTTING HIM UNDER A TRANCE AND DISGUISING HIM AS A FELLOW SIDE-SHOW PERFORMER!
GONZO
THE ASTOUN
TRIPLE-JOIN
WITH RALPH'S FANTASTIC STRETCHING POWERS, EVEN UNDER HYPNOSIS I'M SURE HE HAD NO TROUBLE WITH THIS HUMAN PRETZEL ROUTINE HOKUS COMMANDED HIM TO ADOPT! MAYBE NOW I SHOULD--
EH? SOUNDS LIKE A CAR STARTING OUTSIDE...
RAROOMMM!
IT'S THE "GOON SQUAD" AGAIN... AND IF MY HUNCH IS RIGHT, THEY'RE SETTING OUT ON ANOTHER CRIME-CAPER!
I SUPPOSE I COULD NAB THEM NOW FOR KID-NAPPING-- BUT MY INSTINCTS ARE TELLING ME TO HOLD OFF...
9

...AND VIBRATE INVISIBLY ALONGSIDE FOR THE RIDE UNTIL I FIND OUT WHAT THIS BIZARRE CAPER IS ALL ABOUT!
THEN I'LL MAKE SURE HOKUS BRINGS RALPH OUT OF THAT TRANCE-- BEFORE I TURN HIM AND HIS TWO CIRCUS STOOGES OVER TO THE POLICE!
BUT BACK AT THE BAXXUM BROTHERS CIRCUS SOME TWENTY MINUTES LATER--IT APPEARS SOMEONE ELSE HAS ARRIVED AND DISCOVERED ONE TENT OF GREAT INTEREST...
R-RALPH? OMIGOSH, IT IS YOU, ISN'T IT?
BUT WHAT ON EARTH HAVE THEY DONE TO MY POOR BABY?
GONZO
THE ASTOUNDING TRIPLE-JOINTED MAN!
I TOLD BARRY ALLEN ABOUT THE BAXXUM BROTHERS CLIPPINGS I FOUND... AND WHEN HE TOLD ME THE BAXXUM CIRCUS WAS RIGHT HERE IN CENTRAL CITY--
--I COULDN'T RESIST DRIVING OVER HERE TO LOOK FOR YOU MYSELF!
BUT WHAT'S WITH THE SILLY DISGUISE, HONEY?
IS IT SOMETHING TO DO WITH THE CASE, OR IS--
GOOD GRIEF! HE HASN'T HEARD A WORD I'VE SAID... AND JUDGING FROM THAT BLANK LOOK ON HIS FACE, HE ISN'T SEEING ME, EITHER!
IT'S ALMOST AS IF HE'S IN A... TRANCE!
HMMM... WHAT TO DO! IF RALPH IS OUT OF IT BECAUSE OF A DRUG, I'LL HAVE TO GET HIM TO A DOCTOR!
BUT IF HE'S UNDER SOME SORT OF HYPNOTIC TRANCE... MAYBE I CAN SNAP HIM OUT OF IT MYSELF ...RIGHT HERE AND NOW!
I DON'T KNOW IF A PROFESSIONAL WOULD CONSIDER THIS "APPROACH" VERY SCIENTIFIC--
--BUT THEN, THE KIND OF CHEMISTRY RALPH AND I HAVE ALWAYS SHARED GOES WAY BEYOND WHAT CAN BE MEASURED IN A LABORATORY!
10

A SHIFT IN SCENE IS IN ORDER NOW-- A NUMBER OF MILES AWAY TO THE LOCAL CENTRAL CITY BRANCH OF S.T.A.R. LABORATORIES*-- ONE HALF-HOUR LATER...
S.T.A.R.
...WHERE WE FIND A FAMILIAR CAR PARKED SUSPICIOUSLY CLOSE BY!
*SCIENTIFIC AND TECHNOLOGICAL ADVANCED RESEARCH. --LEN.
AND A PAIR OF SECURITY GUARDS WHO ARE NOT ON GUARD AT ALL-- FOR THEY TOO HAVE BECOME VICTIMS OF A HYPNOTIC SNEAK ATTACK...
BUT WHERE IS THE SCARLET SPEEDSTER, YOU MIGHT WELL ASK? AND WHY HASN'T HE PUT A STOP TO THIS CRIME-IN-PROGRESS?
CAREFUL, BLUBBA! WHATEVER YOU DO, DON'T DROP IT! THAT'S 20 THOUSAND DOLLARS' WORTH OF INTERFERON IN YOUR PUDGY LITTLE HANDS!
DON'T WORRY, HOKUS! I GUARANTEE MISS BLUBBA WON'T HAVE IT FOR VERY LONG!
MONKEY SPIT! WHAT'S THE ELONGATED MAN DOING OUTTA HIS CAGE?
HOKUS, YOU TOLD US THAT TRANCE WOULD BE GOOD FOR A WEEK!
DON'T BLAME HOKUS-- HE DIDN'T KNOW ABOUT "SUE-D"-- THAT'S THE CODE-NAME FOR MY OWN PERSONAL ANTI-HYPNOSIS AGENT!
I SEE YOU TOOK THE TIME TO RECLAIM YOUR OWN COSTUME, MR. DIBNY! HOW THEATRICAL! BUT HOW DID YOU KNOW WHERE TO FIND US?
ELEMENTARY... CONSIDERING THIS PARTICULAR S.T.A.R. BRANCH IS THE ONLY INTERFERON-PRODUCING LAB IN THE STATE!
YOU'RE SMART, DIBNY... AND TOO SLIPPERY FOR YOUR OWN GOOD... NOT TO MENTION OURS!
WHICH IS WHY I'M DOUBLING THIS BOOSTER-CHARGE FROM MY HYPNO-BEEPER!
11

I BELIEVE I'LL PASS ON THE FREE HYPNOSIS-SESSION THIS TIME, IF YOU DON'T MIND!
WILL YOU LOOK AT THAT ARM! AND I USED TO THINK I WAS WEIRD!
NOW, MISS BLUBBA--ALLOW ME TO RELIEVE YOU OF THAT PRECIOUS "LIQUID LOOT"!
YOU MIGHT AS WELL GIVE IT TO HIM, BLUBBA! WE'RE NO MATCH FOR A FIGHTING ELONGATED MAN!
BUT AS UNTHINKABLE AS IT SOUNDS--THE CRIMSON COMET SUDDENLY RACING ONTO THE SCENE IS INDEED A MATCH FOR RALPH DIBNY!
OH--! COULD THAT RED BLUR BE WHO I THINK IT IS, HOKUS?
FLASH-- HAVE YOU LOST ALL YOUR MARBLES? I'VE BEEN TRACKING THIS THIEVING TRIO ALL ACROSS EUROPE!
WHEN THEY'RE NOT PERFORMING FOR THEIR TRAVELING CIRCUS... THEY SPECIALIZE IN STEALING RARE MEDICINE FROM LABS ALL ACROSS THE WORLD--
--NO DOUBT TO SELL IT ON THE BLACK MARKET!
OOFFF!
HOW COME FLASH AND ELONGATED MAN ARE FIGHTING EACH OTHER? I ALWAYS THOUGHT THEY WERE BUDDIES!
WHO CARES WHY THEY'RE AT EACH OTHERS THROATS? THIS IS OUR CHANCE TO ESCAPE AND GET BACK TO MASTER JERO!
12

WHEN I CONFRONTED THEM SIX DAYS AGO IN CHICAGO AND SAID I WAS TURNING THEM IN-- HOKUS CAUGHT ME OFF-GUARD AND DEEP-SIXED ME INTO A TRANCE!
IT'S NO GOOD... I DON'T SEEM TO BE GETTING THROUGH TO BARRY! HE LEAVES ME NO CHOICE!
WITHOUT WARNING, THE DUCTILE DETECTIVE UNCOILS HIMSELF AT THE SPEEDSTER LIKE A HUMAN SERPENT...
SORRY, OLD FRIEND-- BUT I SUSPECT YOU'VE BECOME A VICTIM OF A HOKUS TRANCE YOURSELF!
THAT'S THE ONLY EXPLANATION I CAN COME UP WITH FOR YOUR AIDING AND ABETTING THOSE FREAKY CROOKS!
I'M JUST PUTTING ON THE SQUEEZE ENOUGH TO KNOCK THE WIND OUT OF YOU-- SO I CAN GO FINISH THE ARREST I SHOULD'VE MADE SIX DAYS AGO!
RALPH... RALPH! YOU'VE GOT IT ALL WRONG! I KNOW EXACTLY WHAT I'M DOING!
IT'S GOING TO BE TOUGH FOR RALPH AND ME TO SEE EYE-TO-EYE WHILE HE'S TRYING TO PUT ME TO SLEEP WITH THIS BOA CONSTRICTOR ROUTINE!
SO... IT'S MY MOVE AGAIN!
WHOOAAHHH!
EYYAAHHHH!
LIKE I FIGURED... THE VELOCITY OF MY SUPER-SPEED SPIN CREATED ENOUGH CENTRIFUGAL FORCE TO SEND RALPH FLYING-- AS IF HE WERE POPPED OUT OF A SLING-SHOT!
13

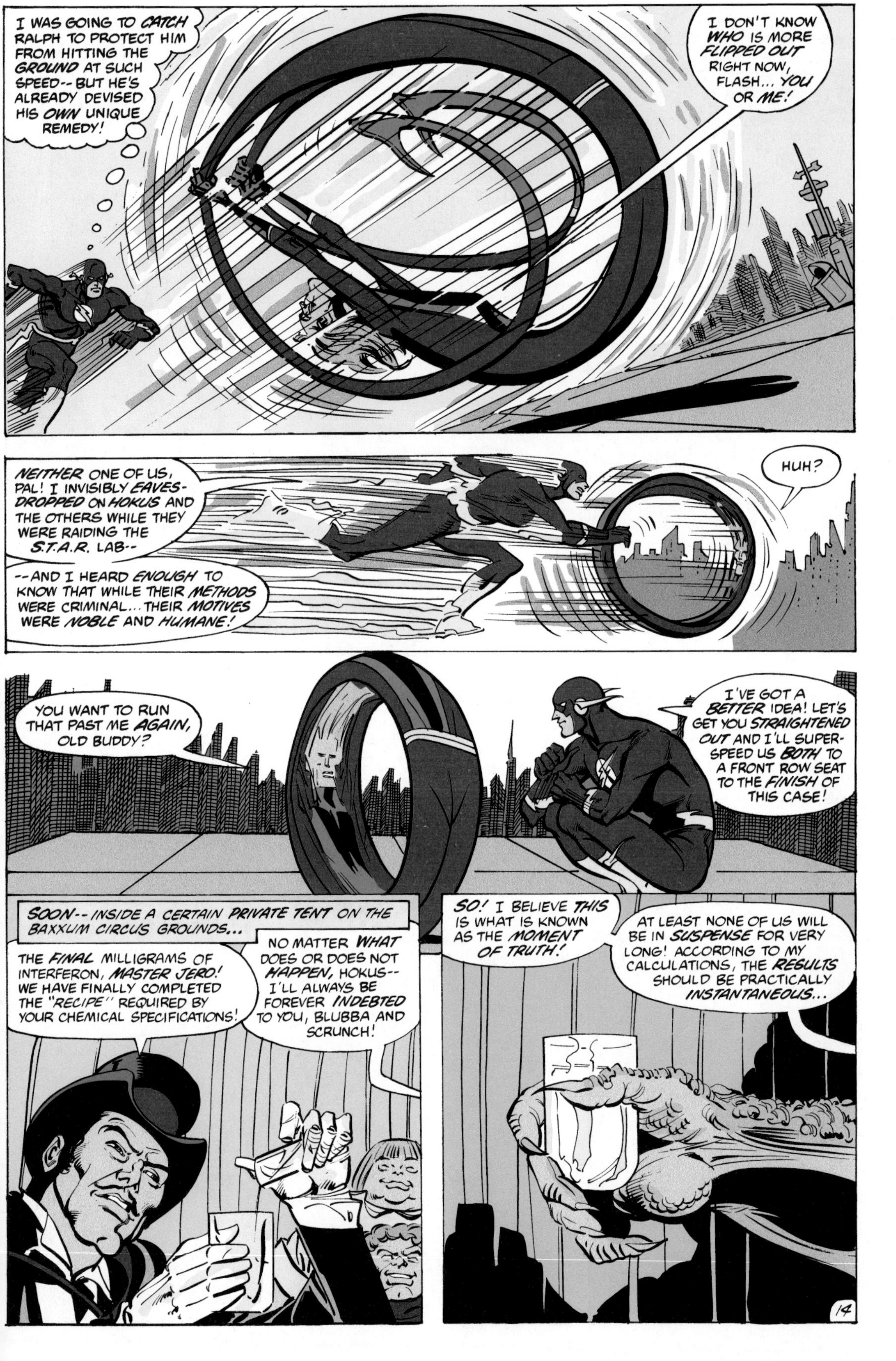
I WAS GOING TO CATCH RALPH TO PROTECT HIM FROM HITTING THE GROUND AT SUCH SPEED-- BUT HE'S ALREADY DEVISED HIS OWN UNIQUE REMEDY!
I DON'T KNOW WHO IS MORE FLIPPED OUT RIGHT NOW, FLASH... YOU OR ME!
NEITHER ONE OF US, PAL! I INVISIBLY EAVES-DROPPED ON HOKUS AND THE OTHERS WHILE THEY WERE RAIDING THE S.T.A.R. LAB--
--AND I HEARD ENOUGH TO KNOW THAT WHILE THEIR METHODS WERE CRIMINAL... THEIR MOTIVES WERE NOBLE AND HUMANE!
HUH?
YOU WANT TO RUN THAT PAST ME AGAIN, OLD BUDDY?
I'VE GOT A BETTER IDEA! LET'S GET YOU STRAIGHTENED OUT AND I'LL SUPER-SPEED US BOTH TO A FRONT ROW SEAT TO THE FINISH OF THIS CASE!
SOON-- INSIDE A CERTAIN PRIVATE TENT ON THE BAXXUM CIRCUS GROUNDS...
THE FINAL MILLIGRAMS OF INTERFERON, MASTER JERO! WE HAVE FINALLY COMPLETED THE "RECIPE" REQUIRED BY YOUR CHEMICAL SPECIFICATIONS!
NO MATTER WHAT DOES OR DOES NOT HAPPEN, HOKUS-- I'LL ALWAYS BE FOREVER INDEBTED TO YOU, BLUBBA AND SCRUNCH!
SO! I BELIEVE THIS IS WHAT IS KNOWN AS THE MOMENT OF TRUTH!
AT LEAST NONE OF US WILL BE IN SUSPENSE FOR VERY LONG! ACCORDING TO MY CALCULATIONS, THE RESULTS SHOULD BE PRACTICALLY INSTANTANEOUS...
14

...THAT IS, ASSUMING MY SERUM PROVES TO BE SUCCESSFUL!
I PROPOSE A TOAST TO MYSELF--
--AND HOPEFULLY, THE END OF THE ACCURSED AFFLIC-TION THAT HAS PLAGUED ME FROM THE DAY I WAS BORN!
...THE SAME DISEASE AN ENGLISHMAN NAME JOHN MERRICK SUFFERED FROM BACK IN THE 1880'S!
HIS APPEARANCE WAS SO UNSIGHTLY, HE WAS NICKNAMED "THE ELEPHANT MAN" AND BECAME WORLD-FAMOUS BEFORE HIS TRAGIC DEATH IN 1890!
NEUROFIBROMATOSIS...
ALTHOUGH THERE'S NO COMPLETE CURE FOR NEUROFIBROMATO-SIS... I THOUGHT MEDICAL SCIENCE WAS ABLE TO AT LEAST CONTROL THE DEFORMITIES!
IN MOST CASES, YES! HOWEVER, YOUNG JERO SUFFERS FROM A VERY RARE FORM OF THE DISEASE-- RESISTANT TO ALL KNOWN DRUGS!
HE USED TO BE PART OF THE BAXXUM SIDE-SHOW... UNTIL HIS CONDITION BECAME SO SEVERE HE WAS FRIGHTENING THE CUSTOMERS!
THE REST OF US TOOK IT UPON OUR-SELVES TO TAKE CARE OF JERO'S NEEDS, KEEPING HIM WITH THE CIRCUS BUT OUT OF SIGHT!
BUT IN SPITE OF EVERYTHING, JERO NEVER ADMITTED DEFEAT-- NOT WITH A GENIUS I.Q. OF 185!
HE SPENT YEARS STUDYING MEDICAL JOURNALS AND EXAMINING HIMSELF-- UNTIL HE FORMULATED AN EXPERIMENTAL CURE FOR HIMSELF... ON PAPER!
IT WAS UP TO THE THREE OF US TO GET HIM THE INGREDIENTS HE NEEDED!
15

I SEE! ONE OF THOSE INGREDIENTS BEING INTER-FERON, THE NEW EXTREMELY EXPENSIVE DRUG NOW BEING MANUFACTURED IN LABORATORIES FOR CANCER RESEARCH!
EVEN THE SMALL AMOUNT YOU NEEDED WOULD'VE COST MANY THOUSANDS OF DOLLARS NONE OF YOU HAD-- SO YOU RESORTED TO STEALING IT!
WE REALIZED WE WERE BREAKING THE LAW-- BUT ALL OF US AGREED WE WOULD GLADLY GO TO JAIL... AS LONG AS WE COULD PROVIDE JERO WITH HIS CURE!
GOOD GRIEF!
THEN I FEAR ALL YOUR GALLANT EFFORTS WERE FOR NAUGHT, MY NOBLE FRIENDS!
OH NO!
FOR AS YOU CAN PLAINLY SEE-- I AM STILL AS I ALWAYS WAS! MY "CURE" HAS BEEN A TOTAL FAILURE!
:CHOKE: I MUST'VE MADE A MISCALCULATION IN MY RESEARCH! BUT I WAS SO SURE...
WHAT IS IT, RALPH-- SOMETHING IN JERO'S NOTES CAUGHT YOUR EYE?
ONE OF THE OTHER INGREDIENTS IN HIS SERUM, FLASH-- GINGOLD EXTRACT! *
I BELIEVE I'M STARTING TO FORMULATE A MEDICAL THEORY OF MY OWN!
* GINGOLD, THE WONDROUS LIQUID OBTAINED FROM A RARE RUBBER TREE THAT ENDOWS RALPH DIBNY WITH HIS AMAZING STRETCHING POWERS! -- LEN.
OVER THE YEARS OTHER PEOPLE HAVE TAKEN GINGOLD... YET ONLY RALPH DIBNY TURNS INTO AN ELONGATED MAN! THE QUESTION IS-- WHY?
I THINK IT'S BECAUSE OF A RARE X-FACTOR I'VE ALWAYS CARRIED AROUND IN MY TYPE O BLOOD!
MR. DIBNY... I HAVE TYPE O BLOOD!
SO YOUR NOTES INDICATED! I'D BE WILLING TO BET THAT IF I GIVE YOU A TRANSFUSION OF A FEW PINTS OF MY BLOOD--
--YOU'D PICK UP ENOUGH OF MY X-FACTOR TO PERMIT YOUR CURE TO DO ITS JOB!
16

SCANT MOMENTS LATER, AFTER THE FASTEST MAN ALIVE HAS RACED TO THE NEAREST HOSPITAL AT SUPER-SPEED TO BORROW THE NECESSARY EQUIPMENT...
MAY YOU ALWAYS BE BLESSED FOR WHAT YOU'RE TRYING TO DO, RALPH DIBNY!
INDEED! I CANNOT FATHOM NOW HOW WE COULD'VE TREATED YOU AND FLASH AS ENEMIES!
AND OUTSIDE THE TENT, AS THE CRUCIAL MOMENTS SLOWLY DRAG ON...
THE TRANSFUSION HAS JUST GOT TO BE THE ANSWER! IT'S GOT TO BE!
IF YOU DON'T STOP PACING, BLUBBA, WITH YOUR WEIGHT YOU'RE GONNA WALK YOURSELF INTO A TRENCH!
UNTIL FINALLY...
LADIES AND GENTLEMEN-- PREPARE YOURSELVES FOR A REAL TREAT-- AS WE PRESENT, FOR YOUR PLEASURE AND DELIGHT...
...THE AMAZING AND ORDINARY MASTER JERO-- COMPLETELY CURED AND NORMAL, JUST LIKE THE REST OF US...
...WELL, MOST OF US, ANYWAY!
HOKUS AND THE OTHERS WILL STILL HAVE TO ANSWER TO THE AUTHORITIES FOR THE INTERFERON THEFTS... BUT UNDER THE CIRCUMSTANCES, THE JUDGE OUGHT TO BE LENIENT!
OH YEAH? AND WHY IS THAT?
BECAUSE JERO TOLD ME TOMORROW HE'S GOING TO START USING THAT GENIUS I.Q. OF HIS TO STUDY LAW! HE WANTS TO BECOME ANOTHER PERRY MASON!
AND I'M NOT ABOUT TO BET AGAINST HIM!
THE END
17

TWO MEN FUSED BY A BIZARRE NUCLEAR EXPLOSION: ONE IS NOBEL PRIZE-WINNING PHYSICIST PROFESSOR MARTIN STEIN: THE OTHER IS TEENAGER RONNIE RAYMOND, AND TOGETHER THEY FORM--
FIRESTORM TM.
THE NUCLEAR MAN
"MULTIPLEX X MEANS MULTIPLE-CHOICE... DEATH!"
...IF WHAT YOU'RE WRITING IS SO INTERESTING THAT YOU CAN'T HEAR MY QUESTIONS, MISTER RAYMOND, WHY DON'T YOU SHARE IT WITH THE REST OF THE CLASS?
BRING ME THAT NOTEBOOK, RONALD. RIGHT NOW!
UH-OH.
ENG. LIT 3
THE STATE OF THE ECONOMY AT THE PR AND AL
MARY, 555-0261
SCHOOL STINKS
ENG. LIT. IS BORING AND SO IS MA/TH = TH
I HATE SOCIAL STUDIES AND SCIENCE AND MATH AND ENGLISH
SNAP
GERRY CONWAY WRITER * DENYS COWON PENCILLER
BOB WIACEK INKER
FEATURING CHARACTERS CREATED BY CONWAY and MILGROM
MILTON SNAPINN LETTERER
PHIL RACHELSON COLORIST
LEN WEIN EDITOR
J-7065
1

WHAT A JAM. WHEN THEY SEE THE SKETCH OF FIRE-STORM IN MY NOTEBOOK, IT MIGHT GET THEM TO WONDERING... ESPECIALLY THAT CREEP, CLIFF CARMICHAEL!
SOMETIMES I THINK CARMICHAEL SUSPECTS THERE'S A CONNECTION BETWEEN ME AND THE NUCLEAR MAN...
HOME WORK
HIGHEST GRADES
ATTENDANCE
...AND THE THING IS, HE'S RIGHT!
BUT I CAN'T REFUSE... IF I DO, I MIGHT GET FLUNKED!
AND I REALLY NEED THIS GRADE IF I'M EVER GONNA --
YOU MUST BE AS BAD WITH YOUR FEET AS YOU ARE WITH YOUR BRAIN, RAYMOND!
OR MAYBE YOU JUST CAN'T SWEAT AND WALK AT THE SAME TIME! HAWHAWHAW!
WHOOA
CARMICHAEL, YOU TRIPPED ME! I'M GOING TO TIE THOSE DUMB SIDEBURNS OF YOURS INTO KNOTS--!
YAH-YAH-YAH. TYPICAL JOCK WISECRACK. TRUST YOU TO TURN TO VIOLENCE!
THAT'S ENOUGH, RONALD. WHERE'S YOUR NOTEBOOK?
MY NOTEBOOK? WHY, IT'S RIGHT OVER...
2

HEY! WHERE'D IT GO? I HAD IT WHEN I FELL DOWN JUST A--
I DON'T HAVE TIME FOR YOU TO SEARCH FOR YOUR LOST PROPERTY, RONALD.
IT'S GETTING CLOSE TO THE END OF THE PERIOD AND I STILL HAVEN'T ASSIGNED THE WEEKEND --
--HOMEWORK.
BRRINNG
SOMETIMES I WONDER IF YOU KIDS DON'T PLAN IT THIS WAY.
GO ON, RONALD. YOU MIGHT AS WELL GO HOME WITH THE REST OF THE CLASS.
LOSE SOMETHING, RONALD?
MY NOTEBOOK! IT MUST'VE SLIPPED UNDER THE DESKS WHEN I TRIPPED.
THANKS A LOT, DOREEN. YOU SAVED MY NECK.
SO THAT'S THE PLAN FOR TONIGHT, RONNIE? MORE BASKETBALL PRACTICE--OR DO WE FOR ONCE GET TO SPEND A FRIDAY EVENING TOGETHER, ALONE?
YOU KNOW COACH BLAKE, DOREEN. HE WANTS BRADLEY HIGH TO WIN THE LEAGUE CHAMPIONSHIP THIS YEAR. AND SINCE I'M THE TEAM'S BEST PASSER...
DON'T SAY IT. I UNDERSTAND. WELL, I'LL MEET YOU AFTER PRACTICE, THEN. BUT DON'T BE LATE...
3

"...BECAUSE I HAVE SOME PLANS OF MY OWN FOR FOR THIS EVENING, AND THEY DON'T INCLUDE TWIDDLING MY THUMBS OUTSIDE A LOCKER ROOM."
DOREEN DAY IS NOT ALONE IN HAVING PLANS FOR THIS EVENING; FOR, EVEN NOW, IN THE HEART OF MANHATTAN, AT THE TOWERING MIDTOWN OFFICE BUILDING HOUSING CONCORDANCE RESEARCH, INC...,
...THE OTHER HALF OF THE FIRESTORM DUAL PERSONA, THE PHYSICIST NAMED PROFESSOR MARTIN STEIN, IS JUST PUTTING PLANS OF HIS OWN INTO ACTION...
G'NIGHT, MARTIN. BE SURE TO TURN OFF THE LIGHTS WHEN YOU LEAVE, OKAY? SEE YOU MONDAY MORNING.
I'M FORTUNATE THE PERSONNEL DIRECTOR DIDN'T FIRE ME FROM THIS JOB, AFTER MY DISAPPEARANCE FROM MY LAST POSTING IN THE SOUTH PACIFIC.*
IT'S GIVEN ME THE OPPORTUNITY I'VE BEEN HOPING FOR,..
*SEE THE PAST THREE ISSUES OF THE FLASH. --LEN.
...THE CHANCE TO USE THIS LAB TO STUDY WHAT EFFECT BEING HALF A SUPER-HERO IS HAVING ON MY METABOLISM!
WHEN RONALD RAYMOND TOLD ME THAT HE AND I SHARED A DUAL IDENTITY AS THE NUCLEAR MAN, I DIDN'T BELIEVE HIM. NOW, I DO BELIEVE...
4

...AND I CAN'T HELP WONDERING WHERE OUR FIRESTORM ALTER-EGO FINDS THE SHEER POWER TO DO WHAT HE DOES.
IT CERTAINLY ISN'T SPONTANEOUS CREATION OF ENERGY, SO HOW CAN--
KRASHH
WORKING LATE, DEAR OLD MENTOR? HOW LIKE YOU...
...AND HOW DESPICABLE! I HATED THAT LITTLE IDIOSYNCRACY OF YOURS WHEN I WAS YOUR ASSISTANT DURING THE DESIGN OF THE HUDSON NUCLEAR FACILITY.
I STILL HATE IT, NOW THAT I AM SOMETHING--FAR MORE!
YOUR VOICE... I KNOW YOU!
OF COURSE YOU DO. I'M DANTON BLACK, FORMERLY YOUR STUDENT--FORMERLY YOUR RIVAL. AN EXPLOSION AT THE HUDSON FACILITY MADE ME WHAT I AM NOW, HOWEVER--YOUR SUPERIOR!
CALL ME MULTIPLEX--
--OR CALL ME YOUR EXECUTIONER!
EITHER NAME WILL DO, BETWEEN OLD FRIENDS.
THAT EXPLOSION DANTON MENTIONED--IT MUST HAVE BEEN THE SAME BLAST THAT FUSED RONALD AND ME INTO FIRESTORM! YES, NOW I REMEMBER...
5

"THERE WAS SOMETHING ABOUT IT IN THE PAPERS AT THE TIME. MULTIPLEX WAS FIRESTORM'S FIRST SUPER-VILLAIN..."
"...BUT WHERE THE NUCLEAR MAN HAS THE POWER OF FUSION..."
"...THE MULTIPLE MENACE GAINS HIS POWER THROUGH FISSION!"
I'VE BIDED MY TIME THESE PAST FEW MONTHS, STEIN. I'VE WAITED FOR JUST THE RIGHT CRIME TO PULL FOR MY COMEBACK!
THEN, WHEN I READ IN A SCIENTIFIC JOURNAL THAT YOU HAD COME TO WORK FOR CONCORDANCE RESEARCH, I SAW MY OPPORTUNITY, AND I SEIZED IT!
CONCORDANCE HAS A WEAPONS DEVELOPMENT CONTRACT WITH THE PENTAGON!
RECENTLY THEY DEVELOPED A NEW FORM OF RADAR, WORTH MILLIONS.
"THE PROTOTYPE MODEL OF THAT RADAR IS KEPT IN A VAULT ON THIS FLOOR."
"NATURALLY, ACCESS TO THE VAULT IS RESTRICTED --AND PROTECTED BY A SOPHISTICATED ALARM SYSTEM."
"THE ONLY WAY INTO THE VAULT AREA IS THROUGH A VENT TUBE BARELY LARGE ENOUGH FOR A SMALL CHILD."
"BY DIVIDING MYSELF A NUMBER OF TIMES, I CAN CREATE SMALLER DUPLICATES OF MYSELF..."
"...EACH ONE TINIER THAN THE ONE BEFORE..."
6

"...ALLOWING 'ME' TO PASS ANY OBSTACLE..."
"...UNTIL I REACH THE HEART OF THE VAULT ITSELF!"
ONCE I BREAK INTO THE VAULT AND STEAL THE PROTOTYPE, I'LL MAKE THE RETURN TRIP EASILY--WHILE PLANTING EVIDENCE THAT WILL LINK YOU, DEAR OLD ENEMY, WITH THE CRIME!
BUT--I MUST CONCENTRATE --TO MAINTAIN MY MENTAL CONTROL!
LOOKING AWAY FROM ME...
...GIVING ME THE CHANCE I NEED TO REACH OUT--AND SUMMON RONALD, FUSING US ONCE MORE INTO THE HERO CALLED FIRESTORM!
NICE PLAN, PROFESSOR, BUT UNKNOWN TO YOU, THERE'S ABOUT TO BE A HITCH...
FOR, AT THIS VERY MOMENT, IN THE SCHOOL GYM AT THE REAR OF BRADLEY HIGH...
WE'VE BEEN SHOOTING BASKETS FOR AN HOUR! GETTING SO SWEATY I CAN HARDLY--
WHEW! COACH SURE IS PUSHING HARD!
--SEE WHERE I'M--
7

KLONG
BROTHER, HE SURE WHONKED HIMSELF GOOD, DIDN'T HE?
LUCKY FOR HIM HE'S GOT SUCH A THICK HEAD.
UH-OH, HERE COMES COACH BLAKE.
YOU GUYS, YOU GUYS! YOU'RE PUBLIC MENACES, THE BUNCH OF YOU!
NOW GET OUTTA MY WAY AND LET ME SEE IF RAYMOND IS --
--HURT?
OKAY, WHO STOLE RAYMOND?
I DON'T GET IT, COACH. HE WAS HERE A MOMENT AGO. HOW COULD HE JUST--
"--DISAPPEAR?" THE ANSWER IS, HE DIDN'T--RATHER, HIS PHYSICAL FORM TRAVELED HALF A DOZEN MILES TO COMBINE WITH ANOTHER...
THE RESULT IS--
FIRESTORM!?
YES, WELL, THERE'S A PROBLEM ABOUT THAT. YOU SEE...
GOOD HEAVENS! NORMALLY, RONALD IS IN CONTROL OF THE FIRESTORM PERSONA, BUT SUDDENLY, THIS TIME-- I AM!
BUT--I'VE NEVER DONE THIS BEFORE! I DON'T KNOW WHAT TO DO!
THEN YOU BETTER LEARN FAST, PROFESSOR! 'CAUSE HERE COMES MULTIPLEX--AND BOY, DOES HE LOOK MAD!
AS YOU MIGHT WELL IMAGINE-- TO BE CONTINUED!

TWO MEN FUSED BY A BIZARRE NUCLEAR EXPLOSION: ONE IS NOBEL PRIZE-WINNING PHYSICIST PROFESSOR MARTIN STEIN: THE OTHER IS TEENAGER RONNIE RAYMOND, AND TOGETHER THEY FORM--
FIRESTORM
THE NUCLEAR MAN
THE RONNIE RAYMOND RULE OF MAXIMUM FOUL-UP: SOMETIMES, WHEN YOU LEAST EXPECT IT, DISASTER COMES ALONG TO TAKE A BITE OUT OF YOUR BACKSIDE.
THIS IS ONE OF THOSE SOMETIMES.
PROFESSOR STEIN, SOMETHING'S GONE SCREWY! YOU SUMMONED ME TO JOIN YOU AS OUR FUSED PERSONA FIRESTORM--
BUT INSTEAD OF ME BEING IN CHARGE OF OUR FUSED SUPER-GUY BODY-- YOU ARE!
I THINK WE'RE IN VERY SERIOUS TROUBLE, DEAR BOY!
THE MULTIPLEX COMPLEX
GERRY CONWAY writer
DENYS COWAN & BOB WIACEK artists
featuring characters created by CONWAY AND MILGROM
BEN ODA letterer
JERRY SERPE colorist
LEN WEIN editor
1

PARTICULARLY UNDER THE CIRCUMSTANCES.
I SUMMONED OUR FIRESTORM PERSONA BECAUSE OUR OLD NEMESIS, MULTIPLEX, HAS RETURNED TO CAUSE US-- OR RATHER, ME--NEW ANGUISH.
MULTIPLEX, OF COURSE, IS MY OLD LAB ASSISTANT, DANTON BLACK.
THE SAME NUCLEAR ACCIDENT THAT JOINED RONNIE RAYMOND AND PROFESSOR MARTIN STEIN INTO THE NUCLEAR MAN--
--GAVE DANTON BLACK THE ABILITY TO SPLIT HIMSELF INTO SEVERAL BEINGS SIMULTANEOUSLY!
I KNOW ALL THAT, PROFESSOR. OBVIOUSLY HE'S BACK TO DO YOU DIRT--MAYBE FRAME YOU FOR A ROBBERY HERE AT CONCORDANCE RESEARCH!
SO SKIP THE FLASHBACK AND LET'S DO SOMETHING!
AH, YES, BUT--AH-- WHAT?
WHATEVER YOU DO, PROFESSOR--
--DO IT QUICK!
CHOOOM
2

I DON'T KNOW WHY YOU'RE JABBERING TO YOURSELF, FIRESTORM...
...OR WHAT MADE YOU COME HERE, TO INTERFERE WITH MY PRIVATE REVENGE ON MARTIN STEIN...
BUT NOW THAT YOU'RE HERE, I'M GLAD.
I LOOK FORWARD TO DISMANTLING YOU, PUNK. LIMB BY LIMB.
I BELIEVE HE BEARS A GRUDGE FROM OUR LAST ENCOUNTER.*
I'LL TRY TO AVOID HIM WHILE I GATHER MY THOUGHTS.
SHARP MOVE, PROFESSOR.
*FROM FIRESTORM #5. --L.
ONLY ONE PROBLEM. I SEE FROM WHAT'S IN OUR MUTUAL MIND THAT MULTIPLEX HAS SENT A WHOLE BUNCH OF LITTLE MULTIPLEXES TO STEAL SOME GIZMO FROM THE CONCORDANCE VAULT.
GOOD LORD, THAT'S RIGHT!
I CAN'T LET HIM STEAL THE NEW RADAR PROTOTYPE MODEL THAT CONCORDANCE DEVELOPED FOR THE PENTAGON! BUT HOW CAN I STOP HIM?
THERE ARE SO MANY POSSIBILITIES... SO MANY ALTERNATIVES TO CHOOSE FROM...!
WISH I COULD HELP YOU, PROFESSOR...
3

NORMALLY, I'M IN CHARGE OF OUR FIRESTORM IDENTITY.
BUT BECAUSE OF A BUMP ON THE OLD CRANIUM, WHICH I JUST PICKED UP DURING A ROUND OF BASKETBALL PRACTICE BACK AT SCHOOL--
--I WAS UNCONSCIOUS WHEN YOU BROUGHT US TOGETHER.
THAT MEANS YOU'RE IN CHARGE, PROFESSOR. FOR A CHANGE, I'M THE BACKSEAT DRIVER. YOU'VE GOT THE WHEEL--SO DRIVE!
IF I MUST, THEN, BY HEAVEN, I WILL!
MULTIPLEX SPLIT OFF PART OF HIMSELF IN SMALLER FORM--
"--AND THOSE INCREASINGLY SMALLER 'MULTIPLEX' CLONES ARE USING THEIR DIMINUTIVE HEIGHT TO ENTER THE VAULT AREA--
"--SLIPPING PAST THE ALARMS BECAUSE OF THEIR SIZE!"
WE'LL PUT A STOP TO THAT RIGHT NOW!
FTOOM
FTOOM
4
YOU NEED PRACTICE, PROFESSOR, ESPECIALLY WHEN YOU USE OUR ATOMIC RE-STRUCTURING POWER TO PASS THROUGH WALLS!
THAT LAST WALL FELT LIKE HOT CHEESE AS WE WENT THROUGH!

I BELIEVE I'M GETTING THE KNACK OF THIS, RONALD.
BY HITTING THE VARIOUS MULTIPLEX CLONES WITH MY NUCLEAR BURSTS, I'M "OVERLOADING THEIR ENERGY CAPACITY!
THE RESULT--THEY'RE POPPING OUT OF EXISTENCE LIKE OVER-EXPANDED SOAP BUBBLES! THIS IS THE SAME METHOD WE USED TO DEFEAT HIM LAST TIME!
THAT'S WHAT WORRIES ME, PROFESSOR.
MULTIPLEX WOULDN'T BE DUMB ENOUGH TO FALL FOR THE SAME TRICK TWICE. I GET THE FEELING WE'RE BEING SET UP FOR A--
--FALL!
KLONG
5

IT'S NOT MUCH, I ADMIT, JUST AN OLD ABANDONED TEXTILE FACTORY IN SOHO, BUT I CALL IT HOME. I HAVE TO, THANKS TO YOU.
IT'S JUST ONE MORE INDIGNITY YOU'VE CAUSED ME...
...ONE MORE REASON I'M GLAD I CAPTURED YOU.
A PITY MY OLD MENTOR STEIN DISAPPEARED. IF I HAD HIM, AS WELL AS YOU, AND THIS RADAR PROTOTYPE, MY JOY WOULD BE COMPLETE.
WHAT ARE YOUR PLANS NOW, BLACK?
OH, I SUPPOSE I'LL HAVE TO FIND A BUYER FOR THE RADAR.
THAT SHOULDN'T BE TOO HARD. IN THE MONTHS I'VE SPENT IN HIDING, I'VE MADE A FEW CONTACTS IN THE UNDERWORLD.
THEY'RE A SLEAZY BUNCH, BUT THEY SHOULD BE USEFUL-- NOT LIKE THAT MANIAC, THE HYENA, WHOM I ALMOST TOOK ON AS A PARTNER SOME MONTHS AGO.*
TOTALLY IRRESPONSIBLE, THAT ONE. WE MET ONCE, THEN HE VANISHED.
*ALSO IN FS #5. --LEN.
NOW IF YOU'LL EXCUSE ME, I HAVE SOME PERSONAL MATTERS TO ATTEND TO.
WHEN I RETURN, WE'LL SEE HOW LONG IT TAKES YOU TO DIE.
HMM, MOST INTRIGUING. I WONDER...
6

THAT LAMP SHOULD TELL ME WHAT I NEED TO KNOW.
YES, AS I EXPECTED! THE LIGHT IS DIMMING...
...AS THOUGH THERE WERE A MOMENTARY POWER DRAIN AFFECTING THE WHOLE BUILDING. I WONDERED WHY BLACK CHOSE AN OLD FACTORY FOR HIS LAIR.
NOW I KNOW. HE NEEDED THE HEAVY-DUTY POWER LINES THAT FEED INTO THE FACTORY TO CARRY THE ELECTRICAL CURRENT HE REQUIRES TO FEED HIS NEEDS AS MULTIPLEX!
THIS CHARADE HAS CONTINUED QUITE LONG ENOUGH!
WH-WHAT? FIRESTORM! BUT YOU WERE BOUND-- SECURELY TIED--!
COME NOW, MULTIPLEX, DID YOU REALLY THINK A FEW STRANDS OF WIRE COULD HOLD A MAN WHO CAN ALTER MOLECULAR STRUCTURE AT WILL?
I CHANGED YOUR BONDS TO GARLANDS OF PLASTIC FLOWERS--
--AND I'D HAPPILY DO THE SAME TO YOU, IF MY POWERS HAD A SIMILAR AFFECT ON ORGANIC MOLECULES! SADLY, THEY DO NOT!
THUS, YOU'LL HAVE TO SETTLE FOR A PRISON TERM!
NEVER!
NEVER!
7

I PROMISED TO DESTROY YOU--
--AND I SHALL!
I GIVE YOU THIS, MY FRIEND, YOU ARE PERSISTENT.
PERSISTENCE, HOWEVER, IS THE VIRTUE OF THE INCOMPETENT.
AND WHILE MY NUCLEAR POWERS CANNOT AFFECT ORGANIC MATERIALS, THEY CAN MANIPULATE THOSE HEAVY DUTY POWER CABLES QUITE HANDILY--
"--CAUSING THEM TO WRAP AROUND THE BOTH OF YOU, CHANGING THEIR ELECTRICAL CHARGE FROM POSITIVE TO NEGATIVE!
SSSSKKKZZ
"INSTEAD OF SUPPLYING YOU WITH ENERGY, THE CABLES WILL DRAIN YOUR ENERGY--
"--UNTIL YOU ARE FORCED TO RECOMBINE INTO ONE BEING, NO STRONGER THAN ANY OTHER MAN.
"AND THAT, DANTON BLACK, IS THE END OF YOUR MULTIPLEX COMPLEX!"
AND SO, NOT LONG AFTER, AS THE NEW YORK FINEST ARRIVE IN ANSWER TO AN ANONYMOUS PHONE CALL...
YOU DID GOOD, PROFESSOR. I'M GLAD I KEPT IN THE BACKGROUND WHILE YOU AND MULTIPLEX TUSSLED.
THERE'S ONE ADDITIONAL FAVOR YOU CAN DO ME, RONALD.
OH? WHAT'S THAT, PROFESSOR?
DON'T EVER GET YOURSELF KNOCKED UNCONSCIOUS AGAIN.
HA HA HA HA
FROM NOW ON, YOU MAY CONTROL FIRESTORM--AND YOU'RE WELCOME TO IT!
THE END

ONCE UPON A TIME...
by LEN WEIN & WALTER SIMONSON
IT WAS A DARK AND STORMY NIGHT.
SUDDENLY, A SHOT RANG OUT.
THE MAID SCREAMED.
A DOOR SLAMMED.

SUDDENLY, A PIRATE SHIP APPEARED ON THE HORIZON.
THE REAPER'S EDGE
AS HE TOUCHED HER HAND, SHE SIGHED.
AND THEY LIVED HAPPILY EVER AFTER.

ANNUAL
DC
1982
$1.00
NO.1
DC COMICS PRESENTS
SUPERMAN
AND THE GOLDEN AGE
SUPERMAN
APPROVED BY THE COMICS CODE AUTHORITY
S-3957

SUPERMAN
A MEETING OF GIANTS
SIDE-BY-SIDE WITH
THE GOLDEN AGE
SUPERMAN
created by JERRY SIEGEL & JOE SHUSTER
MARV WOLFMAN writer RICH BUCKLER & DAVE HUNT artists
JOHN COSTANZA letterer CARL GAFFORD colorist JULIUS SCHWARTZ editor
S-3910
CRISIS ON THREE EARTHS!
1

CHAPTER 1
MILLION-DOLLAR MAYHEM!
HE STRIKES QUICKLY, CRUSHING ALL OPPOSITION WITHIN SECONDS. NOTHING BUT NOTHING STANDS IN HIS WAY...
L BANK
SKRUNCH
BANK
$
$
IT'S LUTHOR! H-HE'S GOT TO BE STOPPED!
STOP
BAM
BAM
BLAM
BAM
STOP HIM? WE CAN'T EVEN SLOW HIM DOWN!
FACE IT, JACKSON-- WE NEED SUPERMAN!
AND, SPEAKING OF WHOM...
LUNCH ON LES CHAMPS ELYSÉES... IT WAS WONDERFUL, DARLING.
WELL, I'VE HAD TO BREAK SO MANY DATES LATELY--
--I FELT I OWED YOU SOMETHING SPECIAL.
MMMMMM! IT WAS, IT WAS! I WISH THINGS COULD BE LIKE THIS FOR US ALWAYS!
SO DO I, BUT I'M AFRAID EVEN THIS DATE HAS TO BE CUT SADLY SHORT!
:SIGH: ANOTHER EMERGENCY?
AFRAID SO, HONEY.
CRIME DOESN'T TAKE OFF LUNCH-HOURS. I GUESS I'M DENIED THAT LUXURY AS WELL!
G
LOIS LANE SAYS NOTHING, BUT THE MAN OF STEEL FEELS HER STIFFEN IN HIS ARMS...
2

RELUCTANTLY, HE LOWERS HER TO THE ROOF OF THE GALAXY BROADCASTING BUILDING, AND...
SUPERMAN, WHAT ARE YOU DOING-- SUPERMAN!?!
WRUNCH
BUT THE ACTION ACE IS ALREADY ON THE MOVE...
TELL ME, SUPERMAN--IS THAT DAILY PLANET GLOBE SUPPOSED TO REPRESENT SOME MANNER OF THREAT?
AH, AT LAST, OLD FRIEND. I'VE WONDERED WHAT HAS TAKEN YOU SO LONG!
WELL, IT DOESN'T, YOU FOOL!
YOU SEE, I'VE COME PREPARED FOR THIS MEETING--
--WITH A SPECIAL KRYPTONITE RAY OF MY OWN DESIGN!
WHICH IS WHY I'M STAYING OUT OF RANGE, LUTHOR.
WHAT YOU CAN'T HIT CAN'T HURT ME!
POLICE
AND, SINCE I WANT TO "SPARE" MYSELF ANY FURTHER GRIEF--
--I THINK IT'S TIME TO "STRIKE" YOU OUT!
SKRUNCH!
LUTHOR, LUTHOR, JUST WHAT AM I EVER GOING TO DO WITH YOU?
WHEN ARE YOU GOING TO REALIZE--AS LONG AS SUPERMAN IS AROUND--CRIME NEVER PAYS!
BAH!
POLICE
3

SOON...
SORRY THAT TOOK SO LONG, LOIS--
--BUT I WANTED TO MAKE CERTAIN LUTHOR WAS SAFELY BEHIND BARS!
AND IF IT WEREN'T THAT, THERE'D BE SOMETHING ELSE!
I'M BEGINNING TO THINK YOU THRIVE ON THESE LITTLE TROUBLES.
COME ON, LOIS--LOOK WHAT HAPPENS WHEN I TAKE A LITTLE SIDETRIP TO PARIS.
DO YOU REALIZE WHAT MIGHT HAVE HAPPENED IF I WEREN'T HERE?
BUT I LOVE YOU, DARLING, AND I WANT TO FEEL THAT YOU LOVE ME!
YOU DON'T THINK I'D LIKE THE SAME?
I MAY BE "SUPER", BUT I'M ALSO A MAN!
BUT BECAUSE I'M SUPERMAN, I'M PLEDGED TO HELPING MANKIND.
AND I FIND AS EACH DAY PASSES BY, I SEEM TO HAVE LESS AND LESS TIME FOR MYSELF.
PLEASE UNDERSTAND, LOIS-- THE WORLD SIMPLY NEEDS ME.
AND YOU NEED THE WORLD, TOO.
LIFE IS LESS COMPLICATED WHEN YOU DON'T HAVE TO GIVE IN TO EMOTION--
--AND JUST SURRENDER TO DUTY!
YOU DO KNOW THE WORLD WAS HERE BEFORE YOU CAME!
IT MAY EVEN HANG IN THERE ONCE YOU'RE GONE!
BUT, IN THE MEANTIME, I STILL CAN'T SHIRK MY DUTY.
I'M SORRY, LOIS. I'M TRULY SORRY!
WGBS
SO AM I, DARLING. SO AM I!
4

EARTH-TWO: AND IN THE LAB OF THIS EARTH'S LUTHOR...
ALL TOO OFTEN HAVE I BEEN DEFEATED BY THAT SUPER-POWERED CRETIN...
...AND ALL TOO OFTEN HAVE I REFRAINED FROM STRIKING BACK WITH ALL THE AWESOME ARSENAL AT MY DISPOSAL.
BUT NO MORE, SUPERMAN!
THIS TIME ALEXEI LUTHOR SHALL BE THE VICTOR!
YOU SEE, SUPERMAN, THIS TIME MY PLAN EXCLUDES YOU, YET WILL HIT YOU WHERE IT HURTS THE MOST!
DAILY STAR
ALL YOUR STUPID FRIENDS WORK AT THE DAILY STAR--
--BUT VERY SOON, MY SUPER MISSILES WILL MAKE THEM LITTLE MORE THAN MERE MEMORIES--
--WHICH SHALL TORTURE YOUR SOUL FOR AS LONG AS YOU LIVE!
YOU MAY NOT DIE, SUPERMAN--BUT THE DEATH OF YOUR FRIENDS WILL DEMORALIZE AND ULTIMATELY DESTROY YOU!
CHAPTER 2 MISSILES OVER METROPOLIS!
5

AND, IN THE OFFICE OF DAILY STAR EDITOR CLARK KENT...
CLARK--I--I CAN'T BELIEVE IT!
THAT YOU WANT TO RUSH INTO MY ARMS AND KISS ME?
NO, YOU BIG LUG--LOOK! UP IN THE SKY--
GREAT SCOTT!
THIS CERTAINLY IS A JOB FOR SUPERMAN!
AND, AS THE MAN OF TOMORROW LEAPS SKY-WARD...
UP, UP, AND AWAYY!
BE CAREFUL, DARLING.
I ALWAYS AM, HONEY.
IT DOESN'T TAKE TWO GUESSES TO FIGURE OUT WHO'S BEHIND THIS.
ONLY LUTHOR IS TWISTED ENOUGH TO RISK KILLING MILLIONS.
WELL, I'LL HAVE TO PUT A CRIMP IN HIS SINISTERLY TAILORED PLANS!
BUT...
BEAUTIFUL! THE STEEL-SKINNED GOON SHOWED UP, BUT MY SUPER-SPEED MISSILES ARE STILL STRONGER THAN HE!
DAILY STAR
OOOF! THAT SENT ME FOR THE PROVERBIAL LOOP!
HAVE TO REMEMBER I'M NOT QUITE AS "SUPER" AS I ONCE WAS.
I WAS MY MOST POWERFUL WHEN I WAS IN MY THIRTIES--
--BUT AS I'VE GOTTEN OLDER, I'VE NATURALLY GROWN A BIT WEAKER.
WELL, THAT'S ALL RIGHT. I BEGAN MY SUPERMAN CAREER JUST BEING ABLE TO "LEAP TALL BUILDINGS".
I GUESS I CAN END IT THE SAME.
6

BESIDES, ONLY BEING "MORE" POWERFUL THAN A LOCOMOTIVE-- AS THEY USED TO SAY ABOUT ME--
--IS STILL POWERFUL ENOUGH TO CATCH LUTHOR'S MISSILES.
HMMM... IT'S TICKING.
IT'S GOING TO DETONATE ANY SECOND NOW.
WELL, I ALWAYS THOUGHT I'D MAKE A GOOD MAJOR LEAGUE PITCHER!
STRIKE ONE, TWO, AND THREE-- THEY'RE OUT!
SKA-BLAMM!
DAILY STAR
AND...
I DON'T BELIEVE IT-- HE DID IT!
WELL, THAT MUSCLE-BOUND FOOL WON'T SURVIVE MY NEXT ATTACK!
YOU SURE ARE CONFIDENT THERE WILL BE A NEXT ATTACK, AREN'T YOU, LUTHOR?
BUT I'M HERE TO BURST THAT BUBBLE OF HOPE!
SUPERMAN? BUT H-HOW?
THOSE MISSILES WERE RADIO-CONTROLLED!
I TRACED THEIR CONTROL-SIGNAL BACK HERE.
AND NOW, MY TWISTED FRIEND, I THINK YOU DESERVE A LITTLE LESSON.
I CAN FIGURE OUT WHAT YOUR SICK PLAN WAS, LUTHOR--
--AND IF YOU EVER TRY TO HURT MY FRIENDS THAT WAY AGAIN...
...I SWEAR YOU'LL RUE THE DAY YOU WERE EVER BORN!
7

CHAPTER 3
A SWITCH IN TIME!
BLAST THAT MAN! I CAME SO CLOSE TO KILLING HIM, BUT, AS ALWAYS, HE PULLS HIS FAT HEAD OUT OF THE FIRE!
WELL, GLOAT FOR NOW, MY DECADES-LONG FOE. ALEXEI LUTHOR WILL NOT REMAIN DEFEATED FOR LONG.
MEAN-WHILE ON EARTH-ONE...
HEY, LUTHOR-- MAYBE THEY SHOULD PUT A REVOLVING DOOR IN YOUR CELL!
LAUGH ON, CRETIN, BUT NO PRISON CAN HOLD ME FOR LONG.
MAYBE, LUTHOR. BUT SUPERMAN WILL BRING YOU BACK HERE AS HE ALWAYS DOES.
SUPERMAN! GAAH, HOW I DESPISE THAT NAME!
BUT IF MY PLAN SUCCEEDS, I'LL FINALLY BE RID OF HIM.
SMITHFIELD! NO ONE IS WATCHING! GET OVER HERE!
I'VE BEEN WAITING FOR YOU, LUTHOR. WAITING SO LONG.
DON'T YOU THINK I KNOW THAT?
WHO PLANTED YOU IN THIS HELL-HOLE ON THE OFF-CHANCE I MIGHT RETURN HERE?
AND WHO OUTFITTED YOU WITH A WAFER-THIN FALSE CHESTPLATE...
...COMPLETE WITH BUILT-IN MICRO-CIRCUITRY?
8

SHORTLY, IN LEX LUTHOR'S CELL...
I PLANNED THIS ESCAPE MONTHS AGO, BUT I HAD NOT ANTICIPATED MY NEEDING IT SO QUICKLY.
EXCELLENT! THE SOLAR-CHARGE FUNCTIONS PERFECTLY! THERE'S BEEN NO POWER LOSS!
SUPERMAN, I'LL ACHIEVE MY VENGEANCE--BUT IN A MANNER NO MORTAL COULD POSSIBLY EXPECT!
THIS IS IT!
AND, ON EARTH-TWO...
ALEXEI LUTHOR! I HAVE COME TO SAVE YOU!
WHAT? WH-WHO ARE YOU?
YOUR COUNTERPART, ALEXEI! ONE WHO ALSO WISHES TO SEE SUPERMAN DIE!
QUICKLY, MAN! TAKE MY HAND! THE TIMING MUST BE PERFECT!
I STILL DON'T UNDERSTAND. WHO ARE YOU?
IF YOU'RE HALF THE GENIUS I AM, ALEXEI, YOU'LL FIGURE THIS ALL OUT SOON ENOUGH!
FAREWELL, MY FRIEND--AND GOOD LUCK!
NOTHING CAN STOP US NOW!
9

TIME TO GET OUT OF HERE AND DOWN TO WORK!
GUARDS! GUARDS! HELP! HELP ME!!
HUH? WHO ARE YOU? THIS IS LUTHOR'S CELL!
I-I DON'T KNOW... I WAS IN THE CITY. THEN SUDDENLY I'M HERE!
LUTHOR MANAGED TO ESCAPE... AGAIN! WE'RE TRULY SORRY ABOUT THIS, MR...?
THORUL...LEN THORUL. NO HARM DONE, EXCEPT FOR MY CLOTHING.
WE CAN GET YOU A SUIT... THAT SHOULD BE NO PROBLEM.
EXCELLENT! LET'S PLEASE HURRY THIS, IF YOU WILL.
AND SEVERAL MINUTES LATER...
IT WORKED! I'M ON EARTH-TWO-- AND I'M FREE!
FREE TO DESTROY THIS WORLD'S SUPERMAN!
THIS SUPERMAN IS UNAWARE OF MY METHODS--DESTROYING HIM SHOULD BE SIMPLICITY ITSELF...
...EVEN AS MY COUNTERPART DESTROYS MY MOST HATED FOE!
THIS TIME, LUTHOR SHALL WIN!
10

MEANWHILE...
MR. LUTHOR--THIS WAY, PLEASE.
IT DIDN'T TAKE LONG TO FIGURE OUT WHAT HAPPENED.
YOU WORK FOR THE OTHER LUTHOR, DON'T YOU?
THAT'S RIGHT, SIR, AND HE INSTRUCTED ME TO MEET YOU AND TAKE YOU TO HIS HIDDEN LABORATORY.
EXCELLENT. YOUR LUTHOR IS A GENIUS, ALMOST AS BRILLIANT AS I AM.
NTENTIARY
SHORTLY...
YES, HIS PLAN SHALL SUCCEED. I'LL MAKE CERTAIN IT DOES.
THE OFFICES OF THE DAILY PLANET...
PERRY LOVED IT, LOIS. IT'S GOING ON PAGE ONE!
I'LL BET YOUR FACE IS RED. I GOT THAT SCOOP OF SUPERMAN BEATING LUTHOR...
...AND YOU WERE RIGHT THERE WITH HIM!
THE OL' OLSEN MAGNIFICENCE IS SHOWING THROUGH AGAIN, EH?
DIM YOURSELF DOWN, 'SUNNY-BOY'!
I DIDN'T EVEN TRY TO GET THAT--CLARK?
WHY ARE YOU SO HAPPY?
DIDN'T YOU HEAR THAT SUPERMAN ALMOST LOST HIS LAST BATTLE?
OH, SURE. BUT, YOU KNOW--SUPERMAN WINS SO OFTEN...
...IT'S GOOD FOR HIM TO LOSE EVERY SO OFTEN.
WE DON'T WANT HIM GETTING A SUPER-SWELLED HEAD, DO WE?
CLARK KENT, YOU'RE INSUFFERABLE!
11

I THOUGHT YOU WERE SUPERMAN'S FRIEND. HOW CAN YOU SAY SOMETHING LIKE THAT?
WELL, I'M ENTITLED TO MY OPINIONS, AREN'T I?
GREAT SCOTT! I'VE GOT TO GET OUT OF HERE!
AND I DON'T HAVE TO STAND HERE AND BE INSULTED LIKE THAT, EITHER.
CLARK, GET BACK HERE...CLARK!
MOMENTS LATER...
I REALLY HATE MAKING LOIS MAD LIKE THAT, BUT SOMETIMES IT CAN'T BE HELPED.
NOT WHEN THERE'S A JOB FOR SUPERMAN!
STILL, ONE DAY I'VE GOT TO START INFUSING CLARK WITH SOME GUTS!
WGBS
HE CAN STILL BE MEEK AND MILD, BUT HE DOESN'T HAVE TO BE THE OFFICE JOKE!
WELL, ONE THING FOR CERTAIN, WHAT'S GOING ON DOWN THERE IS CERTAINLY NO JOKE.
FIRE-COLUMNS SHOOTING UPWARD FROM THE SEWERS...
...AND I DON'T HAVE TO BE THE BATMAN TO GUESS THAT YOU'RE BEHIND THIS!
DON'T KNOW WHO YOU ARE, MISTER, BUT YOU'VE MADE A MISTAKE COMING TO MY CITY!
I HARDLY THINK SO, SUPERMAN--NOT WHEN I'VE COME ALL THIS WAY--
--JUST TO SAY GOOD-BYE!
12

SORRY TO DISAPPOINT YOU, BUT THE ONLY ONE LEAVING IS YOU--
--FOR A NICE, LONG TRIP UP THE RIVER.
DON'T YOU WISH, SUPERMAN!
MY GRAVITY BANDS WILL NOT ONLY SAP YOUR FABLED STRENGTH--
--BUT THEY'LL DRAG YOU TO THE FAR SIDE OF THE UNIVERSE!
RAO! C-CAN'T BREAK FREE...
EARTH-TWO...
DAILY STAR
CLARK, I KNOW IT'S NOT MY BIRTHDAY...
...AND IT'S CERTAINLY NOT OUR ANNIVERSARY, SO WHY THIS LOVELY LOCKET?
NO REASON, HONEY, EXCEPT THAT I LOVE YOU...
...AND THAT SOMETIMES I WONDER WHY I WAITED SO LONG BEFORE I MARRIED YOU.
OH, NO.
ANOTHER EMERGENCY. WHAT'S IT THIS TIME? A RUNAWAY COMET?
NOTHING QUITE SO SPECTACULAR, BUT JUST AS IMPORTANT.
IT'S A YOUNG GIRL... ABOUT TO BE RUN OVER.
OH, MY GOD, CLARK--HURRY!
13

DON'T WORRY, LOIS, I STILL HAVE TWO SECONDS.
MORE THAN ENOUGH TIME.
AND, ACROSS TOWN...
WATCH OUT! MY BRAKES AIN'T WORKIN'!
SKREEE
THEN LET ME TAKE CARE OF THAT PROBLEM, SIR.
I'M SORRY TO HAVE TO BE SO ROUGH, BUT THERE ISN'T TIME TO SLOW YOU DOWN.
FORTUNATELY, YOU'RE STRAPPED INTO YOUR SEAT-BELT.
KRUNCH!
877 HEF
AND YOU SHOULD HAVE LOOKED BEFORE YOU CROSSED! ARE YOU ALL RIGHT?
YEAH, SUPERMAN ...I'M JUST FINE.
WHICH IS MORE THAN I CAN SAY FOR YOU!
BANG! YOU'RE DEAD!
14

I-I'M SHRINKING? BUT HOW--?
HOW THIS WORLD'S LUTHOR FAILED TO DESTROY YOU BY NOW IS BEYOND ME!
BUT I HAVE SUCCEEDED!
LEX LUTHOR HAS WON!
HIS ROBOT ASSASSIN STARES BLANKLY AHEAD EVEN AS LUTHOR REJOICES...
...HIS VICTORY OVER SUPERMAN SEEMS CERTAINLY COMPLETE.
STILL SHRINKING...NOW BETWEEN ATOMS.
THERE'S NOTHING I CAN GRAB ON TO...NOTHING TO STOP ME FROM DWINDLING INTO... NOTHINGNESS.
NOTHING, SUPERMAN--?
CLARK? OH, MY HEAVEN-- CLARK!
LOIS, WE HAVE AN EDITORIAL MEETING!
LOIS--?! WHERE ARE YOU GOING?
WHOEVER THAT WAS SHOT SOME KIND OF RAY AT CLARK!
THAT'S WHAT MADE HIM DISAPPEAR!
MAYBE I CAN BRING HIM BACK THE SAME WAY
Ben's
WELL, WELL, THIS EARTH'S LOIS LANE!
SO, EVEN HERE YOU ARE SMITTEN BY THE EX-TUB OF STEEL?
15

MISTER, I DON'T CARE WHO YOU ARE--
--BUT YOU'RE NOT GETTING AWAY WITH HURTING THE MAN I LOVE!
YOU STUPID FOOL! WHAT ARE YOU DOING?
CLARK TAUGHT ME SELF-DEFENSE. NOW I REALLY NEED IT.
THIS IS THE RAY HE USED...
THANK HEAVEN! IT HAS A REVERSAL SWITCH!
STOP IT, LANE!
TOO LATE, MISTER.
MUCH TOO LATE, LUTHOR.
SKRAK!
LUTHOR? BUT HE DOESN'T LOOK--
HE'S THE OTHER EARTH'S LUTHOR, HONEY...
...WHICH MAKES ME WONDER WHAT'S HAPPENED TO MY ARCH-FOE!
HMMM. CROWDS ARE FORMING. IT WOULDN'T DO FOR LOIS KENT TO HANG AROUND SUPERMAN.
OH, DON'T WORRY ABOUT THAT. I'M A REPORTER--AND YOU'RE CERTAINLY HOT NEWS!
16

STILL, MY OTHER-EARTH COUNTERPART COULD BE IN SERIOUS TROUBLE. I'VE GOT TO WARN HIM.
BE CAREFUL... PLEASE!
MEANWHILE, WHAT OF EARTH-ONE'S METROPOLIS MARVEL?...
THESE GRAVITY CABLES ARE EXERTING THE SAME GRAVITY FORCE AS KRYPTON...
...ROBBING ME OF ABOUT HALF MY POWERS!
NOT TO MENTION DRAGGING ME ACROSS THE GALAXY TOWARD THAT BLACK HOLE!
BUT THIS TRAP JUST MAY HAVE BEEN HIS UNDOING! A BLACK HOLE IS A COLLAPSED STAR WITH AN INCREDIBLE GRAVITY PULL...
IT'S PUTTING A STRAIN ON THESE BINDING CABLES.
I MAY NOT BE PULLED APART FOR AWHILE YET, BUT THEY CAN'T POSSIBLY WITHSTAND THE PRESSURE FOR MUCH LONGER.
THERE--!
JUST WISH I KNEW WHO HE WAS! HE'S OBVIOUSLY BRILLIANT, MAYBE A MATCH FOR LUTHOR--
--AND I CERTAINLY DON'T NEED TWO CRAZED GENIUSES OUT TO GET ME.
WELL, WHOEVER HE IS, HE CAN'T HAVE GOTTEN FAR.
I'LL FIND HIM!
17

WHAT DID YOU DO TO SUPERMAN?
I'VE DESTROYED HIM--
--JUST AS I'LL DESTROY YOU, LOIS KENT!
YOU THOUGHT I WOULDN'T REMEMBER YOU, DID YOU?
IT MAY HAVE BEEN YEARS, BUT ALEXEI LUTHOR DOESN'T FORGET!
BUT...
WHOOOOSH
YOU DON'T SEEM TO SUCCEED EITHER--LUTHOR.
SUPERMAN? BUT I THOUGHT--
I'M FINE, LOIS--
--BUT LUTHOR IS CERTAINLY WORSE FOR THE WEAR.
HE CALLED ME LOIS KENT. HE SAID WE'D MET, BUT WE HAVEN'T.
I DON'T UNDERSTAND THIS, SUPERMAN.
FORTUNATELY, I DO!
THOUSANDS OF MILES AWAY, IN THE FROZEN NORTHERN REGIONS OF THE ARCTIC CIRCLE...
...AND I'M GOING TO GET TO THE BOTTOM OF THIS!
18

SEVERAL MINUTES LATER...
THAT'S OUR ONLY POSSIBLE SOLUTION.
IT'S RATHER DRASTIC, BUT I FEAR YOU'RE RIGHT!
THERE'S A LIMBO DIMENSION BETWEEN OUR TWO EARTHS... WE'LL PLACE THE LUTHORS THERE UNTIL WE HAVE A FINAL SOLUTION.
IT BOTHERS ME. I'VE NEVER PLAYED JUDGE AND JURY BEFORE, BUT WE HAVE TO DO SOMETHING.
THIS WON'T BE FOR LONG, LUTHOR.
I'LL DESTROY YOU, SUPERMAN.
I'LL DESTROY BOTH OF YOU!
THAT, ALEXEI LUTHOR SWEARS!
YOU? WHAT HAVE YOU DONE TO ME, YOU FOOL?
YOU SHOULD HAVE LEFT ME ON MY EARTH.
NOW WE'RE BOTH FLOATING HERE LIKE HELPLESS IDIOTS!
I SHOULD DESTROY YOU AS WELL AS THOSE MUSCLE-BOUND BUFFOONS.
19

ALEXEI, YOU'VE ALWAYS BEEN MORE BLOOD-THIRSTY THAN I.
BUT DO YOU TRULY BELIEVE I HAVE NOT TAKEN PRE-CAUTIONS?
TAKE MY HAND, ALEXEI.
WHAT IS IT THIS TIME?
SHUT UP AND I'LL EXPLAIN!
I ANTICIPATED THAT THOSE SUPER-DOLTS MIGHT SOME-HOW DEFEAT US...
...AND THOUGH I HAD NOT ASSUMED WE WOULD BE SENT TO THIS LIMBO--
--I STILL BUILT A DIMENSIONAL "ESCAPE-CLAUSE" INTO MY SPECIAL SUPER-SUIT.
ONE THAT WILL TRANSFER US TO EARTH!
WHICH EARTH? YOURS OR MINE?
NEITHER ONE, ALEXEI--A THIRD EARTH...
...AN EARTH ON WHICH THERE ARE NO SUPER-HEROES!
AN EARTH FROM WHICH WE CAN PLOT OUR VICTORY!
20

CHAPTER 4
WHEN MENACES MEET!
IT WORKED JUST AS I THEORIZED! THIS SHOULD BE EARTH-THREE!
NOW WE'RE FREE TO MAKE OUR PLANS!
WHAT PLANS? I'VE NO INTENTION OF RETURNING TO OUR EARTHS JUST FOR OUR RESPECTIVE SUPERMEN TO DEFEAT US AGAIN!
THE ONLY PLANS I HAVE ARE TO DESTROY MY WORLD!
DESTROY EARTH? ALEXEI, DESTRUCTION IS ULTIMATELY FUTILE. CONTROL IS FAR MORE SATISFYING.
YOU FOOLS WON'T HAVE THE CHANCE TO DO EITHER.
YOU? I WAS WAITING FOR YOU TO APPEAR!
GOOD GOD! HE LOOKS JUST LIKE--
21

--SUPERMAN, ALEXEI? BUT HE'S NEITHER OF OUR TWO FOES!
SUPERMAN? THAT FILTH!
HE AN' HIS FRIENDS IMPRISONED ME. OH, I EVENTUALLY ESCAPED, BUT I WON'T EVER FORGET THAT HUMILIATION!
BUT IF YOU'RE FRIENDS OF THIS SUPERMAN, I'LL DESTROY--
CALM DOWN, YOU BLUNDERING BUFFOON! MY LIMITED KRYPTONITE CHARGE SHOULD STOP YOU!
YOU CALLED ME BUFFOON?
DON'T YOU THINK I KNOW THAT? I RESEARCHED YOU BEFORE I CAME TO THIS THIRD-RATE WORLD.
I'M NOT LIKE YOUR SUPERMAN. KRYPTONITE STRENGTHENS ME!
YOUR NAME IS ULTRAMAN, AND IF YOU PUT US DOWN, I'LL EXPLAIN.
WE'RE YOUR FRIENDS, NOT YOUR FOES.
IF YOU'RE LYING TO ME, BALD ONE, I SWEAR I'LL CRUSH YOU!
LIE? OH, HEAVEN FORFEND. LEX LUTHOR NEVER LIES.
NOT SO THIS SLUG-BRAINED DOLT WOULD EVER KNOW!
22

FIRST, ALLOW ME TO EXPLAIN WHERE WE COME FROM.
YOUR PLANET IS JUST ONE OF MANY EARTHS-- ALL OCCUPYING THE SAME SPACE--
--BUT EXISTING IN SEPARATE DIMENSIONS. MY FRIEND ALEXEI IS FROM EARTH-TWO. I AM FROM EARTH-ONE. AND THIS IS EARTH-THREE.
BAH! ANY EARTH I AM ON IS EARTH-ONE!
MY FRIEND, OH, MY FRIEND. THE NUMBER IS MERE DESIGNATION.
THEY INDICATE THE ORDER OF DISCOVERY.
THE FIRST DIMENSIONAL CROSSOVER WAS FROM EARTH-ONE TO EARTH-TWO. HENCE THE NUMBERS.
THERE'S NO PEJORATIVE CONNOTATION MEANT HERE.
I KNOW OF THOSE OTHER EARTHS.
I TOLD YOU THEIR HEROES CAPTURED ME AND MY FRIENDS.
AND WE KNOW THAT THIS EARTH HAS NO SUPER-HEROES OF ITS OWN, YET YOU SUPER-VILLAINS HAVE NOT BEEN ABLE TO CONQUER THE PLANET.
WELL, WE CAN HELP YOU, ULTRAMAN-- IF YOU HELP US IN DESTROYING OUR FOES.
CONQUER THIS EARTH? YOU'VE GOT A DEAL, LUTHOR!
AND YOU'VE GOT THE MIND OF A HALF-EATEN CANTALOPE!
SHAKE, PARTNER!
FOOL!
AS AN UNEQUAL ALLIANCE FORMS, ALL PARTIES ARE UNAWARE OF A RATHER FAMILIAR FIGURE LURKING SECRETLY IN THE SHADOWS...
23
THIS IS EARTH-THREE'S LOIS LANE. AND SHE IS ABOUT TO CHANGE THE COURSE OF THREE WORLDS.

CHAPTER 5
THE SUMMONING of SUPERMEN!
PUT THAT DOWN OVER THERE, ULTRAMAN. I'LL GET TO IT LATER.
WHAT ARE YOU DOING WITH AN ION TRACTOR BEAM? THAT ISN'T PART OF OUR PLAN.
I CAN'T PULL THE WOOL OVER YOUR EYES, CAN I, LEX?
I HAVE TO ADMIT I KEEP FORGETTING THAT YOU'RE ALMOST AS BRILLIANT AS I AM.
I WON'T HONOR THAT WITH A RETORT, ALEXEI.
NOW HOW ABOUT AN ANSWER?
VERY WELL, LEX--YOU KNOW ION RAYS CAN PENETRATE THE DIMENSIONAL BARRIER...
YOU'RE NOT SPEAKING TO A GRADUATE SCHOOL DROPOUT. GET TO THE POINT!
VERY WELL, LEX. THE POINT SIMPLY IS--WITH MY ION TRACTOR BEAM--
--I INTEND TO DESTROY EARTHS ONE AND TWO!
WHAT?!?
24

AT THIS SELFSAME MOMENT, ACROSS THE BREADTH OF EARTH-THREE'S VAST METROPOLIS...
YOU WERE RIGHT, MISS LANE. THEY ARE UP TO SOMETHING.
I'M PICKING UP AN EXTREME CONCENTRATION OF ION RAYS.
THAT'S WHY I CAME TO YOU, ALEX -- I CAN CALL YOU ALEX, CAN'T I, DR. LUTHOR?
OF COURSE, MISS LANE.
LOIS.
AND MY IDEA... THE ONLY WAY WE CAN STOP THEM? WHAT DO YOU THINK?
IT'S RISKY, DANGEROUS TO SAY THE LEAST. NOTHING LIKE THIS HAS EVER HAPPENED ON OUR WORLD BEFORE--
--AND FRANKLY, LOIS, THE VERY THOUGHT OF IT FRIGHTENS ME.
BUT YOU ARE RIGHT. THERE IS NO OTHER WAY.
THANK HEAVEN. THEN YOU'LL DO IT!
YOU WERE MY ONLY HOPE, ALEX. YOU'RE THE MOST BRILLIANT MAN OUR PLANET HAS.
ONE MYSTERY DEVELOPS, BUT, IN ANOTHER DIMENSION, ON THE WORLD WE CALL EARTH-TWO...
KAL-L, YOUR WORLD IS AS BEAUTIFUL AS MY OWN.
AND YOUR METROPOLIS IS JUST AS INSPIRING.
THANK YOU FOR ASKING ME HERE. MY TRIPS TO EARTH-TWO HAVE BEEN FEW, BUT I DO ENJOY THEM
MY WIFE SUGGESTED I BRING YOU HERE. I THINK SHE WAS RIGHT.
25

SHE'S ALSO THE ONE WHO SAVED ME FROM YOUR LUTHOR'S TRAP.
YOUR LOIS... YOU LOVE HER VERY MUCH, DON'T YOU?
MORE THAN I EVER THOUGHT I COULD, CONSIDERING HOW ROCKY OUR LOVE-LIFE BEGAN.
SHE WAS ALWAYS SNOOPING AROUND, TRYING TO LEARN MY SECRET IDENTITY. I THOUGHT SHE WAS JUST A PEST THEN.
BUT NOW, I LOVE HER AND I WONDER WHY I RESISTED THE IDEA OF MARRYING HER FOR SO LONG.
I JUST NEVER WANTED TO ADMIT TO MYSELF THAT SHE WAS THE ONLY WOMAN FOR ME. I'M GLAD I FINALLY DID.
WHAT ABOUT YOU AND YOUR LOIS?
OH, I LOVE HER. BUT MARRIAGE--? I DON'T KNOW.
I'VE GOT SO MUCH TO DO. A WHOLE WORLD TO CARE FOR.
IT WOULD BE SELFISH FOR ME TO CARE ABOUT MYSELF WHEN THERE ARE MILLIONS OUT THERE WHO NEED ME.
AND WHAT KIND OF LIFE COULD I GIVE LOIS? I WOULDN'T BE AROUND HALF THE TIME.
YOU DON'T KNOW HOW OFTEN I ASKED MYSELF THOSE VERY QUESTIONS.
I WASTED SO MUCH TIME BEFORE I CAME UP WITH THE ANSWER.
YES, THERE ARE MILLIONS OUT THERE, MANY MORE MILLIONS THAN I COULD EVER HOPE TO HELP.
SO I BECAME OBSESSED WITH HELPING EVERYONE. OH, I DID SO HAPPILY, BUT SOMETHING INSIDE ME WAS MISSING.
26

OUR NAME IS SUPERMAN. THAT'S SUPER AND MAN. AND I WAS ALLOWING MY-SELF TO BE CON-TROLLED ONLY BY THE SUPER.
I FINALLY DECIDED AFTER ALL TOO LONG THAT I DE-SERVED SOME HAPPINESS. THE MAN IN ME HAD A RIGHT TO LIVE.
WELL, ONCE I MADE THAT DECISION SOMETHING HAPPENED. I FOUND A RENEWED VIGOR WITHIN ME.
I HAD LOIS. I HAD HAPPINESS, AND THERE I WAS WITH THIS RENEWED COM-MITMENT TO HELPING OTHERS, TOO.
BECAUSE OF THE LOVE LOIS AND I SHARED, I BECAME AN EVEN BETTER SUPERMAN THAN BEFORE.
I TELL YOU, MARRYING LOIS KEPT MY SANITY TOGETHER. YOU SHOULD--
ATTENTION!
I NEED YOUR HELP!
I AM THE LUTHOR OF EARTH-THREE.
LUTHOR? THEN HE'S A VILLAIN, TOO?
NOT NECESSARILY. REMEMBER, THEIR SUPERMAN IS A VILLAIN NAMED ULTRAMAN.
THEN EXPLAIN WHAT'S HAPPENING TO US. WE'RE BEING ABDUCTED.
MAYBE NOT... REMEMBER, HE ASKED FOR OUR HELP.
LET'S GIVE HIM A CHANCE TO EXPLAIN.
27

CHAPTER 6
EARTH'S FIRST SUPER-HERO!
WHY HAVE YOU BROUGHT US HERE, LUTHOR?
THE WOMAN BEHIND YOU LOOKS LIKE--
LOIS LANE. SHE'S A REPORTER, AND SHE IS THE REASON I'VE SUMMONED YOU HERE
PLEASE, BE PATIENT AND LISTEN. I FEAR BOTH YOUR EARTHS ARE DOOMED IF YOU FAIL TO HEED MY WARNING!
IS THAT A THREAT, LUTHOR?
NO, NO, MY FRIEND... I AM HERE TO HELP...
IT IS MY NAMESAKES YOU HAVE TO FEAR, NOT ME!
AND, AFTER EXPLANATIONS ARE QUICKLY MADE...
THEY'RE INSANE. I ALWAYS KNEW LUTHOR HATED ME, BUT THIS IS BEYOND ANYTHING I THOUGHT HE WOULD TRY.
STAY CALM, MY FRIEND. YOU'RE STILL YOUNG AND YOU TAKE THINGS TOO PERSON-ALLY.
THIS ISN'T BEING AIMED AT EITHER YOU OR ME, NO MATTER WHAT THE LUTHORS MIGHT INSIST.
THE SICKNESS THAT INFECTS THEM WOULD BE THERE EVEN IF WE DIDN'T EXIST.
28

I'M SORRY FOR LETTING MY ANGER GET TO ME. AND I'M SO GLAD YOU'RE HERE TO HELP.
I WAS THE FIRST SUPER-HERO ON MY EARTH. I HAD TO MAKE ALL THE MISTAKES MYSELF.
IT WAS DIFFICULT FOR A VERY LONG TIME TO EX-PLAIN MY PROBLEMS TO OTHERS, EVEN TO THE HEROES WHO FOLLOWED ME.
BELIEVE ME, I CAN CERTAINLY UNDERSTAND.
I THINK ALEX HAS A SURPRISE PLANNED FOR ALL OF YOU. READY?
ALMOST, LOIS.
FOR SOME REASON, OUR PLANET HAS NEVER HAD SUPER-HEROES... ONLY VILLAINS.
I THINK I'VE CONVINCED ALEX THAT IT'S TIME FOR THAT TO CHANGE!
I'VE SPENT MOST OF MY LIFE WORKING ALONE. THERE IS LITTLE GLORY FOR THE TRUE SCIENTIST...
...AND QUITE FRANKLY, GLORY MEANS NOTHING TO ME.
BUT OUR WORLDS ARE IN PERIL. AND IT SEEMS I AM IN A UNIQUE SITUATION...
...ONE THAT FORCES MY DESIRES TO BE PUT ASIDE FOR NOW.
YOU BOTH ARE VICTIMS OF NATURAL DISASTERS-- THE DESTRUCTIONS OF YOUR HOME PLANETS.
IT SEEMS THAT WHAT NATURE DID FOR YOU, SCIENCE MUST DO FOR ME!
29

AS ILL AT EASE AS I AM IN SAYING THIS-- BEHOLD:
EARTH-THREE'S FIRST SUPER-HERO!
DOESN'T ALEX LOOK WONDERFUL?
WHAT ARE YOU GOING TO CALL YOURSELF, LUTHOR?
MAYBE I'M FORCED TO WEAR THIS SUIT AND TO WIELD THE WEAPONS I'VE BUILT INTO IT--
--BUT I WOULD FEEL DOWNRIGHT SILLY GIVING MYSELF A SUPER-HERO SOBRIQUET!
LET ME OPEN THE ROOFTOP DOME AND LET'S GET ON WITH WHAT MUST BE DONE!
I AM UNCOMFORTABLE WITH THE IDEA OF THINKING WITH MY FISTS RATHER THAN WITH MY BRAIN.
THEY'RE GONE, ALEX LEADING THEM.
ALEX... HE DOESN'T KNOW HOW LONG I'VE FOLLOWED HIS CAREER... OR EVEN CARED FOR HIM.
HE'S ALWAYS BEEN SO SHY, YET HE'S ALWAYS DONE HIS WORK SO DILIGENTLY. ALWAYS READY TO DO WHAT MUST BE DONE.
HE'S EVERYTHING I'VE ALWAYS THOUGHT A MAN SHOULD BE...
...AND I... I'VE TURNED HIM INTO OUR FIRST HERO!
MY GOD! THE POSSIBILITIES...
...THE POSSIBILITIES.
30

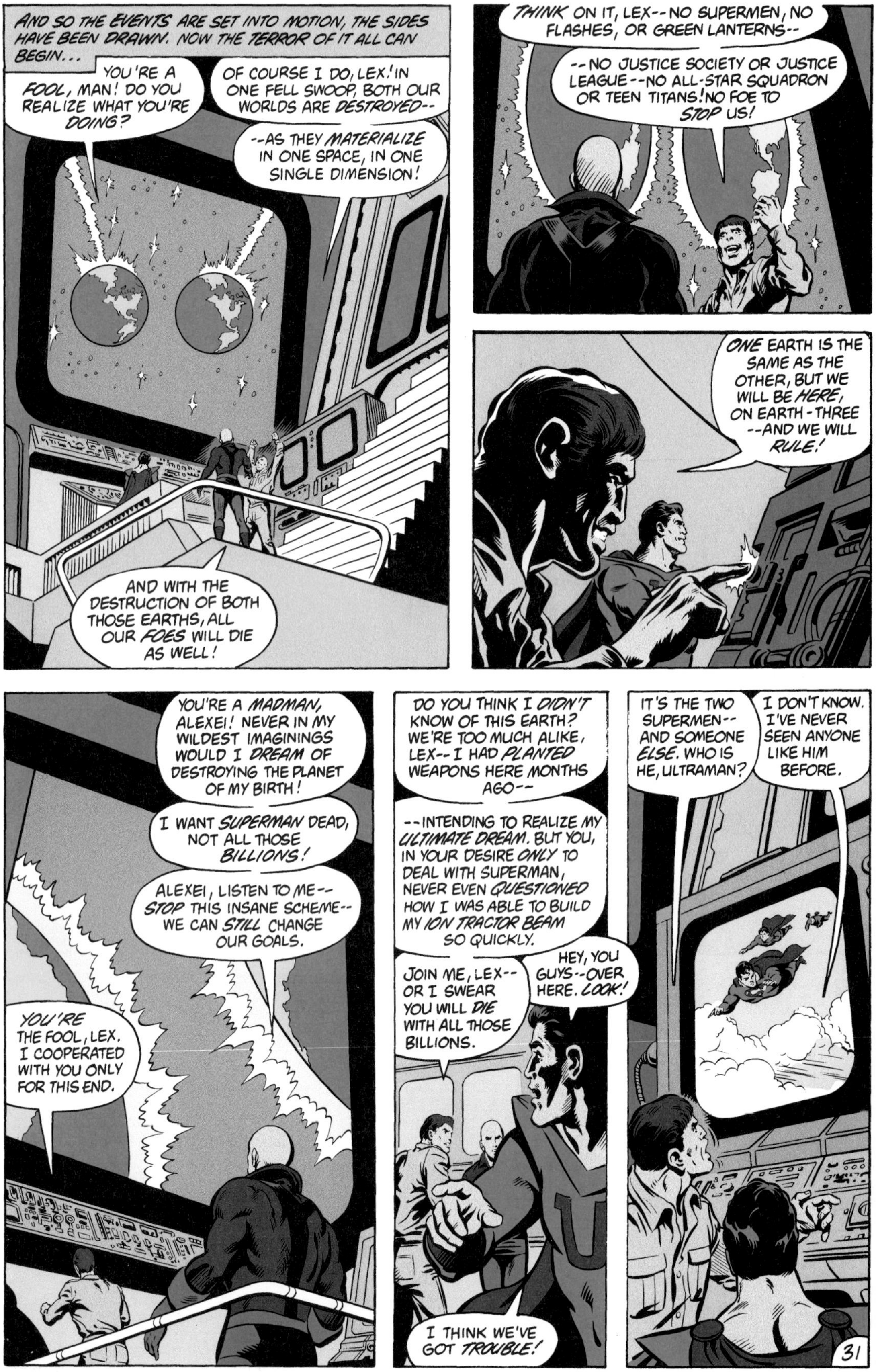
AND SO THE EVENTS ARE SET INTO MOTION, THE SIDES HAVE BEEN DRAWN. NOW THE TERROR OF IT ALL CAN BEGIN...
YOU'RE A FOOL, MAN! DO YOU REALIZE WHAT YOU'RE DOING?
OF COURSE I DO, LEX! IN ONE FELL SWOOP, BOTH OUR WORLDS ARE DESTROYED--
--AS THEY MATERIALIZE IN ONE SPACE, IN ONE SINGLE DIMENSION!
AND WITH THE DESTRUCTION OF BOTH THOSE EARTHS, ALL OUR FOES WILL DIE AS WELL!
THINK ON IT, LEX--NO SUPERMEN, NO FLASHES, OR GREEN LANTERNS--
--NO JUSTICE SOCIETY OR JUSTICE LEAGUE--NO ALL-STAR SQUADRON OR TEEN TITANS! NO FOE TO STOP US!
ONE EARTH IS THE SAME AS THE OTHER, BUT WE WILL BE HERE, ON EARTH-THREE --AND WE WILL RULE!
YOU'RE A MADMAN, ALEXEI! NEVER IN MY WILDEST IMAGININGS WOULD I DREAM OF DESTROYING THE PLANET OF MY BIRTH!
I WANT SUPERMAN DEAD, NOT ALL THOSE BILLIONS!
ALEXEI, LISTEN TO ME--STOP THIS INSANE SCHEME--WE CAN STILL CHANGE OUR GOALS.
YOU'RE THE FOOL, LEX. I COOPERATED WITH YOU ONLY FOR THIS END.
DO YOU THINK I DIDN'T KNOW OF THIS EARTH? WE'RE TOO MUCH ALIKE, LEX--I HAD PLANTED WEAPONS HERE MONTHS AGO--
--INTENDING TO REALIZE MY ULTIMATE DREAM. BUT YOU, IN YOUR DESIRE ONLY TO DEAL WITH SUPERMAN, NEVER EVEN QUESTIONED HOW I WAS ABLE TO BUILD MY ION TRACTOR BEAM SO QUICKLY.
JOIN ME, LEX--OR I SWEAR YOU WILL DIE WITH ALL THOSE BILLIONS.
HEY, YOU GUYS--OVER HERE. LOOK!
I THINK WE'VE GOT TROUBLE!
IT'S THE TWO SUPERMEN--AND SOMEONE ELSE. WHO IS HE, ULTRAMAN?
I DON'T KNOW. I'VE NEVER SEEN ANYONE LIKE HIM BEFORE.
31

IF WE ARE TO RULE THIS EARTH, THEY MUST NOT BE PERMITTED TO THWART MY PLANS!
YOU KNOW YOUR DUTY, ULTRAMAN. DESTROY THEM!
DON'T WORRY ABOUT ME, LUTHOR.
I STILL OWE THEM FOR MY LAST IMPRISON-MENT!
AND ONCE I'VE PAID THEM BACK, I'M COMING FOR YOU!
YOU TREAT ME LIKE SOME MORONIC CHILD, TALK TO ME LIKE I'M AN IDIOT!
WELL, I'M NEITHER, AS YOU AND THESE TWO SUPERMEN SHALL LEARN!
SPAK!
HE'S STOPPED THE TWO SUPERMEN-- HOW CAN I POSSIBLY FIGHT HIM?
THIS IS A FOOLISH MISTAKE, A FLIGHT OF FANCY THAT WILL KILL ME!
BEING A SUPER-HERO ISN'T FOR A SCIENTIST.
YOUR KIND HAS ALWAYS PUT ME DOWN--
NOW IT'S MY TURN, SUPERMAN! MY TURN TO SHOW WHO'S THE MASTER, AND WHO'S THE CLOWN!
TWHOK!
32

MY TURN TO GET BACK AT ALL THOSE WHO HAVE ALWAYS RIDICULED ME--
--DESPITE MY INCREDIBLE POWERS!
YEAH, MAYBE I'M NOT AS SMART AS YOU GUYS--
--BUT I'VE GOT THE POWER!
AND ON THIS WORLD, MIGHT MAKES RIGHT!
H-HE'S CRACKING UP...
...HE HASN'T THE INTELLECT TO USE HIS POWERS--
--AND HE KNOWS IT.
SUPERMAN TUMBLES HELPLESSLY TO THE GROUND. IT WILL TAKE SEVERAL SECONDS FOR HIM TO RECUPERATE...
...ASSUMING HE HAS THOSE PRECIOUS SECONDS... WHICH HE DOESN'T.
THOSE PEOPLE WERE VIRTUALLY BORN WITH THEIR POWERS, YET I'M STILL SUPPOSED TO HOLD MY OWN!
BUT IF I WANT TO SAVE MY WORLD, I DON'T HAVE A CHOICE.
MY GREATEST POWER IS MY MIND... SOMEHOW THAT'S GOT TO BE ENOUGH!
STILL SO WEAK... THE KRYPTONITE WHICH STRENGTHENS HIM MUST SOMEHOW LINGER WITHIN HIM...
THAT CAN BE THE ONLY EXPLANATION AS TO WHY HIS PUNCHES HURT SO.
MY MUSCLES ACHE AND FEEL TERRIBLY SORE, BUT I'VE GOT TO DRIVE THAT PAIN FROM MY MIND...
HAVE TO IGNORE ALL MY AGONIES... AND FIND A WAY OF FIGHTING BACK.
33

ADMIT IT-- BOTH OF YOU SHOUT IT TO THE WORLD! ULTRAMAN IS YOUR BETTER!
ULTRAMAN IS YOUR MASTER!
SWOK
NO USE! JUST BEING BATTERED DOWN...
NO TIME TO RECUPERATE.
ARE YOU REALLY? THEN TURN AGAINST ME, MY FRIEND--
ALL I HAVE IS A SIMPLE BIO-SUIT. SEE IF YOU CAN WREAK YOUR HAVOC AGAINST SOMEONE LIKE ME!
I'LL BE GLAD TO, OLD MAN!
I'LL WIPE THE FLOOR WITH ALL OF YOU!
THEN NO ONE WILL MOCK ME AGAIN!
WHAT'S ALEX DOING? EVEN WITH HIS SUIT, HE CAN'T SURVIVE ONE OF ULTRAMAN'S PUNCHES!
HE'S COMMITTING SUICIDE STANDING THERE!
COME ON-- DO YOUR WORST!
I'LL DO MORE THAN THAT, OLD MAN!
I'LL SHATTER EVERY LOUSY BONE IN YOUR--
WHA--?!
MY HAND--IT'S GOING RIGHT THROUGH YOU!
YOU'RE OBSERVANT, AREN'T YOU, MY FRIEND?
34

WHAT DID YOU DO TO HIM, ALEX?
JUST TURNED HIM INTANGIBLE, SUPERMAN.
I TOLD YOU I PREFERRED FIGHTING WITH MY MIND THAN WITH MY FISTS!
SOMETHING TELLS ME ALEX CAN HANDLE HIMSELF QUITE WELL.
NEED A HAND?
I THINK SO... I'M NOT QUITE AS YOUNG AS I ONCE WAS...
THE PAIN OF HIS PUNCHES HASN'T ALL GONE AWAY.
YOU TWO FIND THE LUTHORS. I'LL CONTROL ULTRAMAN.
BE CAREFUL, ALEX.
MY FRIENDS, BELIEVE ME WHEN I SAY I INTEND TO!
MEANWHILE...
I WON'T LET YOU DO IT, ALEXEI.
THAT'S MY WORLD YOU'RE INTENDING TO DESTROY.
OH, LIGHTEN UP, LEX! WHAT'S ONE EARTH OR TWO WHEN THERE ARE SO MANY SIMILAR WORLDS?
DO YOU OWE ANYTHING TO YOUR EARTH?
HAVE THEY GIVEN YOU ANYTHING BUT GRIEF?
LET THEM GO TO BLAZES WHILE WE RULE THIS EARTH!
NO, ALEXEI, I CAN'T. I'M NOT AS BLOOD-THIRSTY AS YOU ARE!
AND UNLIKE YOU, I'VE STILL GOT FAMILY TO PROTECT!
MY SISTER WON'T BE SLAIN JUST TO GIVE YOU ONE VAIN-GLORIOUS THRILL!
35

DON'T WORRY, LUTHOR, LENA WON'T DIE--
--ANY MORE THAN YOUR FRIEND HERE WILL SUCCEED!
THE SUPERMEN?!?
ARE YOU NOW WITH ME, LEX? DO YOU WANT TO SPEND THE REST OF YOUR MISERABLE EXISTENCE BEHIND BARS?
LET'S DEFEAT THEM HERE AND NOW AND THEN WE CAN SPARE YOUR SISTER EVEN AS YOUR EARTH IS DESTROYED!
I WON'T BE TAKEN BACK TO PRISON, AND I DEMAND SUPERMAN'S DEATH!
ALL RIGHT, ALEXEI, WE TEAM TOGETHER!
YOU CAN'T WIN, LUTHORS...DON'T YOU KNOW THAT BY NOW?
OH, WE SHALL WIN, SUPERMAN--ALREADY THE TWO EARTHS ARE JUST MOMENTS AWAY FROM TOTAL DESTRUCTION!
THEN WE'VE GOT TO SPLIT UP. YOUR POWER IS GREATER THAN MY OWN--CAN YOU TAKE CARE OF THE EARTHS--
--WHILE I HANDLE OUR MUTUAL FOES?
I HAVE A PLAN...
...ONE THAT REQUIRES SOMETHING ALEX POSSESSES.
GOOD LUCK, PAL.
I THINK WE'LL BOTH NEED MORE THAN LUCK!
36

THIS IS GOING TO BE EASY!
I'VE BATTLED MY SUPERMAN TO A STANDSTILL --
--AND YOUR POWERS ARE JUST A SHADOW OF HIS!
DON'T BET ON IT, LUTHOR!
THERE'S MORE THAN JUST POWER THAT MAKES THE MAN!
OH, MY FRIEND, THERE'S NOTHING MORE IMPORTANT THAN POWER.
AS THIS ION BLASTER PROVES!
FZZAKK!
WHOOOMM!
NOW WHAT DO YOU HAVE TO SAY, SUPERMAN?
YOU SEE HOW EASY IT WOULD BE TO DESTROY YOU?
NO, I DON'T.
WHATEVER YOU DO TO ME, YOU WON'T STOP ME!
YOU ARE INTENT ON MAKING THIS KILLING ENJOYABLE, AREN'T YOU?
MY SUPERMAN WOULD HAVE JUST CURLED UP AND DIED BY NOW.
WHY PROLONG THE INEVITABLE?
BECAUSE...YOU MUST... BE STOPPED!
BECAUSE... I MUST BE... THE ONE... TO DO IT...!
37

ALL THROUGHOUT HISTORY, THERE HAVE BEEN PETTY TYRANTS LIKE YOU TWO.
YOU ALWAYS POSSESS THE GREATER WEAPONS, YET THROUGHOUT HISTORY, THERE HAVE BEEN THOSE WHO FOUGHT BACK!
NO DICTATOR HAS EVER SURVIVED FOREVER!
NOT YOU, NOT YOUR POWERS, NOTHING CAN EVER STOP SOMEONE LIKE MYSELF FROM FIGHTING FOR JUSTICE!
BUT EVEN AS EARTH-TWO'S SUPERMAN RISES FROM A PAINFUL ATTACK...
HOW MUCH TIME IS THERE LEFT?
I CAN ALMOST FEEL THE TWO EARTHS MERGING...
...IN THE LIMBO NETHERVERSE WHERE KAL-L AND I SENT THE LUTHORS.
WELL, THIS RAY-DEVICE WILL SEND ME TO THAT LIMBO--
--AND WITH WHAT ALEX GAVE ME...
...I CAN ONLY PRAY THAT THERE'S TIME TO SAVE TWO WORLDS!
38

IT'S ALMOST OVER. RAO, I ONLY HAVE MOMENTS BEFORE THE WORLDS MERGE--
--BEFORE BOTH PLANETS TRY TO OCCUPY THE SAME SPACE AT THE SAME TIME!
THEY'LL DESTROY EACH OTHER IF ALEX'S RAY FAILS.
ALL THOSE PEOPLE WILL DIE... ALL OF THEM INNOCENTS, CAUGHT IN THE LUTHORS' PLOT FOR REVENGE!
WHAT IS IT ABOUT THESE MADMEN? BLAST, I WISH I COULD UNDERSTAND THEM...
...BUT I CAN'T! ALL I CAN DO IS KEEP FIGHTING THEM--
SOMETHING'S WRONG! ALEX'S INTANGIBILITY RAY ISN'T WORKING!
MY PLAN TO MAKE BOTH WORLDS INTANGIBLE--TO LET THEM PASS THROUGH EACH OTHER UNHARMED--IS FAILING--
HOLD IT! I DIDN'T SEE IT ON THE UNDERSIDE OF THE EARTHS... THE TWO LUTHORS' ION TRACTOR BEAM...
ALEX'S RAY USES ION POWER, TOO. BUT IT PROBABLY ISN'T POWERFUL ENOUGH...
...UNLESS I CAN INTERCEPT THEIR BEAM--
--BY PLACING MYSELF DIRECTLY IN ITS PATH!
AAGHHH
39

THE LUTHORS' RAY IS STRONG ENOUGH TO GRAB PLANETS...
...IT'S CERTAINLY STRONG ENOUGH TO TEAR ME APART!
THERE HAS TO BE SOME SORT OF KRYPTONITE BASE TO THE RAY--
--BUT I CAN'T... I WON'T GIVE IN TO IT....!
IF I FAIL TO HOLD BACK THEIR RAY--IF I CAN'T TURN THE TWO EARTHS INTANGIBLE JUST LONG ENOUGH FOR THEM TO PASS HARMLESSLY THROUGH EACH OTHER--
--THEN BILLIONS WILL DIE!
WHATEVER THE RISK TO ME, I'VE GOT TO SUCCEED!
THEY MERGE, THE TWO EARTHS...
...AS SUPERMAN TAKES A WORRIED AND DEEP BREATH.
AND FOR A VERY BRIEF MOMENT, IT SEEMS LIKE SUPERMAN HAS FAILED...
...BUT...
HE SUCCEEDED! THE EARTHS ARE SAVED AND YOUR COMPUTER CONTROL BOARD CAN NOW SHIFT THEM BACK TO THEIR OWN VIBRATORY DIMENSIONS!
ONCE AGAIN YOU'VE BOTH FAILED!
WHY DON'T YOU TWO TAKE THAT AS AN OMEN THAT PEOPLE LIKE YOU WILL NEVER SUCCEED?
40

LATER...
AH, I SEE YOU FARED AS WELL AS I HAVE.
YOU KNOW SOMETHING, I MAY JUST CONTINUE TO WEAR THIS COSTUME.
MY EARTH NEEDS IT.
I HOPE YOU WILL, ALEX. YOU WEAR THE ROLE OF SUPER-HERO WELL.
NOW WE'VE GOT TO RETURN TO OUR EARTHS.
MY COMPUTERS WILL SEND YOU HOME.
AND I WILL RETURN ULTRAMAN TO HIS PRISON.
TAKE CARE, MY FRIENDS... UNTIL WE MEET AGAIN.
EARTH-ONE...
WHY DON'T YOU JUST STAY HERE, LUTHOR?
IT WILL SAVE US BOTH A WHOLE LOT OF TROUBLE.
EARTH TWO...
IN YOU GO, LUTHOR.
BAH!
AND REMEMBER-- I'LL ALWAYS BE WAITING!
A FEW MOMENTS LATER...
HI, HON, I'M BACK!
WHAT HAPPENED THERE? WAS EVERYTHING ALL RIGHT?
IT WAS NOTHING MUCH. BUT I MISSED YOU, HONEY.
I TELL YOU, I'M SO GLAD YOU'RE STILL HERE. I'M SO VERY GLAD.
I LOVE YOU SO MUCH!
41
AND ON EARTH-ONE...
BACK HOME AT LAST! THERE'S LOIS... MAYBE I SHOULD--
LOIS, I'VE GOT AN ASSIGNMENT FOR YOU... IN EUROPE! ARE YOU FREE?
OF COURSE I AM, PERRY. WHAT DO YOU NEED?
BUT...
...BUT...
FIN

REMEMBERING JULIE SCHWARTZ

Julius Schwartz was the most confounding person I've ever known. I'm sure he was as confounding to himself as he was to those around him. The problem—and the source of his genius—was his utter absence of accurate self-awareness. In an era when the product whose renaissance he oversaw was maturing into a medium supported by an increasingly mature and thoughtful readership—that is, the growing preadolescent audience, many of whom were no longer peeling off as they got older—he insisted that he was looking for simple, unsubtle stories for kids. He thought it would do this audience some good, though, to read stories that sparked their sense of wonder. See, Julie thought everyone was like him. He had no idea how smart he was. Consequently, maintaining custody of his audience's fantasies required a smarter audience.

He was teaching us, expanding our perceptions, without telling us he was doing it. He thought he was putting something over on us when actually he was just recognizing us for who we were—who we were becoming.

He once asked his buddy Mort Weisinger why Mort always opened his *Superman* stories the same way. Mort was Julie's oldest friend. They had hung out together since they were 16 and published a science fiction fan magazine together called *The Time Traveller* (with two Ls, which Julie insisted was the correct way to spell it). Mort went on to edit and write while Julie became the first—and for a long time the only—literary agent specializing in science fiction. A few years later they were together again, editing stories for DC Comics' corporate predecessors. Mort ran the entire Superman line in those days.

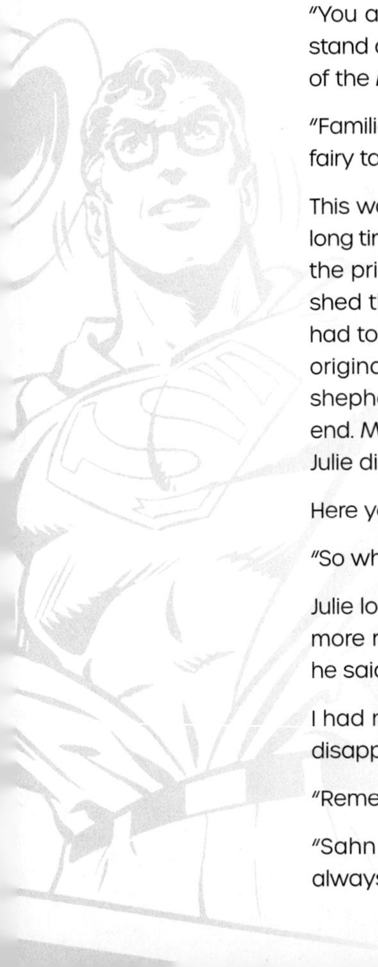

"You always start with the same scene," Julie said to Mort. "The reporters stand around Perry White's office and a caption says, 'One day in the offices of the *Daily Planet*...' Why is that?"

"Familiarity," Mort said. "An understandable frame of reference. I'm publishing fairy tales for children."

This was a very successful formula for Mort. And Julie thought about it for a long time, took it to heart. So when Mort retired from comics and Julie became the principal editor of the Superman line, he tried. A little. But Julie couldn't shed the idea that stories should be original. Inventive. Elevating. Each one had to have something that readers had not seen before. Innovation—brute originality—was what he brought to this age in comics, from the time he shepherded it into existence to the time he closed his long career with its end. Most of it worked and some of it didn't, but you could never claim that Julie didn't leap with all deliberate joy into the deep end.

Here you can see some of where that surge of novelty ultimately led.

"So what're we going to do with your last Superman stories?" I asked.

Julie looked at me a little sheepishly. A sheepish look from Julie was actually more reminiscent of something feral. "I already gave out the assignment," he said.

I had not written a Superman story for a few months, but I was still a little disappointed. "Who?" I said.

"Remember when Alan Moore was here on his way to San Diego?"

"Sahn De-eye-gao," I said, trying to channel Northamptonshire but, as always, coming out New York.

"He grabbed my shirt," Julie said, "got nose to nose and looked at me with those eyes and said, 'You must let me write the last Superman story.' So I said okay."

"Okay, you said? Just okay?"

"He's a wizard. He made me do it."

Nobody made Julie do anything. It was a brilliant choice, as usual. It's called "Whatever Happened to the Man of Tomorrow?" and it's in this book. Incredibly creative, but evocative and respectful of everything that came before. It may be the last story of what we laughingly call the Bronze Age.

Bronze comes after gold and silver because everyone knows that in the Olympics bronze is third place. But that's not what it really means.

First in the story of human civilization was the Stone Age. It was more properly the Wood Age, but archaeologists can find stone tools while the more numerous wooden ones decomposed back into the landscape long before archaeology was a thing. Then came the Iron Age, the centuries just before recorded history, when humans figured out how to smelt ore. They took iron from the earth and turned it into weapons that densely muscled warriors could lift only with both hands and enormous biceps. Conquest at the hands of these guys was as much a result of their being able to carry those things into battle as it was of their skill at using them. But the Bronze Age brought with it more intellectual rigor.

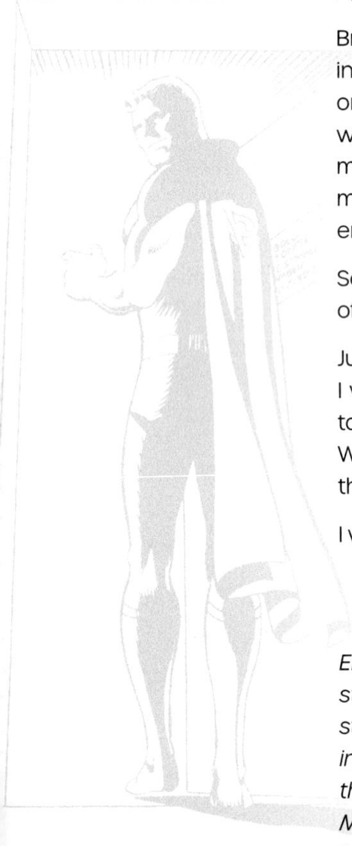

Bronze is an alloy of copper and tin, sometimes with some other metals mixed in. It could contain zinc, maybe a little manganese or aluminum, depending on what the smelter wanted to do with it. Bronze didn't corrode as iron did. It was harder and lighter when it set, and it was far easier to cast precisely. It made a better weapon, and eventually we used it for sculpture and building materials as well. Bronze was civilization's tool. It was sophisticated, complex, enthusiastic—like Julie. Like the stories whose age we call bronze.

So the tales here are some of the best of the end of an era and harbingers of the rise of a new one.

Julie had a client when he was young, a science fiction writer whose name I won't say because you may have heard of him, who got an assignment to write a 65-page story. He counted 65 sheets of typing paper and wrote. When he filled up the 65th page, he stopped and handed in the story. "That's the definition of a hack," Julie said with grudging admiration.

I was asked for a thousand-word essay. That's why, in Julie's honor, it ends here.

Elliot S! Maggin
October 2019

Elliot S! Maggin broke into comics in 1972 with a legendary Green Arrow story originally written as a college treatise. So impressed with Maggin's style was editor Julius Schwartz that Maggin quickly became a key writer in Schwartz's creative stable, penning years of Superman stories as well as the occasional Batman—or, more often, Robin—tale. Now living in California, Maggin continues to write comics as circumstances allow while enjoying a teaching career.

MYSTERIES

In the 1970s, the mystery anthology genre had been a major contributor to DC's sales, with as many as nine or ten titles being published regularly (that doesn't even count the cross-genre books like *Phantom Stranger* or *Weird War Tales*)—the most since the *House of Mystery* opened its doors in 1951. Contributors still included folks who had worked on E.C.'s legendary horror comics, like Carl Wessler and Johnny Craig, as well as young up-and-comers still learning their craft and what seemed like an endless parade of talented artists from the Philippines, led by Tony DeZuniga and then Nestor Redondo. But these were the last days of the genre; title after title met quiet deaths that were less gruesome than the ones in their pages, but just as final.

One last try at turning the trend around was the introduction of serial mystery stories into a couple of the anthologies in an attempt to straddle the divide between the one-off tales that had previously defined the books and the moody success of Marvel's ongoing *Tomb of Dracula*. But DC's vampire didn't prove to have the same ability to rise from the dead...

DC
IS THIS THE END OF...
THE HOUSE OF
MYSTERY
ALL NEW!
60¢
NO. 321
OCT.
APPROVED BY THE COMICS CODE AUTHORITY
FOR SALE
C-445

THE TIME: OCTOBER, 2023. THE PLACE: THE CITY. THE PICTURE:
PORTRAIT OF A DEDICATED COP!
DETECTIVE SERGEANT DEKE BENTON SPRINTS, HIS LUNGS POUNDING AS HE NARROWS THE LENGTH OF PLASTIGLASS SIDEWALK SEPARATING HIM FROM HIS QUARRY--
--NOMAR RAD, WHO SMILES AT THE WARMTH OF THE HUNTER'S BREATH UPON HIS NECK...
J-3268
...AND WHO POSSESSES THAT SUBTLE TOUCH OF MADNESS THAT HAS EARNED HIM THE TITLE OF "CRUELEST MAN IN THE UNIVERSE"--
--A LABEL WHICH EVEN NOW HE PREPARES TO JUSTIFY...
GOOD AND EVIL: THEY ARE SUCH AMBIGUOUS CONCEPTS. WHERE DOES ONE END-- THE OTHER BEGIN?
GOOD AND EVIL: ONE CANNOT HELP WONDERING IF BETWEEN THE TWO THERE CAN EVER BE--
PLING!
--A TRUE VICTOR!
KA-BOOM!
1

DEKE...?
I THINK HE'S COMING AROUND, DOCTOR.
MR. BENTON? MR. BENTON. I'M DOCTOR MARGOLD!
MARY...? CAPTAIN WARING...?
PLEASE, MR. BENTON, DON'T TRY TO TALK. YOU'VE SUFFERED QUITE A BIT OF DAMAGE. WE'VE PUT YOU BACK TOGETHER AS BEST WE COULD, BUT WE HAD TO MAKE CERTAIN... ALTERATIONS!
ALTERATIONS? WH-WHAT ALTER--
OH MY GOD...!
LOOKS LIKE THE DOC REALLY WENT OUT ON A LIMB TO SAVE OL' DEKE'S LIFE. BUT WHAT EFFECT THIS ELECTRONIC TRANSPLANT WILL HAVE ON THE NON-PHYSICAL DEKE BENTON REMAINS TO BE SEEN. SO LET'S TAG ALONG ON A LITTLE MANHUNT, SHALL WE? AND SEE JUST WHO GETS CAUGHT BY...
The LONG ARM of the LAW
STORY: BARRY JAMESON • ART: IRWIN HASEN & DANNY BULANADI • COLORING: BOB LE ROSE
2

WEEKS OF INTENSIVE CARE HEAL TORN TISSUE, MEND SHATTERED BONE--BUT DEEPER WOUNDS STILL FESTER...
I'M TELLIN' YOU, DEKE, THAT ARM GIVES YOU ABILITIES AND POWERS ANY MAN ON THE FORCE WOULD SELL HIS SOUL TO HAVE! IT'S THE MOST HIGHLY-ADVANCED COMPUTERIZED CRIME FIGHTING MECHANISM IN THE WORLD TODAY!
SO HOW COME I FEEL LIKE HALF A TIN MAN? GOT ANY ASSIGNMENTS IN OZ THIS WEEK?
I UNDERSTAND HOW YOU FEEL, DEKE! BUT WHAT ELSE COULD WE HAVE DONE? YOUR ARM WAS GONE. WOULD YOU RATHER HAVE HAD SOME LIFELESS CHUNK OF PLASTIC GRAFTED ON?
THEY ONLY DID WHAT THEY THOUGHT WAS BEST, DEAR!
YEAH...YEAH, I DON'T GUESS THERE WAS MUCH CHOICE!
I HAVE TO GET BACK TO HEADQUARTERS NOW, DEKE. I'LL... TRY TO DROP BY WHEN I CAN.
IF IT'S ANY CONSOLATION, YOU'VE STILL GOT THE NOMAR RAD CASE WHEN YOU GET OUT. IF YOU WANT IT!
THANKS, CAPTAIN--I DO WANT IT.
GOOD AND EVIL: WHERE DOES ONE END--THE OTHER BEGIN...?
I WANT IT VERY MUCH!
3

MONTHS PASS BEFORE YOU CAN RETURN TO THE STREETS--AND BY THEN THE TRAIL IS COLD. SO IT'S UP TO YOU, DEKE BENTON, TO WARM IT UP A BIT...
BAR
WHA--!? BENTON! I- I THOUGHT--
--THAT I ENDED UP IN THE SPOON-FEED WARD? NO SUCH LUCK, WILLIE BOY! NOW, DO YOU GIVE ME THE LATEST ON NOMAR RAD--
--OR DO WE PLAY GAMES?
LOUSY COP--!
OKAY, WILLIE, GAMES IT IS! BUT WE'RE GONNA PLAY BY MY RULES!
AGGH! Y-YOU'RE BREAKIN' MY WRIST, BENTON! L-LEGGO! IT HURTS!
AND IT'S GONNA HURT A LOT MORE, LITTLE MAN, IF YOU DON'T START SINGIN' 'BOUT NOMAR RAD!
O-OKAY, I'LL TALK! I'LL TALK! J-JUST LEGGO, WILL YA?
KRRAK
INFORMATION IS OBTAINED AND LOGGED, STORED AWAY IN THE MYRIAD GLISTENING MEMORY CELLS IN YOUR MICRO-CIRCUITED ARM--
--AND FOR THE FIRST TIME IN YOUR LIFE, DEKE BENTON, YOU THRILL TO THE STRANGELY COLD TASTE OF VENGEANCE...
4

BUT AS THE WEEKS PASS AND THE HUNT PROGRESSES, THERE ARE SOME WHO DON'T UNDERSTAND THE NARCOTIC EFFECTS OF REVENGE--THE NEED THAT KEEPS GROWING, ENGULFING, CONSUMING...
WHAT'S THE MATTER, DEKE? EVER SINCE YOU GOT HOME FROM THE HOSPITAL YOU'VE BEEN LIKE A... DIFFERENT PERSON!
LEMME ALONE!
BUT IF SOMETHING'S WRONG, HONEY--
JUST LEAVE ME ALONE, BLAST IT! I GOT THINGS ON MY MIND!
WHRASH!
AND SO, UNCARING OF ALL SAVE YOUR THROBBING THIRST FOR RETRIBUTION, YOU SEARCH FOR THE ONLY "FIX" THAT CAN SATISFY YOUR GNAWING DESIRE...
YOU SCAN EVERY FACE, PROBE EVERY PAIR OF EYES. YOU QUESTION--AND THEN YOU QUESTION HARDER.
AND WHEN THE QUESTIONING FAILS--
--THERE ARE OTHER METHODS...
5

THUS DOES YOUR ENTIRE LIFE SUBTLY SHIFT INTO A CEASELESS EXERCISE IN FIXATION, FRUSTRATION AND ANGER--
--UNTIL...
RAD--!
STRATA MALL 2
STOP! POLICE! HALT OR--
OOF!
YOU MADE ME LOSE HIM, YOU CLUMSY IDIOT!
YOU MADE ME LOSE HIM!!
I'LL KILL YOU FOR THAT, YOU SCUM! I'LL KILL ANYONE WHO STANDS BETWEEN ME AND NOMAR RAD!
GOOD AND EVIL: WHERE DOES ONE END-- THE OTHER BEGIN..?
IT'S GONE TOO FAR, DEKE, THIS NOMAR RAD THING HAS BECOME AN OBSESSION WITH YOU. YOU ALMOST KILLED AN INNOCENT MAN TODAY--AND THAT MAKES YOU NO BETTER THAN RAD.
I'M AFRAID I'M GOING TO HAVE TO ASK FOR YOUR BADGE, DEKE.
YOU CAN HAVE YOUR LOUSY BADGE, CAPTAIN! 'CAUSE I DON'T NEED YOU!
I'M GONNA GET NOMAR RAD! AND WHEN I DO, HE'S GONNA BELONG TO ME--JUST ME!
6

BENTON-- DEKE--WAIT! YOU CAN'T TAKE THE LAW INTO YOUR OWN HANDS--!
I AM THE LAW-- JUDGE, JURY, AND EXECUTIONER! OR DON'T YOU REMEMBER? YOU MADE ME THE LAW--
--WHEN YOU GAVE ME THIS!
BENTON...! BENTON!
AND SO THE FESTERING BOIL OF HATRED GROWS. UNLEASHED FROM THE CONVENTIONS OF AUTHORITY, IT FLOWS LIKE FIERY QUICKSILVER THROUGH YOUR VEINS--
--BLINDING YOU TO ALL BUT YOUR DARK AND UNWHOLESOME QUEST...
THE COSTS OF OBSESSION ARE HIGH--A CAREER, A REPUTATION, A FAMILY-- BUT THE PAYMENTS DON'T SEEM TO MATTER ANYMORE...
...FOR NOW, AT LAST FREED FROM ANY LINGERING VESTIGES OF HUMANITARIAN CONCERN, YOU FIND YOUR GOALS BECOMING RAPIDLY MORE ACCESSIBLE--
--AS INFORMATION BECOMES EASIER TO OBTAIN...
7

I'M GETTIN' CLOSE NOW. I CAN FEEL IT! THAT ANIMAL IS SOMEWHERE DOWN THERE. SOMEWHERE IN--
--NEW LOS ANGELES: GLEAMING ISLAND HOME OF THE WORLD'S LARGEST CITY...
AFTER A TEDIOUS HOUR WITH CURIOUS CUSTOMS OFFICIALS, YOU'RE BACK ON THE STREETS --TRAVELING THE SHADOWED ALLEYWAYS IN A PART OF THE CITY THAT SEEMS TO HAVE BEEN BUILT OLD...
HEY, YOU! FELLA BACK IN NYOK SAID I COULD GET SOME INFORMATION HERE.
YEAH?
YEAH! 'BOUT NOMAR RAD!
NOMAR RAD, HUH? WHAZZAT, SOME NEW KINDA MIXER OR SOMETHIN'?
CHIRP
CHIRP
SQUAWRK!
OKAY, FELLA, YOU WANNA TALK OR END UP LIKE THIS?
GULP! Y-Y-YOU AINT HUMAN--!
8

MAYBE I'M NOT HUMAN ANYMORE! MAYBE I'M JUST A WALKIN' BUCKET O' BOLTS!
BUT, MISTER, THIS "BUCKET" IS GONNA TURN YOU INTO A COUPLE HUNDRED POUNDS OF BLOODY PULP IF IT DON'T HEAR WHAT IT WANTS TO HEAR! GOT IT?
THUS THE FINAL LEAD IS FERRETED OUT, DRAWING CLOSE THE TIME TO BRING YOUR MASTER CARD INTO PLAY...
SLOWLY, WITH AN ALMOST SADISTIC GLEE, YOU ACTIVATE THE PROGRAM CODED IN SO MANY WEEKS BEFORE: "SEEK OUT AND DESTROY THE CRUELEST MAN IN THE UNIVERSE!"
AT ONCE THE METAL MONSTER GRAFTED TO YOUR SHOULDER BEGINS TO THROB, PULSING WITH AN INNER LIFE--TUGGING OF ITS OWN VOLITION AS IT LEADS YOU ONWARD...
ALL TENSION IS GONE --REPLACED BY THE OVERFLOWING JOY OF THE HUNT, THE TINGLING ANTICIPATION OF THE KILL...
9

THE PULSING... IT'S ALMOST CONSTANT! THIS MUST BE IT! NOMAR RAD IS IN THIS ALLEY! AFTER ALL THE MONTHS, ALL THE PAIN-- HE'S MINE!
MINE!
GOOD AND EVIL: WHERE DOES ONE END--THE OTHER BEGIN...?
WHA--!? THE ALLEY'S EMPTY! MY ARM'S THROBBIN' LIKE CRAZY--BUT THERE'S NO ONE HERE BUT ME!
AND THEN YOU REALIZE, DEKE BENTON. YOU REALIZE WHY YOU ARE HERE... AND WHAT YOU'VE BECOME...
GOOD AND EVIL: WHERE DOES ONE END--THE OTHER BEGIN...?
FINI
10

IS THE PAST IRRETRIEVABLY GONE? CAN A MAN GO BACK AND SEIZE ADVANTAGE OF AN OPPORTUNITY HE ONCE IGNORED? ONE MAN DID CROSS THROUGH TIME ... A SHOCKING EPISODE OF GREED AND DECEIT TO BECOME...
"The MAN WHO DIED TOMORROW"
WHAT HAVE I ACHIEVED IN ALL THESE YEARS, ETHEL? I'M AN UNDERPAID BOOKKEEPER WITH NOTHING TO LOOK FORWARD TO!
I'LL NEVER BE ABLE TO AFFORD ALL THE THINGS I'VE WANTED TO GIVE YOU...!
WE'VE BEEN HAPPY, TED! THAT'S ALL THAT MATTERS!
HOME
STORY: CARL WESSLER
ART: LEE ELIAS
COLORIST: JERRY SERPE
IF I COULD LIVE THE PAST 30 YEARS OVER, I'D NOT MAKE THE SAME MISTAKES...
I'D SET ABOUT GETTING RICH!
J-5768
TRY TO BE CONTENT, DEAR! THERE'S NO WAY TO RE-LIVE-- EVEN ONE DAY!
I DON'T KNOW, ETHEL... THERE ARE TIMES WHEN I FEEL--OH, NEVER MIND. I'M GOING FOR A DRIVE!
1

WHY MUST A MAN BE DOOMED TO A LIFE OF STRUGGLE, NEVER KNOWING *REAL* COMFORT?
IS IT *MADNESS* TO DREAM OF STARTING OVER?
ON THIS BLEAK NIGHT IN 1889, TED BRANT'S MIND DRIFTS BACK THROUGH TIME... HE'S HARDLY AWARE HIS HORSE AND BUGGY ARE DRIFTING INTO THE HILLS...
30 YEARS AGO...THERE WAS MONEY TO BE MADE THEN...THE CIVIL WAR WAS JUST STARTING!
A SNAKE! EASY, NELLIE-- EASY!
THE FRIGHTENED ANIMAL LUNGES FORWARD. TERRIFIED, TED HAULS FRANTICALLY ON THE REINS, BUT...
YAAGH!
UHH...I-I LANDED S-SAFELY... ON THE OTHER SIDE...!
TED BRANT IS NOT AWARE OF THE ASTOUNDING CHANGE THAT HAS COME OVER HIM...
W-WHAT HAPPENED? WHERE'S MY HORSE AND BUGGY?
HOW'D I GET ACROSS...? I FEEL... *SO STRANGE!*
2

HE MOVES AWAY, PUZZLED BY HIS SUDDEN FEELING OF STRENGTH, OF VIGOR--A LIGHTNESS OF SPIRIT. NOT UNTIL HE STOPS AT A LAKE DOES THE TRUTH DAWN ON HIM...
IT... GASP! HAPPENED! I'M YOUNG AGAIN...!
I DON'T KNOW WHY OR HOW IT HAPPENED...
MY WISH WAS HEARD... FATE GAVE ME A SECOND CHANCE!
THIS TIME I'M GOING TO MAKE IT! THIS TIME I'M GOING TO BE RICH!
A MIRACLE! TED BRANT HAS BRIDGED A PHYSICAL AND A TIME GAP! AND SOON HE EXPERIENCES THE THRILL OF REJOINING OLD FRIENDS, SECRETLY SAVORING THEIR VERY VOICES...
BILL GRAHAM AND GEORGE MILLER... I REMEMBER THIS... IT WAS 1861!
GEORGE, OLD FRIEND... BILL! HOW GOOD TO SEE YOU BOTH!
COME DRINK TO MY NEW UNIFORM, TED!
HA! HE HASN'T SEEN US SINCE YESTERDAY!
PATRICK, LET'S HAVE ONE FOR TED, HERE!
ARE YOU GOING TO JOIN UP, TED?
WE CAN'T ALL FIGHT! I'M GOING WITH THE WAR DEPARTMENT TO HANDLE SUPPLIES... FOOD, UNIFORMS. PROBABLY HEAVY EQUIPMENT, TOO...
I'LL BE IN CHARGE, TED! I CAN FIND A PLACE FOR YOU...
THANKS! I'LL KEEP IT IN MIND, GEORGE! I NEED A FEW DAYS TO THINK IT OVER...
DUGGAN'S TA
BAR
3

TED BRANT HASN'T FORGOTTEN THE "FUTURE" HE JUST CAME FROM. HE REMEMBERS HIS WISH TO GO BACK 30 YEARS, TO HAVE THAT BIG CHANCE TO GET RICH, TO GIVE ETHEL THE THINGS SHE'S BEEN DENIED. HE CONTACTS A CERTAIN SHADY INDIVIDUAL...
YOU ALWAYS LOOKED DOWN ON ME! WHY SHOULD I HAVE DEALINGS WITH YOU?
STRICTLY BUSINESS, BULLARD. I HAVE CASH IN THE BANK TO PAY FOR ANYTHING YOU GET ME. NO QUESTIONS ASKED!
75¢
SEVERAL NIGHTS LATER...
THOSE KEGS AND CRATES ARE LABELED "U.S. ARMY"! DID YOU STEAL THEM?
NO QUESTIONS, REMEMBER? SO JUST LOAD UP, PAY UP, AND GET OUT OF HERE!
WHAT DO YOU WANT HERE, MISTER?
I HAVE SOME THINGS YOU CONFEDERATES MIGHT BE INTERESTED IN BUYING!
TAKE YOUR JUDAS'S PAY AND GET OUT! I'VE NOTHING BUT CONTEMPT...
GOOD FEDERAL CASH SALVES MY CONSCIENCE! TOO BAD YOU'RE FORCED TO TRADE WITH ME, GENERAL! SORT OF BRINGS YOU DOWN TO MY LEVEL, EH?
TED BRANT TRAVELS BY NIGHT, SOUTH INTO THE REBEL LINES, HIS HEART POUNDING FURIOUSLY, FEELING ONLY A TWINGE OF CONSCIENCE...
CRACK
CRACK
AS THE CONFEDERACY'S NEED FOR WAR MATERIAL GROWS, HIS PROFITS ALSO GROW... AND WITH IT THE RISK OF LEADEN DEATH FROM UNION GUNS...
HIS JOURNEYS BECOME MORE AND MORE FREQUENT. HIS MONEY PILES UP...
IT DOESN'T TROUBLE YOU TO BUY COTTON FROM THE ENEMY?
DOES IT TROUBLE YOU TO BUY ME? YOU NEED COTTON... I NEED MONEY!
NORTHERN COTTON MFG. CO
SOON HE SELLS TO THE NORTH AND SOUTH! THE FEELING OF GUILT THAT FIRST HAUNTED HIM HAS LONG VANISHED...
4

THE CONSIDERABLE WEALTH TED HAS AMASSED ONLY INCREASES HIS GREED. THERE'S NO SUCH THING AS TOO MUCH MONEY. SOON, HE VISITS A FRIEND IN WASHINGTON...
I'VE BOUGHT A SHIP, GEORGE. I NEED CARGO-- CANNONS, POWDER, SHELLS...
BUT WE CAN BEST SUPPLY OUR TROOPS BY WAGON OR TRAIN, TED!
I...ER...HAVE OTHER CUSTOMERS! I'D MAKE IT WORTH YOUR WHILE...
OTHER...? WHAT OTHER?
I'LL CUT YOU IN FOR HALF OF THE PROFITS!
YOU...YOU'VE BEEN DEALING WITH THE REBELS!
YOU'VE SOLD OUT TO THE ENEMY! YOU'VE BEEN RUNNING CONTRABAND!
PLEASE, GEORGE... TRY TO UNDERSTAND IF I DON'T MAKE IT NOW, I'LL BE POOR FOR THE REST OF MY LIFE!
TRAITOR! I'M GOING TO REPORT YOU!
THEY'D STAND ME BEFORE A FIRING SQUAD! ALL I'VE WORKED FOR, RISKED MY LIFE FOR--WOULD'VE BEEN FOR NOTHING!
RESTAURANT
TED BRANT RETURNS TO HIS HOME TOWN, WHERE HE SEEKS OUT THE ONE MAN HE CAN DEPEND ON...
...I NEED ALL THE CANNONS, SHELLS, GUNPOWDER AND BULLETS YOU CAN GET, BULLARD! $233,450 WORTH!
FINE, BRANT! JUST TELL ME WHERE TO FIND YOUR SHIP!
5

AND IN LESS THAN A WEEK...
YOU'RE GOING TO MAKE ONE LAST BIG KILLING, EH, BRANT?
NEVER MIND MY PLANS. HERE'S THE MONEY!
I FEEL AS IF YANK TROOPS WERE SLOWLY CLOSING IN ON ME! I FEEL AS IF I WERE SMOTHERING!
LACKING FACTORIES OF ITS OWN, THE CONFEDERACY NEEDS THE BIG GUNS, POWDER, SHELLS, RIFLES AND BULLETS-- AS MUCH AS IT DESPISES THE MAN DELIVERING THEM...
A HALF-MILLION BUYS YOU THE SHIP AND EVERYTHING ON IT... ENOUGH TO FIGHT A DOZEN BATTLES!
YOU'LL HAVE YOUR MONEY READY IN A FEW HOURS, BRANT--AFTER WE'VE CHECKED IT ALL AGAINST THIS LIST!
TED BRANT NERVOUSLY WATCHES THE GRADUALLY PALING EASTERN SKY. HE SHUDDERS AS A DEEP FOREBODING CREEPS INTO HIS SUBCONSCIOUS...
A HALF-MILLION DOLLARS... IN FRESH NEW BILLS, BRANT. COUNT IT IF YOU LIKE!
I TRUST YOU... I HAVE TO! DAYLIGHT WILL BE HERE SOON!
NOW-- CAN YOU GIVE ME A FAST HORSE?
I'VE GOT TO GO BACK TO THE OLD HOMETOWN NOW, BACK TO THE BRIDGE... BACK TO 1899!
6

MORNING, AND TED IS BACK IN YANK COUNTRY, NOT TOO FAR FROM HOME...
EVERYONE'LL SEE I'M A MAN OF SUBSTANCE, A MAN TO BE RECKONED WITH! AND ETHEL WILL HAVE ALL THE THINGS SHE'S WANTED!
A SHOT SHATTERS HIS DAYDREAM, A BULLET RIPS BY CLOSE TO HIS HEAD...
BLAST! WHY WASN'T I MORE CAREFUL!
CRACK
CRACK CRACK
DEVIL TAKE 'EM-- THEY'RE AFTER ME!
MY HOME TOWN--! THOSE CONFOUNDED SOLDIERS WON'T RISK SHOOTING SOMEONE ELSE!
OH, GOD, WHY'D THEY HAVE TO BE HERE?
BILL... HE'S LOST A LEG!
TAKE A GOOD LOOK, TED... MAYBE A BULLET YOU SOLD CRIPPLED ME!
TREASON, BRANT-- TREASON!
WHAT IN BLAZES DO I CARE ABOUT HIS LEG? I'VE GOT WHAT I CAME FOR! A FORTUNE IN FEDERAL MONEY! ENOUGH FOR ME TO RETIRE IN LUXURY!
7

TED REACHES THE BRIDGE, SAFETY, THE FUTURE--HIS OWN TIME--WAIT MERE YARDS AHEAD...
THE HORSE WILL BLOCK 'EM OFF TILL I REACH THAT CLOUD!
HE'S A BARE FOOT FROM THAT CLOUD WHEN...
AGH...!
CRACK CRACK CRACK
TED STAGGERS INTO THE CLOUD SEPARATING THE PAST FROM THE FUTURE...
G-GOT TO MAKE... IT... BACK HOME... NEED D-DOCTOR...
AND, IN AN INSTANT, HE HAS BRIDGED SPACE AND TIME AGAIN, INTO 1899, WITH THE MONEY FOR WHICH HE SOLD OUT HIS COUNTRY, HIS FRIENDS, HIS VERY SOUL. ALL ELSE IS AS BEFORE...
ETHEL... HERE'S TED! OUR SEARCH IS OVER!
WHERE'VE YOU BEEN, MAN?
B-BACK...TO THE P-PAST... TO MAKE MY FORTUNE... BACK TO CIVIL WAR...
THOSE ARE TED BRANT'S LAST WORDS...
OH, TED... TED... WHAT HAPPENED..?
SAID HE WENT BACK TO THE WAR... TO GET RICH!
SOMEBODY SHOT HIM IN THE BACK! HE MUST'VE BEEN DELIRIOUS!
8
BUT WHEN THE CURIOUS MEN PRY OPEN THE OLD CHEST...
WHY, IT'S CONFEDERATE MONEY!
TED WANTED TO GO BACK 30 YEARS... TO GET RICH! HE MUST'VE SOLD HIS SOUL... AND FOR WHAT?
POOR TEDDY, THE SOUTH HAD BEEN PAYING TED WITH GOOD FEDERAL MONEY--UNTIL THAT LAST TIME, WHEN THEY GAVE HIM A CHESTFUL OF NEW, FRESHLY-PRINTED, TOTALLY WORTHLESS CONFEDERATE CASH!
THE END

MONTGOMERY CRAIG HAS TWO DISTINCT CHARACTERISTICS THAT SET HIM OFF FROM OTHER MEN.
THE FIRST IS A TOTAL DISREGARD FOR THE FEELINGS OF THE MEN HE DESTROYS IN BUSINESS.
YOU'VE RUINED ME WITH YOUR STOCK MANIPULATIONS, CRAIG!
I HOPE YOU BURN IN HADES!
J-7113
1
THE SECOND CHARACTERISTIC THAT DISTINGUISHES MONTGOMERY CRAIG FROM OTHER MEN IS AN ABSOLUTE AND MORBID TERROR OF--
The DARKNESS!
GERRY CONWAY . writer
CARMINE INFANTINO & JOHN BEATTY artists
. JOHN COSTANZA . letters
CARL GAFFORD . colors
KAREN BERGER editor

IT IS NOT THAT MONTGOMERY CRAIG IS AN UNFEELING MAN...
OH, YOU ROTTEN, LOUSY PIG! YOU STINKING, LOUSY--
IT IS SIMPLY THAT MONTGOMERY CRAIG RESERVES HIS COMPASSION FOR HIMSELF...
MR. WINTON HAS BEEN SENT ON HIS WAY, SIR.
YOUR CAR IS WAITING TO TAKE YOU HOME.
IT'S 6:08, KINGLY. SUNSET IS AT 6:25 THIS EVENING.
WHAT'S THE TRAFFIC SITUATION?
GOOD, SIR. YOU SHOULD MAKE FAIR TIME.
WILL YOU BE NEEDING ME OVER THE WEEK-END, SIR?
I PLAN TO STAY AT HOME THIS WEEKEND, KINGLY.
IF I NEED YOU, I'LL WANT YOU ON CALL.
THERE'S A LIGHT OUT IN THE MAIN CORRIDOR UPSTAIRS.
HAVE IT REPLACED.
2

HOME FOR MONTGOMERY CRAIG IS A GLASS-AND-STEEL TOWNHOUSE ON THE EAST SIDE, WITHIN SNEERING DISTANCE OF THE RIVER...
IT IS A VERY SPECIAL TOWN-HOUSE, IN THE SAME WAY THAT ITS OWNER IS A VERY SPECIAL MAN.
DURING THE DAYLIGHT HOURS, THE HOUSE IS WELL-LIT BY THE SUN, YET THIS IS NOT ENOUGH FOR MONTGOMERY CRAIG.
HE KEEPS LIGHTS ENOUGH FOR AN ORDINARY HOME BURNING DURING THE DAY, AND AT NIGHT--
CLICK!
--HE BURNS LIGHTS ENOUGH TO SET PARIS AGLOW.
FOR YET ANOTHER NIGHT, MONTGOMERY CRAIG HAS SUCCEEDED AT THRUSTING OUT THE DARKNESS.
HE POURS HIMSELF A DRINK, IN CELEBRATION--
-- AND, AS EVERY NIGHT, BREAKS INTO A COLD SWEAT AS HE REMEMBERS...
3

HAITI, IN THE MID 1930'S...
EVERY NIGHT, WITH A VIVIDNESS UNDULLED BY THE PASSAGE OF MORE THAN FORTY YEARS, CRAIG REMEMBERS THE HOT BLISTERING DAY WHEN IT BEGAN, SO LONG AGO...
HIS PARENTS WERE ATTACHED TO THE U.S. EMBASSY, HIS FATHER A FIRST CONSUL, HIS MOTHER THE DAUGHTER OF A WEALTHY BOSTON BRAHMIN...
CRAIG WAS A SPOILED BRAT--
-- AND ON THAT HOT AFTERNOON, THAT INHERITANCE OF ASSUMED PRIVILEGE LED HIM TO MAKE THE MISTAKE OF HIS LIFE.
MONTGOMERY-- MONTGOMERY, COME BACK HERE THIS INSTANT!
HE DIDN'T.
LAUGHING, BREATHLESS WITH EXCITEMENT, HE RAN UNTIL HE HE COULD RUN NO MORE AND FINALLY SOUGHT REFUGE FROM THE HEAT IN A SHOP DOORWAY...
IT WAS A VERY SPECIAL SHOP.
VOODOO.
4

TO HIS CHILD'S MIND, IT WAS A WONDERFUL, MAGICAL PLACE.
HE WANDERED THROUGH THE SHOP, AWED, UNTIL HE FOUND HIMSELF DRAWN LIKE A MAGNET TO ONE PARTICULAR ITEM...
WHAT YOU DO HERE, CHILE?
MOTHER JUJU ASK A QUESTION, SHE 'SPECTS AN ANSWER, CHILE.
WHAT YOU DO HERE?
WH-WHAT BUSINESS IS IT OF YOURS?
AH, HE WAS SUCH A SPOILED CHILD, THE YOUNG MONTGOMERY CRAIG...
...AND THE WOMAN CALLING HERSELF MOTHER JUJU TOOK NOTICE OF HIS CHILDISH SNARL AND RAISED AN EYEBROW COOLY...
BEST YOU STAY AWAY FROM THAT CHARM, CHILE.
IT'LL CALL THE DARKNESS DOWN ON YOU. THAT'S THE TRUTH.
DIRTY OLD WOMAN, IF I WANT IT--
--I'LL TAKE IT!
HE EXPECTED THE OLD WOMAN TO CRY OUT... BUT SHE DIDN'T.
LOOKING BACK, HE SAW HER IN THE SHADOWS-- AND SHE SEEMED ALMOST SAD.
5

THAT NIGHT, IN THE PRIVACY OF HIS ROOM, WITH THE LANTERNS TURNED LOW, HE BROUGHT OUT HIS TREASURE--
--AND DISCOVERED THAT WHAT HAD BEEN SO ENTICING IN THE WANTING WAS SO MUCH BLACK GLASS IN THE ACQUISITION...
JUNK. CRUMMY, CHEAP VOODOO--
--JUNK!
HE HEARD THE CHARM SHATTER WHERE IT FELL IN THE DARKNESS...
...BUT HE PAID NO ATTENTION TO IT AS HE LAY THERE BROODING... PAID NO ATTENTION TO THE SHADOWS THAT SEEMED TO BE DRAWING CLOSER AROUND HIS BED...
...PAID NO ATTENTION TO THE LANTERN AS ITS FLAME SUDDENLY WENT OUT... PAID NO ATTENTION TO THE SILENCE... UNTIL SOMETHING IN THE SILENCE, IN THE DARKNESS--
--TOUCHED HIM.
EEEEEEEE
THEN HE BEGAN TO SCREAM...
6

FROM THAT NIGHT ON, HE'D ALWAYS SLEPT WITH A LIGHT.
HIS PARENTS BROUGHT HIM TO THE BEST PSYCHIATRISTS IN HAITI AND BOSTON, BUT NONE OF THOSE DOCTORS COULD SHAKE MONTGOMERY CRAIG'S TERROR OF-- THE DARKNESS.
ONCE, LONG AFTER HIS PARENTS' DEATH, CRAIG HAD RETURNED TO HAITI AS AN ADULT, SEEKING MOTHER JUJU...
HER SHOP WAS EMPTY AND THE WOMAN HERSELF, PEOPLE SAID, WAS DEAD.
AS A MAN, MONTGOMERY CRAIG CHANNELED HIS FEAR INTO AN AGGRESSIVE, RUTHLESS BUSINESS TECHNIQUE...
UNTIL TODAY, HE'S SURVIVED AND SURVIVED IN STYLE. UNTIL TODAY...
UNTIL TONIGHT.
THE LIGHTS!
WHAT HAPPENED TO THE LIGHTS?
HIS BREATH CATCHES IN HIS THROAT, AND HIS HEART LEAPS.
MONTGOMERY CRAIG STUMBLES FORWARD IN THE DARKNESS, HANDS GROPING... AND SOMETHING IN THE DARKNESS--TOUCHES HIM.
7

FORTY-FIVE YEARS OF NIGHTLY TERROR ARE HEAVY ENOUGH BURDEN FOR ANY MAN'S HEART TO BEAR.
NOW, OVERLOADED AT LAST, MONTGOMERY CRAIG'S HEART SIMPLY--
--STOPS.
KLICK!
I NEVER THOUGHT IT'D HAPPEN SO QUICKLY, BUT NOW THAT IT'S OVER, I'M GLAD. I PLANNED THIS A LONG TIME, CRAIG...
...HATING EVERY MINUTE THAT I LET YOU WALK OVER ME, ME-- YOUR FAITHFUL ASSISTANT.
WHEN THE BOARD OF DIRECTORS MEETS TO PICK YOUR REPLACE-MENT, THEY'LL CHOOSE ME-- I'VE SEEN TO THAT.
A LITTLE BLACKMAIL CAN DO WONDERS. IT'S THE SMALL THINGS THAT RUIN A MAN... LIKE YOUR TERROR OF THE DARK.
IMAGINE A GROWN MAN BEING SO MOR-TALLY AFRAID OF-- EH?
WHAT HAPPENED TO THE LIGHTS? I REPLACED THE FUSE I PULLED. THE LIGHTS SHOULD BE ON...!
SO DARK, I CAN'T--
IIIEEEEEE
...AND SOMETHING IN THE DARKNESS BIT KINGLY IN TWO!
END

CAIN'S GAME ROOM
HEY, HAZEL... HOW'S THE WORK ON YOUR HOUSE COMING ALONG?
JUST FINISHED!... HOP ON... I'LL TAKE YOU OVER TO SEE IT!
IT'S ABOUT TIME YOU DID SOMETHING ABOUT THAT SHACK YOU LIVED IN!
IT'S MAGNIFICENT!
EVEN IF THE INTERIOR DOES LEAVE JUST A LITTLE BIT TO BE DESIRED!
J-7441
MANAK

FROM THE VERY BEGINNING IT WAS A WAR OF NERVES. HARRY HAD COURTED ISADORA FOR ONE REASON... TO INHERIT HER MONEY. IT WASN'T THE FIRST TIME. THERE WERE TWO OTHER "DECEASED" WIVES AND TWO OTHER INHERITANCES IN HARRY'S LIFE BEFORE ISADORA. A KIND OF CAREER YOU MIGHT SAY.
BUT NOW THE MONEY WAS RUNNING LOW AGAIN... HARRY WAS A BIG SPENDER ... AND IT WAS TIME TO HAUL OUT THE CHARM AND MARRY ANOTHER RICH WIDOW, AND HE DID JUST THAT. ISADORA HAD PLENTY SOCKED AWAY. TONS OF IT. UNFORTUNATELY, ISADORA HAD MORE THAN JUST MONEY... SHE ALSO HAD...
GAMES
TOYS
LILAH! PUT THAT DOWN! THAT'S FOR LITTLE BOYS! NOW PICK OUT SOMETHING FOR A SWEET LITTLE GIRL!
BUT I LIKE IT!
SALE
A LOUSE IS NOT A HOME
J-7291
BRUCE JONES writer
JOHNNY CRAIG artist
CARL GAFFORD colorist
KAREN BERGER editor
JOHN COSTANZA letterer
WHAT ABOUT THIS, DEAR... A NICE DOLL HOUSE. WOULDN'T YOUR DOLLIES JUST LOVE IT?
NAGH! DOLLS STINK. HEY, HOW ABOUT THIS?
THE LITTLE BRAT IS IMPOSSIBLE!
1

BUT, DARLING, THAT IS A DOLL... OH DEAR, WHAT A HIDEOUS LOOKING THING! WHAT IS IT?
GENUINE ZULU FETISH DOLL, M'AM! CAME ALL THE WAY FROM SOUTHEAST AFRICA!
IT'S NEAT!
LEGEND SAYS YOU CAN MAKE MAGIC WITH IT... HEH-HEH! IF YOU CAN SPEAK ZULU!
PLEASE, PLEASE CAN I HAVE IT?
I DON'T KNOW... HARRY, WHAT DO YOU THINK?
ABSOLUTELY NOT! IT'S DISGUSTING! PUT IT BACK.
WE'LL TAKE THE DOLL HOUSE. HOW MUCH?
I HATE YOU! I HATE YOU! I HATE YOU!
LILAH!
HARRY SMILES SMUGLY TO HIMSELF... HE'D WON THE FIRST SKIRMISH OF THE WAR...
...STUPID, CRUMMY, DUMB DOLL HOUSE!
IT'S A PERFECTLY LOVELY DOLL HOUSE. EXACTLY WHAT A PROPER YOUNG LADY SHOULD HAVE FOR HER BIRTHDAY!
TOYS
AND AT DINNER...
CHEW YOUR FOOD SLOWLY, LILAH...
I'LL CHEW MY CRUMMY FOOD ANY CRUMMY WAY I FEEL LIKE IT! NOBODY CARED HOW I CHEWED UNTIL YOU CAME AROUND!
LILAH! APOLOGIZE TO MR. COMBS! HE'S NOW YOUR NEW DADDY.
I CAN'T BELIEVE YOU MARRIED THIS CREEP!
LILAH! THAT DOES IT! STRAIGHT TO YOUR ROOM!
NEVER MIND, ISADORA DEAR. CHILDREN MUSTN'T BE DEPRIVED OF THEIR NOURISHMENT. FINISH YOUR SUPPER, LILAH...
...AND AFTERWARDS WE'LL SEE HOW A NICE SPANKING SUITS YOU.
2

AND AFTER DINNER...
COME, LILAH. LET'S TAKE OUR PUNISHMENT LIKE A SOLDIER.
YOU STINK, HARRY COMBS!
HARRY, DO YOU THINK THE CHILD SHOULD BE SPANKED JUST FOR... I MEAN, IT IS HER BIRTHDAY AND--
NOW-NOW, ISADORA. LEAVE THIS TO ME. WE DON'T WANT OUR DAUGHTER GROWING UP TO SOUND LIKE A COMMON GUTTER TRAMP, DO WE?
I HOPE YOU GET CANCER AND FALL OFF A BRIDGE!
MY MY, WHAT AN ACTIVE IMAGINATION! PITY IT'S NOT SMART ENOUGH TO...
AGH!
HA HA HA! HOW GRACEFUL! EVER THINK ABOUT JOINING THE ICE CAPADES, MR. COMBS?
YOU PUT THAT THERE PURPOSELY, DIDN'T YOU?
LISTEN TO ME, YOU DISGUSTING LITTLE WRETCH! YOU CAN TRY ANYTHING THAT UGLY LITTLE MIND OF YOURS IS CAPABLE OF CONJURING, BUT I'VE ALREADY MARRIED YOUR MOTHER AND THERE'S NOTHING YOU CAN DO!
FOR HER MONEY! YOU ONLY WANT HER 'CAUSE WE'RE RICH.
WHACK!
YEOWWWWWW
3

YOU DO LOVE ME, DON'T YOU, HARRY? YOU DIDN'T DO THIS BECAUSE... BECAUSE...
SH-H, BE STILL, MY LOVE. LET THESE BITTER THOUGHTS FLEE YOUR MIND.
IT'S JUST THAT, WELL, I KNOW I'M NOT A PRETTY WOMAN, AND...
HUSH! LISTEN, MY SWEET!... "LAST EVE IN DREAMS I SAW THEE STAND, LIKE QUEENLY NYMPHS FROM FAIRY-LAND-- ENCHANTRESS OF THE FLOWERY WAND, MOST BEAUTEOUS ISADORA!...
...AND WHEN I BADE THE DREAM UPON THY SPIRIT FLEE, THY VIOLET EYES TO ME UPTURNED, DID OVER-FLOWING SEEM WITH THE DEEP, UNTOLD DELIGHT OF LOVE'S SERENITY...
...THY CLASSIC BROW, LIKE LILIES WHITE AND PALE AS THE IMPERIAL NIGHT UPON HER THRONE, WITH STARS BEDIGHT, ENTHRALLED MY SOUL TO THEE!...
OH, HARRY...
SLIMY SLUG... JUST A LOT OF EMPTY AIR...
HARRY! WHAT WAS THAT? SOMEONE'S IN THE HOUSE!
NONSENSE, I'LL SEE.
CREAK
4

GLASSES... WHERE DID I PUT MY GLASSES... CAN'T SEE A THING WITHOUT MY--
ON THE NIGHTSTAND, DEAR...
AHHH...
HOW ENDEARING... THE SWEET ANGELIC NYMPH, WINDING HER WAY TO SLUMBERLAND... HAVEN'T BEEN SKULKING ABOUT THE HALLS TONIGHT, HAVE WE LILAH, MY LOVE?
WELL, NEVER MIND, YOU SHAN'T BE SKULKING ABOUT MUCH LONGER...
SHALL I TELL YOU WHY? BECAUSE VERY SOON THERE'S GOING TO BE A SERIES OF NASTY ACCIDENTS IN THIS HOUSE, ONE OF WHICH YOU, MY DEAR, ARE NOT LIKELY TO SURVIVE!
YOU SEE, THE ONLY THING THAT STANDS BETWEEN ME AND DEAR SWEET ISADORA'S MONEY IS THAT FOUL LITTLE MOUTH OF YOURS--
--AND I INTEND TO SEE THAT THAT MOUTH IS CLOSED FOREVER! DO YOU HEAR ME, LITTLE DREAMER?
SWEET THOUGHTS, PET. UNTIL TOMORROW...
5

TOYS
6

MORNING...
IZZY? ISADORA? WHAT TIME IS IT?
IZZY, DEAREST? WHERE ARE YOU?
...GLASSES, WHERE'D I PUT MY BLAMED GLASSES...
IZZY? HAVE YOU SEEN MY GLASSES, DEAR?...
HEY, WHAT IS THIS? WHERE IS EVERYBODY?...
DARK IN HERE...
MUST'VE GONE TO THE STORE...
WHAT TH-- FRONT DOOR LOCKED... WHY ON EARTH WOULD SHE-- HEY! THE LOCK'S MISSING! BEEN FILED-OFF OR SOMETHING!
IT'S THAT LITTLE BRAT! SHE'S LOCKED ME IN THE HOUSE! LILAH, YOU LITTLE WITCH! I KNOW YOU'RE OUT THERE! I CAN HEAR YOU TALKING! OPEN THIS DOOR IMMEDIATELY!
GOOD GOD, THE WINDOWS! SHE'S PAINTED THEM BLACK! NO WONDER IT'S SO DARK IN HERE!
LILAH! YOU'LL GET A THRASHING FOR THIS! I MEAN IT!
GOT TO GET TO THE CELLAR... GET A CROWBAR OUT OF THE TOOL CHEST AND GET THAT DOOR... HUH?
BLAST! BASEMENT DOOR'S LOCKED, TOO! THE LITTLE MONSTER'S GOT ME TRAPPED IN HERE! I SUPPOSE SHE'LL SET FIRE TO THE PLACE NEXT!
7

LILAH! YOU'LL PAY FOR THIS! I SWEAR IT! WHA... WHO'S THAT, SITTING IN THE LIVING ROOM...
MY GLASSES! NOW WE'LL SEE WHAT THIS IS ALL ABOUT...
YAAAAGGGGGHHHHHHHH
THE DOLL! THE AFRICAN FETISH DOLL! ONLY IT'S... IT'S...
LILAH, NO! NO! PLEASE! DON'T DO THIS! I'LL MAKE IT UP TO YOU! I'LL BUY YOU ANYTHING YOU WANT! PLEASE, LET ME OUT! LET ME OUT OF THIS THING!
BAM
BAM
LILAAAAAAAAAAAAAAAAAAAAA
BAM
BAM
8
I SOB JUST CAN'T BELIEVE HE'D UP AND LEAVE LIKE THAT... LILAH... DID YOU HEAR SOMETHING JUST THEN?
JUST THE WIND IN THE ATTIC, MOTHER... JUST A LOT OF EMPTY AIR...
END

THE FIRST THING I MURDERED WAS MY FEAR! I SPENT HOURS TRACKING IT ACROSS THE CITY, THEN FINALLY CORNERED IT DOWN ON THE DOCKS...
DEAD END
IT FELL TO ITS KNEES, COWERING, PLEADING, AS I STARED INTO ITS TEAR-FILLED RABBIT EYES--
--AND I KNEW THEN I HAD MADE THE RIGHT CHOICE!
J-1307
DYING by DEGREES!
P-P-PLEASE, HARRY-- P-P-PUT THAT GUN AWAY--! YOU C-CAN'T SHOOT ME-- I'M A PART OF YOU--!
HARRY-- PLEASE--! YOU D-D-DON'T KNOW WHAT YOU'RE DOING--!
WRONG, LITTLE MAN--
--DEAD WRONG!
BLAM!
I FINALLY KNOW PRECISELY WHAT I'M DOING!
END
AND, FOR THE FIRST TIME IN MY LIFE, I WAS NOT AFRAID!
1

LEN WEIN writer · GIL KANE & DAN ADKINS artists · JOHN COSTANZA letterer · ADRIENNE ROY colorist · KAREN BERGER editor

"NEW YOU, UNLIMITED" WAS LOCATED ON THE 13TH FLOOR OF ONE OF THOSE NEW PREFAB SKYSCRAPERS THAT SEEM TO POP UP OVER THE WEEKEND...
BUZZZ
A TOO-CUTE RECEPTIONIST BUZZED ME THRU THE WAITING ROOM--
--AND INTO THE CAVERNOUS OFFICES OF THE FIRM'S FOUNDER, ONE NICHOLAS BELL...
WELCOME, MR. MONROE--YOU'RE BACK SOONER THAN EXPECTED!
I TRUST YOU FOUND THE EXPERIENCE... SATISFACTORY?
IT WAS GREAT, BELL--JUST WISH IT HAD BEEN REAL!
I ASSURE YOU, MR. MONROE-- IT WAS QUITE REAL!
AS STATED IN THE NEWSPAPER AD THAT FIRST BROUGHT YOU TO US, THE "NEW YOU" SYSTEM IS DESIGNED TO BRING OUT THE WORST IN YOU--
--QUITE LITERALLY!
THE SECRET OF OUR SUCCESS IS OUR UNIQUE PROCESS OF MANIFESTING YOUR CHARACTER FLAWS IN PHYSICAL FORM SO YOU CAN FINALLY CONFRONT THEM--
--AND THUS PUT AN END TO THEM!
OF COURSE, IF YOU'RE DISPLEASED WITH OUR SERVICE, WE'LL CHEERFULLY RETURN YOUR DOWN PAYMENT--
--AND EVERYTHING ELSE WE TOOK FROM YOU!
HEY--WHOA! I JUST WANT TO BE SURE THIS IS GONNA WORK FOR ME, IS ALL!
YOU'VE GOT TO UNDERSTAND... ALL MY LIFE, I'VE BEEN A NOTHING-- A NOBODY-- STANDING ON THE SIDELINES, WATCHING OTHER GUYS STRIKE IT RICH!
I'VE BEEN MY OWN WORST ENEMY, BELL--TOO NERVOUS, TOO FRIGHTENED, TOO DAMNED INSECURE TO GRAB MYSELF A PIECE OF THE PIE!
THEN, SUDDENLY, YOU AND THIS CRAZY COMPANY COME ALONG AND TELL ME I CAN FINALLY BECOME THE MAN I WAS ALWAYS MEANT TO BE!
THIS MAY BE MY LAST CHANCE, BELL--I CAN'T AFFORD TO BLOW IT!
NOR WILL YOU, MY FRIEND-- WE GUARANTEE COMPLETE SATISFACTION!
2

NOW WHY DON'T YOU GO HOME AND RELAX, MR. MONROE?
WE'LL CONTACT YOU SOON ABOUT YOUR NEXT--AH--THERAPY SESSION.
YEAH--YOU DO THAT, BELL...
...AND THE SOONER, THE BETTER!
HOME, IN MY CASE, WAS YOUR CLASSIC SUBURBAN SPLIT-LEVEL--
--COMPLETE WITH SECOND MORTGAGE, SECOND-HAND FURNITURE, SECOND-HAND MEMORIES--
--AND A WOEBEGONE WIFE, WHO HAD SEEN FAR TOO MUCH DISAPPOINTMENT IN HER LIFE AND FAR TOO LITTLE JOY...
HARRY, I WENT TO THE BANK THIS MORNING.
SO?
SO THERE'S FIVE HUNDRED DOLLARS MISSING FROM OUR SAVINGS ACCOUNT, HARRY.
HALF THE MONEY WE HAVE IN THIS WORLD...
YEAH? SO WHAT IF IT IS?
I WORKED MY BUTT OFF TO EARN THAT MONEY, EMILY-- I BLED FOR IT--
--AND I'LL SPEND IT ANY DAMN WAY I PLEASE!
DON'T YOU SEE? I CAN'T GO ON LIVING LIKE THIS--A NOTHIN' IN A NOBODY WORLD--!
I'M 46 YEARS OLD, EMILY-- I'VE GOTTA TRY TO BE SOMEBODY WHILE I'VE STILL GOT THE CHANCE!
I KNOW THAT, AND I SYMPATHIZE--BUT WHAT ABOUT ME?
I'M NO KID MYSELF ANY MORE, HARRY--NOT EVEN CLOSE!
I SKRIMPED AND SAVED AND HOARDED TO PUT THAT MONEY IN THE BANK!
I WENT WITHOUT, HARRY--SO YOU WOULDN'T HAVE TO!
YEAH--I GUESS MAYBE YOU DID...
...BUT WHAT'VE YOU DONE FOR ME LATELY?
3

FACE IT, EMILY-- YOU'RE A PAIN IN THE NECK, ALWAYS WORRYING, ALWAYS COMPLAINING--!
ALL THESE YEARS I'VE BEEN AFRAID TO TELL YOU THAT--BUT I'M NOT AFRAID ANY MORE, EMILY...
...I'M NOT AFRAID OF ANYTHING!
THAT STILL DOESN'T GIVE YOU THE RIGHT TO SPEND OUR MONEY WITHOUT TALKING TO ME ABOUT IT FIRST.
DOESN'T IT? I'D SAY THAT GIVES ME THE RIGHT TO DO ANYTHING I DAMN WELL PLEASE!
AND IF YOU DON'T LIKE IT, LADY--
--YOU CAN TAKE THIS FARCE OF A MARRIAGE--
--AND SHOVE IT!!
PLEASE, HARRY --DON'T
I'M GOING OUT FOR A WALK, EMILY! MAYBE IT WOULD BE BETTER FOR BOTH OF US IF YOU WERE GONE WHEN I GET BACK!
SOMEHOW IT DIDN'T SURPRISE ME THAT MY WANDERING BROUGHT ME BACK TO "NEW YOU"...
COME IN, MR. MONROE --I'VE BEEN WAITING FOR YOU.
THEN YOU SHOULD KNOW WHY I'M HERE, BELL! I WANT TO SPEED UP MY THERAPY!
I WANT TO BE THAT NEW ME YOU'VE PROMISED-- AND I WANT IT NOW!
THE NEXT THING I MURDERED WAS MY HUMILITY! I CAUGHT UP WITH IT ON A WINDING MOUNTAIN ROAD OUTSIDE THE CITY...
IT WAS DRIVING A DUSTY USED CAR, MUCH LIKE THE ONE THAT I USED TO DRIVE WHEN I THOUGHT THAT WAS ALL I DESERVED--
--UNTIL I LEARNED BETTER!
SKRAK-KRASH!
I DESERVED THE MOON...THE STARS... THE WHOLE BLOODY UNIVERSE...
4

...AND I WOULD STOP AT ABSOLUTELY NOTHING IN ORDER TO GET THEM!
I STARED DOWN OVER THE EDGE AT THE FLAMING, TWISTED WRECKAGE--
--AND, FOR THE FIRST TIME IN MY MISBEGOTTEN LIFE, I FELT PROUD!
RUSH HOUR TRAFFIC WAS AT ITS THICKEST WHEN I FINALLY RETURNED TO THE CITY--AND I RESENTED IT!
WHAT RIGHT DID THESE INSIGNIFICANT LITTLE PEOPLE HAVE TO WASTE MY VALUABLE TIME?
AT THAT MOMENT, I SAW A BREAK IN THE FLOW AND HEADED FOR IT--
HEY-- WHAT--?!?
--BUT SOMEONE ELSE SAW IT FIRST!
THE CAR SPED BY ME, TURNING ONTO THE OFF-RAMP--
--BUT AS IT PASSED, I GOT A GOOD LOOK AT THE DRIVER AND HIS LOVELY PASSENGER...
PUNK! YOU LOUSY PUNK! I WON'T FORGET YOU!
I WON'T FORGET EITHER OF YOU!
I WAS FURIOUS, SEETHING WITH RAGE--
--BUT I KNEW A GOOD WAY TO CHANNEL THAT RAGE INTO SOMETHING USEFUL...
ARE YOU CERTAIN YOU WANT TO CONTINUE AT THIS PACE, MR. MONROE?
MOST OF OUR CLIENTS PREFER TO TAKE THINGS A BIT MORE CAUTIOUSLY, YOU KNOW.
I'M PAYING FOR THIS, BELL--SO I'LL DO IT HOWEVER I LIKE!
AS YOU INSIST!
SO THE NEXT THING I MURDERED WAS ALL MY USELESS SENTIMENT!
C'MON, HARRY--GIVE ME A BREAK! WE GO BACK A LONG WAY TOGETHER, YOU AND I!
DON'T REMIND ME!
ALL YOU'VE EVER DONE IS WEIGH ME DOWN, PAL--
--SO NOW I'M RETURNING THE FAVOR!
5

PLEASE, HARRY, THINK ABOUT THIS-- BEFORE YOU DO SOMETHING RASH!
YOU CAN'T GET RID OF ME THIS EASILY--YOU MUSTN'T! I'M AN IMPORTANT PIECE OF YOU--!
HARRY, YOU NEED ME!
THAT'S WHERE YOU'RE WRONG, LOSER--
--THE NEW HARRY MONROE DOESN'T NEED ANYONE!
BLAM!
EMILY'S FUNERAL WAS ON A FRIDAY--LESS THAN A WEEK AFTER I THREW HER OUT, SHE'D COMMITTED SUICIDE...
I TRIED HARD TO FEEL SOME SORT OF REMORSE--
--BUT, BY THEN, I'D MURDERED THAT TOO!
WITH EMILY GONE, I WAS FREE TO SEEK OUT NEW COMPANIONS--AND, AT AN UPTOWN COCKTAIL PARTY, I FINALLY FOUND WHAT I'D BEEN SEARCHING FOR...
THE SAME BEAUTIFUL BLONDE WHO'D BEEN IN THAT CAR THAT PASSED ME ON THE HIGHWAY...
C'MON, JUDY, I COULD BE GOOD FOR YOU --VERY GOOD!
HARRY, PLEASE--I'M NOT INTERESTED!
NO, YOUR TYPE IS NEVER INTERESTED, ARE YOU--
--NOT IN A MIDDLE-AGED NOBODY LIKE ME!
SMAK!
WELL, FRANKLY, LADY--I'M SICK OF IT!
OOOHH!
THIS MAKES THE SECOND TIME YOU'VE CUT ME OFF COLD, SISTER--BUT I PROMISE YOU THERE WON'T BE A THIRD!
NOBODY MAKES A FOOL OUT OF HARRY MONROE ANY MORE, LADY--NOBODY!!
6

BELL WAS WAITING FOR ME AS USUAL--BUT THIS TIME HE DIDN'T LOOK HAPPY...
YES, MR. MONROE--WHAT NOW?
YOUR SYSTEM ISN'T WORKING, BELL! I'M STILL THE SAME LOSER I'VE ALWAYS BEEN!
WHERE ARE ALL THOSE RESULTS YOU'VE BEEN PROMISING ME?
I TOLD YOU, MR. MONROE--THESE THINGS TAKE TIME.
IF YOU ATTEMPT TO MURDER TOO MUCH TOO QUICKLY, YOU MAY WELL MURDER MUCH MORE THAN YOU BARGAINED FOR!
THAT'S A RISK I'M WILLING TO TAKE!
I'M DESPERATE, BELL--AND I WANT TO BE DONE WITH THIS ONCE AND FOR ALL!
AS YOU WISH, MR. MONROE! BUT, REMEMBER--YOU HAVE BEEN WARNED!
I WAS WAITING FOR MY NEXT "VICTIM" ON A DARKENED MIDTOWN STREET.
BELL HAD SMILED AS HE PROMISED ME THAT THIS WOULD BE MY FINAL MURDER--AND I WONDERED WHAT I WOULD KILL...
MY SHAME... MY PETTINESS... MY JEALOUSY... PERHAPS ALL OF THEM...
ANXIOUSLY, I STEPPED FORWARD, FIRING OVER AND OVER--
BLAM BLAM BLAM
--AND, AS THE SHADOWY FIGURE TOPPLED INTO THE LIGHT, MY HEART CAUGHT DRY IN MY THROAT...
NO... OH, LORD... NO...
IT WAS JUDY, THE YOUNG WOMAN I'D THREATENED AT THE COCKTAIL PARTY IN FRONT OF DOZENS OF WITNESSES...
NO ONE WOULD EVER BELIEVE I HAD KILLED HER BY ACCIDENT--NOT NOW!
I WOULD BE TRIED... CONVICTED... SPEND THE REST OF MY LIFE BEHIND BARS...
THUS, AS THE SOUND OF APPROACHING POLICE SIRENS MINGLED WITH THE SOUND OF MY OWN SOBBING, I REALIZED BELL HAD BEEN WRONG...
POOR JUDY WASN'T MY FINAL VICTIM...
THE LAST THING I MURDERED WAS--MYSELF!
The End

THERE IS AN UNOCCUPIED ROOM IN THE HOUSE OF MYSTERY, FEAR FANS. IT'S HELD VACANT FOR THE NOMADIC "ROMANIES," BETTER KNOWN AS GYPSIES--RESERVED FOR WHENEVER THEY'RE IN THE NEIGHBORHOOD!
PERHAPS YOU'RE WONDERING JUST WHERE THESE WAYFARERS ARE TRAVELLING THESE DAYS... AND WHAT THEY'RE UP TO...
MEET ALGA, QUEEN OF THE GYPSIES, AND SHE'LL SPIN A TALE THAT WILL ANSWER YOUR QUESTIONS...
COME CLOSER... TO THE LIGHT OF THE FIRE... FOR ITS KNOWING FLAMES SHALL TELL OLD ALGA IF THE ROMANIES CAN TRUST YOU... FOR IF THEY CANNOT, THEN YOU MAY BE ONE WHO WILL STUMBLE ON A ROOT OF...
THE SERPENT TREE
WRITER: JACK C. HARRIS
ARTIST: NESTOR REDONDO
LETTERER: ESPHIDYM
COLORIST: JERRY SERPE
EDITOR: KAREN BERGER
J-7132
A SULTRY SUN STEAMS THE SIDEWALKS OF MINGWILTON, A SMALL, SEEDY CITY IN THE HEART OF THE SOUTH.
DILLSDA EMPLOY AGENC
MR. DILLSDALE... THERE'S A GENTLEMAN TO SEE YOU.
YEAH? SEND 'IM IN.
A JOB? WELL, C'MON IN, PAL! I AIN'T GOT ALL FLAPPIN' DAY!
THERE IS EAGERNESS AND CURIOSITY HERE... AND THERE IS HATE...
Come closer, my dear and listen to me
And you shall hear of the Serpent Tree
With roots in Eden, and limbs in Hell,
The devil stands as its sentinel...

... AND THE HATE QUICKLY CAUSES THE EAGERNESS TO FADE.
C'MON, GYPSY... I KNOW YOUR KIND DON'T KNOW HOW TO DO MUCH MORE 'N STEAL...
WE CALL OUR PEOPLE ROMANIES, SIR, AND MY SKILLS ARE MANY.
THE INTERVIEW IS BRIEF... AND ALL THE YOUNG ROMANIE LEAVES WITH IS NOTHING MORE THAN AN ADMIRING GAZE...
HMMM... HIS LOOKS WOULD BE ENOUGH FOR ME TO HIRE HIM.
THERE'S NO NEED TO FILE THAT ONE, JENNIFER, MY DEAR. THERE JUST AIN'T NO JOBS FOR THAT YOUNG GYPSY FELLA.
OHH--!
BESIDES, THEM GYPSIES GOT GOLD STASHED ALL OVER!
'ND AFTER ALL, DEAR JENNY... AIN'T I MAN ENOUGH FER YOU AROUND HERE?
MISTER DILLSDALE, I HAVE TOLD YOU ABOUT YOUR ADVANCES...
RAMOND KNOWS WHAT IT'S LIKE TO BE UNWELCOME, FOR HIS PEOPLE HAVE ALWAYS BEEN OUTCASTS...
JUST KEEP AWAY FROM ME OR I'LL QUIT!
NOW... WHERE WOULD YOU GO? AND WHO ELSE WOULD HIRE A GOLD DIGGER LIKE YOU?
YOU'RE DESPICABLE!
"DESPICABLE"? NOW WHERE'D'YA SUPPOSE SHE HEARD A WORD LIKE THAT? SHE SURE SHOWS HER INFATUATION WITH ME IN A STRANGE WAY!
2
Where'er the Gypsy makes his stand,
The Serpent Tree does e'er expand,
And by bond in blood once is made,
Those untrue can ne'er evade!

THE INSULTS THROWN AT JENNIFER LOGAN BY HER LUSTFUL BOSS COULD HARDLY BE CLASSIFIED AS INSULTS... FOR THEY ARE STATEMENTS OF TRUTH...
GOLD! THAT FAT OLD SLOB SAID ALL THESE GYPSIES HAD GOLD STASHED AWAY!
MISTER RAMOND... I'VE HEARD OF GYP--UMM, ROMANIES SINCE I WAS A CHILD BUT I'VE NEVER MET ONE...
WHA--? THAT GYPSY BOY'S DONE CAST A SPELL ON MY WOMAN--!
THE AIR IS CHARGED... THE HEAT WRITHES THROUGH THE CITY LIKE A SERPENT... GREED SURFACES... AND THERE IS STILL HATE.
AND AT AN ENCAMPMENT ON THE FAR EDGE OF THE CITY...
THE ANXIOUS GIRL NOTICES NOT THE STARES OF THE DARK PEOPLE AROUND HER NOW...
YOU RISK MUCH BEING HERE, JENNIFER. I SOUGHT A JOB TO SEE IF ATTITUDES HAVE CHANGED. BUT THERE IS STILL MUCH HATE FOR MY PEOPLE!
DO NOT DRAW BACK. THIS IS ALGA. YOU WOULD CALL HER OUR GYPSY QUEEN!
STAND CLOSE TO THE FIRE, MY DEAR... SO THAT I MIGHT SEE IF YOU CAN BE TRUSTED BY THE ROMANIES...
"DO YOU WONDER HOW WE ROMANIES HAVE SURVIVED SO VERY LONG THOUGH WE BE OUTCASTS WHEREVER WE DWELL...?
"'TIS 'CAUSE OF THE SERPENT TREE PLANTED IN THE GARDEN OF EDEN BY THE PRINCE OF LIARS HIMSELF...
"WE KNOW THE SECRETS OF THE TREE... AND IT BEARS ITS FRUIT FOR US..."
BUT KNOW THIS-- WHOSOEVER LIES TO A ROMANIE, FOR THEM A NEW BRANCH GROWS ON THE SERPENT TREE!"
3

AND LIES OF LOVE... YES, THOSE ARE THE VILEST OF UNTRUTHS INDEED!...
TAKE ME AWAY FROM HERE, RAMOND... SHE-- SHE'S FRIGHTENING ME...
DON'T BE AFRAID OF ALGA, JENNIFER... SHE IS OF THE OLD WAYS.
AND LIKE MANY OF OUR PEOPLE, SHE FEARS OUR MIXING WITH OUTSIDERS...
AND MAYBE YOU'LL LET ME IN ON WHERE SOME OF THAT GYPSY GOLD MIGHT BE...
VERY TOUCHING...
MISTER DILLSDALE! YOU--YOU FOLLOWED US!?
CALL ME ADAM... BUT YOU'RE CURSED NOW, JENNY, AND HE'S GONNA HAVE TO PAY FOR IT!
BLAAAM
NOOOOOOO!
HER MIND WHIRLS... HER BOSS HAS TRULY GONE OVER THE EDGE IN JEALOUSY, AND HER LIFE IS IN DANGER. THE GREED IN HER HEART STILL SURFACES TO HER BRAIN AND SHE PANICS AT HER OWN THOUGHTS...
BUT ALL THOUGHTS ARE ERASED--BLANKED OUT, WHEN JENNIFER LOGAN ENTERS A CLEARING AND COMES FACE TO FANGS WITH...
THE SERPENT TREE!
OH MY GOOOOOODDDDD!!!
4

JENNIFER! SPEAK THE TRUTH IN YOUR HEART! SPEAK THE TRUTH OR THE TREE WILL SPELL YOUR DOOM!
OH MY LORD... MY LORD...
THE TRUTH! HURRY!
I... I ONLY... CAME WITH YOU... BECAUSE OF THE GOLD!
I DON'T CARE FOR YOU--OR ANYONE! IT'S THE TRUTH! PLEASE... PLEASE...?
JENNIFER..?
SO HE DESERTED YOU HERE IN THE MIDDLE OF THE WOODS, DID HE? LEFT YOU HERE FOR ME?
The tree... it was the tree...
YOU'RE FREE NOW, JENNY... FREE FROM THAT GYPSY SPELL!
AND AS FOR THIS HERE TREE...
IT'S JUST THE PLACE TO SEAL OUR... ENGAGEMENT! HEH...HEH...
AD + JL
YES... ADAM...
5

NO ONE TOOK NOTICE OF THE DEPARTURE OF THE ROMANIE TRIBE... JUST AS NO ONE TOOK NOTICE OF A SMALL WEDDING THAT TOOK PLACE IN THE OFFICE OF A JUSTICE OF THE PEACE...
JUSTICE OF THE PEACE
I DO... HEH...HEH... HEH...
I...I...
AND NO ONE REALLY TOOK ANY SPECIAL NOTICE OF A CERTAIN HONEYMOONING COUPLE...
HEH... HEH... HEH...
AND IT WASN'T UNTIL MIDNIGHT THAT THE MOTEL'S MANAGER AND A LOCAL POLICE OFFICER DID NOTICE SOMETHING... AMISS...
EEEEYAAAA
AND AFTER A HASTY ENTRY TO THE... BRIDAL SUITE...
LORDY! THERE...THERE WAS A SNAKE IN HIS BED!
HE...HE'S A GONER-- AND HIS WIFE LOOKS LIKE SHE'S GONE OFF THE DEEP END!
AD + JL
AND, Y'KNOW, THEY NOTICED THE STRANGE MARKING ON THE BELLY OF THAT SNAKE, TOO...
SO, REMEMBER, DEAR READERS... IF YOU MEET A ROMANIE, BE TRUTHFUL...AND NOT A SNAKE IN THE GRASS!

DC
DO YOU DARE ENTER...
THE HOUSE OF
MYSTERY
50¢
ALL NEW!
NO. 290
MAR.
APPROVED BY THE COMICS CODE AUTHORITY
BEGINNING: AN UNFORGETTABLE NEW SERIES... "I...VAMPIRE!"
JOE KUBERT

BEGINNING: A SENSATIONAL NEW SERIES IN THE FEAR-SHROUDED HOUSE OF MYSTERY TRADITION!
"MY MIND IS ASWIRL WITH SO MANY IMAGES -- FRIENDS, LOVERS, DEMONS -- ALL ROLLING INTO ONE INDECIPHERABLE WHOLE...
"AS THE YEARS PASS, IT BECOMES INCREASINGLY HARDER TO TELL WHERE THE DARK LINE BETWEEN GOOD AND EVIL -- BETWEEN THE SHIMMERING GATES OF HEAVEN AND THE STEAMING PITS OF HELL -- TRULY LIES. AND NOWHERE IS THIS CONFUSION MORE EVIDENT THAN WITHIN MY OWN HEART.
"I HAVE SEEN SO MUCH -- I HAVE BORNE THE DEVIL'S FLAMING CROSS -- YET STILL I SURVIVE..."
J-6489
1
I...VAMPIRE!

J.M. DeMATTEIS *writer/creator* • TOM SUTTON *artist* • JOHN COSTANZA *letterer* • ADRIENNE ROY *colorist* • LEN WEIN *editing & guidance*

"MARY, QUEEN OF BLOOD, IS IN THE HOTEL LE GRANDE,' THE EERIE VOICE ON THE PHONE HAD WHISPERED--AND THESE TWO HAD BEEN THE FIRST TO ARRIVE IN RESPONSE TO THE CALL...
HOTEL LE GRANDE
WELL, DEBORAH--WHAT DO YOU SEE?
LOOKS LIKE HER--BUT WHO KNOWS? WE'VE BEEN FOOLED BEFORE...
LET ME LOOK, GIRL. MY EYES MAY BE OLD--BUT THEY'RE SHARP.
DON'T GRAB, MISHKIN!
"DEBORAH DANCER AND DIMITRI MISHKIN WERE SO LOST IN THEIR TASK THAT THEY FAILED TO NOTICE THE WILD-EYED WOLF THAT LEAPT SILENTLY ONTO THE ROOF WITH FURTIVE GRACE...
"BUT THE FERAL BEAST SOON MADE ITS PRESENCE KNOWN WITH A GUTTURAL...
GRROOOOWWRRRRRRRR
ASSUME A DEFENSIVE POSTURE, DEBORAH!
DON'T WORRY ABOUT ME, OLD MAN. WORRY ABOUT YOURSEL--
HEY, WAIT! LOOK AT THAT THING--IT'S...
"...CHANGING! WITHIN A PRETERNATURALLY THICK VEIL OF FOG THE BEAST WAS BEING TRANSFORMED...
"...AND FROM THE CENTER OF THE MISTY CLOAK...
"...I EMERGED!"
GOOD EVENING, DEBORAH...MISHKIN...
OH, ANDREW--IT'S YOU!
I THOUGHT IT WAS ONE OF THEM!
2

I DIDN'T MEAN TO STARTLE YOU--BUT THE WOLF-FORM IS PERFECT FOR ROOFTOP TRAVEL.
OH, I DON'T MIND, ANDREW...
ACH! YOU BOTH ACCEPT THESE PERVERSIONS SO CASUALLY!
BELIEVE ME, MISHKIN-- I DO NOT ACCEPT MY...CONDITION...
...CASUALLY...
"MISHKIN AND I HAD BEEN ASSOCIATES FOR YEARS-- BUT STILL HE FEARED ME--LOATHED MY UNDEAD WAYS. AND I COULD NOT BLAME HIM...
"...FOR HE HAD NOT KNOWN ME BEFORE. HE HAD NOT KNOWN THE CHEERFUL LORD ANDREW BENNETT OF QUEEN ELIZABETH'S COURT...
"...HE'D NEVER HEARD ME LAUGH--OR RAISE MY VOICE IN JOYOUS SONG...
"I WAS A FAR DIFFERENT MAN THEN. I'D BECOME SOMETHING OF A LEGEND AT COURT THANKS TO MY DARING EXPLOITS DURING THE WAR WITH SPAIN...
"...BUT I MUCH PREFERRED BEING LIONIZED FOR MY BALLADS OF PEACE...
"...FOR I SAW NO GLORY IN WAR. I SAW ONLY THE CORPSES OF INNOCENTS-- SENT TO THEIR DEATHS FOR REASONS THEY COULD NEVER TRULY COMPREHEND...
"...AND IT MADE ME SICK. NO DOUBT THAT WOULD SURPRISE MISHKIN...
"AND HOW WOULD THE OLD RUSSIAN REACT TO THE SIGHT OF ANDREW BENNETT IN LOVE?
"AS IF THE WORD 'LOVE' COULD DO JUSTICE TO THE INEFFABLE FEELING THAT UNITED ME WITH MY DARLING... MARY..."
3

"MARY SEWARD WAS THE QUEEN'S PERSONAL HANDMAIDEN. SHE WAS ALSO THE WOMAN I TREASURED ABOVE ALL WHO LIVED. SHE WAS MY LIGHT-- MY LIFE...
"MARY UNDERSTOOD ME--ACCEPTED ME UNCONDITIONALLY--MADE EVERY INSTANT NEW AND PRECIOUS...
"SHE HAD AN INTUITION-- A WAY OF SEEING INTO THE HEART OF THINGS-- THAT OFTEN BORDERED ON THE PSYCHIC. AND LIKE A FOOL I MADE JOKES OF HER GIFTS...
ANDREW-- PLEASE DON'T GO RIDING TONIGHT. SOMETHING FEELS WRONG.
ANOTHER VISION, BELOVED...?
YOU'D DO WELL TO KEEP THESE THINGS QUIET-- OR THE QUEEN WILL BURN YOU AS A WITCH! HA-HA-HA!
TILL... LATER, ANDREW...
TILL LATER, BELOVED!
"SO OFF I WENT--AS I DID EVERY EVENING. I ENJOYED THE SOLI-TUDE-- THE SILENCE...
"...AND THE DARK...
LORD BENNETT... IS THAT YOU...?
"THE OLD MAN APPEARED FROM NOWHERE: A GHOST RIDING A WAVE OF MOONLIGHT...
DO I KNOW YOU, GOOD SIR? IT IS HARD TO PIERCE THIS GLOOM...
"HIS VOICE WAS ENCHANTING-- HIS TONES SOMBER YET MELLIFLUOUS...
EVEN AT THE SUN'S HEIGHT YOU WOULD NOT KNOW ME, LORD. YOUR SOUL IS TOO PURE AND THUS YOUR EYES WILL NOT SEE.
"I FELT SOME-HOW DRAWN TO HIM--LIKE A CHILD TO ITS MOTHER'S BREAST..."
SEE...? SEE WHAT...?
SEE THAT YOUR VISION OF A JUST UNIVERSE IS A LIE...
...THAT THE GOODNESS YOU EMBRACE IS A SHAM!
4

"HIS CRIMSON EYES WERE ENTICING--MES-MERIZING--MY WILL DRAINED LIKE BLOOD FROM A WOUND...
BOW DOWN TO ME, LORD--AND PEER INTO THE BLACK HUB OF THE UNIVERSE...
...LOOK BEYOND MAN'S LIMITED PERCEP-TION AND SEE THE CORE OF EVIL--OF DESPICABLE DEBAUCHERY!
"HIS AGED, CRACKED LIPS PARTED...
I WILL TEACH YOU THE TRUTH I ALONE HAVE LIVED WITH--FOR FIVE HUNDRED YEARS...
"...AND I KNEW WHAT HE WAS...
"...BUT--GOD FORGIVE ME--I WAS HELP-LESS TO RESIST. THE BLOOD POURED FROM ME IN A SEEMINGLY-ENDLESS FLOW--UNTIL...
ANDREW... MY LOVE...
MARY...?'
"WAS IT HALLUCINATION--SUBCONSCIOUS PROJECTION--PSYCHIC LINK...? I CANNOT SAY...
"...BUT THE SIGHT OF THAT FACE--AND ALL IT MEANT TO ME--FLOODED ME WITH STRENGTH--WITH A VITAL CLARITY... AND I ACTED!
AWAY FROM ME, DAMN YOU!
UGHH!!
LIFE IS NOT THE HORROR YOU PERPETRATE!
THERE IS DIGNITY IN THE WORLD--THERE IS MEANING IN THIS LIFE...
...AND SUCH AS YOU CANNOT BE ALLOWED TO CORRUPT THESE FRAGILE TRUTHS!
"I REMEMBERED THE LEGENDS THAT HAUNTED ME AS A CHILD--LEGENDS OF THE CREATURE THAT THE IRISH CALLED DEARG-DUL...
"...I KNEW WHAT HAD TO BE DONE TO DESTROY THIS INHUMAN FILTH...
"...AND I DID IT!
"BUT MY TRIUMPH HAD COME TOO LATE--I'D LOST MORE BLOOD THAN I'D REALIZED...
M-MARY...
"MY VISION BLURRED--MY INSIDES TURNED TO SLIVERS OF ICE...
"...AND--IN THE YEAR OF OUR LORD, 1591--I DIED..."
5

"FOR THREE DAYS AND NIGHTS UNHOLY SLEEP TOOK ME-- AND WHEN I FINALLY RETURNED TO MY OPULENT QUARTERS WITHIN THE CASTLE...
WHY IS ANDREW AVOIDING ME--WHY DOESN'T HE LEAVE HIS ROOMS?
HE MUST KNOW HOW WORRIED I AM. THERE'S SOMETHING WRONG HERE--SOMETHING TERRIBLY WRONG. I JUST...
...KNOW IT...?
M-MARY!
OH SWEET LORD-- THE DREAMS I'VE BEEN HAVING-- THE DREAMS OF THE OLD MAN WITH SATAN'S EYES...
...THEY WERE TRUE!
"TREMBLING, I DROPPED THE CHALICE OF DEER'S BLOOD AND--IN WRACKED SOBS OF TORMENT-- TOLD MARY MY TALE...
"...AND WHEN I'D FINISHED...
A-ANDREW--I LOVE YOU MORE THAN LIFE ITSELF.
I MUST BE BY YOUR SIDE... FOR ALL ETERNITY... MAKE ME... WHAT YOU ARE, MY LOVE.
N-NO...
"BUT THE SURGING BLOOD-LUST AND THE ACHING LONE-LINESS IN MY DAMNED SOUL SAID... YES...
"THREE NIGHTS OF AGONIZED WAITING LATER, SOMETHING AROSE-- BUT IT WAS NOT MY MARY..."
OH, ANDREW--I NEVER DREAMED THAT IT WOULD BE LIKE THIS. I FEEL SO STRANGE-- SO WONDERFUL!
THERE IS POWER IN ME--ALL THE UNBRIDLED POWER OF HELL AT MY COMMAND!
WE ARE SUPERIOR TO THE HUMAN RABBLE NOW, ANDREW! WE CAN HAVE THIS KINGDOM IN OUR HANDS-- NO ONE CAN STOP US!
WE SHALL BE RULERS ON A THRONE OF BLOOD!
WH-WHAT ARE YOU SAYING, MARY?!
YOUR WORDS ARE TWISTED AND UNCLEAN... LIKE HIS! I HAVE MADE YOU A THING LIKE HIM!
YOU DARE REJECT ME AFTER I GAVE UP MY LIFE FOR YOU?!
YOU SHALL PAY FOR THIS INDIGNITY, ANDREW BENNETT --BY THE DEVIL, YOU'LL PAY!
6

MARY... NO! YOU MUST...
...UNDERSTAND...
"THAT NIGHT I VOWED THAT I WOULD FIND HER AGAIN--THAT I WOULD SAVE THE SOUL THAT I HAD DESPOILED...
"EVEN IF IT TOOK FOREVER!
"I STALKED HER ACROSS THE CONTINENTS AND ACROSS THE CENTURIES--AND LONG WAS THE TRAIL OF GORE SHE LEFT BEHIND.
"WE BOTH TOOK MANY NAMES--WE BOTH TOOK MANY LIVES--AND SOME DAY I WILL SPEAK OF THOSE GRIM ENCOUNTERS...
"...BUT NOT NOW, FOR...
...TIME'S GROWING SHORT, ANDREW. WE'VE GOT TO MOVE IF WE'RE GOING TO CATCH HER!
TIME SEEMS TO HAVE RUN OUT, DEBORAH...
...FOR SHE HAS SENT HER MINIONS TO CATCH US!
AND WHAT THE MISTRESS WANTS, FEEBLE-MIND--THE MISTRESS GETS.
YOU THINK MY AGE HAS ROBBED ME OF MY REASON, VERMIN?
THEN IT IS YOU WHO HAVE THE FEEBLE MIND!
"MISHKIN ACTED IMPETUOUSLY, AS USUAL. BUT, AFTER ALL, HE WAS A YOUNG MAN OF SEVENTY-TWO AND I COULD FORGIVE SUCH IMPULSES IN ONE WHO HAD NOT LIVED ONE-FOURTH MY LIFETIME...
7

"THE ROOFTOP EXPLODED IN VIOLENCE THEN, AND I MARVELED AT HOW MY MARY'S SPHERE OF INFLUENCE HAD GROWN OVER THE FOUR HUNDRED YEARS I'D BEEN PURSUING HER.
"WHO WOULD HAVE THOUGHT THAT QUEEN ELIZABETH'S GENTLE HAND-MAIDEN WOULD ONE DAY COMMAND SUCH A FORCE OF UNGODLY KILLERS...
"... AND THAT THOSE KILLERS WOULD ONLY BE ONE SMALL PART OF AN INTERNATIONAL ORGANIZATION WITH ARMS, EYES, AND EARS IN ALL STRATA OF SOCIETY...
"... WITH OPERATIVES IN CORPORATE TOWERS, CRIMINAL LAIRS, HOUSES OF WORSHIP, AND HOUSES OF GOVERNMENT?
"ANY WONDER THEN WHY I WENT BERSERK AT THE VERY SIGHT OF HER PUPPETS?
"ANY WONDER WHY ALL REASON WAS LOST IN A HAZE OF PRIMOR-DIAL SAVAGERY?
YOU CAN BREAK MY NECK, ANDREW BENNETT-- BUT YOU CANNOT KILL ME...
JUST AS YOU CANNOT DESTROY THE BLOOD RED MOON!
"THE BLOOD RED MOON! IT WAS AN APT NAME FOR MARY'S OBSCENE AGENCY...
"... AN AGENCY I HAD SWORN TO SMASH--TO DRIVE BACK INTO THE REEKING DIRT FROM WHICH IT CRAWLED...
YOU ARE POWER-LESS AGAINST US, BENNETT-- FOR WHAT HARMS US-- HARMS YOU!
"TRUE. BUT I WAS NOT ALONE...
"... THERE WERE OTHERS WHO COULD WIELD THE POWER... AND USE IT!
AWAY, UPUIR*! LET THE HOLY WAFER'S LIGHT DRIVE BACK YOUR CONSUMING DARK-NESS!
YOU TELL 'IM, MISHKIN! AND IT GOES DOUBLE FOR ME!
*UPUIR IS THE RUSSIAN NAME FOR THE UNDEAD.--LEN.
8

"HER PAWNS FLED LIKE THE COWARDLY BEASTS THEY WERE-- WHILE I WAS PAINFULLY REMINDED OF JUST WHO AND WHAT I WAS...
G-GET THOSE THINGS... AWAY... Y-YOU'RE MAKING ME... ILL...
OH, ANDREW-- I'M SORRY. I DIDN'T MEAN TO--
PFAW! HE'LL BE FINE, GIRL-- HIS KIND DOESN'T DIE EASILY... AS YOU WELL KNOW!
"DEBORAH DANCER LOVED ME-- IT WAS TRAGICALLY OBVIOUS-- BUT THAT LOVE COULD NEVER BE RETURNED. MY HEART WAS ENSLAVED TO ONLY ONE WOMAN...
MARY!!
THOSE UPUIR WERE TRYING TO DISTRACT US WHILE SHE ESCAPED!
ESCAPE? NOT NOW-- WHEN WE'RE...
...SO CLOSE!
ANDREW... WAIT!
NO, DEBORAH--YOU MUST LET HIM GO TO HER...
"FRANTICALLY I FLEW-- BEATING LEATHERN WINGS AGAINST THE CHILL NIGHT WIND...
"...THE MOMENT --AT LAST-- SEEMED AT HAND...
"...I WOULD HAVE HER...
"...AND NO ONE-- NOT GOD--NOT LUCIFIER--WOULD STAND IN MY WAY!
9

"TREMBLING, I REACHED INTO THAT BLACK MACHINE--LITTLE CARING THAT THE CHAUFFEUR WAS GETTING AWAY...
"...ALL I CARED ABOUT WAS...HER!
"NOT THAT I KNEW WHAT I'D DO WITH HER NOW THAT I HAD HER.
YOU LOOK SLIGHTLY DUMBFOUNDED, BELOVED. WHERE IS THE ELOQUENT SPEECH I ONCE ADORED...
...WHERE ARE THE FLOWERY PHRASES AND THE WORDS OF GENTLE GRACE?
"SOMETHING WAS AMISS. THIS WAS MARY'S FACE...BUT THE VOICE WAS DEEPER--THE ARMS TOO THIN...
"...I'D BEEN DUPED...
HOW EASY TO MAKE A FOOL OF YOU, ANDREW BENNETT! THE MISTRESS SAID IT WOULD BE SO!
IT WAS ONE OF OUR OWN THAT CALLED YOU HERE--JUST SO WE COULD HUMILIATE YOU--TEAR DOWN YOUR WALLS OF EGO!
AS YOU STAND THERE GAWKING--YOUR BELOVED MARY IS SETTING INTO MOTION A PLAN THAT WILL SPELL THE FINAL TRIUMPH OF THE BLOOD RED MOON! HA HA HA HA!!
"I LET HER GO--WHAT USE TO DALLY WITH PAWNS WHILE THE CHESS-MASTER RAN FREE?
LOOK AT HIM, MISHKIN--HE NEEDS SOMEONE TO COMFORT HIM...
LEAVE HIM ALONE, GIRL--THERE IS NOTHING EITHER OF US COULD SAY TO EASE HIS TORMENT...
"I OVERHEARD MISHKIN'S TROUBLED WHISPERS--AND KNEW HE WAS RIGHT...
THERE MUST BE AN END TO THIS MADNESS, MARY...
...THERE MUST BE AN END!
"BUT LITTLE DID I KNOW THAT THE STRUGGLE THAT HAD LASTED FOUR HUNDRED YEARS--WAS ONLY BEGINNING...
10

COMIC BOOK COLLEGE

Comic books were a passion that grabbed me at a very early age and never let go. (I've said it before, and I'll say it again: I don't recall a time when I *didn't* read comics.) Sure, I moved on to Dostoyevsky, Bradbury, Hesse, and Vonnegut, but I never abandoned Lee, Kirby, Broome, Kane, and the other comic book masters who inspired and nurtured me growing up.

I was always creative, obsessed with drawing, playing guitar, writing stories and songs. In many ways, these things weren't just my passions: they were what defined me. They *were* me. Which meant that I didn't just want to read comics, I wanted to *write* them—as desperately as I wanted to be a rock 'n' roll star.

In the late 1970s, when I was taking my first awkward steps as a comic book writer (until then I'd been making my living, such as it was, playing in rock 'n' roll bands and working as a music journalist), I had a very simple rule that served me well: *The editor is always right.* I was hungry to work, and the people sitting behind the desks handing out the assignments held the keys to the kingdom I so desperately wanted to enter. More important: they had knowledge and experience they were willing to share.

Over the years, young writers have occasionally come to me for guidance, and some of them, when offered advice, become instantly defensive, wasting their time and mine by explaining exactly why they don't need to *take* that advice, why their stories are just fine, thank you, and shouldn't be altered. "Well, if it's just fine," I've often wondered, "what are you coming to *me* for?" I never saw things that way. I *wanted* to learn; I wanted to grow as a writer and soak in all that wisdom my editors had amassed.

The truth, of course, is that the editor *isn't* always right. Sometimes they're spectacularly wrong, and it's a writer's responsibility to stand up for himself and his work and, when necessary, to challenge his editors, but a neophyte writer still grappling with the fundamentals of his craft would do well to save his battles for a later date. One thing I intuited in those early days was that no matter what the editor asked of me—short of requesting something morally or artistically abhorrent, which, for the record, never happened—I could take it as a challenge, and, more important, *learn something from it.* I looked at those early years at DC Comics as my Comic Book College: I was an overeager freshman and, happily, I had a trio of superb professors. And the first of them was a young man named Paul Levitz.

I made several aborted attempts to enter the comic book business before my success: five years earlier, I'd written a script sample and sent it to Marvel Comics. I had no clue what a comic book script looked like, and I'm sure that what I submitted was less than brilliant. The assistant editor who read my sample thought so too, and told me just that, in no uncertain terms. (I've learned, over the years, that it's important to encourage new talent regardless of the face value of their work. Even if the samples you're evaluating are abysmal, you have to find something encouraging to say. Humans—especially the sensitive, neurotic, artistic variety—desperately need encouragement. The smallest crumb of kindness becomes a mountain of hope. I suspect that nameless assistant editor was overwhelmed, having a rough day, and simply couldn't bear to plow through yet another wretched submission. But he could have made my day much brighter by simply saying, "You're not there yet, kid, but keep at it. Don't give up.")

A year or two later, DC began a short-lived apprentice program: a rare opportunity for novices to be trained by seasoned pros in the craft of writing for comics. Aspiring writers were encouraged to submit their work, and those with the best submissions would be chosen for the program. I decided to write a Justice League script, a fact I now find hilarious: team books are difficult for even the most experienced writer—I don't think I've ever mastered the form—but there I was, 19 years old and ready to give it my all.

I didn't make it into the program (frankly, I didn't deserve to), but I received some extremely helpful feedback from a woman on the DC staff named Val Eads. It was the first time I was encouraged by a professional, and it meant the world to me. Understand: I was just some kid from Brooklyn who grew up in a lower-middle-class family. My father worked for the New York City Parks Department, raking leaves and shoveling snow in a local park. My mother was a switchboard operator. Growing up, I'd never encountered anyone even vaguely resembling a professional writer or artist. (My best friend's older brother was a working musician, part of a Las Vegas lounge act; that was the closest I ever came to hobnobbing with the rich and famous.) Making it as a writer seemed about as easy as scaling the Monolith from Kubrick's *2001*—which is why that small encouragement from Val was so important to me. (Ms. Eads, if you're out there, God bless you!)

A few years later, a fellow student and comic book fanatic at Brooklyn College, Warren Reece, actually made it over the Monolith: he got a job at Marvel, working in the production department. Warren very kindly submitted some of my material to the folks at Marvel editorial, but I never received a response (which, in some ways, was worse than being rejected). Warren then encouraged me to submit some samples to *Crazy* magazine (Marvel's attempt at a *Mad*-style humor publication). Truth is, I had no interest in writing for *Crazy*—I possessed zero skills in that arena—but, miraculously, editor Paul Laikin bought one of my pitches and, even more miraculously, I got a check in the mail with Spider-Man's picture on it. (Blessings to Mr. Laikin and Mr. Reece both.) I'd hoped that selling something to *Crazy* would get me an in with the comic book side of Marvel, but it didn't. Still, it allowed me to say that I was a (kinda/sorta/maybe/but not really) professional.

Not long after that, I sent another batch of samples to DC. (I still have them filed away in my office: a Superman script, a Plastic Man script, and an original piece called *Stardust*—which was a very raw prototype for what would, seven or eight years later, evolve into *Moonshadow*.) I got a letter back from Somebody's Assistant saying, "We're not going to buy Superman scripts from a writer we've never heard of, but Paul Levitz is looking for material for *House of Mystery* and *Weird War Tales*." These were two of the many anthology comics—they called them mystery books in those days because, after the witch-hunting of the Wertham era, the companies were still reluctant to use the word *horror*—that DC was then publishing. Each title had multiple five- to eight-page tales, most of them supernatural stories with a *Twilight Zone*-ish twist ending. I'd never read the anthologies, hardly knew they existed, but you can bet I ran out and bought a stack of them, devoured them, and quickly (perhaps *too* quickly) developed some story ideas that I mailed off to Paul.

Given how raw my material was at the time, I wouldn't have blamed Paul if he'd tossed my pitches into the trash, but instead he took the time to analyze the stories and offer constructive (sometimes *bluntly* constructive) feedback. His reply, dated August 22, 1977 (yep, that's still in the files, too), very politely, succinctly—and accurately—tore my stories to shreds. The last line was a classic: "You're welcome to submit more ideas in the future, but I suggest you use a professional typing service or type more slowly. The physical presentation of your manuscripts leaves something to be desired." He was right: this was the troglodytic era before computers, and, in my hunger and enthusiasm, I had crossed things out, scrawled in the margins, and written up and down the sides of the paper.

Paul's criticism didn't bother me. The only thing that mattered was that wondrous phrase, "You're welcome to submit more ideas in the future." Which is what I immediately did: submitted again (and again) until, finally—this must have been November of that year—I made an appointment to go up to DC (a thrill in itself) and meet with Paul. I walked into the office to find a skinny kid who, despite being only 20 at the time—I was an ancient 23—had been working at DC since high school. With the attempted mustache clinging to his lip and his extremely serious demeanor, he seemed like the world's oldest young person. (Or perhaps the world's youngest old person?)

I remember sitting across the desk from Paul, nervous and intimidated, pitching ideas. When he actually liked one of my stories and asked me to work up a draft, I had a moment of dizzying, euphoric confusion: *Wait a minute...WAIT a minute! Is he saying he actually wants me to WRITE this?!*

The story in question—which eventually saw print in *House of Mystery*—was called (brace yourselves) "The Lady Killer Craves Blood." (I warned you.) Illustrated by Gerry Talaoc, the story was based on the Son of Sam killings that had traumatized New York the previous summer. In my version, the Sam-like maniac murders a woman, not knowing that her husband is (what a brilliant twist!) a vampire. The vampire then hunts down the serial killer and, still mourning his lost love, submits himself to the obliterating rays of the morning sun. All in eight pages!

The short stories were the perfect way to learn the comics form. You had five to eight pages to develop a complete plot, a full character arc, sharp dialogue, and moody narration. (Many of those shorts were so packed with plot that they could easily have been expanded to fill a complete issue.) The anthologies weren't high-profile—I still think of them as the vaudeville of comics, the place you went to learn your craft till you were ready for Comic Book Broadway—and you got to master your craft, or at least wrestle with it, without the whole world watching and judging your every move.

A week or so after that first meeting, back to DC I went, my first-draft script in hand, ready for Paul's dissection of my work. "No more than five panels per page," he wrote, on a piece of yellow lined paper (I've got that in the files, too), "no more than 35 words per panel, no more than two sentences per caption, clear transitional captions, don't forget your splash panel." I raced home, wrote another draft, incorporating Paul's suggestions (well, I took them as *orders*: believe me, I counted *every damn* word in each panel) and then, to my astonishment and delight, the next time we met, he bought it. What followed remains one of the greatest, most magical moments of my professional life: Paul Levitz shook my hand, looked me square in the eye, and said, "Welcome to the business." I didn't need the D train: I could have floated back to Brooklyn.

I continued writing stories for Paul well into 1978, and, thanks to him, I had the honor and privilege of working with artists far more skilled at their craft than I was at mine. Those anthologies were home to veterans—masters!—like Steve Ditko, Dick Ayers, Gil Kane, Dan Spiegle, and Don Newton, as well as newer but no less talented artists like Marshall Rogers and Tom Sutton.

After six months of studying at Paul's feet, two wonderful things happened: (1) I was assigned my first full-length story—what the cover copy eventually called "a bonus-length, 22-page thriller!"—for *Weird War Tales*, and (2) my rate was raised from $13.00 a page to what seemed an exorbitant $15.00 a page. There's an old Warner Bros. cartoon where Daffy Duck, having found a pile of gold, shouts, "I'm rich! I'm wealthy! I'm independent! I'm socially secure!" Well, that's how I felt. But somewhere between the day I turned in the script and the day the check arrived, that security evaporated...

...and DC imploded.

In June of 1978, the company—which had gone through an expansion the previous year, the so-called "DC Explosion"—laid off staff and canceled something like 40 percent of its line. Marginal creators like myself found themselves cut off—I remember sitting in the DC waiting room with Paul as he gently explained the situation to me—and my march to comic book glory abruptly ended. (My band broke up right around the same time, so you can imagine my gloomy state of mind.) When my *Weird War* check arrived, I somehow managed to live off that $330.00 for the entire summer. It helped that I had four roommates and the rent was cheap.

I continued on with music journalism, eventually getting a foot in the door at *Rolling Stone*, but I never gave up on comics. When I got a call from DC editor Jack Harris early in 1979 (no doubt on Paul's recommendation) about contributing to a new science fiction anthology, *Time Warp*, I couldn't say yes fast enough. Jack was a genuinely warm, welcoming guy who taught newbies like me through enthusiasm and encouragement. He'd sometimes sit in the office and edit the scripts with me sitting across from him, telling me what he'd changed and why—and always with a smile and a positive spin. *Time Warp* was the crowbar that reopened DC's doors for me. I was soon working with both Jack and Paul and feeling very much a part of the DC family. (Around that time, I sent my dear friend Karen Berger up to the office to meet Paul. He was looking for an assistant, and Karen, who'd just graduated from Brooklyn College with a journalism degree, was looking for a job. They hit it off, and the rest is—quite literally—comic book history.)

That family expanded when the late, great Len Wein joined to the DC staff. Despite being just past 30, Len was already a legend in the industry. This was the writer who, with the equally legendary Bernie Wrightson, created the groundbreaking *Swamp Thing* series. Unless you were around when that book debuted, you can't really grasp how truly revolutionary *Swamp Thing* was, how different it was from everything that had come before it. I remember being floored by the emotional power of the art, the pulp poetry of the language, and the big beating heart at the story's core. You couldn't read an issue of *Swamp Thing* without feeling something, without being moved.

If that series was all Len had done, his place in comic book heaven would still be secure, but he was also the guy who co-created Wolverine, one of the most popular and successful characters in the medium's history; resurrected and revitalized the X-Men franchise; had memorable runs on everything from *Justice League* to *Hulk* to *Batman* to *Spider-Man*; and, oh, yes, was editor-in-chief of Marvel Comics along the way.

Which is why, when I entered his office in the spring of '79, I counted myself among the lucky ones: I didn't realize just how lucky I was until I got to know Len. There are some writers whose work you admire, but then you meet them and it's impossible to make the leap from the words on the page to the person across the table. There seems to be some great cosmic disconnect—and, yes, a great disappointment as well. (It's unfair to expect writers or actors or musicians to somehow be the embodiment of their art—the work alone should be more than enough—but we hope for it nonetheless.) With Len, though, the man and the work were one. He was just like his stories: charming, funny, eloquent, and all heart.

In a very short time, Len became not just my editor, but my friend and mentor. He saw a spark of something special in my stories and, through his patient guidance, he helped to fan that spark into a flame. There I was, an insecure, working-class kid from Brooklyn, uncertain of my own talent, wondering if I could really make it as a writer—and there was the legendary Len Wein providing the answer: "If you want it, you absolutely can." You can't put a price on that.

The same can be said of the entire time I spent as a student at DC University. I look back with great warmth, and great *gratitude*, on those days crafting short, spooky tales for the classic anthologies, hanging on every word that Professors Levitz, Harris, and Wein uttered. Those three gifted gentlemen gave so much of themselves so freely, and because of their generosity and wisdom, I've had a long career traversing the worlds of comics, television, film, and novels. I will never stop being grateful to them—and to those oddball "mystery books" that were my entry into the unique and magical world of comic books.

J.M. DeMatteis
October 2019

Born and raised in Brooklyn, New York, J.M. DeMatteis was a professional musician and music journalist before he entered the comic book field. He has written for nearly all of the major DC and Marvel icons—including memorable runs on Spider-Man *and* Justice League *(the latter of which won him an Eisner Award)—as well as authoring a celebrated series of original graphic novels that includes* Seekers Into the Mystery, The Last One, Mercy, *and* Brooklyn Dreams. *His groundbreaking creation, the Eisner-nominated* Moonshadow *(illustrated by Jon J Muth) was hailed in Gene Kannenberg Jr.'s* 500 Essential Graphic Novels *as one of the finest fantasy comics ever created, and his children's comic* Abadazad, *launched in 2006, grew into an acclaimed three-book series published by Disney.*

In addition to his contributions to the printed page, DeMatteis has written extensively for the screen, including the animated films Constantine: City of Demons *and* Superman: Red Son *and episodes of* Justice League Unlimited, Batman: The Brave and the Bold, Ben 10, *and* Marvel's Spider-Man.

In his spare time he teaches Imagination 101, a three-day workshop that explores the practicalities and metaphysics of writing for comics, graphic novels, and animation. He's also the founder of the story consultation service Creation Point, which offers in-depth guidance for both the professional and aspiring writer. DeMatteis lives and works in upstate New York.

THE LAST BATTLES

From the opening battle cry of 1952's *Our Army at War* #1, DC's war titles were among its steadiest sellers, and many of their contributors provided work throughout their almost four decades of unbroken publication. Bob Kanigher was the original editor for the first half of the line's existence, and he was also the principal writer for those comics until peace broke out and World War II finally ended, four decades late. Joe Kubert, while not the original artist on *Sgt. Rock*, was indisputably the definitive one, and Sam Glanzman's 16-year run on the Haunted Tank feature rivaled Russ Heath's earlier one.

But as the wars wound down, these titles also introduced many new creators to the field—especially talented students from the new Kubert School in Dover, New Jersey, a veritable factory for thoughtful and skilled comic artists like Steve Bissette and Rick Veitch. From the late 1950s on, the war comics had balanced serials with short stories, and the backups featured a wide variety of art styles, particularly after Kubert took over editorial chores from Kanigher. In the waning days of the genre, a number of new features were tried, like the Creature Commandos, but to no noticeable effect. It seemed clear that readers either wanted conventional

BATTALION SGT. MAJOR RICHARD J. BISSETTE REPORTING-- WITH A TRUE STORY ABOUT C BATTERY, ONE UNIT OF THE 206TH FIELD ARTILLERY BATTALION ATTACHED TO THE 86TH INFANTRY BRIGADE... STATIONED SOMEWHERE IN KOREA...DURING THE HEIGHT OF THE KOREAN WAR!
THE BRIGADE HAS ORDERS TO PULL BACK 40 MILES... AND IT'S UP TO K CO. AND BATTERY C TO STAY BEHIND AND BUY THE 24 HOURS THEY NEED TO MAKE THE MOVE!
1300 HRS--THE OPERATION BEGINS! K CO. REMAINS BEHIND, HOLDING ENEMY PROBES BACK AS THE 86TH INFANTRY BRIGADE MAKES ITS WAY TO AND ACROSS-
-THE BRIDGE!! ...WHERE BATTERY C IS POSITIONED...
J-6104
...ITS SIX HOWITZERS READY TO PROVIDE HEAVY FIRE TO COVER K CO.! WHEN THE LAST MEN OF K CO. HAVE CROSSED THE BRIDGE, C BATTERY WILL BLOW THE BRIDGE TO KINGDOM COME!! 1930 HRS--TWO OUTPOSTS ARE SET UP...
ONE: CAPT. WESTOVER AND HIS RADIO OPERATOR, OVERLOOKING THE MAIN ROAD TO THE BRIDGE...
I'VE GOT NUMBER TWO: OVERLOOKING A SMALL DIRT ROAD! WITH ME ARE RADIOMAN SP4 ROBERTS AND RIFLEMAN PFC MILLER.
WE ARE THE "LOOSE ENDS" OF THIS OPERATION! WE STAY BACK--CALLING IN HOWITZER FIRE TO COVER K CO.--UNTIL THE LAST MAN CROSSES THE BRIDGE! EVEN IF IT MEANS JUMPING OUT OF THE FRYING PAN--
--INTO THE FIRE!
STORY: SGT. MAJ. RICHARD J. BISSETTE
ART: SRBISSETTE
1

0520 HRS -- WE'VE SET UP OUR OUT-POST, LOOKING OVER A DIRT ROAD... ALL QUIET HERE, THOUGH WE CAN HEAR HEAVY FIRE AND SEE THE SMOKE BEYOND THE HILL...
0600 HRS -- CO. K IS FALLING BACK, THEIR POSITION UNDER FIRE! CAPT. WESTOVER CALLS IN FROM HIS OUTPOST FOR HEAVIER FIRE FROM BATTERY C.! ALL CREWS ARE FIRING!
0620 HRS --
ROBERTS! GET BATTERY C ON THE LINE!
ENEMY TROOPS AND FOUR TANKS MOVIN' UP DIRT ROAD--TRYIN' TO CUT OFF K CO.!
BATTERY C FIRES IN SIX ROUNDS -- LEAVING ONE TANK BURNING. THE OTHERS MOVE OUT OF SIGHT WHILE THE TROOPS LAY LOW BY THE SIDE OF THE ROAD.
0720 HRS -- ROBERTS PICKS UP A CALL FROM WESTOVER'S OUTPOST...
...THE REDS ARE ALL AROUND US... MOVING UP THE HILL...
IT WAS THE LAST WE EVER HEARD FROM THEM!
2

1015 HRS -- CO. K IS IN SIGHT OF THE BRIDGE AND UNDER HEAVY FIRE. C BATTERY IS FIRING JUST IN FRONT OF THEM... TRYING TO HOLD THE ENEMY BACK!
1025 HRS--
ROBERTS! CALL IN MORE FIRE FROM C BATTERY! GOTTA KEEP THE REDS PINNED!
TWO TANKS TRY TO MAKE A RUN FOR IT, LEAVING ONE BURNING-- THE OTHER OFF THE ROAD ON ITS SIDE! ENEMY TROOPS ARE BETWEEN US AND THE MAIN ROAD -- THEY ARE COMING UP TOWARDS US--
1040 HRS -- WE ARE NOW CALLING IN FIRE ALMOST ON OUR OWN POSITION!
ROBERTS HAS BEEN HIT IN THE BACK AND THE RIGHT ARM -- BUT--HE'S STILL OPERATING THE RADIO!
PFC MILLER IS DOING ONE HECK OF A JOB WITH HIS RIFLE--KEEPING THE REDS OFF US. I'VE BEEN HIT IN MY LEFT LEG AND LEFT SIDE... A LOT OF BLOOD, BUT NO PAIN --YET!
3

1125 HRS -- THE SECOND PLATOON OF K CO. IS CROSSING THE BRIDGE. A LOT OF WOUNDED...
1145 HRS -- THE LAST OF K CO. CROSSES THE RIVER. THE MAIN ROAD IS UNDER VERY HEAVY FIRE!
1205 HRS --
DICK... WE'VE GIVEN YOU ALL THE TIME WE CAN! THE BRIDGE BLOWS IN TEN MINUTES! WE'VE GOT TO MOVE OUT AFTER SHE GOES!
WE CAN'T MAKE THE BRIDGE! GIVE US ALL THE FIRE YOU CAN AND WE'LL BREAK FOR THE RIVER-- AND SWIM ACROSS! ROBERTS IS HURT BAD... BUT... WE'RE COMING HOME!
WE'RE TEARING DOWN THE HILL FOR THE RIVER. HALF WAY DOWN WE ALMOST RUN OVER SIX REDS COMING UP!
MILLER OPENS UP AND DROPS TWO OF THEM!
WE CAN SEE THE RIVER ABOUT A HALF MILE AHEAD OF US -- THEY'VE JUST BLOWN THE BRIDGE!
4

C BATTERY IS GIVING THE HILL A REAL GOING-OVER...
WE REACH THE RIVER BANK... MILLER AND I TAKE OFF OUR HEAVY JACKETS AND BOOTS.
BOY, THE RIVER SURE IS COLD! BUT--IT'S OUR ONLY WAY HOME. I CAN MAKE OUT SOME OF OUR BOYS WAITING ACROSS THE RIVER. WE MUST DESTROY OUR JEEP AND RADIO. WHILE MILLER UNDRESSES ROBERTS, I PUT OUR CLOTHES IN THE JEEP--AND FIRE A ROUND AT THE GAS TANK!
WE HIT THE WATER--LIT BY THE BURNING JEEP! MILLER AND I HELP ROBERTS ACROSS.
THE NEXT THING WE KNOW, WE'RE BEING HELPED OUT OF THE FREEZING WATER BY OUR GUYS. WHEN WE TOLD THEM WE WERE GOING TO SWIM ACROSS, THE WORD WENT OUT--AND OUR STRONGEST SWIMMERS WERE TRUCKED TO THE RIVER BANK.
1230 HRS--C BATTERY GAVE THE ORDER C.S.M.O. (CLOSE STATION MARCH ORDER) AND WE STARTED THE 40 MILE TRIP TO REJOIN OUR BATTALION. BATTERY C AND CO. K HAD HELD THE BRIDGE... GIVING THE BRIGADE THE 24 HOURS THEY HAD TO HAVE!
THE END

DURING THE CIVIL WAR THE GREAT PLANTATIONS SUPPLIED THE CONFEDERATE ARMY AND SLAVE LABOR FREED THOUSANDS OF MEN FOR FIGHTING. LOCATED FAR BELOW THE MASON-DIXON LINE, THESE PLANTATIONS HAD BEEN SAFE UNTIL THE UNION REGIMENTS MADE UP OF FORMER SLAVES BEGAN RAIDING BEHIND ENEMY LINES...
THE FORMER SLAVES KNEW THE LAND WELL. SOMEHOW THE WORD GOT TO THOSE IN BONDAGE-- GET READY! MOSES IS COMIN'--
PLEASE, MOSES... LET ME REST OR I'LL DIE... I'M...
MOVE... OR DIE NOW!
STORY: VAL EADS ART: RICK VEITCH
DEAD MEN CAN'T ANSWER QUESTIONS!
GO DOWN MOSES
1

COMBAHEE PLANTATION'S NEARLY 1000 SLAVES ARE THE BACKBONE OF THE SUPPLY LINE. FOR THEM, LINCOLN'S PROCLAMATION HASN'T SOFTENED THE LASH...
...OR SWEETENED A BITTER HOPE!
"GO DOWN, MOSES... TELL DE OL' PHAROAH."
JUNE 2, 1863...
PORT ROYAL HEADQUARTERS
GENERAL DAVID HUNTER
VERY WELL, SERGEANT-- BEGIN PREPARATIONS FOR THE RAID ON COMBAHEE!
YES, SIR.
LOOK AT THESE MAPS-- INCREDIBLE!
THAT BLACK SCOUT, MOSES, IS WORTH HIS WEIGHT IN GOLD-- IF HE CAN GET AROUND ENEMY LINES LIKE THAT!
2

I'VE TAKEN ONLY ENOUGH MEN TO MAN THE BOATS!
WE'LL BE **OVERLOADED** COMIN' BACK!
EVERY MAN HERE **WANTED** TO GO!
DARK SOON... **LET'S START!**
LET'S GO, YOU MEN!
REMEMBER--**DON'T** FIRE ON THE BARNS UNTIL YOU HEAR OUR GUNS ON THE RIVER! THEN... LEAD THE PEOPLE TO THE SHORE!
THERE'S THE **FALSE CHANNEL MARKERS!**
KEEP TO **THIS** SIDE... AND LET OFF THE SQUAD.
3
WE MADE IT... THERE IT IS!
LET'S GET DOWN TO THOSE BARNS!
WHERE'S MOSES AN' THEM BOATS?

WHUP
THEY'RE HERE!
WHOUMPP
YANKEES ON THE RIVER!
HOW'D THEY GET PAST THE SHALLOWS?
WE MARKED THE **WRONG CHANNEL!**
RUN FOR YOUR FREEDOM!
4

SUPPLY BARNS BURNT... OVER 800 SLAVES FREED... GUNS DESTROYED... EXTRAORDINARY!
WHERE IS MOSES? I WANT TO SHAKE HIS HAND!
MOSES IS DOWN WITH SOME OF TH' NEW FREED SLAVES!
SOME OF THE CHILDREN AND OLD FOLKS IS SICK!
WELL, THEN... I'LL GO DOWN THERE TO SEE HIM!
MOSES-- THIS IS GENERAL HUNTER. HE WANTS TO MEET YOU!
PLEASED T' MEET YOU, GENERAL!
HARRIET TUBMAN..."BLACK MOSES"... THE ONLY WOMAN WHO EVER LED AN AMERICAN ARMED EXPEDITION AGAINST ENEMY FORCES! BECAUSE THE ARMY REFUSED TO INDUCT A WOMAN, SHE FOUGHT AS A CIVILIAN "VOLUNTEER" AND WAS NEVER PAID FOR HER SERVICES. SHE DIED IN 1913, PENNILESS... BUT FREE!
THE END

MT. VERNON, VIRGINIA... 1781...
HE'S A LIVING LEGEND! I-I CAN'T PAINT THE PORTRAIT OF A -- LEGEND!
MAYBE I KIN TELL YOU SOMETHIN' ABOUT GEN WASHINGTON, MR. CONSTABLE!
IT WAS AT VALLEY FORGE--ONE COLD, CRUEL WINTER'S NIGHT...
JIM'S DESERTIN'!
STOP 'IM!
WHAT FOR?
WINTER SOLDIER!
RIC ESTRADA 1972
BOB KANIGHER'S GALLERY OF WAR
G-1034

BUT... WE'RE SENTRIES-- AIN'T WE? WE'VE GOT T' STOP JIM FROM DESERTIN'...
YEAH? WE'LL ALL BE DEAD HERE... LESS WE DO THE SAME!
WE AIN'T NO ARMY -- WE'RE JUST A BUNCH O' FROZEN SCARECROWS!
HURT YOURSELF, SON?
N-NO -- GEN. W-WASHINGTON, S-SIR!
SENTRIES... ARREST THIS MAN!
2

PRISONER-- DO YOU HAVE ANYTHING TO SAY BEFORE THE SENTENCE OF THIS COURT-MARTIAL IS READ?
NO, GENERAL! CAN'T SAY... I DIDN'T GIT... A FAIR TRIAL!
IT IS THE SENTENCE OF THIS COURT THAT YOU BE EXECUTED BY FIRING SQUAD...
...FOR DESERTION! AT DAWN-- TWO DAYS HENCE!
COWARDS SHOULD BE HANGED-- GENERAL!
THE SENTENCE OF EXECUTION STANDS!
3

GEN. WASHINGTON--!
WRITING TO YOUR MOTHER, SON?
YOU TRIED TO DESERT, SON-- BUT YOU'RE NOT A COWARD!
COME WITH ME!
I- I- I'VE SURE TRIED-- GENERAL! B-BUT HOW KIN I TELL MY MOTHER I'M BEIN' SHOT FOR BEING A COWARD!
PRISONER-- HALT!
AT EASE, SENTRY! I'LL BE RESPONSIBLE FOR HIM!
4

VALLEY FORGE, SON-- A FROZEN HELL FOR THE CONTINENTAL ARMY OF THE UNITED STATES!
BUT THERE WON'T BE A UNITED STATES OF AMERICA... UNLESS WE CAN DRIVE THE BRITISH ARMIES FROM OUR LAND!
THERE ISN'T A MAN HERE WHO ISN'T DREAMING OF DOING EXACTLY WHAT YOU DID, SON... RUN AWAY FROM THIS FREEZING DESOLATION!
WHAT CHANCE DOES AN ARMY LIKE OURS HAVE-- AGAINST THE SEASONED, VICTORIOUS BRITISH?
I NEED YOUR HELP, SON--TO PUT STEEL IN THE SOULS OF YOUR STARVING, FREEZING, FEARFUL COMRADES!
I NEED YOU TO DO SOMETHING FAR BRAVER THAN FACING THE BAYONETS OF THE ENEMY!
W-WHAT, GENERAL?
5

DAWN OF THE SECOND DAY...
IMAGINE, MOM... GEN. WASHINGTON ASKED ME--ME!--TO SET AN EXAMPLE IN FRONT OF THE FULL ARMY! TO SHOW 'EM HOW A REAL SOLDIER KIN FACE GUNS WITHOUT BLINKIN'! SO WHEN THEY MEET THE ENEMY THEY'LL ACT JUST LIKE ME!
The general says I'm the real hero--because I'll be facin' death alone. He says he'll be proud of me! An' he'll never forget me! Well, Mom--time to go! Don't cry--Your Lovin' Son...
Jim
FIRE!
THERE'LL BE NO MORE DESERTERS AFTER THIS, GENERAL! YOU CAN REST EASY NOW!
REST EASY? I'LL BE SEEING THAT BOY'S FACE... IN MY DREAMS... EVERY NIGHT... FOR THE REST OF MY LIFE!

WHAT A FEARFUL BURDEN FOR A MAN TO CARRY!
IT EXPLAINS THE SECRET SORROW BEHIND HIS EYES!
BUT HOW DO *YOU* KNOW OF THIS HAPPENING?
I-I AM JIM'S *MOTHER!*
I'M READY TO PAINT YOUR PORTRAIT, GEN. WASHINGTON!
FOR POSTERITY!!
MAKE WAR NO MORE

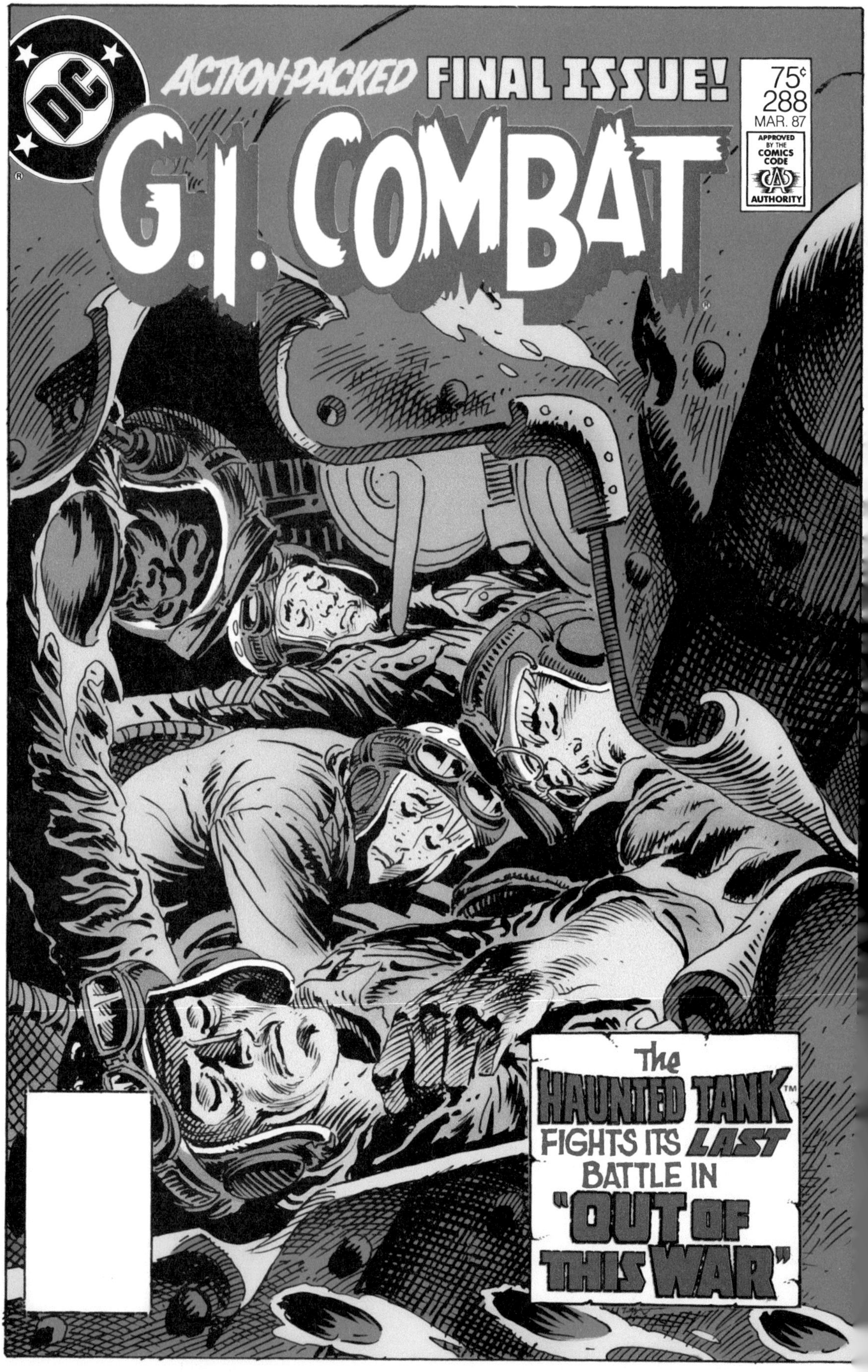
ACTION-PACKED FINAL ISSUE!
75¢
288
MAR. 87
APPROVED BY THE COMICS CODE AUTHORITY
G.I. COMBAT
The HAUNTED TANK FIGHTS ITS LAST BATTLE IN "OUT OF THIS WAR"

MANNED BY A YANK CREW, FLYING THE DEFIANT REB BANNER OF ITS GHOSTLY GUARDIAN, J.E.B. STUART, FAMED CONFEDERATE GENERAL OF THE CIVIL WAR... FOREVER BLAZING NEW PAGES OF COMBAT... THAT'S...
PART ONE
THE HAUNTED TANK
...THE AWOL DOG TAGS
BRUMMMM!
BRUMMMM!
BRUMMM!
0630 HOURS. AS THE SUN RISES, 28 MILES WEST OF THE RHINE RIVER, DRIVERS REV THE ENGINES OF THEIR SHERMAN TANKS...
THE CACOPHONOUS ROAR AWAKENS LT. JEB STUART...
NEVER OVER-SLEPT BEFORE!
C'MON, MEN... WAKE UP! RISE AND SHINE! THERE'S A WAR ON!
SO WHAT ELSE IS NEW?
HEY, WHAT'S THIS? ONE OF MY DOG TAGS IS... MISSING!?
B4903

LOOTENANT--! I'M MINUS A DOG TAG!
SAME HERE!
ME, TOO!
I BEEN WEARING MINE SO LONG, I FEEL NAKED WITHOUT IT!
WITH ALL THE FIGHTING WE'VE BEEN IN, NO WONDER THEY CAME LOOSE AND WE LOST 'EM!
SO WHAT! ONE'S ALL WE NEED! THE OTHER'S FOR THE BURIAL DETAIL!
SO STAY ALIVE, BOYS... UNTIL WE GET NEW ONES!
AM I SEEING THINGS... OR IS ANOTHER CREW TAKING OUR TANK!?
SKIPPER-- SKIPPER!
WHAT'S GOING ON HERE?
ACCORDING TO AIR RECON, THE LUDENDORFF BRIDGE AT REMAGEN IS STILL STANDING! WE'VE GOT TO HELP THE INFANTRY CAPTURE IT BEFORE THE GERMANS BLOW IT UP!
IF WE DO, IT'LL SAVE COUNTLESS LIVES THAT WOULD BE LOST IN A RIVER CROSSING, CAPTAIN. I REMEMBER THE 36TH INFANTRY DIVISION HAD 7,000 CASUALTIES CROSSING THE RAPIDO RIVER IN ITALY!
2
OUT OF THI

LOOTENANT! D'YA SEE WHO'S TAKIN' OUR PLACE!?
I MUST BE FLIPPIN'--!
NO YOU AIN'T-- THOSE GUYS--
THEY'RE OUR DOUBLES!
THEY'RE US!?
GNRRRRR
KIPPER-- DON'T GNORE E... AS F I DIDN'T EXIST!
THIS ISN'T A DREAM... OR A NIGHTMARE! WE'RE NOT GHOSTS!
OH, YEAH? THEN HOW COME WE'RE THE ONLY ONES WHO KNOW WE'RE HERE?
HOW CAN WE BE HERE... AND IN OUR TANKS AT THE SAME TIME?
AND WHY IS EACH ONE OF US MISSING HIS DOG TAG?
WE'RE LIKE OUR DOG TAGS... HALF AWOL!
war!
3
EDITOR: MURRAY BOLTINOFF
COLORS: JERRY SERPE
LETTERS: Gaspar
ART: SAM GLANZMAN
CREATED & WRITTEN BY ROBERT KANIGHER

RATATAT!
RATATAT!
HEADS UP, GUYS! KRAUT FIGHTER STRAFING THE FIELD!
YOU LOUSY BUZZARD! COME ON, COME ON...
COME ON INTO MY SIGHTS SO'S I CAN NAIL YOU!
POW! POW! POW!
VIIP!
VIIP!
TZING!
VIIP!
VIIP!
BHEEE!
THE AA GUN CREW GOT STITCHED--!
LET'S TAKE OVER!
WATCH ME PLANT THAT FLYIN' SWASTIKA SIX FEET UNDER!
4

C'MON-- C'MON!
WHAT'S HOLDING YOU UP, RICK?
WHY DON'T YOU FIRE--?
I'M TRYIN'-- I'M TRYIN'!
THIS PIECE AIN'T JAMMED!
IT'S LOADED...
...BUT--NOTHIN'S HAPPENIN' AT ALL...
IT'S LIKE I AIN'T FIRIN'--LIKE I AIN'T EVEN HERE!
THAT KRAUT PILOT WOULD'VE BLASTED US-- IF HE SPOTTED US...
...BUT TO HIM, WE AIN'T HERE EITHER!
5

LOOK AT THAT! THE MEDICS DON'T SEE US, TOO! WHAT'S HAPPENED TO US?
I DUNNO... BUT IT BEATS THE HELL OUTTA ME!
WE'RE NOWHERE-- WE'RE LOST... SOMEWHERE!
WE'RE NOT LOST TO THE GOOD LORD!
HE HAS HIS EYE ON THE HUMBLEST SPARROW.
HE WILL NOT FORGET US!
WE MUST HAVE FAITH IN HIM...
...NO MATTER WHERE WE ARE...
...HE HAS HIS EYE ON US, TOO!
WE WON'T FIND THE ANSWER JUST STANDING HERE! WE CAN'T LET ANOTHER CREW TAKE OUR PLACE AS IF WE WERE DEAD... NO MATTER WHO THEY ARE!
THAT JEEP'S THE ONLY ONE THAT WASN'T STRAFED! LET'S GRAB IT, AND CATCH UP TO OUR TANK BEFORE, IT REACHES THE BRIDGE!
YOU SEE WHAT I SEE? THAT JEEP... SPEEDIN' AWAY... BY ITSELF...
YEAH! WE MUST BE HAVIN' HALLUCINATIONS FROM BATTLE FATIGUE!
6

PART 2
...DEADLY DECOY
YESTERDAY'S PATROL SEEMED LIKE A MILLION YEARS AGO...
COLUMNS OF SMOKE AT 12 O'CLOCK!
THAT MUST BE WHERE BLUE PATROL RADIOED IT WAS BEING SHELLED BY PANZERS!
SERGEANT!
GET OFF THE ROAD... SO WE CAN HIT THE KRAUTS FROM THE RIGHT FLANK!
HANG ON, FELLERS! HERE WE GO, EARNIN' OUR PAY!
WE'VE BEEN FIGHTING SO LONG WITHOUT REST, I FEEL LIKE I'M HANGING ON WITH MY FINGERNAILS!
PRAYER WILL GIVE YOU STRENGTH, EDDIE!
I'M PRAYIN', DEACON, I'M PRAYIN'... I JUST DON'T WIND UP IN A BODY BAG!
BAMM
BAMM
HARRY'S STILL IN ACTION AGAINST THREE OF 'EM!
BOB'S AND ROY'S TANKS ARE FLAMERS... BUT THEY TOOK TWO PANZERS WITH 'EM!
STEP ON IT, SERGEANT! BEFORE HE'S KAYOED TOO!
BAM!
7

WE'LL TAKE 'EM ON THE RUN IN TURN... AT 3, 12, AND 9 O'CLOCK... WHERE THEIR ARMOR IS THINNEST!
RICK--IT'S YOUR SHOW NOW! FIRE AT WILL!
I DON'T DREAM ABOUT GIRLS NO MORE, EDDIE... ONLY PANZERS!
BUT IF YOU DON'T KNOCK THESE BABIES OUT, YOU'LL NEVER DREAM OF A GIRL AGAIN!
BLAM!
BLANG!!
8

ONE DOWN! TWO TO GO!
BAM!
GREAT SHOOTING, RICK! RIGHT ON THE MONEY! ONLY ONE MORE TO GO!
WATCH IT! HE'S TRAVERSING HIS 88 TO NAIL US!
BLAAANG!
BAM!
MAN, AM I DIZZY! THAT SHOT GAVE ME 88 HEAD-ACHES...
OUT OF THE WAY, RICK! I'LL FIRE!
THREE STRIKES, AND THEY'RE ALL OUT!
HARRY-- YOU'RE IN THE CLEAR!
BLANG
BLAM!
9

GET US OUT, JEB--WE'RE TRAPPED IN THIS FLAMIN' COFFIN!
LET'S GO, MEN--ON THE DOUBLE!
NO USE--CAN'T GET NEARER WITH OUR FIRE EXTINGUISHERS! FIRE'S TOO INTENSE!
FOR GOD'S SAKE, JEB... I'M BEING BURNT ALIVE... PUT ME OUT OF MY AGONY... JEB... PLEASE...
ARGHNNN
I SHOULD'VE GONE IN AFTER HIM! AT LEAST, I SHOULD'VE TRIED!
YOU OUTTA YOUR SKULL, LOOTENANT?! YOU COULDN'T DO NOTHIN' TO SAVE HIM!
IT AIN'T YOU, JEB! IT'S THE WAR! IT'S THIS STINKIN' WAR!
THE WAR-- THE WAR!
FIRST, IT KILLED ARCH... THEN SLIM...
WE FOUGHT IN NORTH AFRICA...SICILY...ITALY... FRANCE...
BUT THE WAR NEVER ENDS!
THIS WAR WILL NEVER END TILL WE'RE ALL DEAD!
WELL, I'VE HAD ENOUGH! I WANT OUT!
WE DID OUR JOBS!
I WISH TO GOD SOMEONE ELSE TAKES OUR PLACE!
10

HOURS AGO, WE WERE SOLDIERS. NOW, NO ONE KNOWS WE'RE ALIVE. WE'RE LIKE GHOSTS... CHASING OUR TANK TO THE LUDENDORFF BRIDGE!
MY WISH FOR US TO BE REMOVED FROM THIS WAR TURNED INTO A CURSE!
BUT WE'RE STILL SOLDIERS-- WE'RE NOT GOING TO LET SOME-ONE ELSE SIT IN OUR HOT SEATS AND DO OUR JOBS!
THE BRIDGE... STILL STANDING! WHY HAVEN'T THE GERMANS BLOWN IT UP?
11

"WHY ARE THEY SO DETERMINED TO KEEP US FROM CAPTURING IT WHEN THEY COULD HAVE EASILY DESTROYED IT?!"
VIP!
VIP!
VIP!
WHAM!
BEEOW
SPANGG!
THERE'S THE GENERAL! BUT WHY IS HE THERE... WHEN THE FIGHTING'S HERE... AT THE BRIDGE?
SERGEANT! GET CRACKING!
THERE MUST BE A PATH DOWN FROM THIS RIDGE TO THE WATER'S EDGE!
GENERAL! YOU HAVE ALL THE ANSWERS! WHAT HAPPENED TO US?
GENERAL -- CAN'T YOU HEAR ME?
NOTHIN' HERE, LOOTENANT!... NO PATH! NOTHIN'!
MAYBE WE BETTER GET BACK TO THE BRIDGE.
12

NUTS! WE RUN OUTTA GAS, LOOTENANT!
RRRP!
THAT UNDERBRUSH-- IT CAMOUFLAGES A TUNNEL!
LET'S SEE WHERE IT LEADS TO!
NO WONDER AIR RECON WOULD NEVER SPOT IT--
...IT LEADS UNDER THE RIVER!
A SHERMAN!??
THE CREW'S HAD IT!
WHRAM!
BWEEEEE!
ZIP!
ZIP!
LOOTENANT-- LOOK!
ONLY ONE TANK IN THIS WAR FLIES A REB BANNER!
YEAH... OURS!
MOUNT UP!!
IT--IT'S ME...
...WEARING MY OTHER DOG TAG!
WE'RE BACK IN BUSINESS! MAN YOUR GUNS!
13

THIS GUY'S **ME!**
THEY'RE **ALL** OF US!
THEY TOOK OUR PLACES...
...AN' FOUGHT AN' DIED TO THE LAST MAN!
THE KRAUTS ARE FIGHTING **ON** THE BRIDGE...TO COVER THEIR PANZERS COMING ACROSS UNDER THE RIVER IN THE TUNNEL THEY BUILT!
IF WE DON'T STOP 'EM, THEY'LL CROSS... CIRCLE AROUND... AND SLAUGHTER OUR MEN **AT** THE BRIDGE!
OPEN FIRE-- FIRE!
BUDDA BUDDA
BUDDA BUDDA!
TOO MANY OF 'EM TO STOP!
BAM!
RATATAT!
ONLY **ONE** THING TO DO--
RICK-- ELEVATE YOUR .75 CANNON AS HIGH AS YOU CAN!
CHUNNG!
FIRE!-- FIRE!-- FIRE!
BAM BAM
14

KNOCK IT OFF, RICK! YOU BROUGHT DOWN THE ROOF!
NOW LET'S GET OUTTA HERE BEFORE WE'RE DROWNED LIKE THE PANZERS
RUMMBLE!
ROARRRRRRR
WHO... WHO WAS HE?
WHO WERE THEY--?
15

GENERAL -- CAN YOU SEE ME NOW?
I WAS UNDER ORDERS NOT TO TELL YOU BEFORE, JEB... BUT SOME FORCE FAR GREATER THAN A GHOSTLY GENERAL... GRANTED YOUR WISH!
BUT WISHES DON'T ALWAYS COME TRUE THE WAY YOU EXPECT! ONLY PART OF YOU AND YOUR CREW WERE REMOVED FROM THIS WAR!
THE OTHER HALF REMAINED... UNTIL YOU WERE READY TO COME BACK AGAIN!
FOR A WHILE, YOU WERE LOST TO HUMAN SIGHT-- LIKE YOUR SINGLE DOG TAG!
BUT WHEN YOU RETURNED... TO PUT YOUR LIVES ON THE LINE AGAIN... YOUR OTHER SELVES VANISHED!
NOW YOU ARE WHOLE AGAIN... BACK IN THE WAR!
LIKE MY DOG TAGS!
THE BRIDGE-- WE CAPTURED IT!
YES, JEB... BUT ONLY WE--YOU AND YOUR CREW, AND I...
...KNOW WHAT MILITARY HISTORY WILL NEVER RECORD--THE SECRET BATTLE IN THE TUNNEL THAT MADE IT POSSIBLE!
The End

SGT. ROCK
ALL NEW! 60¢
NO. 368 SEPT.
APPROVED BY THE COMICS CODE AUTHORITY
TZIINNNG
LOOK OUT, SAR-
JOE KUBERT
30 KMS
THIS IS THE 1ST PAGE OF THE 30TH ANNIVERSARY STORY APPEARING IN THIS ISSUE OF SGT. ROCK!
C-930

SGT. ROCK OF EASY CO.
TAKE COVER, KID! TAKE CO-
IN WAR, ALL IT TAKES IS ONE SHOT--A SCREAMIN' PIECE OF POWDER-CHARGED AIR-DRIVEN METAL--TO TURN A WARM, LIVIN' AN' BREATHIN' KID INTO A LUMP OF DEAD MEAT!
JOE KUBERT '82
30 YEARS OF DOGTAGS
CREATED & WRITTEN by: ROBERT KANIGHER / LETTERS: ANDY KUBERT / COLOR: TAJANA WOOD

WHREE EEEEEEEEEE
A PATTERN OF INCOMIN' MORTARS EXPLODED ALL THE COLOR OUTTA THE WORLD...
WHUMP
WHRAM
EEEEE
THE KID LAY IN A CRUMPLED HEAP...BLOOD TRICKLIN' FROM HIM LIKE BLACK THREADS--
H-HE TOOK THAT SLUG... FOR ME!
THE KID LASTED ONLY ONE DAY ...IN THIS DAMNED WAR!
THE MORTARS KEPT THUMPIN' DOWN... BUT--I DIDN'T HEAR 'EM!
I-I'VE HAD A BELLYFUL O' SLAUGHTER!
BLAM
LOOK! ROCK'S TAKIN' OFF!
WE GOTTA BRING THE SARGE BACK BEFORE--
EYES FRONT!
ROCK KNOWS WHAT HE'S DOIN'!
THE KRAUTS'LL BE ATTACKIN' ...SOON AS THE MORTAR FIRE LIFTS!
WHAM
WHUMP

ME AN' EASY WERE 30 KILOMETERS FROM THE RHINE...BUT-- MY HEAD WAS SOMEWHERE ELSE! IN NORTH AFRICA... WHERE A PANZER WAS PINNIN' US DOWN...
BLAM
RATATAT
V'IP
Z'IP
LITTLE SURE SHOT--EASY'S POINT--LAY WOUNDED IN THE PATH OF A STEEL JUGGERNAUT...
MEDIC-- DON'T TRY'N' BE A HERO!
WHAT "HERO" ROCK? BUT--HOW'D I TELL MY MOM THAT "HER SON THE DOCTOR" LET HIS FIRST PATIENT DOWN?
RATATATAT
RATATATATAT
THE TANK WAS FIRIN' AT ANYTHIN' THAT MOVED! AN' LEVY, THE MEDIC, WAS MOVIN'--
ZING
ZIP
V'IP
BWEEE
3

VROOSH
THAT MOMENT GAVE ZACK A CHANCE TO LET FLY WITH A ROCKET...
WHUMP
LEVY'D SAVED LITTLE SURE SHOT'S LIFE...
HE WORE HIS DOGTAGS ONLY TWO MONTHS! HARDLY LONG ENOUGH TO GET 'EM WARM...
A ROAD HAS MARKERS ... THE WAR HAS 'EM, TOO!
C'MON, EASY! THERE'S A WAR ON!
THERE WAS ANOTHER G.I. WHO WAS ALWAYS ON THE EDGE OF WHAT WAS HAP-PENIN'... THE GUYS CALLED HIM MOUSE...
ONE DAY THE AFRIKA KORPS HIT US WITH A BARRAGE...
TAKE COVER! SET UP HOUSEKEEPIN' FOR AN ATTACK... AFTER THE SHELLIN'!
MOUSE WAS IN A SHELLHOLE WITH A COUPLE OF GUYS... WHEN THE SHELLIN' LIFTED--
4

THEN--MOUSE MOVED!
FTOOM
PIECES O' SMOKIN' CORDITE WERE STILL FALLIN' TO THE GROUND WHEN I FOUND HIS DOGTAG...
THAT WAS ONE MOUSE THAT HAD THE HEART OF A LION!
THEN...WHEN EASY MOVED TO SICILY...WE HAD SOME GUYS WHO'RE ALWAYS PLAYIN' CARDS! THE DEALER...ACEY-DEUCY...WINNER...POKER FACE...AN' LOSER!
RATATATATATAT
BUT THEY ALL LOST...ATTACKIN' AN ENEMY M.G. NEST CONCEALED IN AN OLD TEMPLE...
5

THEY'D JOINED THE ARMY TOGETHER...THEY DIED TOGETHER...
HERE'S ALL THAT'S LEFT... A HANDFUL OF DOGTAGS!
I WONDER WHO HELD THE WINNIN' HAND? IN WAR--I GUESS EVERY-ONE'S A LOSER!
C'MON-- EASY! THERE'S A WAR ON!
AMONG THE COMBAT-HAPPY JOES THAT'D MADE IT INTO ITALY AN' SLUGGED THEIR WAY UP "THE BOOT" TOWARDS ROME--WAS SLEEPIN' BEAUTY!
ZZZZZZZZZZ
THAT'S THE ONLY GUY I KNOW WHO KIN MARCH IN HIS SLEEP!
EVEN CHOW TIME DIDN'T KEEP SLEEPIN' BEAUTY FROM SNORIN'!
ZZZZZZZZ
WHRAM
BLAM
ZZZZ
THE SHELLIN' STARTED FROM ATOP MONTE CASSINO... EVERY EASY JOE WAS WAITIN' FOR THE ONE WITH HIS NUMBER ON IT--EXCEPT SLEEPIN' BEAUTY!
6

HE WAS STILL SLEEPIN' WHEN A DIRECT HIT FROM A SCREAMIN' EIGHTY-EIGHT BURIED HIM!
KER-WHAAAAM
I PULLED HIS BLOODY DOGTAGS OUTTA THE MUCK THAT'D BE SLEEPIN' BEAUTY'S LAST RESTIN' PLACE...
AIN'T NOBODY GOIN' TO WAKE HIM NOW...HE CAN SLEEP FOREVER!
EASY WAS IN THE INVASION...D-DAY... IN AN LCI HEADIN' FOR THE BEACH! GUYS WERE SWEATIN'...PRAYIN'... THROWIN' UP IN THEIR HELMETS BECAUSE OF THE HEAVY SEAS...
LCI 104
WHAT'RE YOU READIN', BOOKWORM?
TOLSTOY'S "WAR AND PEACE," SARGE!
AND...IT'S THICK ENOUGH TO BE MY "BULLET-PROOF" VEST!
BUT WHEN EASY WADED THROUGH THE HELL BURSTIN' LOOSE AROUND THE LANDIN'...
BOOK-WORM!
WAR and PEACE
THE ONLY THING YOU'D'VE LEARNED 'BOUT "WAR AND PEACE" IS THERE'S NO PEACE IN THIS WAR!
7

ON THE MURDEROUS HEDGE ROWS OF NORMANDY, LITTLE PHIL AN' BIG PHIL WERE HUNG UP LIKE SPOILED FRUIT...
BWEEEE
LITTLE PHIL--BIG PH--
TZING
RATATAT
WHILE EASY FLATTENED THE ENEMY M.G. NEST ON THE OTHER SIDE...I KEPT ON ADDIN' TO MY COLLECTION!
IT DON'T... EVER...END!
THERE WAS ONE GREEN APPLE WHOSE NAME I NEVER GOT A CHANCE TO KNOW...IN THE WINTRY WIND AN' IRON-HARD GROUND OUTSIDE BAS-TOGNE...
EIGHTEEN YEARS OLD! NOW...NOTHIN' BUT A SET O' DOGTAGS!
THE ENEMY FOUGHT FOR EVERY YARD WE GAINED! A CROOKED-CROSSED BUZZARD SCRATCHED WHISTLIN' WILLIE--HORSELAUGH--AN' SWEET TOOTH FROM EASY'S ROSTER!
RATATAT
YOU GUYS NEVER WORE THESE LONG ENOUGH... TO EVEN TARNISH 'EM!
I'M EASY'S TOPKICKER... ...THE GUYS DEPEND ON ME TO LEAD 'EM--SAFELY!
BUT...I FAIL 'EM--I ALWAYS FAIL!
8

WHEN THE KID GOT KILLED SAVIN' MY SKIN... 30 KILOMETERS FROM THE RHINE... I WALKED AWAY FROM EASY! NO MORE DOGTAG COLLECTOR FOR ME...
I WALKED, ALL RIGHT... IN A CIRCLE-- BACK TO EASY-- TRAPPED AT THE CROSSROADS!
BLAM
WHRAAM
ENEMY TANK'S GOT EASY BOXED IN!
I'M-- RIGHT BACK WHERE I STARTED FROM!
THE SHELLIN' STOPPED-- AN' I SAW WHY--
PANZER GOIN' IN FOR THE KILL!
I PRIMED A GRENADE AS I SCRAMBLED UP THE TANK'S BACKSIDE...
KLANK
KLANK
9

WHREEEEE
BLANNNG
ROCK OUTFLANKED THAT TANK... AN SLAMMED IT OFF OUR NECKS!
I WAVED EASY PAST ME...
MOVE IT-- THERE'S A WAR ON!
I LOOKED AT THE KID'S DOGTAG... SEEIN' ALL THE OTHER DOGTAGS I'D COLLECTED THROUGH NORTH AFRICA... SICILY...ITALY... FRANCE...GERMANY...
THEY WEIGHED A TON--WHY SHOULDN'T THEY?
I WAS HOLDIN' THIRTY YEARS O' DOGTAGS!
END

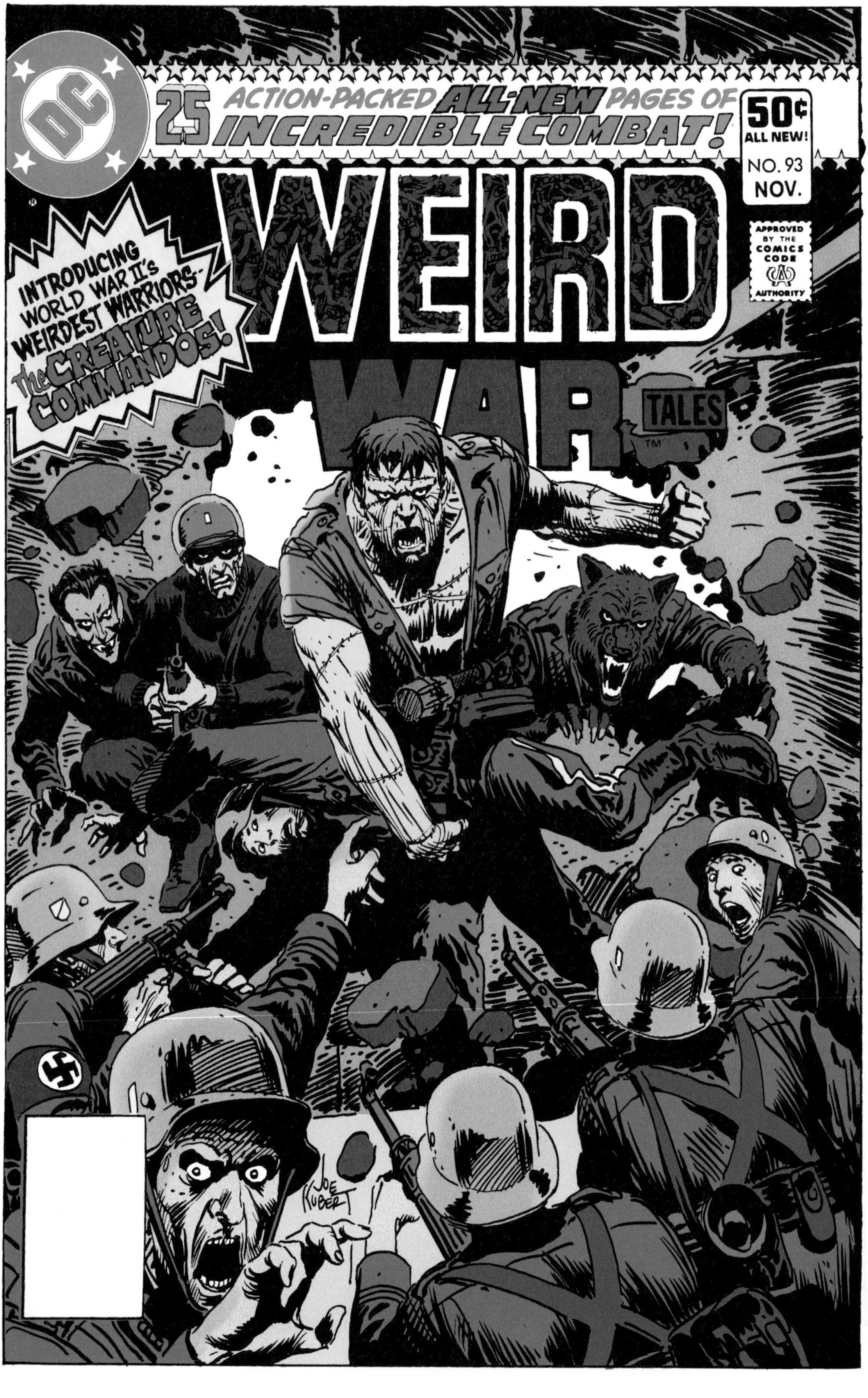
DC
25 ACTION-PACKED ALL-NEW PAGES OF INCREDIBLE COMBAT!
50¢ ALL NEW!
NO. 93
NOV.
APPROVED BY THE COMICS CODE AUTHORITY
WEIRD WAR TALES
INTRODUCING WORLD WAR II's WEIRDEST WARRIORS-
The CREATURE COMMANDOS!
JOE KUBERT

IN A CENTURIES-OLD CASTLE IN THE HEART OF NAZI-OCCUPIED FRANCE, A BIZARRE TABLEAU UNFOLDS--AS THE CREAM OF HITLER'S KILLER ELITE COME FACE-TO-FACE WITH THE WEIRDEST WARRIORS OF ALL...
The CREATURE COMMANDOS!
OKAY, GENTLEMEN--IT APPEARS THE TIME FOR DISCRETION IS PAST--WE'VE GOT A WIDE-OPEN FIGHT ON OUR HANDS!
LEAVE, VELCRO...WHEN THERE IS GLORIOUS BLOOD... AND DEATH..?!
WE SHOULD JUST TURN AROUND AND LEAVE YOU TO THE WOLVES, SHRIEVE--IT'S WHAT YOU DESERVE!
WRITER- J.M. DE MATTEIS
ARTISTS- PAT BRODERICK & JOHN CELARDO
COLORIST- ADRIENNE ROY
LETTERER- BEN ODA
EDITOR- LEN WEIN

IT BEGINS AT A MIDWEST ARMY BASE-- ON A WIND-SWEPT SPRING DAY IN 1942...
SECURITY IS TIGHT ON THE BASE--AND EVEN THE USUALLY WELL-INFORMED TOP BRASS THAT PASS THROUGH THE HEAVILY GUARDED FRONT GATES KNOW NEXT TO NOTHING ABOUT THE MYSTERIOUS...
PROJECT M TOP SECURITY CLEARANCE
...PROJECT "M"!..
FROM ACROSS THE NATION AND ACROSS THE GLOBE, THEY CAME: GENERALS, ADMIRALS, SENATORS-- AND THEIR UNEASY ATTENTION IS LOCKED ON A SOLITARY FIGURE...
...LIEUTENANT MATTHEW SHRIEVE OF U.S. ARMY INTELLIGENCE...
NOW THAT WE ARE ALL HERE, SIRS--I THINK WE CAN BEGIN...
I WANT TO TALK TO YOU ALL ABOUT THE DARK REALMS-- THE UNDERSIDE OF MAN'S CONSCIOUSNESS...
...THE REALMS WHERE WE KEEP OUR PERSONAL MONSTERS IN MENTAL CHAINS...
NOW LOOK HERE, SON-- I DIDN'T LEAVE THE WAR AND COME RUNNING HERE JUST TO LISTEN TO SOME TRIPE ABOUT THINGS THAT GO BUMP IN THE NIGHT!
JUST WHAT THE DEVIL HAVE YOU ARMY BOYS GOT GOING THAT'S SO ALL-FIRED IMPORTANT?!
FIRSTLY, ADMIRAL...
...THIS PROJECT IS THE RESULT OF A COMBINED EFFORT OF ALL OUR ARMED FORCES--NOT TO MENTION A NUMBER OF CIVILIAN GROUPS...
SECONDLY, IF YOU'LL JUST TURN YOUR ATTENTION TO THE SCREEN BEHIND ME--I BELIEVE ALL OF YOUR...AH... WELL-INTENTIONED QUESTIONS WILL BE ANSWERED!
THE LIGHTS DIE...BLACKNESS DESCENDS...
2

...AS THE FILM-SCREEN FLARES INTO ANIMATE LIFE...
AS MANY OF YOU ALREADY KNOW, INTELLIGENCE HAS LONG BEEN INTERESTED IN AIDING THE WAR EFFORT NOT JUST ON A PHYSICAL LEVEL...
...BUT ON A PSYCHOLOGICAL ONE AS WELL!
WE RESEARCHED THE SUBCONSCIOUS ARCHETYPES-- THE SYMBOLS OF FRIGHT AND HORROR THAT ALL MEN SEEM TO SHARE REGARDLESS OF SOCIAL AND CULTURAL CONDITIONING...
...AND THEN WE SET ABOUT SCIENTIFICALLY RE-CREATING THEM! THAT WAS THE BIRTH OF PROJECT "M" ...FOR MONSTER!
"THIS IS WARREN GRIFFITH --A 4F OKLAHOMA FARMBOY WITH A PROBLEM: HE SUFFERS FROM LYCANTHROPY*...
"...A CONDITION THAT A TEAM OF SPECIALLY-SELECTED SCIENTISTS AND MEDICAL MEN MANAGED TO MANIFEST PHYSICALLY IN OUR YOUNG VOLUNTEER.
*A FORM OF INSANITY IN WHICH THE PATIENT IMAGINES HIMSELF A WOLF. --LEN
"NEXT CAME SGT. VINCENT VELCRO--WHO WISELY MANAGED TO AVOID A THIRTY YEAR SENTENCE IN AN ARMY BRIG BY JOINING PROJECT "M!"
"FOR SIX MONTHS, HE WAS INJECTED WITH A COMPOUND COMPOSED OF EXPERIMENTAL CHEMICALS AND BLOOD EXTRACTED FROM THE NEW MEXICAN VAMPIRE BAT, AND THE RESULT WAS... INTRIGUING.
FINALLY, THERE WAS A GOOD-HEARTED MARINE PRIVATE NAMED "LUCKY" TAYLOR--WHOSE LUCK RAN OUT WHEN HE STEPPED ON A LAND MINE ON SOME GOD-FORSAKEN ISLAND IN THE PACIFIC...
"OUR SURGEONS WORKED FOR WEEKS ON END PUTTING "LUCKY" BACK TOGETHER AGAIN... ALBEIT NOT THE WAY HE WAS ORIGINALLY CONSTRUCTED..."
THE FILMED IMAGE FADES AS THE SEA OF HIGH-RANKING OFFICIALS RISE IN A TSUNAMI OF OUTRAGE...
WHAT IS THIS NONSENSE?
BE CALM, SIRS, BE CALM AND BEHOLD...
HOW DARE YOU CALL US TOGETHER TO HEAR SUCH IDIOCY!
ENOUGH OF THIS!
SLAM
3

...THE CREATURE COMMANDOS!
A SLIGHTLY MELODRAMATIC ENTRANCE, SIRS-- BUT ONE THAT I THINK GETS THE POINT ACROSS QUITE EFFECTIVELY!
YOU EXPECT US TO BE FOOLED BY SOME LUDICROUS HOLLYWOOD COSTUME JOB?
I AM APPALLED, LIEUTENANT!
APPALLED, YOU STINKING BUFFOON? YOU DON'T KNOW THE MEANING OF THE WORD!
FIRST UNDERSTAND WHAT IT IS TO BE TRANSFORMED INTO SOME KIND OF REPUGNANT THING--AND THEN BE APPALLED!
THIS IS NO "HOLLYWOOD COSTUME JOB," GENERAL-- LUDICROUS THOUGH IT MAY BE! YOU AND YOUR ILK HAVE MADE ME A CREATURE THAT NEEDS HUMAN BLOOD TO SURVIVE...
...AND I WILL HAVE YOURS!!
GRIFFITH--GET VELCRO...STOP HIM!
THE MAN-WOLF ANSWERS WITH A SUB-GUTTURAL GROWL AS HE LEAPS WITH THE SAVAGE GRACE OF A BEAST...
...AND LANDS WITH THE FRAGILE CLUMSINESS OF A BOY...
DAMN! SCIENCE-BRANCH SAID GRIFFITH'S CONDITION WAS UNSTABLE--THAT HE'D CHANGE BACK AND FORTH UNCONTROLLABLY--
BUT DID IT HAVE TO BE NOW?
4

"LET'S HOPE 'LUCKY' CAN HANDLE THIS!"
SO, MY MAMMOTH FRIEND--YOU SEEK TO STOP ME, TOO?
THEN HAVE AT ME, LUMMOX! LET'S SEE WHAT YOU'RE...
...MADE OF...?!
WHEN THE SURGEONS REBUILT "LUCKY" TAYLOR'S BODY, THEY NEGLECTED TO GIVE HIM VOCAL CHORDS--AND THUS HE SAYS NOTHING. HE MERELY FLASHES FRUSTRATION FROM THE DAPPLED DEPTHS OF HIS PALE-BLUE EYES...
...AND DOES WHAT HE HAS TO...
AND WHEN THE SOUND AND THE FURY HAVE SOMEWHAT SUBSIDED...
LIEUTENANT SHRIEVE, THESE ...COMMANDOS OF YOURS ARE A MENACE!
THEY ARE A TERRIFYING, REPREHENSIBLE ASSORTMENT OF INHUMAN DREGS--AND I HOPE THAT I NEVER SET EYES ON THEM AGAIN!
Y-YES, SIR, GENERAL--BUT I--
DON'T INTERRUPT ME, SON!
I SAID I NEVER WANT TO SET EYES ON THEM AGAIN AND I MEANT IT--BUT THAT DOESN'T NEGATE THE FACT THAT THEY MAY BE THE MOST EFFECTIVE SECRET WEAPONS THIS COUNTRY HAS EVER SEEN!
SIR...?
"SO YOU TAKE YOUR CREATURE COMMANDOS, LIEUTENANT--AND YOU TEACH THOSE DAMNABLE NAZIS THE TRUE MEANING OF THE WORD FEAR!"
THE BRASS DIDN'T WASTE MUCH TIME GETTING US INTO FRANCE--DID THEY, SHRIEVE?
CAN THE CHATTER, VELCRO--AND MOVE! WE'VE GOT A SCHEDULE TO MEET!
5

NEXT STOP-- CASTLE CONQUEST!
WHAT'S THIS CASTLE CONQUEST, SHRIEVE? OR AREN'T YOU PERMITTED TO TELL YOUR LITTLE GUINEA PIGS?
IT'S AN OLD FRENCH STRONGHOLD THAT'S BEEN TAKEN OVER AND RE-MODELED BY THE GERMANS, VELCRO. THEY'RE CONDUCTING EXPERIMENTS THERE. WE HAVE TO STOP THEM.
AND THAT IS ALL I CAN TELL YOU.
WHO CARES... WHY WE'RE GOING... IT IS THE COMING SLAUGHTER... THAT MATTERS...
YOU KNOW, MISTER GRIFFITH-- I THINK I PREFER YOU AS AN IGNORANT FARM-BOY...
I TOLD YOU ONCE BEFORE, SHRIEVE-- CAN THE CHATTER...
"...AND MOVE!!"
I BELIEVE THE LUMMOX IS TRYING TO COMMUNICATE WITH US, SHRIEVE.
AND WITH GOOD REASON...
...THE NAZIS HAVE SPOTTED OUR PLANE!
THAT'S ONE MORE SCORE TO SETTLE!
OH, SPARE US! YOU KNOW THERE'LL BE NO TEARS SHED FOR OUR POOR FALLEN COMRADES...
WHOOM!
...NO TEARS AT ALL.
BUT ONE GLANCE AT THE MAN TRAPPED WITHIN THE GNARLED MIS-SHAPEN PATCH-WORK FORM WOULD PROVE THE BLOOD-DRINKER WRONG...VERY WRONG.
6

AN HOUR'S TRAMP THROUGH COLD, FORBIDDING WOODS FINALLY BRINGS THE CREATURE COMMANDOS TO THEIR GOAL. BUT ARRIVAL DOES LITTLE TO RAISE THEIR DULLED SPIRITS...
AND YOU SAY ALL WE HAVE TO DO IS DESTROY THIS FORTIFICATION? YOU ARE A FOOL, SHRIEVE...
WE CREATED YOU WITH CERTAIN TALENTS, VELCRO, NOW'S THE TIME TO...
"...USE THEM!"
WELL, IT HAS BEEN TOO MANY HOURS...
...SINCE I LAST HAD...
VAS...?
...A SATISFYING MEAL...
AND, THOUGH VINCENT VELCRO MAY BE SOMEWHAT SATIATED--
--THE FEAST OF BLOOD FOR SOME...
DE-LIGHTFUL...
...IS JUST BEGINNING!
KRACK
7

LIKE FURTIVE DEMONS, THE THREE NON-MEN AND THEIR COLD-BLOODED LEADER CREEP DEEPER INTO THE HEART OF CASTLE CONQUEST...
...AND MANY SOULS ARE SENT TO FINAL REST ALONG THE BLOOD-STAINED WAY...
...AND THEN...
IF OUR INFORMATION IS CORRECT-- THE ROOM WE'RE LOOKING FOR SHOULD BE JUST AROUND THIS...
...TURN...
OKAY, GENTLEMEN-- IT APPEARS THAT THE TIME FOR DISCRETION IS PAST-- WE'VE GOT A WIDE-OPEN FIGHT ON OUR HANDS!
MEIN GOTT!
AND AS THE CREATURE COMMANDOS CUT THROUGH THE AMAZED GERMANS LIKE SABERS SLICING THROUGH MEN OF WAX...
"LUCKY"-- BEFORE ANY MORE OF THEM COME...
...WE'VE GOT TO GET THROUGH THAT DOOR!
THE MONSTROUS MAN-BRUTE NODS HIS MASSIVE HEAD...
...AND IN A MATTER OF SECONDS-- TEN FEET OF REINFORCED STEEL DOOR IS SO MUCH SCRAP METAL!
BA-WHOOM!
NO--YOU MUST STOP THIS ATTACK!
THE VOICE FROM WITHIN IS FAMILIAR-- BUT SO OUT OF PLACE HERE IN THIS FORTRESS OF EVIL...
...STILL, THERE IS NO DENYING THE FACE AND FORM OF PRESIDENT FRANKLIN D. ROOSEVELT...
PLEASE, YOUNG MEN --THERE HAS BEEN A MISTAKE...
MISTAKE MY FOOT, YOU TIN-PLATED PHONY!
PING!
PING!
PING!
8

INSTANTLY, THE FANTASTIC TRUTH BECOMES CLEAR AS GLISTENING GLASS!
YOU'VE GOT IT, "LUCKY" --THAT'S NOT ROOSEVELT ...IT'S A MECHANICAL RINGER!
SPRONG
LOOK AROUND--EISENHOWER... STALIN... CHURCHILL--THEY'RE CONSTRUCTING A HORDE OF THESE THINGS! ANDROID DUPLICATES FOR THE NAZIS TO SLIP IN SECRETLY!
THINK OF IT-- THE ALLIED NATIONS BEING RUN BY THIRD REICH PAWNS!
IT IS A BEAUTIFUL PLAN--IS IT NOT?
A PITY YOU WILL NOT LIVE TO SEE IT COME TO FRUITION!
OH, I DON'T KNOW ABOUT THAT...
HIT 'EM!
AND HIT THEM, THEY DO--WITH ONE OF THE MOST INCREDIBLE, SENSE-STUNNING DISPLAYS OF PURE POWER EVER RECORDED IN THE ANNALS OF WAR..
VELCRO--GRIFFITH--"LUCKY" --WE'VE GOT TO GET OUT OF HERE!
BUT WHAT ABOUT THE ANDROIDS?
NO QUESTIONS --JUST GET US OUT!
9
"JUST GET US OUT!"
THOSE WORDS RING IN THE AIR AS THE COMMANDOS PLOW THROUGH THE SEEMINGLY ENDLESS WAVES OF GERMAN FLESH...
...BUT FOR ONE, AT LEAST... IT IS NOT EASY. HE KNOWS THE TOLL SUCH MADNESS TAKES ON THE HUMAN SOUL--AND HE WEEPS FOR THOSE HE HAS SLAIN...
OH NO... NOT NOW... I CAN'T CHANGE NOW!
FOR ANOTHER--THERE IS ONLY HORROR AND CONFUSION...

GRIFFITH--YOU HAVE GOT THE ROTTENEST TIMING..!
S-SORRY, LIEUTENANT...
TIME FOR APOLOGIES LATER...
...IF WE SURVIVE!
THEY LEAP...
...THEY RUN...
...IN TIME!
WHAT IN HELL WAS THAT?
THAT WAS A SPECIALLY-CRAFTED EXPLOSIVE THAT I WAS CARRYING IN MY BAG...
BA-BA-WHOOM!
YOU MEAN IF W-WE HADN'T GOTTEN OUT IN T-TIME..?
AGAIN YOU TOYED WITH US--MANIPULATED OUR FATES AS IF WE WERE JUST CHATTEL!
WE MAY HAVE THE FORMS OF MONSTERS, SHRIEVE--BUT YOU--YOU HAVE THE MONSTROUS SPIRIT!
VELCRO, PLEASE ... I'M VERY TIRED...
...YOU CAN CALL ME ALL THE NAMES YOU'D LIKE...
...AFTER WE GET HOME...
THERE IS HATRED BETWEEN THESE MEN--THERE IS ANGER AND RESENTMENT. BUT THERE IS ALSO THE UNVOICED THOUGHT...
...THAT THEY HAVE JUST BEGUN TO CARVE A NEW LEGEND...IN THE WEIRD WAR...

DAD'S ARMIES

We always had comics in our house when I was growing up. They were all over the place, lying around in bedrooms, bathrooms, living rooms...everywhere. And I guess I took them for granted since they were always around. I never bought comics from the newsstands, except for a few odd Archie books when we were on vacation. And since the only comics my dad brought home were from DC, I had never read any Marvel titles until my father brought some home from the DC offices in the late 1970s. I guess at that time DC and Marvel had worked out some kind of a trade deal for comp copies.

My favorites, though, were always the DC war comics. Not because I loved war, but because I liked the historical context of them along with the real-life settings. They were different from the superhero stories, more believable, because they were either based on true stories or included real characters. The TV show *Combat* with Vic Morrow and the film *Patton* with George C. Scott were some of the first war pictures I can remember watching and being enthralled by as a child. To this day, the modern movies that resonate with me are things like *Saving Private Ryan* and *Full Metal Jacket*.

My father's comics were like those films. To me, even though Sgt. Rock wasn't a real person, he was believable and lifelike. His stories were grounded, especially when they were drawn by my dad, Russ Heath, John Severin, or Sam Glanzman. The way my father and his fellow artists drew the characters, they each had their own identity. They acted their own way. They had personalities. Different body types. Different postures. They laughed and cried. Yes, some of their adventures were over-the-top, but they were done in a way that grabbed you by the seat of your pants and sucked you right in.

I had long conversations with my dad about those stories, and we discussed the ways in which he approached them. He was usually open about his process, but he wouldn't elaborate too much. A lot of what he said was, "I drew that in that way because that's the way I felt at the time." Funny, because the great Frank Miller gave me the same answer when I asked him how he approached some of his work.

My father came from a European background, having left Poland just before the beginning of World War II. His mother, father, and sisters had all arrived in the United States via Ellis Island by the time he was two years old. A lot of his family who stayed behind in Europe were killed during the war. In retrospect, I think that this may have been the reason he was so prolific with his war comics. Even though he hadn't been able to fight the Nazis himself (he was drafted into the U.S. Army during the Korean War), he turned the pain of that loss into energy for his work.

My father began his career when he was very young, around 12 years old. He was a prodigy. At that time, he was known for his superhero work, but his interests and artistic style leaned toward the more realistic (for superheroes, anyway) characters. I may be biased, but to me his depictions of Hawkman and Hawkgirl are the best renditions of those heroes ever made, mainly due to his naturalistic style. When he drew them flying, he gave them a real sense of believability. He made those characters move in such a way that it seemed plausible that a man and woman could dress up as hawks and fly around.

He often told me that even though he enjoyed the superheroes, he was more comfortable drawing and relating to characters that were based in reality. Looking at Sgt. Rock, Enemy Ace, The Losers, *G.I. Combat*, and *Tarzan*, it's clear that this preference held true. In the last decade or so of his career, he also focused more on his own creator-owned work—*Tor* (the caveman character that he created in the 1950s), *Yossel*, *Fax from Sarajevo* (based on the real-life drama of his friend Ervin Rustemagic), *Jew Gangster*, and *Dong Xoai* (based on true stories from the Vietnam War).

Our Army at War #196 includes one of my favorite Sgt. Rock tales. Entitled "Stop the War, I Want to Get Off!," it was to me a combination of Charles Dickens's *A Christmas Carol* and the classic Jimmy Stewart film *It's a Wonderful Life*, with maybe a few *Twilight Zone* episodes tossed in. It's also a good example of my father's love of history, which is clearly demonstrated by all the attention he paid to the historical figures that show up in it. He reflected on that story quite a few times with me, and I mentioned to him that even though it was first published back in 1968, it was and still is one of my favorite things he had ever done. Anytime I would compliment him, though, he would humbly brush it off by saying he couldn't even look at that old work now because it might embarrass him. I would just sit there and shake my head.

In his studio at his school, my father had piles of reference books beside his drawing table. I would often catch him sitting back in his chair, engrossed in one of those books. He was a stickler for accuracy, always telling me to reference anything that was real or previously established in the story. "The drawings have to look believable and credible," he would tell me, "or else you will lose your audience."

He also used models for reference. There was a red Fokker Triplane model hanging from his studio ceiling to aid in drawing the Enemy Ace stories, and he had an actual German World War II helmet as well as an American World War II helmet. He never had any of the weapons, though. Those were all drawn from books.

Interestingly, he would often use Russ Heath's drawings of rifles, machine guns, and tanks for reference; a good example is the German Tiger tank drawn by Russ in the story "Easy's First Tiger" (*Our Army at War* #244). My dad loved Russ's work and all the detail that he put into the drawings; he said that Russ's work was better to look at than actual photographs. I had the opportunity a few years back to meet Russ and tell him what my father said. It brought a huge smile to his face.

As a kid, I used to travel with my father to the DC offices on occasion. It was a lot of fun to go into Manhattan and hang out at DC. From what I remember, he would drive in maybe once a week when he was an editor. With the promise of lunch or dinner in NYC (or a stop at the Red Chimney hamburger stand in Secaucus, New Jersey), I would sit in my father's office and listen to him and Bob Kanigher talk (and sometimes yell) about stories, or discuss cover ideas as my dad quickly sketched them out. I remember meeting Jenette Kahn, Julie Schwartz, Carmine Infantino, Joe Orlando, Jack Adler, Len Wein, and Ernie Colón during those visits, along with so many others. I got piles of comics to keep me busy and out of the way, and I read every one of them.

After I graduated in 1984 from the Joe Kubert School of Cartoon and Graphic Art (now known simply as the Kubert School), one of my first jobs was to take over pencilling and inking *Sgt. Rock*. At that point my father had handed off the editorial duties of the war books to Murray Boltinoff, but when I took on the assignment, I made sure that my dad would still oversee whatever I did. This being my first big comics gig, I was extremely nervous, and I wanted his input and guidance.

He would spend hours with me going over my work—not only correcting and discussing layouts, but also talking about everything from the actual drawing of the comics to life in general and how it reflected on the work that he was doing. He would discuss when to use those circle "insets" of close-ups to convey emotion, and how to "frame out" an area that you wanted the reader to focus on by putting something in the foreground—such as showing little "clothespin figures" walking across a landscape with smoke rising from an exploded tank leading the reader's eye to some larger figures above it.

He would also discuss his future projects with me. *Yossel*, a World War II-era story set in the Warsaw ghetto, presented what my father thought his childhood might have been like if his parents had not left Poland before the German invasion—a very personal project that meant a lot to him. *Jew Gangster*, in which he reflected upon parts of his actual childhood in Brooklyn, was another.

I loved those talks. And so did he.

You'll see a lot of my father in my work, him being the huge influence on me that he was. He had such natural drawing and storytelling abilities that it's difficult to put into words how good he really was. It was so easy for him. And he gave me the encouragement and guidance that I needed to shape my own career.

Andy Kubert
February 2020

Andy Kubert began his career at DC Comics illustrating the highly successful Batman Versus Predator *series. He then went on to draw Marvel Comics' popular* X-Men *title, which was consistently a sales juggernaut and remained their top-selling comic during his six-year run. Also at Marvel, Andy drew the original* Wolverine: Origin *and* Marvel 1602 *miniseries, for which he collaborated with* New York Times *bestselling author Neil Gaiman. For DC, Kubert has illustrated the bestselling* Batman and Son *(with Grant Morrison),* Flashpoint *(with Geoff Johns),* Batman: Whatever Happened to the Caped Crusader? *(again with Neil Gaiman), and* Dark Knight III: The Master Race *(with the legendary Frank Miller, along with writer Brian Azzarello and inker Klaus Janson). He recently finished the six-issue miniseries* Superman: Up in the Sky *with multiple Eisner Award-winning writer Tom King.*

OTHER WORLDS

Genre fiction is all about familiarity with a hint of surprise: a constant search for tropes that the reader will recognize and enjoy repeatedly, as long as each individual story takes the characters somewhere fresh. The 1980s saw the end of two more genres that had been part of DC's mix for decades—science fiction and westerns—as well as the demise of DC's only long-running sword and sorcery title, *Warlord*.

Mike Grell originally developed *Warlord* as a newspaper strip, but after he became a regular contributor to DC, he launched the series in the periodical format. Uniquely for the time, Grell both wrote and pencilled a long run of issues, and even stepped in occasionally to serve as an inker as well, as in the example that follows here.

Science fiction anthologies had been a steady, if modest, part of the DC line during the 1950s and 1960s, and *Time Warp* was a brief attempt to see if their magic could be rekindled with a mix of new and established talent. Sadly, the day for all of DC's anthologies was ending, regardless of their content.

Lastly, westerns had been very successful for DC in the 1950s, then faded away even before that genre lost its hold on the television audience. But a couple of unconventional western titles survived into the 1980s. *Jonah Hex* featured a scarred and bitter ex-Confederate as its hero, and the series had only two writers over the course of its long run: co-creator John Albano and Michael Fleisher, represented here with a story illustrated by *Hex*'s other co-creator, Tony DeZuniga. Let's ride with them into the sunset...

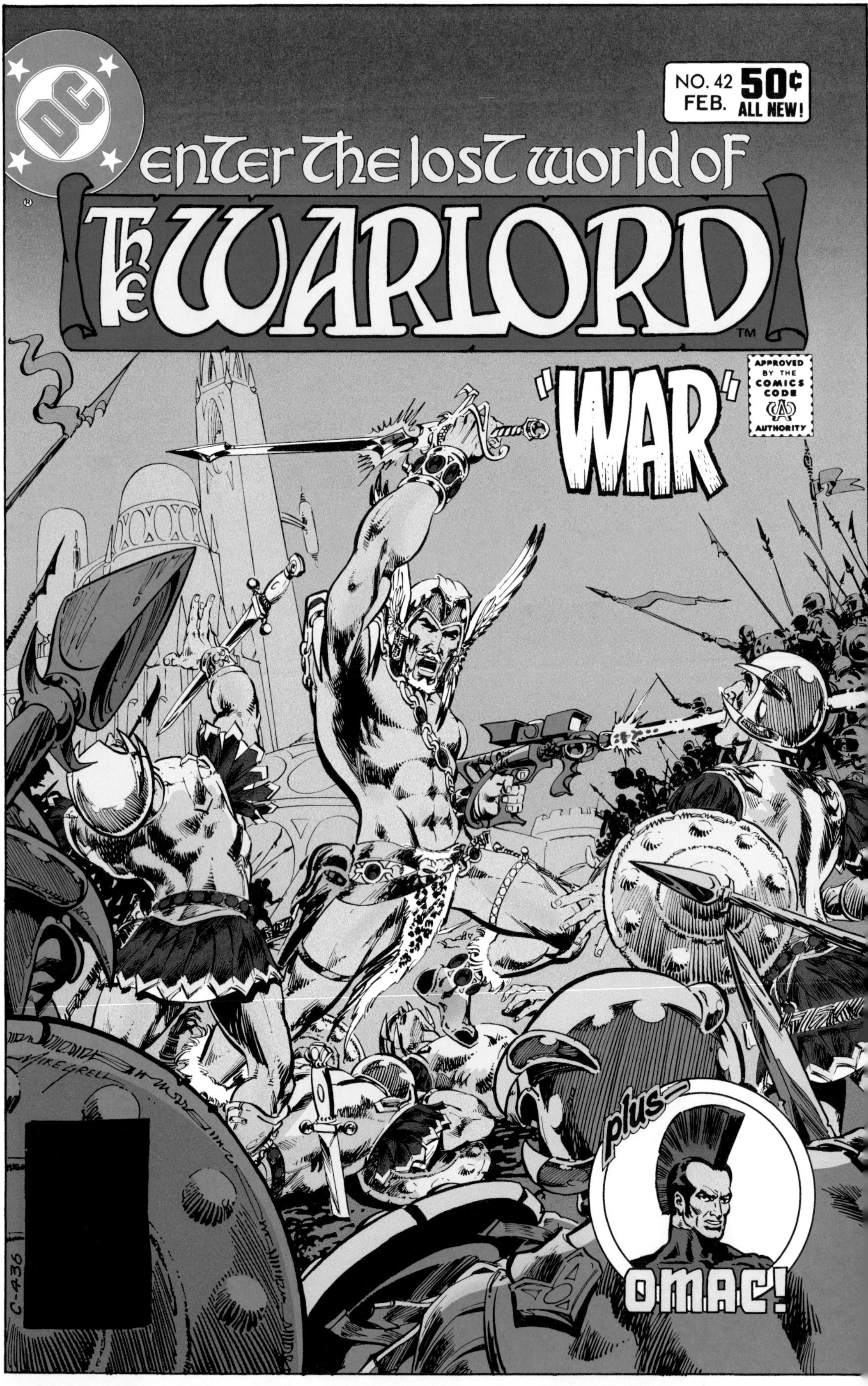
NO. 42
FEB.
50¢
ALL NEW!
enter the lost world of
The WARLORD
TM
APPROVED BY THE COMICS CODE AUTHORITY
"WAR"
plus—
OMAC!
C-436

BEYOND THE GREAT FIRE MOUNTAIN IN FOREST EBONDAR, LIES THE SHINING CITY OF SHAMBALLAH, ITS GOLDEN TOWERS REACHING TOWARD THE ETERNAL SUN THAT CASTS ITS RAYS OF LIFE UPON THE WORLD WITHIN OUR WORLD...
J-7023
BUT LIFE WALKS HAND IN HAND WITH DEATH, AND TRAVIS MORGAN AND HIS FELINE COMPANION, SHAKIRA, APPROACHING THE END OF THEIR LONG JOURNEY, FIND THE COUNTRYSIDE BATTLE SCARRED AND BARREN...
THAT'S THE THIRD ONE! THOSE POOR DEVILS NEVER HAD A CHANCE.
THEY MUST HAVE BEEN TRYING TO REACH THE CITY... NOT THAT IT WOULD BE ANY SAFER THERE!
A LOW GROWL ESCAPES SHAKIRA'S THROAT, AS A DISTANT SOUND REACHES HER SENSITIVE EARS...
LET'S JUST PRAY WE HAVEN'T COME ALL THIS WAY TOO LATE! WHA--?
YES, I HEAR IT NOW. LET'S HAVE A LOOK.
STOP COMPLAINING. I DON'T NEED A BACKSEAT DRIVER!
IF YOU'RE SO MUCH BETTER AT THIS THAN I AM, WHY DON'T YOU DO A LITTLE OF YOUR OWN WORK FOR A CHANGE?
1

IN THE SAVAGE WORLD OF SKARTARIS, LIFE IS A CONSTANT STRUGGLE FOR SURVIVAL. HERE, BENEATH AN UNBLINKING ORB OF ETERNAL SUNLIGHT, ONE SIMPLE LAW PREVAILS: IF YOU LET YOUR GUARD DOWN FOR AN INSTANT YOU WILL SOON BE VERY DEAD.
The WARLORD®
written and illustrated by
MIKE GRELL
WAR
COLORIST:
Adrienne Roy
LETTERER:
John Costanza
EDITOR:
Jack C. Harris
2

3

FROM HIS LOFTY PERCH, MORGAN LOOKS DOWN ON A SIGHT THAT QUICKENS HIS PULSE AND SENDS A TREMOR OF EXCITEMENT THROUGH HIS BODY...
SO! IT'S ALREADY BEGUN! THEY'RE BRINGING IN A RAM TO BREECH THE GATES OF SHAMBALLAH!
THE SITUATION MUST BE FAR WORSE THAN I EXPECTED! THE THERANS WERE THWARTED IN THEIR LAST ATTEMPT TO CONQUER TARA'S PEOPLE-- I KNEW IT WOULDN'T BE LONG BEFORE THEY TRIED AGAIN.
THE HOUNDS OF WAR ARE LOOSED UPON THE LAND! THE BATTLECRY HAS SOUNDED AT LAST!
I KNEW THIS WOULD COME. KNEW IT! DREAMED OF IT!
GOD HELP ME... I'VE LONGED FOR IT!
TELL ME, MORGAN, WHY DO MEN MAKE WAR ON THEIR BROTHERS?
THIS PARTICULAR WAR GOT STARTED BECAUSE THE THERANS REGARD THE SHAMBALLANS AS AN INFERIOR RACE, TO BE SUBJUGATED AND ENSLAVED.
NO ONE HAS THE RIGHT TO PUT ANOTHER HUMAN BEING IN CHAINS! SO, TARA'S PEOPLE DID THE "UNTHINK-ABLE"-- THEY FOUGHT BACK! NATURALLY, AN IDEA LIKE FREEDOM OF CHOICE COULD BE A VERY DANGEROUS THING, SO THE THERANS HAVE VOWED TO CRUSH THE SHAMBALLANS AS AN EXAMPLE TO THE OTHER PEOPLES OF SKARTARIS, THE AUTHORITY MUST NEVER BE QUESTIONED!
AND YOU, MORGAN-- WHY DO YOU MAKE WAR?
I ONCE HAD A DREAM FOR THIS WORLD OF YOURS, SHAKIRA. I SAW SKARTARIS AS A PLACE WHERE ALL MEN COULD LIVE IN FREEDOM AND EQUALITY, WITH EQUAL JUSTICE FOR THE SMALLEST AND THE GREATEST! MAYBE THAT DREAM STILL BURNS SOMEWHERE IN MY SOUL.
OR MAYBE IT'S SIMPLY THAT I NEVER FEEL SO ALIVE AS WHEN THE SCENT OF BLOOD AND SOUND OF BATTLE ARE IN THE AIR AND A STOUT BLADE IS IN MY HAND!
4

AND SO YOU WILL JOIN THIS BATTLE--PERHAPS FOR A CAUSE... PERHAPS FOR YOURSELF.
SOMEWHERE BEHIND THOSE GOLDEN WALLS, TARA IS WAITING FOR ME. I'VE LET HER DOWN TOO MANY TIMES IN THE PAST. NEVER AGAIN!
WHEN THIS BATTLE IS FOUGHT, I'LL BE AT HER SIDE.
THAT ALL SOUNDS VERY NOBLE, BUT HOW WILL YOU GET THROUGH? THE THERANS WILL HAVE THROWN UP BATTLE LINES ALL AROUND THE CITY.
DON'T WORRY! I'LL FIND A WAY...
...OR I'LL MAKE A WAY!
IT'S A HOPELESS GESTURE! WHAT COULD YOU ACCOMPLISH?
MAYBE NOTHING-- BUT I CAN AT LEAST BE WITH HER.
FINE! JUST DON'T EXPECT ME TO WATCH YOU DIE!
AND WITH THAT, MORGAN PUTS SPURS TO HIS WARHORSE AND THUNDERS OFF TO MEET DESTINY, LEAVING BEHIND A TINY FIGURE, TREMBLING, PERHAPS WITH ANGER.
PERHAPS.
5

STRAIGHT INTO THE FACE OF DEATH PLUNGES THE MAN CALLED THE WARLORD, HIS MIGHTY BLADE CLUTCHED IN A POWERFUL HAND THAT SWINGS DEATH IN A GLITTERING ARC OF DESTRUCTION! NO ORDINARY MAN THIS, BUT THE MIGHTIEST WARRIOR EVER TO STRIDE THE SAVAGE WORLD OF SKARTARIS!
6

SO COMPLETE IS THE SURPRISE OF HIS ATTACK THAT MORGAN HAS NEARLY WON THROUGH BEFORE HIS ENEMY CAN RESPOND. FOR A MOMENT, THE PATH TO THE CITY GATES STANDS CLEAR...
BUT PERVERSE FORTUNE TAKES A HAND IN THE FORM OF AN UNSEEN GOPHER HOLE...
AND IN THAT MOMENT, THE DOORWAY OF OPPORTUNITY IS SLAMMED SHUT!
IN THE AFTERMATH OF THE BATTLE, THOSE FORTUNATE ENOUGH TO BE NEARBY AND STILL SURVIVE WOULD REPORT THAT THE STRANGE WARRIOR SMILED SAVAGELY IN THE FACE OF DEATH AND CLUTCHED A BLADE THAT PULSED AND THROBBED WITH INHUMAN POWER! AND THEN...
7

...ALL HELL BROKE LOOSE!
ABOVE THE SHRIEK OF HIS SLASHING BLADE WHICH GREW LOUDER EACH TIME IT DRANK THE BLOOD OF ANOTHER VICTIM, THE WARRIOR WAS HEARD TO SHOUT ONE NAME...
..."TARA!"
AND THEN HE SPRANG THROUGH THE THRONG OF WARRIORS AS HIS FALLEN STEED REGAINED ITS FEET...
...AND WAS GONE!
8

SHORTLY, DEEP WITHIN THE SHELTERING FOREST...
THROUGH A HAZE OF PAIN, A MURMURING VOICE COMES TO MORGAN...
HUH? WHO--?
OH... IT'S YOU!
HAVEN'T YOU HAD ENOUGH?
WHAT DOES IT TAKE TO QUENCH THAT UNHOLY THIRST OF YOURS?
THE MIGHTY BLADE SQUIRMS IN MORGAN'S GRASP, AND, FOR A MOMENT, THE LIGHT OF THE HELLFIRE STONE BURNS WITHIN HIS SOUL.
THEN...
SHUT UP!
AND AS THE SIREN SONG OF THE BLADE FALLS SILENT, MORGAN SOMEHOW SENSES A GREAT VICTORY.
9

WELL, MORGAN, YOU CAN'T JUST LEAVE THIS THING STICKING OUT OF YOUR BODY. SO DO IT!
AAAARRRGH
A NAUSEATING WAVE OF BLACKNESS SWEEPS OVER MORGAN--HIS SENSES REEL, AND...
AND AS MORGAN LIES UNCONSCIOUS, THE FATES ARE WEAVING ANOTHER STRAND INTO THE TAPESTRY OF HIS DESTINY...
LADY J.
BATTERED BY THE SEA, PARCHED BY THE SUN, JENNIFER MORGAN TOSSES IN FITFUL SLUMBER AND DREAMS OF HER SAVAGE FATHER...
LADY J
... AND RELIVES THE TRAGIC MOMENT WHEN, WHILE ATTEMPTING TO RETURN TO THE OUTER WORLD, HER YACHT, THE "LADY J." BECAME A DEATH SHIP!
10

ALONE NOW IN A SAVAGE WORLD, SHE MUST FIGHT TO SURVIVE... IF SHE CAN!
FOR JENNIFER MORGAN, THE NIGHTMARE IS JUST BEGINNING...
LOOK, MASTER! LOOK WHAT THE SEA HAS BROUGHT! IS SHE NOT BEAUTIFUL?
YES! YES! I UNDERSTAND! I WILL OBEY!
AND AT THAT VERY MOMENT, A THOUSAND LEAGUES DISTANT...
I LEAVE YOU ALONE ONCE, AND LOOK WHAT HAPPENS! CAN'T YOU DO ANYTHING RIGHT?
WHA--? SHAKIRA!
HOW LONG WAS I--?
MY GOD! THE CITY--!
--STILL STANDS!
THE SIEGE CONTINUES, BUT THE THERANS HAVEN'T BROKEN THROUGH... YET.
YOU CAME BACK! WHY?
I THOUGHT YOU MIGHT BE ABLE TO USE THIS!
11

A LASER RIFLE!
YOU WENT BACK TO THE ATLANTEAN ARMORY!
WELL, SOMEONE HAD TO KEEP YOU FROM KILLING YOURSELF!
GOOD LUCK, MORGAN! I HOPE SHE'S WORTH IT!
DOES THIS MEAN... GOODBYE?
NO. IF I KNOW YOU, WE'LL MEET AGAIN... SOONER THAN YOU THINK!
AND, WITH THAT, TRAVIS MORGAN'S COMPANION OF MANY ADVENTURES WORKS HER WONDROUS TRANSFORMATION AND IS QUICKLY LOST IN THE JUNGLE...
WELL, COME ON, HORSE! LET'S DO IT!
12

IMPOSSIBLE! NO MAN IN HIS RIGHT MIND WOULD EVEN ATTEMPT IT! YET, AGAINST IMPOSSIBLE ODDS, TRAVIS MORGAN ONCE AGAIN CHARGES INTO THE FACE OF DEATH! A SAVAGE WAR CRY ISSUES FROM THE THROAT OF A MAN ONCE CIVILIZED, NOW GONE TOTALLY SAVAGE... A MAN WHOSE LEGEND IS WRITTEN IN BLOOD AND FLAME ACROSS A SAVAGE WORLD... A MAN CALLED THE WARLORD!
13

THE BANSHEE WAIL OF MORGAN'S MIGHTY SWORD MINGLES WITH THE SCREAMS OF THE DEAD AND DYING AS IT SLAKES ITS UNHOLY THIRST AND, IN MORGAN'S LEFT HAND, A WEAPON FROM A LONG DEAD CIVILIZATION DEALS BURNING DEATH TO ALL WHO WOULD DARE GAZE INTO THE RUBY EYE!

HACK, SLASH AND SLAY! ENEMIES' FACES SWIRL BEFORE HIM THROUGH A BLOOD-RED HAZE, AS HE DEALS DEATH AND DESTRUCTION TO ALL WHO COME WITHIN REACH OF HIS TERRIBLE WEAPONS... UNTIL, AT LAST, TRAVIS MORGAN STANDS ALONE AT THE GATES OF SHAMBALLAH!
15

AND AS THE INVADING ARMY FALLS BACK BEFORE MORGAN'S TERRIBLE ONSLAUGHT...
WELL, ARE YOU GOING TO OPEN THE GATES...OR ARE YOU GOING TO LEAVE ME OUT HERE?
AS THE MASSIVE GATES SWING WIDE...
BY HEAVEN, THIS IS THE MAN THEY CALL THE WARLORD!
THEN OUR SALVATION IS HERE! FOR, TRULY, THE GOD OF WAR STRIKES THROUGH HIS HAND!
SAVE IT! THEY'LL BE BACK WHEN THEY GET THEIR COURAGE UP AGAIN!
LET ME GUESS -- YOU GUYS ARE THE HEAD HONCHOS AROUND HERE, RIGHT?
WE -- AH -- ARE THE COUNCIL OF ELDERS! WE WISH TO THANK YOU FOR--!
CAN IT! TAKE ME TO YOUR QUEEN... NOW!
BUT, SIR. SHE IS NOT IN THE CITY. SHE HAS GONE TO KAAMBUKA TO--!
NOT IN THE CITY!?!!
16

THAT'S IMPOSSIBLE! SHE LEFT KAAMBUKA WELL AHEAD OF ME. SHE SHOULD HAVE REACHED SHAMBALLAH LONG AGO, UNLESS--!
OH, MY GOD!
17
NEXT ISSUE: "BERSERK!" ON SALE: DEC. 23RD

THE SHIP IS ALONE IN THE COLD HEART OF SPACE.
IT SOARS SILENTLY THROUGH THE VACUUM--A GIANT MUTE TRAVERSING THE TRACKLESS VOID.
BUT, WITHIN THE U.S.S. DOG STAR, THERE IS A TUMULTUOUS RACKET! ALERT-SIRENS SQUEAL THEIR WARNINGS-- COMPUTER CONSOLES HUM AND CLATTER--
--AND, ABOVE THE DIN, THE COLD, CONFIDENT VOICE OF CAPTAIN SUZANNE WOO IS HEARD, BARKING ORDERS TO A NERVOUS CREW...
WATCH THOSE POWER-METERS, LIEUTENANT O'HARE! WE MAY BE THE FIRST SHIP EVER EQUIPPED WITH A FASTER-THAN-LIGHT WARP DRIVE--
BUT ONE MISCALCULATION AND WE'LL ALSO BE THE LAST!
The SAVIOURS!
J.M. DE MATTEIS-STORY
GIL KANE-ARTIST
ADRIENNE ROY-COLORIST
1

I DON'T THINK YOU'LL HAVE TO WORRY ABOUT BLOWING THE ENGINES, CAPTAIN--
-- WE MADE IT THROUGH IN ONE PIECE.
UNTIL NOW, THE CREW OF THE DOG STAR THOUGHT THEY'D BE PREPARED FOR THIS MOMENT--FOR THE INSTANT WHEN THEIR VESSEL WOULD WARP THE VERY FABRIC OF THE UNIVERSE AND ENTER HYPER-SPACE...
...THEY WERE WRONG...
LOOK AT IT, CAPTAIN. HAVE YOU EVER SEEN SUCH INDESCRIBABLE BEAUTY?
WHAT A SIGHT!
THIS IS A SCIENTIFIC EXPEDITION, LIEUTENANT-- SO PLEASE SPARE US YOUR POETIC OUTBURSTS!
YES, CAPTAIN...
... BUT MUST YOU LASH OUT AT ALL BEAUTY JUST BECAUSE IT IS DENIED TO YOU? WHY MUST YOU BE SO UNFEELING?!
2

BUT, BENEATH CAPTAIN WOO'S ICY EXTERIOR, IS A SOUL IN TORMENT...
DAMN THEM ALL! THEY'LL NEVER UNDERSTAND WHAT IT MEANS TO BE... UGLY.
I'D TRADE THE GLORIES OF MY CAREER IN THE FLEET IN AN INSTANT IF I COULD ONLY GAZE INTO THE MIRROR AND SEE--
THE CAPTAIN'S REVERIE IS SUDDENLY CUT SHORT BY A VIOLENT...
WHAT THE DEVIL WAS THAT?!
FA-THOOOM!
CAPTAIN WOO-- IT'S THE ENGINES-- ONE OF THEM RUPTURED! THE SHIP IS--
I KNOW, LIEUTENANT! WITH THAT ENGINE GONE--
"--WE'RE BEING RIPPED RIGHT OUT OF HYPER-SPACE! I ONLY HOPE THE SHIP ISN'T RIPPED APART, TOO!"
IF ONLY HOPING COULD MAKE IT SO.
THE DOG STAR EMERGES FROM THE BOWELS OF HYPER-SPACE TO FIND ITSELF CRIPPLED AND LOST-- FLOATING, LIKE ERRANT, COSMIC DUST THROUGH AN UNKNOWN, UNCHARTED SECTOR OF SPACE!

IN THE WEEKS THAT FOLLOW-- STILL ANOTHER UNFORSEEN TRAGEDY OCCURS...
THIS DISEASE IS SPREADING THROUGH THE SHIP LIKE A PLAGUE, CAPTAIN! IN ANOTHER FEW DAYS THERE WILL BE NO ONE LEFT ALIVE ON THIS VESSEL!
BUT WHAT IS IT, O'HARE?
RADIATION LEAKAGE FROM THE DAMAGED ENGINES! IT'S EATING AWAY AT EVERY ONE OF US! AND WE CAN'T STOP IT!
YOU MEAN-- THIS UGLINESS AWAITS US ALL?!
THE AWFUL PROPHECY COMES TRUE-- AND IN A MERE FORTY-EIGHT HOURS...
C- CAPTAIN... WE ARE THE... ONLY ONES LEFT... ALIVE ON BOARD...
DEATH IS NOT... A TERRIBLE THING, LIEUTENANT... BUT TO DIE WITH BODIES SO WARPED...
AND THEN, A WARM, LILTING VOICE-- LIKE THE VOICE OF A GOD-- ECHOES ACROSS THE BRIDGE...
CAPTAIN WOO, LET US HELP.
CAPTAIN...
YES... I HEAR IT, TOO!
LOOK TO YOUR VIEW SCREEN, CAPTAIN-- AND SEE US. SEE YOUR SAVIOURS.
BE PATIENT-- WHILE WE BRING YOU ABOARD.
LOOK, LIEUTENANT! THAT'S BEAUTY! IT'S LIKE... A CATHEDRAL IN SPACE...
4

THERE IS A SOFT GONGING SOUND-- FOLLOWED BY A GENTLE DESCENT INTO DARKNESS, AND THEN...
WELCOME, PEOPLE OF EARTH.
WE GREET YOU WITH LOVE IN OUR HEARTS.
WE ARE ONLY TOO SORRY THAT WE DID NOT HAPPEN UPON YOUR VESSEL BEFORE THE REST OF YOUR CREW PERISHED.
A PITY WE COULD NOT SAVE THEM, AS WELL.
WITH OUR SCIENCE, WE WILL BE ABLE TO TRANSFER YOUR CONSCIOUSNESS INTO FORMS GROWN IN OUR BODY BANKS.
YOU WILL NOT DIE.
LIKE YOU? BUT YOU'RE NOT HUMANS SUCH AS WE--
WHO CARES, CAPTAIN-- WE'LL BE ALIVE! BUT ...FOR HOW LONG?
FORMS AS LOVELY AS OUR OWN-- WHICH WILL BE YOURS TO DWELL IN FOR ETERNITY.
THINK OF IT, TO BE IN SUCH A BODY FOR ETERNITY!
IT'S LIKE A MIRACLE!
BUT AS THE RADIATION SICKNESS COURSES THROUGH HIS BODY, LT. O'HARE GASPS-- HIS WORDS BARELY AUDIBLE...
...YOU DON'T UNDER-STAND... YOU'RE BLINDED...BY DESIRE... BUT IF YOU LIVE...IT DOESN'T MATTER...
WHAT DID YOU SAY, O'HARE?
LIEUTENANT O'HARE...?
UNCONSCIOUS, THE LIEUTENANT CANNOT ANSWER.

LESS THAN AN HOUR LATER...
FEAR NOT, CAPTAIN WOO. ALTHOUGH YOUR BODIES HAVE BUT MOMENTS TO LIVE-- YOU SHALL SURVIVE.
NOT ONLY THAT-- BUT WE HAVE REPAIRED YOUR DAMAGED ENGINES-- AND CLEANSED YOUR DISEASED STARSHIP.
YOU WILL BE ABLE TO RETURN HOME.
CAPTAIN WOO SMILES-- HER HEART BURSTING WITH INEFFABLE JOY...
TH-THANK YOU...
... FOR BRINGING ME THE GIFT...
6

THE RADIO MESSAGE COMES SIX WEEKS LATER-- AND TREMENDOUS CROWDS FLOCK TO THE J.F.K. INTERNATIONAL SPACEPORT FOR THE HERALDED RETURN OF THE U.S.S. DOG STAR...
THE PEOPLE CHEER WILDLY AS THE SHIP GLIDES IN LIKE A TRIUMPHANT EAGLE...
HOW CAN THEY HELP BUT BE SURPRISED WHEN THE MAIN DOORS DILATE AND THE GARBLED, INHUMAN SHRIEK BARRELS OUT FROM THE SHIPS METALLIC ENTRAILS...
AND HOW CAN THEY NOT RUN IN MAD TERROR, AS THE FILTHY, FETID-SMELLING THINGS COME SHAMBLING DOWN THE RAMP-- DRIPPING SLIME FROM THEIR GELATINOUS FORM! ONE IS SCREAMING IN A DISGUSTING DISTORTION OF HUMAN TONGUE:
NO, THE CROWD CANNOT POSSIBLY KNOW OF CAPTAIN WOO'S HORRIBLE MISTAKE. FOR, INDEED, THE ANGELIC, GOD-LIKE BEINGS HAD BEEN THE PETS-- WHILE THE FOUL MONSTROSITIES HAD BEEN THE MASTERS!
I AM SUZANNE WOO!!
QUIT YOUR SCREAMING, CAPTAIN. WE'RE ALIVE AND WILL STILL BE ALIVE WHEN ALL OF OUR "FELLOW HUMANS" ARE DEAD AND GONE!
JUST THINK-- YOU AND I-- WOO AND O'HARE ARE EARTH'S NEW ADAM AND EVE! HA, HA HA, HA, HA, HA!
END

EVIL! THIS IS WHAT THEY LOOKED LIKE,,,
RITES OF SPRING
...MEN! AND THEY WERE EVIL!
CREATURES OF DARKNESS, SPAWNED IN HATRED, NURTURED BY FILTH--
DEFILERS! SPOILERS! WRECKERS!
TRUVA HEARS--
--BUT SHE DOES NOT BELIEVE!
TURNING AWAY FROM THE TEACHER, SHE HEARS--
PSST! YOUNGSTER!
YOU NOT SWALLOWING THAT, ARE YOU?
STORY: DENNY O'NEIL
ART: DICK GIORDANO
LETTERING: MILT SNAPINN
COLORIST: ADRIENNE ROY

NOT TRUE, WHAT TEACHER SAYS! REASON SHE TALKS LIKE THAT IS THERE NOT ANY MEN ANY MORE--NOT SINCE THE PLAGUE HUNDRED YEAR AGO!
MEN ALL DIE! WE WOMEN COME DOWN HERE--
--UNDERGROUND!
UP TOP, DISEASE--AND MONSTERS!
WE LEARN TO MAKE BABIES IN THE LABORATORY AND--
BUT IF MEN AREN'T BAD, WHY DO WE HATE THEM?
'CAUSE WOMEN NEED MEN SAME A MEN NEEDED WOMEN--
--AND FOLKS ALWAYS HATE WHAT THEY NEED AND CAN'T HAVE!
YOU BABBLING YOUR LIES AGAIN, OLD WOMAN?
GET OUT! YOU KNOW YOU'RE NOT SUPPOSED TO BE IN THE TEEN QUARTERS!
AS FOR YOU, TRUVA--INSTEAD OF LETTING HER FILL YOUR HEAD WITH TRASH, YOU SHOULD BE AT WEAPONS PRACTICE!
GO...BEFORE YOU FIND YOURSELF ON PUNISHMENT DETAIL!
DISCONSOLATELY, THE GIRL ENTERS A SHORT-CUT SHE ACCIDENTALLY FOUND MONTHS EARLIER, A LONG-ABANDONED TUNNEL...
SOMETHING FAINT AND DELICIOUS TEASES HER NOSTRILS...
2

AIR-- BUT AIR SUCH AS SHE HAS NEVER IMAGINED!
SHE FOLLOWS IT TO ITS SOURCE--
--A CRACK IN THE WALL, CAUSED BY A THING SHE RECOGNIZES AS A TREE ROOT...
SLOWLY, SHE REALIZES THE ROOT MUST HAVE PUSHED FROM ABOVE-- AND THAT BY FOLLOWING IT SHE WOULD REACH THE SURFACE!
BUT A RUDE VOICE JARS HER--
TRUVA! WHERE ARE YOU?
A MINUTE LATER, SHE REACHES THE FIRING RANGE, WHERE--
WE MUST PRACTICE THE KILLING ARTS, WOMEN--
--FOR IF ANY CREATURE FROM UP TOP SHOULD REACH OUR UNDERGROUND PARADISE, WE MUST DESTROY IT!
...READY...
...FIRE!
FOM FOM FOM
3

AT THE REGULAR TIME, THE LIGHTS ARE DIMMED FOR THE SLEEP PERIOD...
BUT FOR TRUVA, SLEEP IS IMPOSSIBLE!
TORMENTED BY INNER STIRRINGS SHE CAN NOT NAME, SHE ARISES--
--AND, DIMLY AWARE OF WHAT SHE MUST DO, GLIDES TO THE GUN RACK AND TAKES A PISTOL...
THEN, AS THOUGH DRAWN BY AN INVISIBLE CORD, SHE HURRIES TO THE SHORTCUT--
FOR A LONG MOMENT, SHE SIMPLY STANDS, FILLING HER BEING WITH THE MARVELOUS PERFUME THAT SEEPS FROM THE CRACK IN THE WALL, TINGLING WITH A PHANTOM EXCITEMENT...
WITH A THRILL OF BOTH DANGER AND ANTICIPATION, ASTONISHED AT HER OWN BOLDNESS, SHE SLIPS INTO THE BREECH--
--AND, TREMBLING, CLIMBS UPWARD TOWARD AN EERIE GLOW.
AFTER MINUTES THAT ARE ETERNITIES, SHE REACHES HER DESTINATION, BLINKS AT A LIGHT THAT STINGS HER EYES, AND WHEN HER VISION CLEARS, GASPS...

COLORS AND BRIGHTNESS AND SOUNDS AND A SUBTLE PERFUME SUCH AS SHE HAS NEVER IMAGINED...
HER HEART POUNDS AND SHE GROWS DIZZY WITH JOY--!
SO UTTERLY TRANSPORTED IS SHE THAT AT FIRST SHE IS NOT AWARE OF A HUMAN VOICE--
--A VOICE SCREAMING...
HELP!
INSTINCTIVELY, SHE GRASPS HER WEAPON--
--AND RUNS TO A HORRIFYING SCENE...
SHE DOES NOT NEED TO THINK, FOR SHE HAS TRAINED FOR THIS VERY MOMENT! SHE REACTS--
5

THEN, THE FINAL ASTONISHMENT--
YOU... YOU'RE A WOMAN!
I'VE BEEN SEARCHING FOR MONTHS! I THOUGHT THERE WERE NO FEMALES LEFT!
NO, TRUVA DOES NOT NEED TO THINK--
--FOR SHE HAS TRAINED--
--SHE REACTS...
FOM FOM FOM
THE BLAST HURLS HIM BACK AND HE FALLS NEXT TO THE OTHER MONSTER!
WORDS FORM ON TRUVA'S LIPS: "I'M SORRY."
BUT SHE DOES NOT SPEAK THEM ALOUD! INSTEAD, SHE TURNS...
...AND WITH THE JOY DYING WITHIN HER, MOVES TOWARD HER WORLD...
6
END

MORE PAGES OF GUT-GRABBING WESTERN ACTION!
IN THIS ISSUE: TEJANO!
60¢
U.K.20p
ALL NEW! MORE PAGES!
NO. 54
NOV.
JONAH HEX
APPROVED BY THE COMICS CODE AUTHORITY
THE STRAP TIGHTENS AROUND YOUR NECK WITH EVERY TURN...! ADIOS, HEX!
"EL PAPAGAYO" RETURNS!

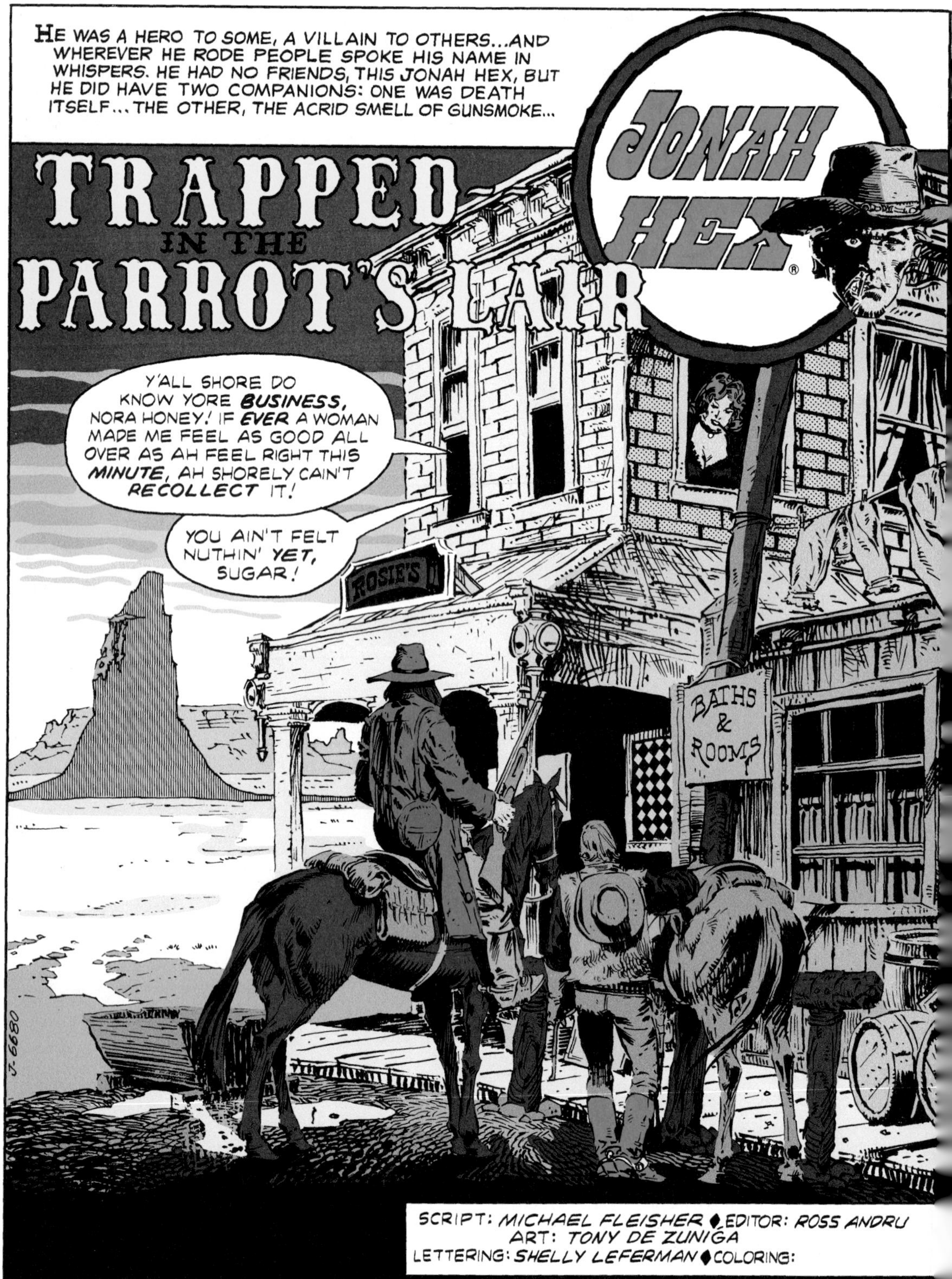

HE WAS A HERO TO SOME, A VILLAIN TO OTHERS...AND WHEREVER HE RODE PEOPLE SPOKE HIS NAME IN WHISPERS. HE HAD NO FRIENDS, THIS JONAH HEX, BUT HE DID HAVE TWO COMPANIONS: ONE WAS DEATH ITSELF... THE OTHER, THE ACRID SMELL OF GUNSMOKE...
JONAH HEX®
TRAPPED IN THE PARROT'S LAIR
Y'ALL SHORE DO KNOW YORE BUSINESS, NORA HONEY! IF EVER A WOMAN MADE ME FEEL AS GOOD ALL OVER AS AH FEEL RIGHT THIS MINUTE, AH SHORELY CAIN'T RECOLLECT IT!
YOU AIN'T FELT NUTHIN' YET, SUGAR!
ROSIE'S
BATHS & ROOMS
J. 6680
SCRIPT: MICHAEL FLEISHER ♦ EDITOR: ROSS ANDRU
ART: TONY DE ZUÑIGA
LETTERING: SHELLY LEFERMAN ♦ COLORING:

YOU JUST WAIT TILL WE GET THROUGH WASHIN' THE TRAIL GRIME OFF THIS SEXY BODY OF YOURS --
--AND THEN WE'LL--
THE LADY'S RIGHT, HEX! A MAN STINKS AS MUCH AS YOU DO, WHY HE'S JUST GOTTA DO SOMETHIN' ABOUT IT QUICK AS HE CAN!
AIN'T THET A FACT, BROTHER BARLOW?
HUH--!?
WHAM!
IT SHORELY IS, BROTHER HANK! WAY AH LOOK AT IT, IT AIN'T HARDLY CHRISTIAN FER A MAN TUH BE SMELLIN' LIKE A PIG PEN AT HIS OWN FUNERAL!
WHYN'T YOU JUST RUN ALONG NOW, GIRLIE? AFTER ALL, ANYTHIN' YOU WUZ PLANNIN' ON DOIN' TUH JONAH HEX HERE, ME'N BROTHER HANK HERE COULD DO IT TWICE AS GOOD!
WHY, WHEN ME'N BROTHER HANK HERE WUZ JUST KNEE-HIGH TO A COUPLA TADS, WE USED TUH DO THIS DARN NEAR EVER' TIME ONE'A PAW'S HOGS WENT AN' ROLLED IN THE MUD!
2

FIRST WE--
WHU--!?
AAAHH!
TSAK
GNNGHHH!
G-GET OUTA HIS WAY, BARLOW! HOW'M AH GONNA GET OFF A CLEAR SHOT IF'N YUH DON'T GET UP OUT'N THE WAY?
AH'M AFRAID YORE BABY BROTHER CAIN'T HEAR YUH, SONNY!
HE'S WAY TOO BUSY THINKIN' BACK TUH THEM GOOD OLD TIMES WHEN YOU AN' HIM WUZ JUST KNEE-HIGH TO A COUPLA TADS!
HUH--!?
BDOW
BDOW
BLASTED SHORT-BARRELLED SMITH AND WESSONS!...
3

AH NEVER WILL UNDERSTAND JUST WHY IN TARNATION JESSE JAMES LIKES 'EM SO MUCH!
'CAUSE AS FAR AS AH'M--
EEEK!
JONAH HEX! JUST LOOK WHAT YOU'VE DONE! THERE'S BLOOD AND WATER SPLASHED ALL OVER MY FRESH-POLISHED FLOOR! THAT'S TWO DOLLARS I'M GOING TO BE ADDING TO YOUR BILL!
TWO DOLLARS!? HOLY HANNAH!
THET'S ONE DOLLAR FER THE BATH...TWO DOLLARS FER THE FLOOR! AIN'T THERE NUTHIN' IN THIS PLACE YOU FOLKS DON'T CHARGE FER?
NOT HARDLY, SUGAR! BUT HERE--
--HERE'S A LITTLE SOMETHING ON THE HOUSE!
4

SOON...
LOOKA THERE, MA! COMIN' DOWN THE STREET! IT'S JONAH HEX, THE FAMOUS BOUNTY HUNTER!
COUNTY
WHA--!? JONAH HEX? I-IT CAN'T BE!
KIN I GO SAY HELLO TO 'IM, MA? KIN I? HUNH?
NO, WILBUR! YOU MOST CERTAINLY MAY NOT! YOU ARE GOING TO GROW UP TO BE A DENTIST, LIKE YOUR FATHER! NOT A... A HIRED GUNSLINGER!
THEN COULDN'T I JUST MAYBE PET HIS HORSE, MA? PLEASE?
TELEGRAPH OFFICE
AW, MA!
QUICK! I-I WANT TO SEND A TELEGRAM! HURRY!
5

NOW IT IS EVENING. AND MANY MILES AWAY, IN A WHITE-COLONNADED PLANTATION HOUSE ON THE OUTSKIRTS OF RICHMOND, VIRGINIA...
THEN HE'S REALLY DEAD! YOU'RE ABSOLUTELY CERTAIN HE'S REALLY, TRULY DEAD!
AIN'T NOBODY IN THE WORLD EVER BEEN DEADER THAN HE IS, MR. TURNBULL! ONCE THE SMOKE CLEARED AFTER THET DYNAMITE BLAST WENT OFF--
--THE ONLY THING LEFT'A JONAH HEX WUZ A FEW SCRAPS'A CONFEDERATE GRAY STILL CLINGIN' TO THE BARBED-WIRE FENCE OUTSIDE OF FORT CHARLOTTE! *
EXCELLENT, GENTLEMEN! EXCELLENT! THEN THIS CLEARLY DOES CALL FOR A ROUND OF CHAMPAGNE!
*FOR DETAILS, CHECK OUT "RETURN TO FORT CHARLOTTE," IN JONAH HEX #36. ED.
I HEREBY PROPOSE A TOAST, GENTLEMEN! A TOAST TO--
BEGGIN' YO' PARDON FO' INTERRUPTIN', SUH! TELEGRAM JUST COME IN FROM CLEMENTINE SPRINGS, SUH!
MY WORD, SOLOMON! HAVE YOU FORGOTTEN YOUR MANNERS? CAN'T YOU SEE THAT WE'RE CELEBRATING?
JONAH HEX BE ALIVE, SUH! HE BE ALIVE AND WELL IN CLEMENTINE SPRINGS!
BLAST!
SPTAK!
6

THIS... THIS IS INTOLERABLE!
INTOLERABLE!
SIR! YOUR HAND! I-IT'S BLEEDING,
HERE! LET ME--
WILL NO ONE HELP ME AVENGE THE BLOODY DEATH OF MY ONLY SON? WILL NO ONE HELP ME RID THE EARTH OF THAT VILE MAGGOT JONAH HEX?
YESSIR! WE'LL DO IT FOR YOU, SIR!
WE'LL RIDE TO THE END OF THE EARTH IF WE HAVE TO, AND WE WON'T COME BACK HERE UNTIL WE'VE FOUND JONAH HEX AND PUT HIM IN HIS GRAVE!
HOTE
BEEN A RED-LETTER DAY, ALL RIGHT! AIN'T OFTEN AH TAKE A BATH AN' KETCH TWO OWLHOOTS ALL IN THE SAME AFTER-NOON!
AH JUST HOPE THE BED AH'M 'BOUT TUH GO TUH SLEEP ON TURNS OUT TUH BE MORE OF A BARGAIN THAN THET MISERABLE EXCUSE FER A MEAL AH JUST ATE IN THET RESTAURANT!
ROOM NUMBER TWELVE, MR. HEX! JUST TURN RIGHT AT THE TOP OF THE STAIRS!
7

FER ONE THING, THET STEAK THEY GIVE ME WUZ ABOUT AS APPETIZIN' AS SUCKIN' ON AN OLD BOOT! AN' AS FER THET STRAWBERRY SHORTCAKE...
...AH'VE SEEN TASTIER LOOKIN' WHIPPED CREAM RUNNIN' DOWN THE INSIDE WALL OF A BARN!
ROOM TWELVE, HE SAID! WELL, THAR'S EIGHT... TEN...!
10
8
HERE IT IS! ROOM NUMBER TWELVE!
10
8
12
12
YOU SO MUCH AS TWITCH, MISTER, AN' YO'RE GONNA FIND YORE BRAINS SQUISHIN' ALL AROUND IN THE BOTTOM OF YORE BOOTS!
QUÉ? *
*SPANISH FOR "WHAT?"
8

PLEASE, SEÑOR HEX! Y-YOU MUST NOT SHOOT ME! NOT AFTER I HAVE TRAVELED ALL THIS WAY TO SPEAK WITH YOU!
WHO THE--!?
HAVE YOU FORGOTTEN ME SO SOON, SEÑOR HEX? IT IS ME, COL. SANCHEZ! DO YOU NOT REMEMBER HOW I ONCE HIRED YOU TO PERFORM A VITAL MISSION FOR THE MEXICAN GOVERNMENT? *
OH YEAH! AH REMEMBER, ALL RIGHT!
*IN JONAH HEX #9-10.--ED.
Y'ALL HIRED ME TUH TRANSPORT A FORTUNE IN GOLD INGOTS FROM VERA CRUZ TUH MEXICO CITY, AN' ALMOST ENDED UP GETTIN' ME PLANTED IN BOOT HILL BY EL PAPAGAYO* AN' HIS ARMY OF CUTTHROAT BANDIDOS!
SI, SEÑOR HEX!
*SPANISH FOR "THE PARROT."
IT IS EL PAPAGAYO WHOM I HAVE COME TO SPEAK TO YOU ABOUT NOW!
OKAY, COLONEL! COME ON INSIDE! BUT AH CAIN'T SEE AS HOW THAR'S REALLY THET MUCH LEFT FER US TUH SAY 'BOUT EL PAPAGAYO, SEEIN' AS HOW HE'S A DEAD MAN!
I FEAR EL PAPAGAYO IS NOT SO DEAD AS WE THOUGHT, SEÑOR HEX! IT IS TRUE THAT HE WAS KNIFED IN THE BACK BY THE WOMAN ESTRELLITA--*
*IN JONAH HEX #10.--ED.
--BUT HE WAS FOUND BY PEASANTS, SEÑOR HEX, AND NURSED BACK TO HEALTH, AND NOW HE IS VERY MUCH WEETH US, AND CAUSING MUCH MISCHIEF IN MY COUNTRY WEETH HIS BANDIDO ARMY!
SO? WHUT KIN AH DO 'BOUT IT?
9

YOU, SEÑOR HEX, ARE THE ONLY MAN WHO HAS EVER ENTERED EL PAPAGAYO'S STRONGHOLD AND RETURNED ALIVE TO TELL THE TALE! *
IT EES FOR THAT REASON THAT MY PRESIDENTE HAS AUTHORIZED ME TO OFFER YOU TEN THOUSAND AMERICAN DOLLARS TO INVADE "THE PARROT'S" STRONGHOLD AND BRING HIM BACK TO US DEAD OR ALIVE!
* IN JONAH HEX #2.--ED.
THE NIGHT IS A CLOAK OF VELVET STUDDED WITH PLATINUM STARS AS A LONE HORSE-MAN CLAD IN CONFEDERATE GRAY GALLOPS ALONG THE BANK OF A DRIED-OUT RIVER-BED AS IT WRITHES TORTUOUSLY THROUGH THE VILLA ROJO CANYONS OF NORTHERN MEXICO LIKE A PURPLE GASH ON THE UNDERBELLY OF A GREAT BLACK SNAKE...
WHILE HIGH ATOP THE CANYON RIM...
IT EES A GRINGO, JOSÉ! AND HE EES ALONE!
HE MUS' BE ONE MUY* UNHAPPY HOMBRE TO THROW AWAY HIS LIFE FOR NOTHEENG JUST TO RIDE ALONE INTO THE STRONGHOLD OF EL PAPAGAYO!
* VERY.
SI, JOSÉ! IT EES A FAVOR WE ARE DOING FOR THEES POOR UN-HAPPY GRINGO TO PUT HEEM QUICKLY OUT OF HIS MISERIES!
KPOW! KPOW! KPOW!
10

WHIIIIIII!
VIP!
VIP!
VIP!
GOOD SHOOTING, GARCIA! YOU GOT HEEM!
EET WAS NOTHING, JOSE! EET IS ALWAYS A SIMPLE THEENG TO SHOOT THE GRINGOS AT NIGHT--
--BECAUSE THEIR WHITE TEETH--
HUH--!?
GO ON, GARCIA! DON'T BE SHY!
TELL ME ALL 'BOUT HOW EASY IT IS TUH SHOOT GRINGOS AT NIGHT!
WHA--!?
PRESENTLY...
AH FIGGER YOU GENTS'LL PROB'LY MANAGE TUH WORK YORESELVES LOOSE IN A COUPLA HOURS, AN' IF'N AH WUZ YOU, AH'D JUMP RIGHT ON THEM CAYUSES AN' NOT STOP RUNNIN' TILL AH'D REACHED THE YUCATAN!
11

'CAUSE LAST TIME AH OUTSMARTED A COUPLA EL PAPAGAYO'S SENTRIES, HE WENT AN' GUTTED 'EM WI'F THET SABRE OF HIS RIGHT ON THE SPOT! *
*IN JONAH HEX #2.--ED.
SO LONG, BOYS!
MMMPF!
MMMPF!
BUT AT THAT VERY MOMENT...
MADRE DE DIOS! * THEES GRINGO, HE HAS TIED UP JOSÉ AND GARCIA AND NOW RIDES TOWARD OUR ENCAMPMENT DISGUISED IN JOSÉ'S CLOTHING!
*MOTHER OF GOD.
I MUST GO QUICKLY, AND PRAY THAT I CAN WARN EL PAPAGAYO IN TIME!
AND SO, A SHORT WHILE LATER...
WELL, HERE AH AM! AN' UNLESS MUH MEMORY'S STARTIN' TUH DESERT ME IN MUH OLD AGE, THET LARGE ADOBE HUT ON THE RIGHT IS WHAR EL PAPAGAYO HANGS HIS SOMBRERO AT!
12

OF COURSE, GETTIN' INTUH THIS PLACE WUZ THE EASY PART!
IT'S GETTIN' OUT AGAIN WHUT'S LIABLE TUH GET A MITE STICKY!
BAM! BAM!
YES? WHO EES IT?
PLEASE FORGIVE ME, PAPAGAYO! I--
OH, IT EES YOU, JOSE! COME IN! COME IN!
THERE IS NO NEED TO ASK FORGIVENESS OF YOUR OLD FRIEND! MY HOUSE IS YOUR HOUSE! YOUR HOUSE IS MY HOUSE! BESIDES, FOR NEARLY A HALF HOUR NOW, I HAVE BEEN EXPECTING YOU--
-- JONAH HEX--!!
WHU--!?
13

EES THAT NOT RIGHT, PEPITO? IS EET NOT RIGHT THAT FOR A HALF HOUR NOW WE HAVE BEEN EXPECTING A VISIT FROM OUR GOOD FRIEN' JONAH HEX?
SQUAWWK!
EET HAS BEEN A LONG TIME SINCE LAST I SEE YOU, SEÑOR HEX, BUT I HAVE THOUGHT ABOUT YOU MANY TIMES! I HAVE THOUGHT ABOUT EXACTLY HOW I AM GOING TO KEEL YOU!
AND, IN YOUR HONOR, I HAVE EVEN TAUGHT PEPITO A NEW WORD, SEÑOR HEX!
TELL ME, PEPITO! WHEN WE CATCH JONAH HEX, HOW ARE WE GOING TO KEEL HIM, EH?
SQUAWWK! SLOWWLY! SQUAWK!
HA HA HA! PEPITO, HE IS THE SMARTEST PAPAGAYO IN THE WHOLE WIDE WORLD, IS THAT NOT SO, SEÑOR HEX?
WHAM!
UNNGHH!
SQUAWWK!
WHA--!? SEÑOR HEX, HE MUST NOT HAVE LIKED YOUR NEWEST TRICK, PEPITO! LOOK AT HEEM! IT IS STILL EARLY, AND ALREADY HE IS FAST ASLEEPING!
SOON...
HOLY HANNAH! W-WHAR IN THUNDERATION AM AH?
14

UH-OH! OL' PAPAGAYO'S GOT ME ALL TRUSSED UP LIKE A CHRISTMAS TURKEY AT THE BOTTOM OF AN OLD DRY WELL!
NORMALLY, THE DONKEY TURNIN' THET WOODEN SHAFT IS WHUT BRINGS UP THE WATER FROM DEEP UNDERGROUND--
--BUT PAPAGAYO'S MODIFIED THE APPARATUS SO THET EVER' TIME THE BURRITO DOES A TURN AROUN' THE WELL, HE TIGHTENS THIS RAWHIDE NOOSE AROUN' MUH (UNNGGH) NECK!
WELL THIS CLEARLY AIN'T NO PLACE FER A FRESH-FACED YOUNG BOUNTY HUNTER LIKE MUHSELF TUH BE IN!
AH JUST HOPE THEM NASTY MEXES AIN'T CONFISCATED--
--MUH PARDNER MISTER BOWIE SO'S AH KIN REQUISITION HIS HELP IN--
--GETTIN' OUTA THIS MESS!
WHEW! IT SHORE DO FEEL GOOD TUH BE ABLE TUH BREATHE AGAIN!
NOW IF'N AH KIN JUST CUT AWAY THE REST'A THESE BLASTED THONGS--
--MEBBE, JUST MEBBE--
15

--AH KIN GET ENOUGH OF A HANDHOLD ON THESE SLIPPERY OLD WALLS--
--TUH GIVE MUHSELF HALF A TINKER'S CHANCE OF CLIMBIN' THE HECK OUTA HERE!
SO FAR, SO GOOD! NOW--
SO! EET IS AS EL PAPAGAYO TOLD ME!
WHU--!?
YOU ARE ONE MUY TREECKY HOMBRE, EH, SEÑOR HEX?
WELL YOU ARE NOT TREECKY ENOUGH TO--
THUK!
UNNGH!
WHO--!?
QUICKLY, SEÑOR HEX! CLIMB OUT OF THE WELL AND COME WITH ME! PRONTO!
AND SO NOT MAKE A SOUND! IF WE ARE SEEN, EET WEEL MEAN A SLOW DEATH FOR US BOTH, DO YOU COMPRENDE?*
YEAH, AH COMPRENDE!
*UNDERSTAND.
BUT THET DON'T MEAN AH AIN'T AWFUL CONFUSED 'BOUT WHUT'S GOIN' ON HERE! WHO IN TARNATION ARE YOU? AND WHY'RE--
I AM CARMELITA, THE WOMAN OF EL PAPAGAYO!
16

BUT I AM ALSO IN THE PAY OF COL. SANCHEZ TO SPY ON THE BANDIDOS!
HURRY! THERE ARE OUR CABALLOS! * I WEEL LEAD YOU PAST THE SENTRIES UNTIL YOU ARE SAFELY AWAY FROM THE BANDIDO CAMP!
*HORSES.
YOUR PISTOLAS * AND YOUR OWN CLOTHES ARE IN YOUR SADDLE-BAGS! YOU CAN PUT THEM ON ONCE YOU ARE SAFELY AWAY FROM HERE!
*PISTOLS.
NOW, SEÑOR HEX! IF YOU VALUE YOUR LIFE, RIDE LIKE THE WIND!
PRESENTLY...
WHOA!
THIS EES AS FAR AS I CAN GO WEETH YOU, SEÑOR HEX! I MUST RETURN TO EL PAPAGAYO'S SIDE BEFORE HE BEGINS TO MISS ME!
I ADVISE YOU TO STOP AND REST AWHILE IN THEES MEADOW! FOR NOW, AT LEAST, YOU ARE SAFE FROM EL PAPAGAYO!
THE LADY KNOWS WHUT SHE'S TALKIN' 'BOUT, HEX! YO'RE SAFE FROM EL PAPAGAYO, ALL RIGHT!
WHU-!?
BUT LORD, YOU SHORE AIN'T SAFE FROM US!
17
TO BE CONTINUED--!!

IN THIS ISSUE: TEJANO!
60¢
U.K.20p
ALL NEW! MORE PAGES!
NO.55
DEC.
APPROVED BY THE COMICS CODE AUTHORITY
JONAH HEX
C-726

HE WAS A HERO TO SOME, A VILLAIN TO OTHERS... AND WHEREVER HE RODE PEOPLE SPOKE HIS NAME IN WHISPERS. HE HAD NO FRIENDS, THIS JONAH HEX, BUT HE DID HAVE TWO COMPANIONS: ONE WAS DEATH ITSELF... THE OTHER, THE ACRID SMELL OF GUNSMOKE...
JONAH HEX®
"TRAIL OF BLOOD!"
AH'LL BET IT FEELS REAL GOOD TUH'VE GOTTEN CLEAN AWAY FROM EL PAPAGAYO, DON'T IT, HEX?
WHU--!?
BEST ENJOY THET GOOD FEELIN' WHILE YOU STILL KIN, YOUNGSTER, 'CAUSE YOU SHORE AS BLAZES AIN'T 'BOUT TUH GET AWAY FROM US!
SCRIPT: MICHAEL FLEISHER ARTIST: TONY DE ZUÑIGA
LETTERER: SHELLY LEFERMAN COLORIST: BOB LE ROSE EDITOR: ROSS ANDRU
*YOU CAUGHT THE SENSES-SHATTERING ACTION HERE, LAST ISSUE ED.

YUH DID A REAL GOOD JOB BRINGIN' 'IM HERE, CARMELITA! HERE! OL' MAN TURNBULL SAID FER US TUH GIVE YUH THIS!
TURNBULL!? WHY, YOU NO-GOOD CONNIVIN' FEMALE!
YOU TOL' ME YOU WUZ WORKIN' FER THE MEXICAN GOV'MENT, SPYIN' ON EL PAPAGAYO AN' HIS BANDIDOS!
HA HA! I AM WORKING FOR ANYONE, MR. HEX--
--ANYONE WHO HAS THE--
VIP
GHAAA!
HUH--!?
WHO--!?
RIFLE FIRE! COMIN' FROM ATOP THET BLUFF! EVERBODY GET DOWN!
IT'S EL PAPAGAYO! IT HAS TUH BE! HE MUSTA FOUND THET SENTRY ME AN' HER KILLED* AN COME OUT AFTER US!
YOU ARE SO RIGHT AS ALWAYS, SEÑOR HEX! MY POOR OLD FRIEND PABLO, I DID INDEED FIND HEEM!
*LAST ISSUE--ED.
2

THEES EES YOUR MUCHO GOOD FRIEND EL PAPAGAYO WHO IS SPEAKING TO YOU, SEÑOR HEX! AS YOU CAN SEE, I HAVE ALREADY KILLED THE PUTA* WHO BETRAYED ME, AND NOW I AM GOING TO KEEL YOU AND ALL YOUR FRIENDS WHO ARE DOWN THERE WEETH YOU!
*TRAMP.
WHUT IN TARNATION'S HE TALKIN' BOUT? WE AIN'T YORE FRIENDS! WHY, WE'S JUST RODE ALL THE WAY F'UM VIRGINIA TUH KILL YOU OURSELF!
OH YEAH? WELL, WHYN'T YOU GO UP THAR ON THET BLUFF AN' TRY TELLIN' HIM THET!
LISTEN TO ME, GRINGOS! THROW DOWN YOUR RIFLES AND YOUR PISTOLAS*! SURRENDER TO ME AND TO MY MEN!
YOU HAVE MY WORD OF HONOR AS A BANDIDO CHIEF THAT I WEEL KEEL YOU ALL QUEECKLY, AND NOT SLOWLY!
*PISTOLS.
WHATTA YOU THINK, MICAH?
WHUT'S THAR TUH THINK ABOUT, SHENANDOAH? WE CAIN'T SURRENDER! WE GOTTA STAND AN' FIGHT!
UH-HUH! WE STAY AN' FIGHT, WE'S JUST ALL GONNA GET SLAUGHTERED!
LIKE IT OR NOT, WE'S GONNA HAVE TUH RUN FER IT!
AH FIGGERED THET'S THE KINDA SOLUTION YOU'D COME UP WITH, HEX!
QUIT RUNNIN' YORE MOUTH, MICAH, AN' START HELPIN' ME SET FIRE TUH THIS HERE BUFFALO GRASS! IT'S GREEN, WHICH MEANS IT'LL SEND UP LOTSA SMOKE! AN' BY THE TIME THEM MEXES CIRCLE ROUND IT, WE KIN BE ON OUR CAYUSES AN' BEATIN' A TRAIL OUTA HERE!

YEAH, WELL MEBBE WE DO GOTTA RUN FER IT, HEX! BUT THET SHORE DON'T MEAN WE GOTTA TAKE YOU ALONG WITH US NOW, DO IT?
TELL THIS DUMB GALOOT TUH PUT HIS IRON AWAY, MICAH!
AND SO, WITHIN MOMENTS...
PAPAGAYO! LOOK! THE GRINGOS HAVE SET FIRE TO THE BUFFALO GRASS! THEY ARE ESCAPING!
DO NOT WORRY, EMILIO! THE AMERICANOS ARE FEW, AND THEY ARE FAR FROM HOME! BEFORE THEY CAN CROSS THE RIO GRANDE RIVER BACK INTO THE UNITED STATES, WE SHALL DESTROY THEM ALL!
THE FOLLOWING MORNING, OUTSIDE A STATELY ANTE-BELLUM MANSION ON THE OUTSKIRTS OF RICHMOND, VIRGINIA, MANY HUNDREDS OF MILES AWAY...
YASSUH, MR. TURNBULL! TODAY BE THE TWELFTH ANNIVERSARY OF THE DAY WHEN YOUNG MASSUH JEB BE KILLED WITH A WHOLE LOTTA OTHER MEN WHILE THEY WUZ ESCAPIN' FROM THE UNION ARMY PRISON CAMP AT FORT CHARLOTTE, SUH!
HE'S RIGHT, PEE-WEE! HEX MAY DESERVE KILLIN', BUT HE'S ALSO THE BEST MAN WITH A SIXGUN WE GOT! TILL WE'RE OUTA THIS MESS, WE'S BEST OFF KEEPIN' 'IM ALIVE!
4

THAT IS CORRECT, SOLOMON! ON THAT BLACK DAY, TWELVE YEARS AGO, MY SON AND SCORES OF HIS COMRADES WERE SLAUGHTERED LIKE CATTLE WHEN JONAH HEX DELIBERATELY LED THEM INTO A UNION MASSACRE FROM WHICH ONLY A HANDFUL ESCAPED ALIVE!
BUT FROM THE ASHES OF THAT FOUL MASSACRE, SOLOMON, HAS RISEN THE FORT CHARLOTTE BRIGADE, SURVIVORS OF THE MASSACRE--ALONG WITH THEIR FRIENDS AND KIN--WHO HAVE SWORN TO WREAK VENGEANCE ON JONAH HEX!
EVEN AS WE SPEAK, SOLOMON, FOUR OF THE BRIGADE'S MOST COURAGEOUS MEMBERS HAVE PURSUED JONAH HEX INTO MEXICO, WHERE WITH THE ALMIGHTY'S BLESSING, THEY--
BEGGIN' YO' PARDON, SUH!
BUT EVER SINCE MASSUH JEB AND MASSUH JONAH BE JUST BOYS PLAYIN' TOGETHER, SUH, YOU AN' ME HAS ALWAYS KNOWN JONAH HEX, AND THAT HE BE A BRAVE MAN, AN' NEVER COWARDLY!
PERHAPS JONAH HEX IS NOT A COWARD, SOLOMON!
BUT HE IS A TRAITOR! HE--
AN' JONAH HEX ALLUZ SAY, MASSUH TURNBULL, THAT THE FORT CHARLOTTE MASSACRE BE AN ACCIDENT, SUH! THAT HE NEVER--
OF COURSE HE SAYS THAT! WHAT ON EARTH DO YOU EXPECT HIM TO SAY?

YOU DON'T ACTUALLY BELIEVE THOSE HORRENDOUS LIES OF HIS, DO YOU, SOLOMON?
A-AH DON'T KNOW, SUH!
YOU'RE A GOOD MAN, SOLOMON! YOU ARE THE FINEST BLACK MAN IT HAS EVER BEEN MY HONOR TO KNOW! BUT YOU ARE A NAIVE MAN, IF ON THE BASIS OF ALL THE EVIDENCE, YOU CAN STILL BELIEVE IN JONAH HEX'S INNOCENCE!
NOW PLEASE, SOLOMON! EXCUSE ME FOR A FEW MOMENTS! ON THIS DAY, ON THIS BLEAK DAY... I WANT TO SPEND A FEW MOMENTS ALONE WITH MY SON!
YASSUH!
MEANWHILE...
C'MON, MICAH! WHUT'RE WE WAITIN' FER? LET'S KILL HEX NOW AN' BE DONE WITH IT!
YOU KNOW AS WELL AS AH DO THET WE VOTED ON THIS LAST NIGHT, PEE-WEE, AN' THE VOTE WUZ NO! EL PAPAGAYO AN' HIS BANDIDOS COULD HIT US AGAIN AT ANY TIME!
AH'VE TAKEN HEX'S GUNS AWAY FROM 'IM, BUT UNTIL WE'S SAFELY ACROSS THE RIO GRANDE, WE'RE KEEPIN' HEX ALIVE!
GET THE HIC LEAD OUT, HEX! WE'S HIC MOVIN' OUT!
6

SOON...
JUST WHUT'S YORE STAKE IN ALL THIS, BOY? ME'N YORE PARDNERS HERE, WE ALL FOUGHT IN THE 7TH CAVALRY T'GETHER DURIN' THE WAR! THEY MAY HAVE THEIR FACTS ALL WRONG 'BOUT WHUT HAPPENED AT FORT CHARLOTTE, BUT AT LEAST THEY GOT SOME BITTER MEMORIES TUH HELP 'EM KEEP THEIR GRUDGE ALIVE!
BUT YOU, WHY WHEN APPOMATTOX HAPPENED, YOU WUZN'T HARDLY MORE'N SEVEN OR EIGHT YEARS OLD, WHICH IS PROB'LY WHY THET THAR UNIFORM FITS YOU LIKE A--
SHUT YORE MOUTH, YOU YANKEE PIG! AH GOT AS MUCH RIGHT TUH WEAR THIS UNIFORM AS ANY MAN!
MEBBE AH WUZN'T OLD ENOUGH TUH BE AT FORT CHARLOTTE WHEN YOU JUDAS-GOATED ALL THEM GOOD MEN TUH THEIR DOOM, BUT MUH PAW WUZ! HE DIED THAR ON ACCOUNTA YOU!
AN' EVER SINCE AH WUZ KNEE HIGH, AH SWORE AH'D AVENGE HIS DEATH BY HELPIN' THE MEN HE RODE WI'F PUT YOU IN YORE GRAVE!
NOW YOU LISTEN TUH ME, SONNY! AH AIN'T 'SPECTIN' YOU TUH BELIEVE THE TRUTH, BUT AH'M GONNA TELL IT TO YUH ANYWAY!
AH NEVER BETRAYED THEM MEN AT FORT CHARLOTTE! THE UNION COMMANDER THAR TRICKED US ALL INTUH TRYIN' AN ESCAPE SO'S HE COULD HAVE A GOOD EXCUSE FER GUNNIN' US ALL DOWN!* NOW MUH VERSION OF WHUT HAPPENED MAY NOT BE SPICY ENOUGH FER YORE LITTLE BOY'S TASTES--
*SEE JONAH HEX #35.--ED.
--BUT IT'S STILL THE--
PTOO!
WHU--!?
WHY, YOU GRIMY-FACED LITTLE--
LEGGO THE KID, HEX!
7

LEGGO THE KID OR AH'LL...
MICAH! THET FEATHER! GRAB SHENANDOAH! MAKE HIM GET AWAY FROM THET--
FEATHER? WHUT FEATHER?
OUT WITH IT, HEX! WHUT IN TARNATION'RE YOU--
FEATHER? HERE'S THE HIC FEATHER!
LOOKS LIKE A HIC LI'L RED PARROT'S--
HUH--!?!
SHENANDOAH! NO--!!
GHAAAAAA
8

A-A JUNGLE PIT-TRAP! THEM MEXICANS HAS WENT AN' BUTCHERED SHENANDOAH IN A --
WHU--!? MY RIFLE!
YUH BLASTED IDIOTS! WHUT'S THE MATTER WI'F YUH? HAS THE BLASTED SUN PUT Y'ALL TUH SLEEP?
UNNGH!
AAAAGH!
KPOW KPOW KPOW
KEEL THE GRINGOS!
SLIT THE THROATS OF THE YANKEE PIGS!
HUH--!?
WHU--!?
CLICK!
BLAST YOU, PEE-WEE! AIN'T YOU EVEN GOT BRAINS ENOUGH TUH LOAD UP YORE RIFLE WI'F MORE'N THREE CURSED SHELLS?
YANKEE!? AH'LL SHOW YUH WHO'S A YANKEE, YOU SONUVAGUN!
WHOK!
UNNHHH!

SAY YOUR PRAYERS, LEETLE GRINGO!
GASP!
I WEEL--
AAGGHH!
AAAHHH!
THUK!
BDAM BDAM
YAAAHH!
MICAH!
QUE!?*
SO YOU WANTA KNOW "WHAT," EH?
*WHAT!?
UNNGHH!
THUG!
BDAM
MICAH! ARE YOU--
NO GOOD! HE'S DEAD!
10

BDAM
BDAM
WELL, THESE HERE MEXICANS AIN'T GONNA BE SCARFIN' DOWN NO MORE TORTILLAS FER BREAKFAST, THET'S FER DARN CERTAIN!
M-MR. HEX! WHUTEVER YOU MAY'VE DID AT FORT CHARLOTTE, AH... AH WANT YUH TUH KNOW AH'M GRATEFUL TO YUH FER SAVIN' MUH LIFE A FEW SECONDS AGO.
YOU DON'T GOTTA BE GRATEFUL TUH HIM, KID! WHUTEVER HEX DONE, HE DONE TUH SAVE HIS OWN SKIN--
--'CAUSE HE KNOWS AS WELL AS AH DO THET IN ORDER FER HIM TUH GET CLEAR'A THEM BANDIDOS, HE NEEDS US AS MUCH AS WE NEED HIM!
SO YOU GET THIS STRAIGHT, HEX! YOU GET IT REAL STRAIGHT! AH'M GONNA LET YOU STAY ALIVE JUST TILL WE CROSS THET RIO GRANDE RIVER, AN' THEN AH'M GONNA KILL YUH MUHSELF!
PAPAGAYO! LOOK! JONAH HEX AND TWO OF HIS GRINGO COMPADRES* ARE ESCAPING! IN JUST A FEW HOURS MORE THEY WEEL REACH THE RIVER AND ESCAPE US FOR GOOD!
NO, EMILIO! THEY WEEL NOT ESCAPE US! FOR, AS ALWAYS, EL PAPAGAYO IS HAVING A MUCHO FINE PLAN! RIGHT, PEPITO?
SQUAWWK!
*COMPANIONS.

AND SO, HOURS LATER, AS THE SUN SETS...
WELL THAR SHE IS, HEX! SOON'S WE'S CROSSED THE RIVER ON THET THAR FERRY-BOAT, YORE LICENSE ON STAYIN' ALIVE IS GONNA HAVE PLUMB RUN OUT!
THET'S A TRUE FACT, AIN'T IT, TIMMY BOY?
Y-YESSIR!
ONLY REASON AH KEPT YOU ALIVE THIS LONG, HEX, WUZ AH FIGGERED WE MIGHT HAVE SOME MORE RUN-INS WI'F THEM MEXICAN FRIENDS'A YORES!
BUT HERE WE BEEN RIDIN' ALL DAY, AN' WE AIN'T SEEN HIDE NOR...
HEY! WHAR IN TARNATION ARE THE TWO OLD COOTS WHO RUN THIS FERRY?
HOW IN BLAZES'RE WE S'POSED TUH GET ACROSS THE RIVER IF'N THEY AIN'T AROUN' TUH FERRY US?
HELLOOO! IS ANYBODY TUH HOME?
12

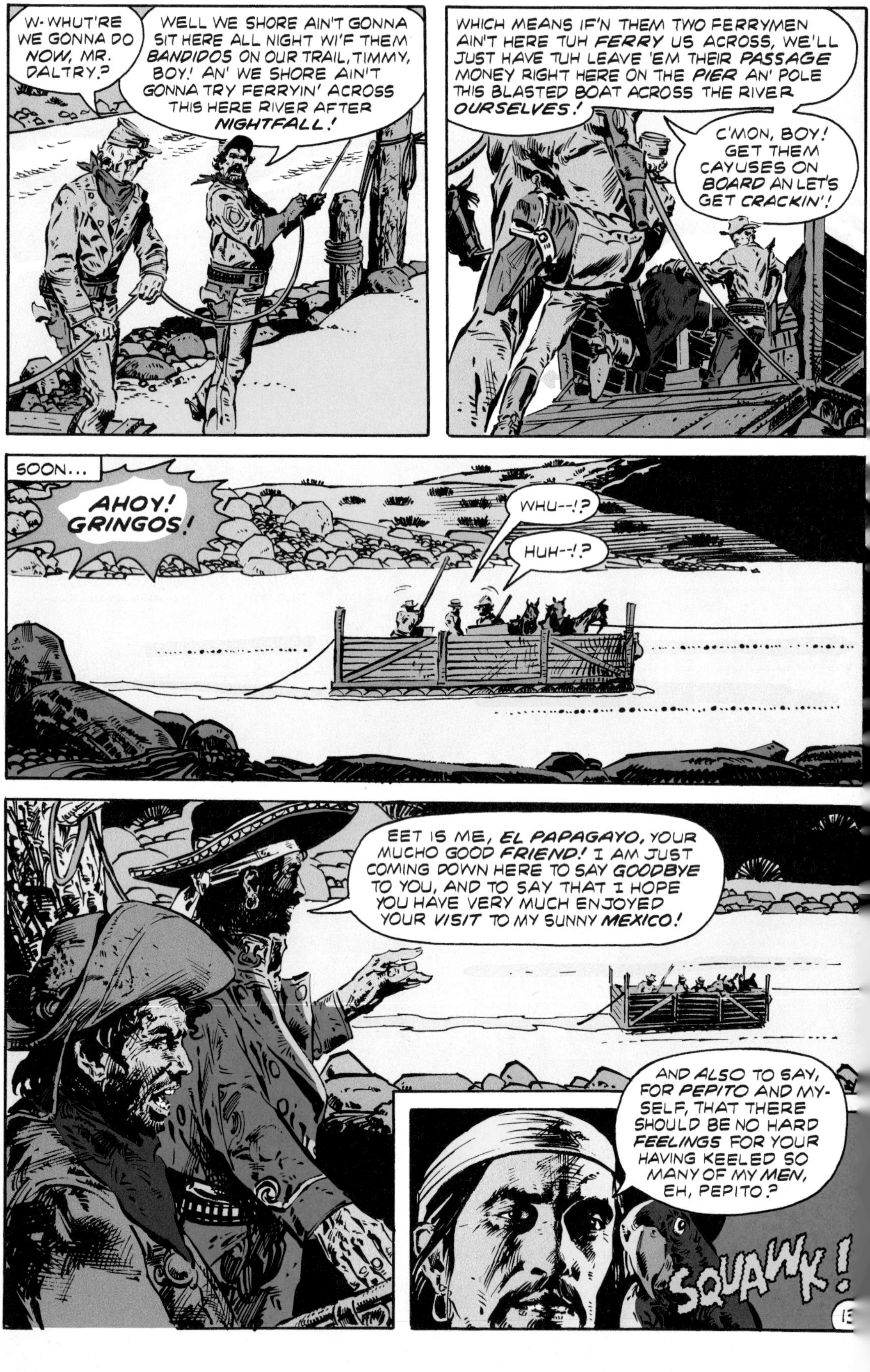
W-WHUT'RE WE GONNA DO NOW, MR. DALTRY?
WELL WE SHORE AIN'T GONNA SIT HERE ALL NIGHT WI'F THEM BANDIDOS ON OUR TRAIL, TIMMY, BOY! AN' WE SHORE AIN'T GONNA TRY FERRYIN' ACROSS THIS HERE RIVER AFTER NIGHTFALL!
WHICH MEANS IF'N THEM TWO FERRYMEN AIN'T HERE TUH FERRY US ACROSS, WE'LL JUST HAVE TUH LEAVE 'EM THEIR PASSAGE MONEY RIGHT HERE ON THE PIER AN' POLE THIS BLASTED BOAT ACROSS THE RIVER OURSELVES!
C'MON, BOY! GET THEM CAYUSES ON BOARD AN LET'S GET CRACKIN'!
SOON...
AHOY! GRINGOS!
WHU--!?
HUH--!?
EET IS ME, EL PAPAGAYO, YOUR MUCHO GOOD FRIEND! I AM JUST COMING DOWN HERE TO SAY GOODBYE TO YOU, AND TO SAY THAT I HOPE YOU HAVE VERY MUCH ENJOYED YOUR VISIT TO MY SUNNY MEXICO!
AND ALSO TO SAY, FOR PEPITO AND MYSELF, THAT THERE SHOULD BE NO HARD FEELINGS FOR YOUR HAVING KEELED SO MANY OF MY MEN, EH, PEPITO?
SQUAWK!
13

AND EMILIO, AND ALL MY OTHER BANDIDOS, THEY WEESH FOR ME TO SAY VAYA CON DIOS,* AND WE ARE ALL HOPING YOU COME BACK TO VISIT US VERY, VERY SOON!
HEX! BLAST IT, MAN, PICK UP THET FERRY POLE! WHUT IN TARNATION DO YOU THINK YO'RE...
WHUT'S IT LOOK LIKE AH'M DOIN', YOU MORON? AH'M RUMMAGIN' THROUGH ALL THESE CRATES WHUT'RE PILED ON HERE, LOOKIN' FER THE--
*GO WITH GOD.
-- DYNAMITE--!
GASP Q-QUICK, HEX! HEAVE IT OFFA HERE!
NO TIME FER THAT! BESIDES, THAR AIN'T NO TELLIN' HOW MUCH MORE OF IT THEY PLANTED ON HERE!
NOW JUMP, BOTH OF YUH! A'FORE THIS WHOLE FLOATIN' MATCH-BOX WE'S RIDIN' ON GOES--
BOOOOOOM!
14

H-HEX! SAVE ME! GLUB! P-PLEASE! AH CAIN'T GLUB SWIM!
ALL RIGHT, BOY! HANG ON! AH GOTCHA!
NOW, C'MON, BOY! DON'T GO TUH SLEEP ON ME! START FROG-KICKIN' WITH THEM LEGS AN' SEE IF'N YOU CAIN'T HELP GIVE THIS HERE PARTNERSHIP OF OURS A LITTLE EXTRA PADDLEWHEEL POWER!
WITH POWERFUL STROKES, JONAH SLICES HIS WAY THROUGH THE SURGING, ANGRY CURRENT. AND SOON...
OKAY, BOY! Y'ALL KIN STOP GASP KICKIN' NOW! 'CAUSE WE'S MADE IT!
WE'S FINALLY--
YEAH, HEX! WE'S MADE IT, ALL RIGHT!
BUT THIS IS WHAR THE LINE ENDS, HEX! THIS IS WHAR AH PAY YOU BACK FER THE EVIL DEED YOU DONE THET BLACK DAY AT FORT CHARLOTTE!
N-NO, MR. DALTRY! DON'T DO IT! I-IT AIN'T FAIR!
15

IT AIN'T FAIR TUH SHOOT 'IM AFTER ALL HE--
FAIR? NOW HOW IN BLAZES WOULD YOU BE KNOWIN' WHUT'S FAIR, BOY? WHY, YOU WUZN'T HARDLY EVEN WET BEHIND THE EARS WHEN THIS YANKEE PIG TRAITOR WENT AN' BETRAYED ALL THEM GOOD MEN AT FORT CHARLOTTE!
NOW AH'LL ADMIT AH AIN'T WITHOUT A TOUCH OF ADMIRATION FER YOU, HEX! AH'LL ADMIT TO THET! BUT A VOW'S A VOW, HEX! AN' THET DAY AT FORT CHARLOTTE--
--AH SWORE THET--
NO, MR. DALTRY! IT AIN'T FAIR TUH KILL 'IM NOW! YOU LEAVE HIM ALONE!
HUNH--!?!
YOU LEAVE 'IM ALONE, AN' LET 'IM RIDE AWAY FROM HERE A FREE MAN, OR SO HELP ME AH'M--
WHY YOU PIMPLY-FACED LITTLE WHELP! YO'RE A TRAITOR, TOO!
KPOW
TIM--!!
UNNGH!
A TRAITOR TUH ME, A TRAITOR TUH YORE POOR DEAD PAW, A TRAITOR TUH EVERY BRAVE CONFEDERATE IN THE FORT CHARLOTTE BRIGADE!
THET'S ENOUGH MOUTH OUTA YOU NOW, HEX!
16

NOW YO'RE-- AAGGHH!!
KPOW
A-AH COULDN'T JUST LET 'IM GO AN' KILL YUH, MR. HEX! N-NOT AFTER ALL THE BRAVE THINGS YUH DONE!
WHUTEVER YOU DONE THET DAY AT FORT CHARLOTTE, AH...AH FORGIVE YUH! AN' MUH PAW...IF MUH PAW WUZ ALIVE TO-DAY, AH KNOW HE'D FORGIVE YUH, TOO!
WHEN AH GET BACK HOME TUH VIRGINIA, AH'M GONNA TELL 'EM ALL WHUT KINDA MAN YOU REALLY ARE, MR. HEX! AN' MEBBE WHEN AH'M THROUGH TELLIN' 'EM, THEY WON'T WANT TUH...
SHH! STAY QUIET, BOY!
TRY AN'--
...TUH.....
DEAR LORD, WHUTEVER IS THAR ABOUT LIFE THET MAKES DARNED NEAR EVERYTHIN' TURN OUT SO SAD?
END?

WE'D ALL BE MILLIONAIRES

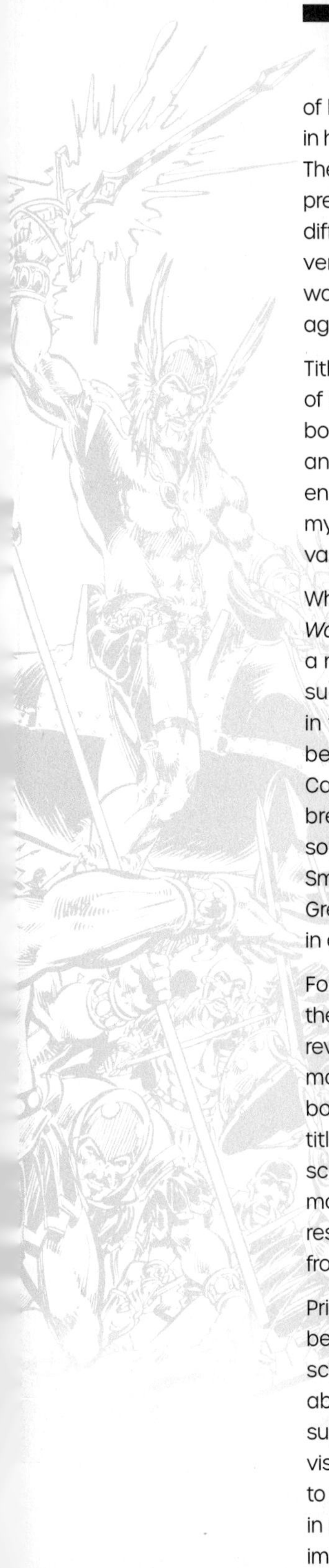

"If we could accurately predict trends, we'd all be millionaires."

This has been the observation of comic book publishers and editors throughout the history of the medium. All have wanted to produce material that sells, but achieving that goal has always involved a lot of blind chance. Superman was just lucky. There was no way anyone involved in his creation and eventual publication could have been certain of his success. The same was true with every other character or genre that comics publishers presented to their public. Would readers buy a new concept? Would they buy a different take on an established popular hit? Would they accept a comic book version of their favorite novel, movie, or television show? There was only one way to find out for sure: run it up the flagpole and see who saluted it. Throw it against the wall and see if it stuck. Publish it and see if it sold.

Titles such as *Warlord*, *Jonah Hex*, and *Time Warp* were all perfect examples of this thinking. They represented just some of the genres presented in comic books—specifically, sword and sorcery, western and frontier, and science fiction and fantasy. The complete list of comics' diverse variety of genres is nearly endless; other notable categories include superheroes, war, supernatural and mystery, crime and detective, humor and animated, romance, and infinite variations and combinations thereof.

Why did some particular books capture an audience at a particular time? Take *Warlord*, for example. The sword and sorcery prose genre found itself enjoying a new surge of popularity in the 1960s following the rediscovery of characters such as Robert E. Howard's Conan the Barbarian, which was first published in the 1930s in the pulp magazine *Weird Tales*. Beginning in 1966, Ace Books began reprinting the Conan stories—expanded on by writers L. Sprague de Camp, Lin Carter, and Björn Nyberg—in new paperback collections that featured breathtaking new cover paintings by Frank Frazetta. Many other sword and sorcery heroes followed, and when writer Roy Thomas and artist Barry Windsor-Smith adapted Conan for Marvel in 1970, the genre was rekindled in comics. Mike Grell's *Warlord* was DC's third foray into this realm (the feature initially appeared in a tryout title, *1st Issue Special* #8), but it proved to be its most long lasting.

For many years, science fiction and fantasy titles held their own alongside the superheroes and the supernatural and mystery books. (In the case of the revered E.C. Comics series *Weird Science* and *Weird Fantasy*, they were actually more popular among their creators than their readers, who preferred horror books like *Tales from the Crypt*.) DC's claims to science fiction fame were the titles *Strange Adventures* and *Mystery in Space*. Both were edited by former science fiction literary agent Julius Schwartz, who peppered his books with as many scientific facts as possible. The *Time Warp* stories were an attempt to resuscitate this love for science fiction in comics, but they also moved away from the more positive scientific stories toward darker, psychological tales.

Printed science fiction, whether gadget based or emotion based, has, ironically, become its own worst enemy, because it often inspired its readers to become scientists and researchers, and they, in turn, made the concepts they'd read about into reality—and rendered the fiction that inspired them obsolete. The super-technology of yesterday's stories is now, literally, at our fingertips. We've visited the moon. Our robots have landed on other planets. We're actually ready to meet aliens (and many believe we already have). The astounding advances in movie special effects have allowed the film industry to dazzle our eyes with imagery that brings even the most implausible scientific concepts to life. Science fiction on the printed page—text and comics alike—now struggles to keep up.

Westerns had their heyday on the silver screen in the 1940s with heroes such as Gene Autry, Roy Rogers, and Hopalong Cassidy, and their stars began to fade as time passed and interest in cowboy films gave way to other genres. However, when the new medium of television began expanding at an astonishing rate in the 1950s, networks were hungry for programming, and the old westerns provided ready-made content that easily edited down to 30- or 60-minute formats. As a result, westerns enjoyed a TV-fueled resurgence in popularity that quickly spilled over into comics.

Of course, western and frontier characters had been in comic books from the beginning. As superheroes' popularity declined in the early '50s, often it was the western heroes who took their places. *All-Star Comics* #57, appearing near the end of 1950, was the final adventure of the Justice Society of America; issue #58 unceremoniously became *All-Star Western*. A year earlier, frontier hero Tomahawk had pushed Robin off the cover of *Star Spangled Comics*, and before that the western version of Johnny Thunder had nudged Green Lantern off his cover spot in *All-American Comics* (which evolved into *All-American Western*). The Silver Age of comics began just a few years later, though, and superheroes soon reclaimed their top-dog status. By the time the Justice League debuted in *The Brave and the Bold* #28, there were only two or three western and frontier titles left.

Jonah Hex was born in a restart of *All-Star Western* in the 1970s, aided by borrowing elements from the supernatural and mystery realms. However, his relevance, like that of his Old West predecessors, slowly waned as time and technology moved inexorably forward.

Why does one genre thrive and another fail? Why does a successful genre fade into obscurity? Why is something popular today and forgotten tomorrow? Why do some return while others are lost forever? The truth is, trends always come and go. Ever since the end of World War II, comic books have grappled with a constantly fluctuating array of interfering forces—everything from censorship to television, from distribution changes to the economy, from population shift to the weather. Fortunately, many of the bygone favorites of yesterday have been preserved, ready to be enjoyed again or to be rediscovered by a new generation.

Warlord and *Jonah Hex* joined *Time Warp* on the turned pages of fondly remembered history. Why? Some reasons are hinted at here, but these could be debated endlessly. After all, if we could accurately predict trends, we'd all be millionaires.

Jack C. Harris
October 2019

Jack C. Harris is a former editor and writer for DC Comics. Beginning his career as one of the legendary "Woodchuck" assistant editors in the mid-1970s, he oversaw such classic titles as Green Lantern, World's Finest Comics, Legion of Super-Heroes, *and* House of Mystery, *as well as cult classics such as Mike Grell's* Warlord *and Steve Ditko's* Shade, The Changing Man. *He was also the original editor of Tony Isabella's* Black Lightning *and Gerry Conway's* Firestorm. *As a writer, Harris penned the adventures of, among others, Wonder Woman, Batgirl, Supergirl, Black Canary, Robin, Adam Strange, Isis, Kamandi, and Gravedigger. He created the new version of the Ray and authored the graphic novel* Batman: Castle of the Bat, *illustrated by Bo Hampton. Harris also did work for Marvel, Archie, Dark Horse, and other comics publishers. He is a retired professor from the School of Visual Arts in New York, where he taught a course on writing for comics.*

ENDINGS AND BEGINNINGS

Some other interesting changes emerged in the early 1980s as the marketplace shifted. The long-running television cartoon *Super Friends* ended its run, as did its companion comic book of the same name, itself the last survivor of a group of TV tie-ins launched in the previous decade. *Blackhawk*, a slightly unclassifiable title (was it a war comic? an adventure series? for one very unfortunate moment, a superhero mag?) that had nonetheless persevered since the Golden Age of Comics with only short interruptions, had its last flight. And Slam Bradley, a DC star from the days before Superman, popped up for one last round.

Another holdover from a bygone age, the *Superman* newspaper strip (actually a revival of the original classic series, originally launched with the title *The World's Greatest Superheroes*) would sputter out. Adventure strips just weren't practical in the tiny spaces newspapers were devoting to their remaining comics, and it was a devilishly hard form for comic book writers to adapt to as well.

Occasional toy tie-ins had been a staple of the DC line since the 1960s, but the 1980s newcomer *Masters of the Universe* got a very special treatment—a launch comic bound into several DC titles as a supplement, followed by tiny

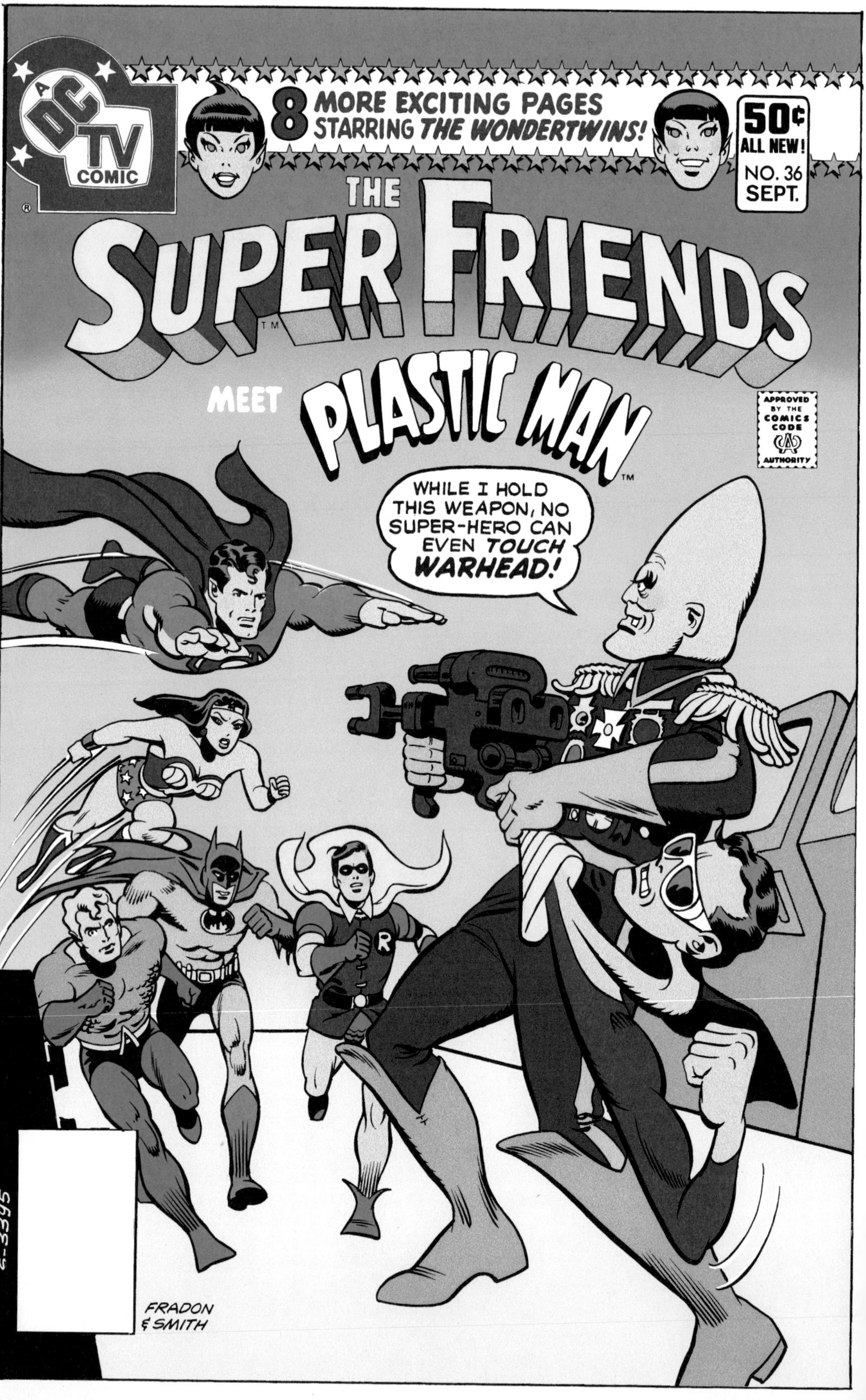
A DC TV COMIC
8 MORE EXCITING PAGES STARRING THE WONDERTWINS!
50¢ ALL NEW!
NO. 36 SEPT.
THE SUPER FRIENDS
MEET PLASTIC MAN
APPROVED BY THE COMICS CODE AUTHORITY
WHILE I HOLD THIS WEAPON, NO SUPER-HERO CAN EVEN TOUCH WARHEAD!
FRADON & SMITH
G-3395

ZAN AND JAYNA, ALIEN TEEN-AGERS FROM THE PLANET EXOR, HAVE COME TO EARTH, WHERE THEY ARE BEING TRAINED IN THE USE OF THEIR POWERS BY THE FIVE GREAT HEROES: SUPERMAN, WONDER WOMAN, BATMAN, ROBIN AND AQUAMAN--
THE SUPER FRIENDS
THAT'S OUR SUSPECT, PLASTIC MAN-- THE ONE WE BELIEVE HAS BEEN ROBBING MILITARY BASES AND WAREHOUSES OF VALUABLE ARMAMENTS!
HIS NAME IS RUPERT C. NALL-- BUT HE'S BETTER KNOWN AS...
WARHEAD!
WHERE DO WE GO TO NAB HIM, CHIEF BRANNER?
HEY, WAIT A MINUTE! THIS IS SUPER FRIENDS, NOT ADVENTURE COMICS! SO WHAT ARE PLASTIC MAN, HIS PAL WOOZY WINKS, AND CHIEF BRANNER OF THE NATIONAL BUREAU OF INVESTIGATION DOING HERE?
LOOKS VERY THREATENIN' TO ME!
S-3408
PATIENCE... THE SUPER FRIENDS WILL BE ALONG IN TIME TO TEAM UP WITH PLASTIC MAN WHEN...
WARHEAD STRIKES AT GOTHAM
WRITER: E. NELSON BRIDWELL
PENCILLER: RAMONA FRADON
INKER: VINCE COLLETTA
LETTERER: MILT SNAPINN
COLORIST: JERRY SERPE
EDITOR: JULIUS SCHWARTZ

WE BELIEVE HE'LL STRIKE EITHER AT THE GOTHAM CITY ARMORY, THE GOTHAM NAVAL BASE, GOTHAM AIR BASE, OR THE GOTHAM DIVISION OF S.T.A.R.* LABS!
GOTHAM! THEN WHY NOT LEAVE THIS JOB TO THE BATMAN?
*SCIENTIFIC AND TECHNOLOGICAL ADVANCED RESEARCH.
FOR ONE THING, HE ISN'T AN N.B.I. AGENT!
AND FOR ANOTHER, THE BATMAN HASN'T BEEN SEEN IN GOTHAM FOR THE PAST WEEK. HE MUST BE ON SOME MISSION OF...
OH, WHY DO I BOTHER TO TELL YOU? YOU DON'T EVEN BELONG HERE, WINKS!
IZZAT SO?
WHEN PLAS AND I CATCH THAT WARHEAD CREEP, YOU'LL BE BEGGIN' ME TO JOIN THE N.B.I.!
UH--NO DICE, WOOZY!
STOP
I'M AFRAID YOU WON'T BE ALONG ON THIS JOB!
PLAS! YOU CAN'T LEAVE ME BEHIND!
BUT--
YOU NEED ME!
--IF YOU GO WITH ME, WHO'LL BE LEFT TO PROTECT THIS CITY AGAINST THE FORCES OF EVIL?
YEAH--YOU'RE RIGHT! I CAN'T DESERT THE PEOPLE WHO DEPEND ON ME!
THAT'S THE SPIRIT, WOOZY!
-WHEW- NOW AT LEAST WOOZY WON'T BE MESSING UP MY MISSION IN GOTHAM!
ONAL BU AU OF
I ONLY HOPE HE DOESN'T MESS THINGS UP TOO BADLY HERE!
2

AT THIS POINT, LET'S EAVESDROP ON OUR VILLAIN-- WARHEAD HIMSELF!
OUR PLANS ARE COMPLETED FOR THE RAID ON THE GOTHAM ARMORY!
GOSH, BOSS-- AIN'T WE GOT ENOUGH WEAPONS YET?
EXPLOSIVES
DANGER
EXPLOSIVES
EXPLOSIVES
DANGER
NO, YOU IDIOT! I WON'T STOP TILL MY CRIMINAL ORGANIZATION IS THE BEST-ARMED FORCE IN THE WORLD!
OW!
WHATTA YA GONNA DO--CHALLENGE THE U.S. AN' RUSSIA TO A SHOWDOWN?
YOU HAVE NO IMAGINATION--NO SUPREME AMBITION! WITH MY ARMS STOCKPILE, THERE'S NOT A GANG THAT WON'T THROW IN WITH ME--
--INCLUDING THE MOB, AND EVERY REVOLUTIONARY AND TERRORIST GROUP ON EARTH!
BUT WHAT IF THE SUPER-HEROES COME AFTER US?
YES, THAT IS A PROBLEM! THE JUSTICE LEAGUE ALONE HAS OVER A DOZEN MEMBERS,,,
,,,NOT TO MENTION THE TEEN TITANS!
UH,,, DIDN'T THE TEEN TITANS DISBAND?
THAT'S WHY I TOLD YOU NOT TO MENTION THEM!
OUR FINAL CAPER HERE WILL GET US THE WEAPON TO USE AGAINST THE SUPER-GUYS! BUT NOW IT'S TIME TO TAKE THE ARMORY!
MATCHES, YOU STAY HERE WITH THE RESERVES!
GOTCHA, BOSS!
EXPLOSIVES
3

AND IN A CERTAIN UNDERWORLD HAUNT...
HULLY CHEE! CAN THAT BE WHO I THINK IT IS?
GIN 1.00
IT IS! "EEL" O'BRIAN! I AIN'T SEEN OR HEARD OF YA IN YEARS! I THOUGHT YA WAS DEAD!
HI, SCRAPPY! HOW'S TRICKS?
OH, FINE--TWO ON THE ROCKS, SADIE--BUT WHERE YA BEEN, EEL?
NO CREDIT
AROUND! BANGLADESH, NICARAGUA, UGANDA, IRAN...
HEY... ALL THEM PLACES HAD REVOLUTIONS! YA DON'T MEAN...
LONG AS I'M PAID, IT DON'T MATTER WHO I FIGHT FOR!
SAY, IT'S FUNNY YOU SHOWIN' UP TODAY, EEL! THERE'S A GUY LOOKIN' FOR MEN WHO KNOW HOW TO HANDLE WAR WEAPONS!
Y'DON'T SAY! TELL ME MORE!
I CAN'T--YET! I'LL GET THE WORD OUT YOU'RE IN TOWN! MEANWHILE... WATCH THE NEWS AND SEE WHAT HAPPENS AT THE ARMORY TONIGHT!
THE ARMORY, YOU SAY?
YEAH--I'LL WANTA GET THE DETAILS!
4

LATER, AT THE ARMORY, AS WARHEAD'S GANG STRIKES...
BARAAMMMM
THAT'S IT, MEN! BLAST 'ER OPEN!
OKAY, GANG! THE HARDWARE IS OURS FOR THE TAKING!
YOU'VE ALL GOT YOUR ASSIGNMENTS!
CAN'T SEEM TO GET THIS TANK'S HATCH OPEN!
UUUHH!
CUT IT OUT! THAT TICKLES!
YIPE!! A TALKING TANK?!
TANK, MY SIDE-ARMS! THAT'S PLASTIC MAN!
HOW RIGHT YOU ARE, WARHEAD! AND YOU'RE MY PRISONER--!
5

AT THAT CRITICAL MOMENT...
OW-OOO... MY HEAD!
WHAT--?
PLASTIC MAN!? NEVER EXPECTED TO FIND YOU HERE!
I GOT A TIP ABOUT THIS ROBBERY AND...
OOO! SO DID I, ROBIN! BUT I THOUGHT YOU WERE HANGING AROUND HUDSON UNIVERSITY THESE DAYS!
RETREAT, MEN-- BEFORE HE RECOVERS!
I--UH--THOUGHT I'D BE NEEDED HERE-- WITH THE BATMAN OUT OF TOWN!
AND I'M WORKING ON THE CASE FOR THE N.B.I.!
HMM... WARHEAD AND COMPANY BEAT IT OUT OF HERE!
IT'LL TAKE ME A WHILE TO GET MYSELF BACK INTO SHAPE!
I'LL STICK AROUND TILL YOU DO!
AND TO THINK I GOT RID OF WOOZY SO HE WOULDN'T BOLLIX THINGS UP!
6

IN CASE YOU DON'T KNOW, PLASTIC MAN HAS BEEN USING A SECRET IDENTITY, CHANGING HIS FEATURES TO BECOME...
EEL! YOU HEARD ABOUT--
--THE WAY THAT GANG YOU WERE TOUTING ME ON BOTCHED THE JOB? YEAH! I AIN'T SO SURE I WANTA TIE UP WITH 'EM!
WHO COULD FIGURE THEM SUPER-CHARACTERS WOULD TURN UP?
BUT I HEAR WARHEAD'S GOT THE BIGGEST JOB EVER PLANNED FOR THE NAVY YARD TOMORROW!
PLANNIN' EM IS ONE THING--PULLIN' 'EM OFF IS ANOTHER!
SOON AFTER, IN A DINGY HOTEL ROOM...
HOPEFULLY, THERE'LL BE NO ROBIN TO GET IN MY WAY THIS TIME!
AND THE FOLLOWING DAY, AT THE GOTHAM NAVY YARD...
I NEVER THOUGHT WE'D EVER BE STEALIN' SOME-THIN' FROM A NAVY YARD!
THEY GOT A NEW PROTOTYPE WE'RE GONNA HEIST --
"--A FULL-SIZED ATOMIC SUBMARINE, LOADED WITH ATOMIC MISSILES!"
7

HOW COME NO GUARDS? THEY MUSTA HEARD US BLASTIN' THROUGH THE FENCE!
I GUESS THEY DECIDED IT WASN'T SMART OR SAFE TO FIGHT US!
THERE'S THE SUB! GET READY TO BOARD HER!
THE MISSILE'S COLORED KINDA FUNNY, AIN'T IT?
OH, I DON'T KNOW! I KIND OF LIKE RED AND YELLOW!
YIPES! THAT PLASTIC PEST AGAIN!
ONCE MORE, AT THAT CRUCIAL MOMENT...
HEY!
WHAT'S GOT HOLD OF MY ARM?
NOW TO NAB-- GREAT WAVES!
8

OH, OH! ANOTHER GOOF-UP!
YEOWWW!
I WAS JUST ABOUT TO CAPTURE THEM WITH MY LASSO WHEN YOU GOT IN MY WAY!
I GOT IN YOUR WAY?
OOHH!
OH, ALL RIGHT-- I SUPPOSE WE ACTUALLY FOULED UP EACH OTHER!
--JUST LONG ENOUGH FOR THE GANG TO ESCAPE!
THAT'S THE BAD NEWS! THE GOOD NEWS IS THAT THIS MAKES TWO JOBS IN A ROW THEY'VE FAILED TO GET WHAT THEY WERE AFTER!
SOON AFTER, THE EEL CONTACTS SCRAPPY AGAIN...
IT AIN'T I DON'T TRUST YA, EEL, BUT WARHEAD IS MIGHTY TOUGH-- AND HE SAYS NOBODY'S TO TALK ABOUT THE NEXT CAPER TO A LIVIN' SOUL!
ONLY TWO OBJECTIVES LEFT, SO...
OKAY, THEN DON'T MENTION THE AIR BASE ROBBERY!
WHY--UH-- WHAT MAKES YA THINK HE'S HITTIN' THERE?
YOUR FACE, SCRAP! I KNEW IT'D GIVE YOU AWAY IF I GUESSED RIGHT!
AND IF IT HADN'T, I'D HAVE KNOWN THE TARGET WAS S.T.A.R.!
9

THE AIR BASE, THE FOLLOWING DAY...
LAND FAST, MEN! DITCH YOUR HANG-GLIDERS AND SWARM INTO THAT BOMBER! IT'S THE NEWEST LONG-RANGE MODEL!
NO, YOU DON'T! I'M NOT LETTING ANYONE GET AWAY WITH THIS PLANE!
I DON'T SEE ANYTHING THAT LOOKS LIKE IT COULD BE PLASTIC MAN--AND THERE'S NO SIGN OF THEM OTHER HEROES, EITHER!
OKAY! GUN HIM DOWN!
THE SLUGS ONLY BOUNCE OFF HIM! HE MUST BE SUPERMAN!
SUPERMAN? NO WAY! HE AIN'T BUILT ANYTHING LIKE THAT!
BLAM!
BDAM
VRAM
TAKATAKA
RIGHT! BUT MY RUBBERY BODY CAN TAKE ANY SHAPE--AND JUST ABOUT ANYTHING WILL BOUNCE OFF IT!
NO--NO--NOT HIM AGAIN!
AND NOW, BOYS--I'VE GOT YOU COVERED!
10

MUST WE SAY IT AGAIN? AT THIS DECISIVE MOMENT...
WHAT THE SAM HILL?
WHAT A BREAK! A BIG WIND SUDDENLY CAME UP--HITTIN' HIM LIKE A SAIL!
NO TALK-- RETREAT!
GOT YOU, PLASTIC MAN!
SORRY TO HAVE CAUSED YOU THIS TROUBLE!
YOU MEAN THIS IS YOUR DOING, SUPERMAN?
I'M AFRAID SO--JUST AS I LET LOOSE A BLAST OF SUPER-BREATH TO BLOW THEM DOWN, YOU SPRANG UP RIGHT IN THE PATH!
ALL I CAN SAY TO YOU SUPER-FRIENDS IS--
WE'VE GOT TO STOP MEETING LIKE THIS!
THE FOLLOWING DAY, AT WARHEAD'S BASE...
THIS IS HIM, WARHEAD! AN EXPERT WITH WAR WEAPONS!
"EEL" O'BRIAN, EH? HEARD A LOT ABOUT YOU.
LIKEWISE, PAL!
BUT WHAT'S YOUR BIG PLAN, ANYWAY? YOU GONNA SELL THESE THINGS YOU TAKE?
NAW--I'M KEEPING 'EM! I PLAN TO BUILD THE BIGGEST, MOST POWERFUL ARMED FORCE IN THE WORLD!
C'MON--YOU AIN'T ANOTHER OF THEM GUYS WHO ARE OUT TO RULE THE WORLD?
11

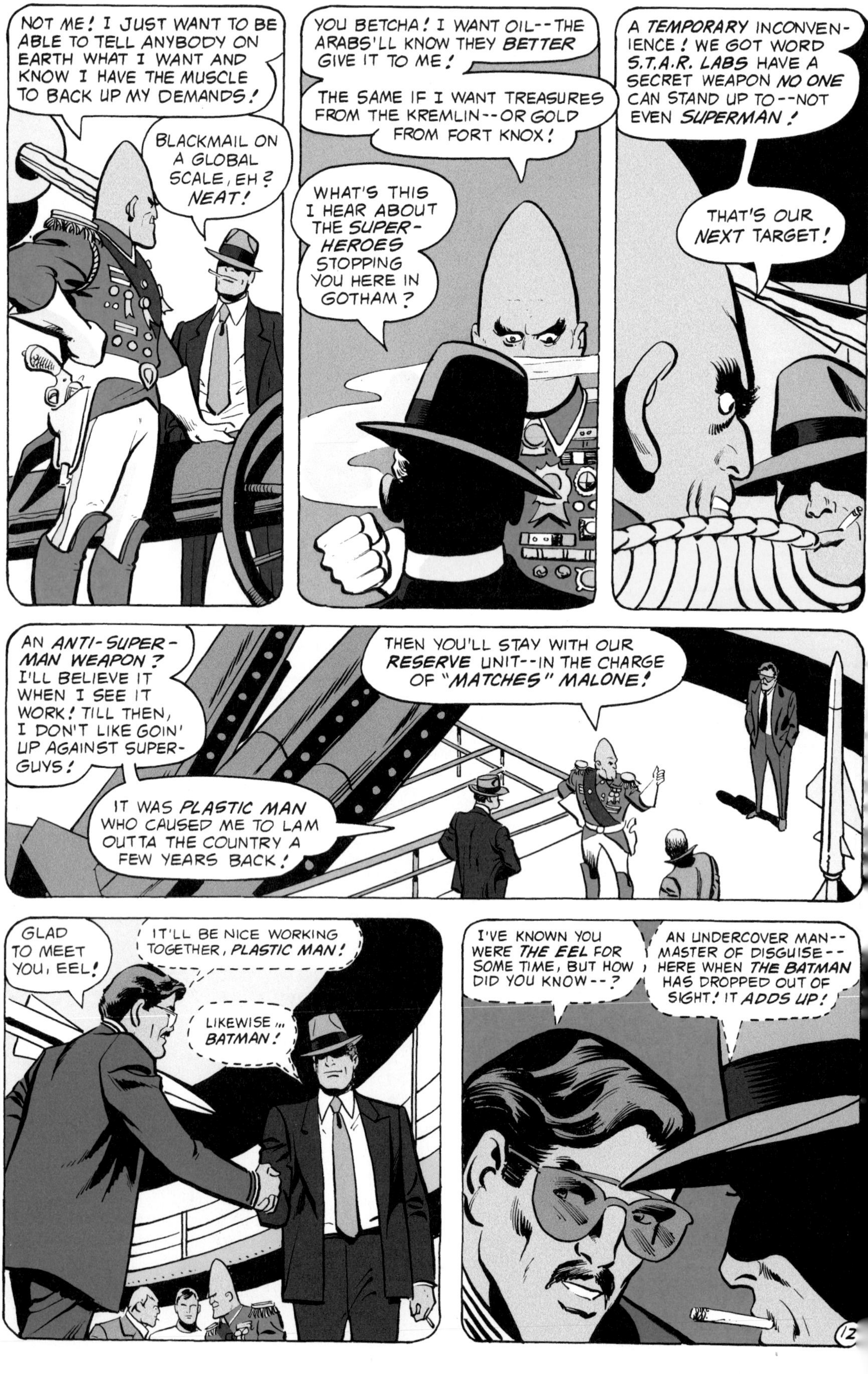

NOT ME! I JUST WANT TO BE ABLE TO TELL ANYBODY ON EARTH WHAT I WANT AND KNOW I HAVE THE MUSCLE TO BACK UP MY DEMANDS!
BLACKMAIL ON A GLOBAL SCALE, EH? NEAT!
YOU BETCHA! I WANT OIL--THE ARABS'LL KNOW THEY BETTER GIVE IT TO ME!
THE SAME IF I WANT TREASURES FROM THE KREMLIN--OR GOLD FROM FORT KNOX!
WHAT'S THIS I HEAR ABOUT THE SUPER-HEROES STOPPING YOU HERE IN GOTHAM?
A TEMPORARY INCONVENIENCE! WE GOT WORD S.T.A.R. LABS HAVE A SECRET WEAPON NO ONE CAN STAND UP TO--NOT EVEN SUPERMAN!
THAT'S OUR NEXT TARGET!
AN ANTI-SUPERMAN WEAPON? I'LL BELIEVE IT WHEN I SEE IT WORK! TILL THEN, I DON'T LIKE GOIN' UP AGAINST SUPER-GUYS!
IT WAS PLASTIC MAN WHO CAUSED ME TO LAM OUTTA THE COUNTRY A FEW YEARS BACK!
THEN YOU'LL STAY WITH OUR RESERVE UNIT--IN THE CHARGE OF "MATCHES" MALONE!
GLAD TO MEET YOU, EEL!
IT'LL BE NICE WORKING TOGETHER, PLASTIC MAN!
LIKEWISE... BATMAN!
I'VE KNOWN YOU WERE THE EEL FOR SOME TIME, BUT HOW DID YOU KNOW--?
AN UNDERCOVER MAN--MASTER OF DISGUISE--HERE WHEN THE BATMAN HAS DROPPED OUT OF SIGHT! IT ADDS UP!
12

AND YOU KNOWING MY IDENTITY -- PLUS THE FACT THAT SOMEONE WAS TIPPING YOUR PALS TO WARHEAD'S JOBS...
NO WONDER YOU'RE A TOP N.B.I. MAN! I THINK WE CAN USE YOUR HELP!
HEY, YOU TWO -- WHAT'S ALL THE GAB ABOUT?
JUST BRIEFING OUR NEW RECRUIT ON WHAT TO DO IN CASE YOU NEED US!
GOOD! WE DON'T WANT ANY SLIP-UPS! WE'RE LEAVING NOW!
AWAIT ORDERS -- 'CAUSE THIS TIME, WERE DEFINITELY GETTING WHAT WE'RE AFTER!
YOU MEAN WHAT YOU'RE ASKING FOR!
EEL -- WAIT IN THE OTHER ROOM TILL I'M READY FOR YOU!
ALL RIGHT, MEN -- FORMATION 6-A!
NOT BAD, BOYS!
NOT BAD?
I'D SAY IT'S PERFECT!
GOOD GRAVY! WHAT IS THAT?
13

STRIKE!
A SWITCH TO COSTUMES AND...
HEY, WHAT--? THE BAT-MAN--AND PLASTIC MAN!
IN PERSON! THESE ROPES WILL HOLD YOU TILL THE POLICE ARRIVE!
THERE WERE TWO OTHERS WHO GOT AWAY. ONE LOOKED LIKE MALONE--DIDN'T RECOGNIZE HIS PAL!
NOW IF WE CAN ONLY BEAT WARHEAD TO THE LABS...
IF YOU DON'T MIND UNORTHODOX TRAVEL, HANG ON--
--AS I SPRING FOR THIS SHORT CUT!
WTAB
AND I THOUGHT WONDER WOMAN'S INVISIBLE PLANE WAS BIZARRE!
FINE WINE
Rose
SOON, AS WARHEAD AND HIS CRIMINAL TROOPS ARRIVE AT S.T.A.R. ...
BADOOOOMM
BLAST OPEN THE PLACE!
14

HIT THE VAULT! IF THOSE HEROES SHOW UP AGAIN, I WANT THAT WEAPON IN MY HANDS!
THAT DOES IT! NOW FOR THE ULTIMATE HERO DESTROYER!
BABABABOOM
THERE IT IS! MADE OF CRYSTAL, JUST LIKE THE REPORTS SAID!
MINE AT LAST! IT WILL MAKE ME INVINCIBLE!
AT THAT VERY INSTANT, OUTSIDE THE VAULT...
BOSS! BRING THAT THING HERE! THERE COME THE SUPER-GUYS!
15

KEEP COOL, MEN! AS LONG AS I HAVE THIS, NO SUPER-HERO CAN GET CLOSE TO ME!
BUT WARHEAD FAILS TO NOTICE A TINY MOSQUITO PERCHED ON THE WEAPON...
FORM OF WATER VAPOR!
ONCE I'VE KILLED SUPERMAN, NO ONE'LL DARE CROSS ME!
READY... AIM...
FIRE!
AND THE MOSQUITO AND WATER VAPOR? WATCH THEIR NEXT CHANGE...
SHAPE OF A SLEET STORM!
FORM OF A FALCON!
16

CAN'T SEE FOR THIS SLEET IN MY EYES!
AND WHEN THE "ONE-MINUTE" WAR IS OVER...
WE PLANTED THE "SECRET WEAPON" STORY TO LURE WARHEAD. AT FIRST, WE SIMPLY PLANNED FOR ZAN TO BE THE WEAPON --
-- BUT WHEN PLASTIC MAN SHOWED UP, IT SEEMED BETTER FOR HIM TO HAVE THE JOB, WHILE ZAN PROVIDED A CRYSTAL COATING!
WELL, THAT WRAPS UP ANOTHER CASE --
-- BUT I'D HAVE DONE IT QUICKER WITHOUT THEIR "HELP"! FROM NOW ON, I'LL STICK WITH WOOZY!
END
NEXT ISSUE:
THE GIRL OF STEEL COMES TO GOTHAM CITY TO TEAM WITH THE SUPER FRIENDS! BUT THE EVIL WEATHER WIZARD STIRS UP "BAD WEATHER FOR SUPERGIRL" ALSO: A SOLO STORY OF IRELAND'S HERO...
JACK O'LANTERN!
ON SALE JULY 24! IT'S A DATE!

DC
FULL-LENGTH NOVEL EXCITEMENT
BLACKHAWK
ALL NEW!
60¢
NO. 258
MAY
APPROVED BY THE COMICS CODE AUTHORITY
THE END OF BLACKHAWK ISLAND!
C-357

All at once, I heard the thunder,
Heard it rumble, long and loud.
All at once, I saw my parents,
Vanish in the mushroom cloud.
All at once, the house I lived in,
Was just sticks and bricks and stone.
All at once, the population,
Was just Spot and me alone.
I recall when Miss Delaney,
Said, "To Progress, pin your hopes!"
That was when she was my teacher.
Now, she's just some isotopes.

I SUPPOSE IT ALL STARTED WITH ALBERT EINSTEIN. BRILLIANT MAN, THAT EINSTEIN. MAYBE EVEN A LITTLE TOO BRILLIANT FOR THIS WORLD AT THIS TIME.
WAY BACK IN 1905, HE FORMULATED THE THEORY OF RELATIVITY. HE SAID THAT E=MC² AND I GUESS IT DOES.
DON'T BE ASHAMED IF YOU DON'T UNDERSTAND IT. I SURE DON'T.
IN 1934, DR. ENRICO FERMI BECAME THE FIRST MAN EVER TO SPLIT THE URANIUM ATOM, THUS UNLEASHING ATOMIC POWER. IT WAS A MAJOR BREAKTHROUGH AND HE OWED IT ALL TO EINSTEIN'S THEORY.
THE NAME OF ALBERT EINSTEIN CARRIED CONSIDERABLE WEIGHT. F.D.R. WAS SUITABLY IMPRESSED AND A TWO-PART PLAN WAS PUT INTO EFFECT...
FORTUNATELY, GERMANY WAS FAR BEHIND. OR WERE THEY? AT THAT VERY MOMENT, THEIR IMMEDIATE GOAL WAS...
THE DEATH O
WRITTEN BY MARK EVANIER • ILLUSTRATED BY DAN SPIEGL

IN '38, FERMI WON THE NOBEL PRIZE. IN '39, HE TRIED TO CONVINCE THE NAVY THAT THE U.S. SHOULD START DEVELOPING AN ATOM BOMB. HE WARNED THAT, IF THE U.S. DIDN'T, GERMANY MIGHT HAVE ONE FIRST.
THE NAVY GAVE HIM A POLITE, "DON'T CALL US, WE'LL CALL YOU."
SOON AFTER, FERMI'S ASSOCIATES PREVAILED UPON EINSTEIN HIMSELF TO GET INTO THE ACT. THEY CONVINCED HIM TO WRITE A LETTER TO PRESIDENT ROOSEVELT URGING THAT THE U.S. START AT ONCE...
PART ONE: STOP GERMANY'S ATOMIC RESEARCH. F.D.R. ARRANGED FOR BRITAIN TO DESTROY THE HEAVY-WATER PLANT AT RJUKAN, NORWAY AND AN ATOMIC RESEARCH LAB IN TRONDHEIM, NORWAY...
PART TWO: BUILD THE BOMB IN THE U.S.! HOWEVER, EVEN WITH THE WORLD'S GREAT SCIENTISTS --MANY OF WHOM HAD FLED GERMANY--IT WOULD TAKE YEARS.
BLACKHAWK™ ISLAND!
LETTERED BY CARRIE McCARTHY • COLORED BY CARL GAFFORD • MARV WOLFMAN, EDITOR

ONLY A FEW PEOPLE KNOW WHERE BLACKHAWK ISLAND IS LOCATED. OR SO BLACKHAWK AND HIS MEN WOULD LIKE TO BELIEVE...
PY YIMINY! THAT BE THE FINAL PIECE OF HAY!
"FINAL PIECE OF HAY?" WHAT IS ZAT?
OLAF MEANS, "THE LAST STRAW."
YOU BAN DESTROY MY PICTURE OF SONJA HENIE! IT BE PERSONALLY AUTOGRAPHED!
OLAF, ZE RUBBER-STAMP SAYING "PLEASE SEE MY MOVIE" DOES NOT CONSTITUTE ZE "PERSONAL AUTOGRAPH."
DOT IS DUMB PLACE TO HANG IT-- NEAR DART BOARD!
HENDRICKSON! IS OUR SHARP-SHOOTER'S AIM GOING BAD?
HE GIF ME ONE MORE PEEP OF TROUBLE, I SHOW YOU AIM! I SHOW YOU HOW I SLICE A SWEDE INTO TWELVE INDIVIDUAL SLICES!
WELL, I JUST HAD ME A PEEK AT OUR FEARLESS LEADER...
WHAT'S HE UP TO?
WHAT'S HE BEEN UP TO, THE LAST SIX DAYS AND NIGHTS?
STANDING WATCH ON STANISLAUS.
YOU GOT IT. HE'S STILL SITTING THERE, WORRYING 'BOUT OL' STAN. ALL DAY AND ALL NIGHT, THAT'S ALL HE DOES...
HE'S GOING TO MAKE IT... HAVE TO KEEP TELLING MYSELF THAT. THAT'S WHAT THE DOCTORS ALL SAY...
I BELIEVE IT. AND MY SITTING HERE WON'T DO A BIT OF GOOD. I OUGHT TO GO WASH UP...
...THOUGH MAYBE I'LL SIT HERE, JUST A LITTLE LONGER.

IF YOU STAY THERE ANY LONGER, WE'RE GOING TO HAVE TO START FEEDING YOU INTRAVENOUSLY.
REALLY. HE'LL BE FINE. AND YOU CAN TRUST ME TO WATCH HIM. THAT'S WHY ALLIED SENT ME.
UH? OH, YEAH. I KNOW, I--WELL, IT'S JUST THAT I SHOT HIM.
DID YOU KNOW IT WAS HIM YOU WERE SHOOTING?
OF COURSE NOT! I WOULD DIE BEFORE I'D SHOOT ONE OF MY OWN MEN.
THEN IT WAS AN HONEST MISTAKE. HE'LL UNDERSTAND THAT. WHY CAN'T YOU?
"WHY CAN'T YOU?" A GOOD QUESTION, BLACKHAWK THINKS: IF ONLY IT WERE THAT EASY...
...BECAUSE STANISLAUS IS STILL HERE, ALIVE ONLY BY A TECHNICALITY. AND THERE HE SHALL REMAIN FOR DAYS MORE.
TWENTY MINUTES LATER...
ALLIED IS BEATING THE BUSHES, LOOKIN' FOR PROFESSOR MERSON. THAT GUY'S SLIPPIER'N A GREASED PIG.
THEY'VE GOT TO KEEP AT IT. A BRILLIANT MIND LIKE HIS ON THE NAZI PAYROLL CAN ONLY MEAN TROUBLE. I'M SURPRISED CHOP-CHOP LET HIM GET AWAY...
YOU KNOW, RECONNAISSANCE SAID THAT THE NAZIS WERE MOVING HEAVY RESEARCH SUPPLIES INTO A CASTLE IN THE KESLAVIK MOUNTAINS.
WANT US TO GO HAVE A LOOK-SEE?
COULDN'T HURT.

THE NURSE IS WATCHING STANISLAUS SO, SHORTLY, THE SONG OF THE BLACKHAWKS RINGS OUT...
MEN OF IRON STRIKE NO FEAR... WHEN BRAVE HEARTS HOLD FREEDOM DEAR... WE'RE THE BLACKHAWKS!
...ALAS, ONE VOICE SHORT.
BLACKHAWK! I RADIO ALLIED. DEY SAY DEY KEEP GOOD EYE ON THE CASTLE. LOTS OF EQUIPMENT GO IN BUT NO SCIENTISTS. DEY BELIEF KRAUTS CHANGE PLANS.
ALLIED RECONNAISSANCE HAS BEEN WRONG BEFORE. THIS IS WORTH US CHECKING FOR OURSELVES.
BEFORE THEY KNOW IT, THEY ARE THERE AND ANDRE TAKES THE LEAD...
ANDRE! GET BACK IN FORMATION! YOU'RE FLYING TOO CLOSE TO THAT CASTLE!
AU CONTRAIRE, MSSR. BLACKHAWK! IT IS SO EASY TO SEE THAT ZE CASTLE-- SHE IS NO THREAT!
MISSILE AT SIX O'CLOCK! BANK!
BLAAM
I AM HIT!
CLEAR OUT, MEN! IF ANDRE IS GOING TO LAND NOW, HE'S GOING TO NEED LOTS OF ROOM!

ZIS IS ANDRE! I AM ATTEMPTING TO LAND ON ZE MESA.
ANDRE! THIS IS BLACKHAWK! YOU'RE COMING IN TOO FAST!
ANDRE! BREAK THROTTLE! YOU'RE GOING TO GO RIGHT OFF THE EDGE!
LEAVE IT TO ME.
VOILA! THE PLANE, SHE IS LANDED!
THE OTHERS LAND QUICKLY IN A NEARBY FIELD...
I'VE TOLD YOU BEFORE! YOU STAY IN FORMATION! YOU DO NOT GO ON AHEAD WITHOUT PROPER ORDERS...
AND THAT LANDING SITE YOU CHOSE... THE MOST DANGEROUS PLACE TO LAND A DAMAGED PLANE...
AH, BUT IT ALL WORKED OUT FINE, DID IT NOT? LET US INVESTIGATE!
"IT ALL WORKED OUT FINE!" ONE OF THESE DAYS, ANDRE, IT AIN'T GONNA WORK OUT FINE.
EVER SINCE HITLER INVADED FRANCE, OUR FRENCH BUDDY'S BEEN TAKIN' CHANCES GALORE.
ALL RIGHT-- BE ON YOUR GUARD. THEY KNOW WE'RE HERE AND--
RRRRUMMMBLE
YUMPIN' YIMINY! IT BE A EARTHQUAKE!
DONNERWETTER!
I HEAR MACHINERY! WHERE'S IT COMING FROM?
7

THE TREMBLING STOPS AS QUICKLY AS IT CAME--BUT THE LAST JOLT CAUSES THIS...
OLAF! QUICK! FIND SOME ROPE!
THEY DO FIND ROPE--AND ARE ON THEIR WAY DOWN WITHIN SECONDS...
ANY SIGN OF HIM?
WITHIN THE CASTLE, TWO GERMAN SCIENTISTS ARE BUSY...
MIT DER BLACKHAWKS SO CLOSE, VE CANNOT TAKE CHANCES. BURN EVERYTHING. IT WAS GOOD WE GOT RADIO-SIGNAL FROM AUTOMATIC SKY-TURRET AND CAME BACK.
BERLIN HAS COPIES OF IT ALL. VE GET IN DAS SCHAUFEL AND GO!
LOOKS LIKE HE'S OKAY!
LUCKY THING YOU'RE LIGHT ON YOUR FEET, OLAF.
I NOT FEEL TOO PRETTY LUCKY, BLACKHAWK. BUT NOTHING BROKE.
8

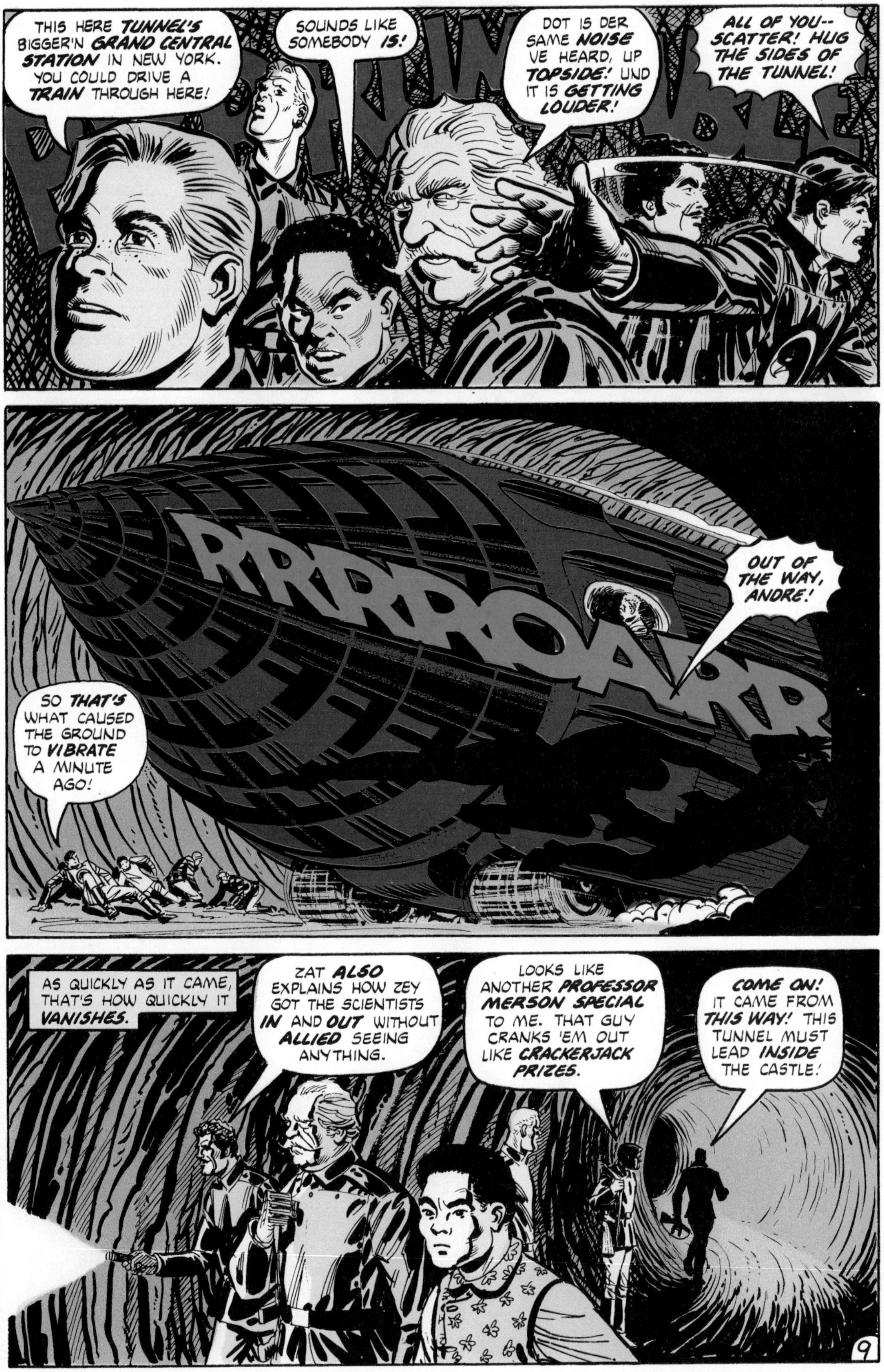
THIS HERE TUNNEL'S BIGGER'N GRAND CENTRAL STATION IN NEW YORK. YOU COULD DRIVE A TRAIN THROUGH HERE!
SOUNDS LIKE SOMEBODY IS!
DOT IS DER SAME NOISE VE HEARD, UP TOPSIDE! UND IT IS GETTING LOUDER!
ALL OF YOU-- SCATTER! HUG THE SIDES OF THE TUNNEL!
RRRRROARR
OUT OF THE WAY, ANDRE!
SO THAT'S WHAT CAUSED THE GROUND TO VIBRATE A MINUTE AGO!
AS QUICKLY AS IT CAME, THAT'S HOW QUICKLY IT VANISHES.
ZAT ALSO EXPLAINS HOW ZEY GOT THE SCIENTISTS IN AND OUT WITHOUT ALLIED SEEING ANYTHING.
LOOKS LIKE ANOTHER PROFESSOR MERSON SPECIAL TO ME. THAT GUY CRANKS 'EM OUT LIKE CRACKERJACK PRIZES.
COME ON! IT CAME FROM THIS WAY! THIS TUNNEL MUST LEAD INSIDE THE CASTLE!
9

IT DOES--BUT ALL THEY FIND IS...
ASHES! THEY BURNED ALL THEIR NOTES! IT WOULD APPEAR THIS LAB HAS SERVED ITS PURPOSE.
NEEN! I KNOW THOSE SNEAKY KRAUTS. THEY NEVER AS THOROUGH AS THEY LIKE TO BELIEVE. WE SEARCH, WE FIND THINGS! YOU SEE.
AND SEARCH, THEY DO--FOR TWO HOURS, IN EVERY CRANNY. UNTIL...
THEY BAN BURN EVERYTHING!
NOT QUITE! THIS HERE FILE SLIPPED DOWN NEXT TO THIS COUNTER AND THEY MISSED IT. LOOKS LIKE IT'S THEIR BIG, HOTSHOT REPORT TO OL' ADOLPH.
WHAT DOES FILE SAY?
DEAR LORD...
IT SAYS WE'RE IN A WHOLE MESS O' TROUBLE. US AND EVERYONE IN THE WHOLE WIDE WORLD.
A HASTY CRY TO THE OTHERS AND...
IF THIS FILE IS CORRECT...IF THE NAZIS HAVE DEVELOPED AN ATOMIC BOMB, HITLER HAS THIS WAR WON.
NO WAY TO STOP HIM. NO WAY.
EXCUSE ME... WHAT IS THIS "ATOMIC BOMB?"
SOMETHING THAT EXISTED ONLY IN THEORY UNTIL NOW. IT'S A BOMB THAT HARNESSES THE POWER OF THE ATOM...THE GREATEST FORCE NATURE KNOWS.
SUCH A BOMB COULD DESTROY WHOLE CITY BLOCKS ...EVEN THE WHOLE CITY... EVEN A COUNTRY!
MAYBE EVEN THIS WHOLE PLANET!
OH, GOD...
THIS IS NOT ZE END OF ZE WORLD! IF THEY CAN DEVELOP ONE, ZE ALLIES CAN DEVELOP ONE! EVERY NATION WILL!
WHAT!? YOU WANT EVERYONE TO HAVE AN ATOM BOMB?
10

WHY NOT? YOU CANNOT STOP PROGRESS. IF EVERY NATION HAS ONE, WARS WILL END MORE QUICKLY. IT IS MORE HUMANE THAN ZE WAY WE FIGHT NOW!
ANDRE, I THINK THAT MUSTACHE WAX YOU USE HAS TURNED YOUR BRAIN INTO CRÊPES SUZETTES! YOU'RE LOCO!
EVERY TWO-BIT LOONY HITLER WILL BE BLOWING UP DOWNTOWN NEWARK!
VE NEED TO FIND THOSE SCIENTISTS UND FAST!
THEY DROVE OFF IN THAT OVER-SIZED MECHANICAL GOPHER. HOW DO WE FIND THEM?
EASY. WE JUST FOLLOW THE TUNNEL.
WE DON'T HAVE A CAR BUT--
CHUCK! HOW LONG DO YOU THINK IT WOULD TAKE FOR YOU TO DISMANTLE MY PLANE AND REASSEMBLE IT DOWN IN THAT TUNNEL?
GIVE ME TOOLS AND ONE HOUR AND YOU GOT IT!
AN INSANE IDEA? PERHAPS. BUT THE STAKES CALL FOR NOTHING LESS. QUICKLY, CHUCK TAKES BLACKHAWK'S PLANE APART...
ITS PIECES ARE PASSED DOWN THE ROPE USED EARLIER TO FIND OLAF.
FINALLY, IT IS DONE...
CHOP-CHOP AND I WILL TRY AND FIND THAT MACHINE! YOU FOUR HEAD BACK TO BLACKHAWK ISLAND AND ALERT ALLIED ABOUT THE DIGGING MACHINE.
BUT DO NOT MENTION THE BOMB. NOT YET.
11

HOW FAR DO YOU THINK THIS TUNNEL GOES?
JUDGING FROM THAT DIGGING MACHINE, THEY COULD GO ALL UNDER THE CONTINENT. WHICH MEANS THEY COULD PLANT THEIR BOMB, ANYWHERE.
WHAT HAPPENS IF WE DON'T FIND THEM AND THEY DO HAVE AN ATOM BOMB?
THEN EVERYONE HAD BETTER START LEARNING HOW TO SPEAK GERMAN AND GOOSE-STEP... 'CAUSE THE BALL GAME IS OVER!
FLYING ABOVE GROUND, THE FOUR RETURNING BLACKHAWKS MAKE FAR BETTER TIME TO BLACKHAWK ISLAND...
CHUCK--NOW IN COMMAND--GETS ON THE RADIO...
...ANY WORD ON ANYTHING UNUSUAL UNDERGROUND... RADIO ANY RUMORS TO US, NO MATTER HOW INCREDIBLE.
CHUCK! I JUST LOOK IN ON STANISLAUS! HE THERE BUT NURSE GONE!
I TELL YOU--IT'S DAYS LIKE THIS, I WISH I WERE BACK IN TEXAS, SLIPPIN' IN THE COW PASTURE.
SHE WOULDN'T LEAVE STAN--NOT UNLESS SOMETHIN' WERE REALLY WRONG!
NOISE FROM SUPPLY ROOM! SOUNDS LIKE SHE IN THERE!
SOUNDS LIKE A STRUGGLE, TOO. BUST THE DOOR DOWN!
12

KA-RASH
LAISSEZ-MOI TRANQUILLE! PLEASE NOT TO BOTHER US.
"BOTHER YOU?" I DANGED NEAR PUT A BULLET IN YOU! WHAT IN THE NAME OF FLORENCE NIGHTINGALE WERE YOU DOING IN HERE!!?
I THINK THEY SMOOCH-SMOOCH.
I KNOW WHAT THEY WERE DOING! THE WORLD'S ABOUT TO GO KABLOOEY AND CASANOVA HERE THINKS IT'S THE SENIOR PROM!
IT IS JUST ZAT SHE IS SO... ATTRACTIVE. I WAS ENTRANCED.
LISTEN, PIERRE! THIS MAY COME AS NEWS TO YOU BUT THERE'S A WAR ON! YOU KNOW: WHERE PEOPLE FALL DOWN AND DON'T GET UP!?
THIS AIN'T A GAME WHERE EVERYONE'S ISSUED THEIR OWN ATOM BOMB AND WE HOPE THEY DON'T DETONATE IT AND INTERRUPT YOU MAKIN' WHOOPEE.
I DON'T KNOW WHAT MAKES YOU TICK, FRENCHY. MAYBE WHEN ONE OF YOUR "DARING STUNTS" GETS SOMEBODY KILLED, YOU'LL FINALLY GET SERIOUS.
I JUST HOPE IT ISN'T ME!
BY NOW, BLACKHAWK HAS LOGGED NEARLY A HUNDRED MILES ...UNDERGROUND.
DO YOU HEAR SOMETHING?
IT'S THE SOUND OF THAT MACHINE... AND I'M AFRAID IT'S GETTING LOUDER!
13

HERE THEY COME! GET OUT!
YOU DON'T HAVE TO TELL ME TWICE!
CRUNNCH
WE'RE UNDERGROUND-- AND AT LEAST A HUNDRED MILES FROM WHERE WE CAME IN.
--WHICH MEANS THAT, UNLESS THERE'S ANOTHER ROUTE BACK TO THE SURFACE, THIS WAY, WE'RE STUCK. LET'S START HIKING.
WE CANNOT RADIO FROM DOWN HERE. PERHAPS VE SHOULD GO BACK AND TELL HERR HIMMLER THAT VE JUST KILLED SOME BLACKHAWKS.
NEIN! THEY VILL HEAR ABOUT IT. VE MUST GO ARM THE TEST-BOMB!
THE TWO NAZI TECHNICIANS ARE IN ERROR...
...FOR THOSE BLACKHAWKS ARE VERY MUCH ALIVE AND, SOON, ARRIVING AT...
THIS APPEARS TO BE WHERE THEY GOT INTO THAT INFERNAL MACHINE. BUT WHERE DOES THE LADDER LEAD? JUST WHERE ARE WE?
ONLY ONE WAY TO FIND OUT...
14

KONNEN SIE SICH BITTE BEEILEN, ICH HABE MICH VARSPATET.
YOU KNOW WHAT THAT LANGUAGE MEANS.
IT MEANS WE'RE NOT IN BROOKLYN.
UPSTAIRS, A PRESENTATION IS BEING MADE, HEREBY TRANSLATED FROM THE GERMAN...
HERE IS THE FINAL PIECE OF RESEARCH, HERR HIMMLER. TOGETHER WITH WHAT BERLIN ALREADY HAS, THIS TELLS HOW TO MAKE THE BOMB.
I UNDERSTAND THAT THE TECHNOLOGY IN THIS BOOK, YOU STUMBLED ONTO LARGELY BY ACCIDENT. AM I INFORMED CORRECTLY?
YES, HERR HIMMLER. PLEASE TO BE EXTRA-CAREFUL WITH THESE NOTES. AS YOU REQUESTED, THEY ARE THE ONLY COPY.
I SEE. AND WHAT WOULD HAPPEN IF THIS NOTEBOOK WERE LOST?
THEN WE COULD PRODUCE THE BOMB ONLY THANKS TO THE KNOW-LEDGE THAT I HAVE IN MY HEAD.
AS YOU REQUESTED, I SHARED MY DISCOVERY WITH NO ONE ELSE.
EXCELLENT...
NOW THAT THE SECRET IS MINE AND MINE ALONE, DER FUHRER AND I MAY DISCUSS A SLIGHT CHANGE IN OUR RELATIONSHIP...
SUCH AS HIM SERVING ME.
BLAM
GUNTHER? GIVE THE SIGNAL TO COMMENCE WITH THE DEMONSTRATION TEST OF THE BOMB, IMMEDIATELY. HEIL HITLER!
...FOR NOW.
15

WAS IST LOS? DAS IST MEIN!
DIE BLACKHAWK-- MMPPHH.!
YOU DON'T KNOW HOW LONG I'VE WAITED TO MEET YOU, HIMMLER.
RUFEN SIE DIE GESTAPO! EINE INVASION HAT SICH EREIGNET!
UH-OH. IT LOOKS LIKE THIS LIBRARY DOESN'T LIKE US CHECKING OUT BOOKS.
HERE! YOU TAKE HIM!
HIMMEL!
WE'D BETTER FIND ANOTHER WAY OUT OF HERE AND FAST!
16

THE SIRENS COME, ALMOST IMMEDIATELY...
SCREEEEEEEEEEEEEEE
THIS IS HIMMLER'S PALACE WE'RE IN! THIS MUST BE WEWELSBURG! WE'RE IN THE MIDDLE OF NAZI GERMANY!
THEN LET'S GET OUT OF THE MIDDLE OF NAZI GERMANY WITH THIS BOOK! THERE MUST BE SOME PLANES OUTSIDE!
SURE ENOUGH: OUTSIDE, GASSED AND WAITING FOR A COURIER, IS ONE...
OOOF!
YOU KNOW HOW TO FLY A MESSERSCHMITT?
WE'RE ABOUT TO FIND OUT!
IN MOMENTS, THEY ARE AIRBORNE...
THERE THEY ARE! SHOOT THEM DOWN! KILL THEM!
THEY ARE OUT OF RANGE, HERR HIMMLER.
ALERT ALL ENCAMPMENTS! I WANT THEM KILLED! I WILL NOT REST UNTIL THOSE VERDAMMT BLACKHAWKS ARE ALL DEAD! EVERY ONE OF THEM!
BUT THE PLANE IS TOO FAST. WORD REACHES EACH ANTI-AIRCRAFT POST LONG AFTER THE CRAFT HAS PASSED...
ALL RECOGNIZED IT AS HERR HIMMLER'S PERSONAL COURIER AND LET IT GO...
17

THEY SELECTED A TEST SITE TO DEMONSTRATE THE POWER OF A "SMALL" ATOM BOMB. BUT THE EXACT LOCATION IS IN CODE.
WE'RE HEADING FOR BLACKHAWK ISLAND. ANDRE CAN BREAK THE CODE. I ONLY HOPE IT DOESN'T TAKE LONG...
GOD KNOWS WHAT THOSE NAZIS WILL BLOW UP TO SHOW THEIR "POWER."
SOON...
I DO NOT BELIEVE IT! A NAZI PLANE IS ABOUT TO LAND! HERE!
ON BLACKHAWK ISLAND? GOTTA BE SOME KRAUT WITH A DEATH WISH! LET'S GO WELCOME HIM!
CHUCK! HENDRICKSON! IT'S US! FIND ANDRE! HE'S GOT TO DECODE SOMETHING FAST! THE NAZIS ARE LAUNCHING AN ATOM BOMB AT SOMEPLACE!
IT TAKES ANDRE LESS THAN FIFTEEN MINUTES TO BREAK THE CIPHER...
IT IS ZE TRANSPOSITION CODE...GROUPS OF LETTERS TO REPRESENT ONE AND SO ON...
NEVER MIND THAT! TELL US QUICK-- WHERE IS THE BOMB HEADED?
ZE BOMB IS HEADED HERE-- TO BLACKHAWK ISLAND!
DEAR GOD...
EVACUATION PROCEDURE! EVERYONE OFF THE ISLAND, NOW!
18

WITHIN SECONDS, A DRILL HAS COME TO LIFE!
GOOD THING DER GROUND CREW IS ALL ON LEAVE!
CHUCK! CHECK THE VISITOR BARRACKS!
WE GET STANISLAUS INTO PLANE, ALL RIGHT!
ANDRE! YOU GET THE VISITOR BARRACKS!
WITHIN TWO MINUTES, THE BLACKHAWKS--STANISLAUS, INCLUDED--ARE OFF THE ISLAND, HEADING AWAY...
A SAFE DISTANCE AWAY--ON ANOTHER ISLAND--THEY LAND.
ALLIED REPORTS A ROCKET OF SOME SORT, HEADED DEAD-ON FOR BLACKHAWK ISLAND!
THAT'S IT. WE GOT EVERYONE OUT, JUST IN TIME.
LOOK!
19

20

SIX MEN STAND, CHILLED TO THE MARROW BY WHAT THEY HAVE SEEN. IT IS MANY MINUTES BEFORE ONE OF THEM CAN FIND WORDS...
WE'LL REBUILD! WE'LL FIND ANOTHER ISLAND FROM WHICH TO MOUNT OUR OPERATIONS. I'M MORE DETERMINED THAN EVER TO STOP THE NAZIS.
THE BOOK! THE BOOK WITH THE FORMULA TO BUILD THESE BOMBS... WHERE IS IT?
BLACKHAWK HAD IT LAST.
I DROPPED IT BACK ON THE ISLAND. IT'S GONE.
MAYBE THAT'S FOR THE BETTER. MAYBE EVEN WE SHOULDN'T POSSESS SUCH A WEAPON.
SOMEONE VILL INVENT IT AGAIN, SOMEDAY.
TRUE. MAYBE SOMEDAY, IT'LL EVEN BE USED BY THE RIGHT PEOPLE FOR THE RIGHT REASON.
BUT I CAN'T HELP FEEL THAT, THE LESS ATOM BOMBS THERE ARE AROUND, THE BETTER OFF WE ALL ARE.
21

BACKWARDS THINKING! WE ONLY LIVE BY TAKING ZE CHANCES! ZE ATOMIC AGE, SHE IS HERE! WE CANNOT DENY IT.
CERTAINLY, I TAKE RISKS WHEN WE ARE IN COMBAT-- RISKS TO WIN FASTER! ZE ATOM BOMB IS JUST SUCH A RISK...
TROUBLE IS, A BOMB LIKE THAT KILLS THE WRONG PEOPLE.
IN A WAR, THERE ARE NO "WRONG PEOPLE." ZE LIFE OF EVERYONE IS ON ZE LINE. WHEN WE ALL HAVE ZE SAME WEAPONS, ZE GAME IS FAIR.
YOU STILL THINK THIS IS A GAME? AFTER WHAT WE'VE JUST SEEN?
WHERE IS NURSE?
VHAT?
THE NURSE! THE NURSE WHO BAN TAKE CARE OF STANISLAUS. SHE WAS ON ISLAND. WHO RESCUE HER?
YOU WERE--
I THOUGHT YOU--
WE'RE ONLY HUMAN. WE CAN'T SAVE EVERYONE!
I KNOW. I KEEP REMINDING MYSELF, EVERY TIME SOMETHING LIKE THIS HAPPENS.
AND YOU KNOW WHAT ELSE OCCURS TO ME--?
I THINK ANDRE HAS JUST STARTED TO TAKE THE WAR SERIOUSLY.
ALMOST THE END...
22

Spot and I are very happy,
Ever since the town went boom.
Now there is no school to go to.
I don't have to clean my room.
Things are peaceful with no problems,
No adults to yell and shout.
Then again, today I noticed,
All Spot's fur is coming out.
And my skin is slowly turning,
Green and yecchy, blue and squirmy.
Since the bomb they dropped on Christmas.
Happy New Year, Dr. Fermi!

SLAM BRADLEY
Created by JERRY SIEGEL & JOE SHUSTER
THE "TOO MANY COOKS..." CAPER!
LEN WEIN WRITER • JIM APARO ARTIST
TATJANA WOOD COLORIST • PAUL LEVITZ EDITOR
EVERYBODY LOVED ARCHIE EVERGREEN. IN HIS 20 YEARS AS BEAT COP, DETECTIVE, AND FINALLY INSPECTOR--THEN THE 18 YEARS THAT FOLLOWED AS ONE OF THE BUSINESS'S BEST PRIVATE EYES, ARCHIE HAD HELPE A LOT OF PEOPLE, TOUCHED A LOT OF LIVE ...
SO NOW, ON THE EVE OF HIS RETIREMENT, A LOT OF ARCHIE'S FRIENDS FROM ALL OVER THE COUNTRY HAD GATHERED HERE IN THE SKYTOP BALLROOM TO PAY HIM THEIR RESPECTS...
J-7087
YEAH, EVERYBODY SURE LOVED ARCHIE EVERGREEN AL'RIGHT...
...EVERYBODY, THAT IS, EXCEPT THE CREEP WHO KILLED HIM!
BLAM
AARRGH

LIKE A SACK OF SOFT POTATOES, ARCHIE FELL INTO MY ARMS, HIS BACK WET WITH HIS OWN BLOOD...
SLAM... H-HELP ME, SLAM...
DON'T WORRY, OLD BUDDY--I'M HERE! SLAM IS HERE!
WHO DID THIS TO YOU, ARCH? CAN YOU TELL ME WHO DID THIS?
IT WAS DOMINION... VICTOR DOMINION... I'VE BEEN TRYING TO NAIL HIM... FOR MONTHS NOW...
...BUT IT LOOKS LIKE... HE NAILED MEEEE
ARCHIE?
AW, NO.
SLEEP WELL, OLD BUDDY--I PROMISE I'LL EVEN THE SCORE!
THAT MAY NOT BE EASILY DONE, FRIEND!
WHOEVER THE KILLER WAS, HE'S NO LONGER OUT THERE!
I'D LIKE TO KNOW HOW ANYONE COULD HAVE BEEN OUT HERE TO BEGIN WITH!
THIS WINDOW OVERLOOKS THE RIVER--AND THE NEAREST HIGH GROUND IS MILES AWAY ON THE OPPOSITE SHORE!
EVEN WITH THE HIGHEST-POWERED RIFLE WITH A TELESCOPIC SIGHT, THERE'S NO CONCEIVABLE WAY ANY-ONE COULD'VE POSSIBLY PEGGED AN ACCURATE SHOT THROUGH THAT WINDOW!
SO THE QUESTION IS NOT ONLY WHO KILLED ARCHIE EVERGREEN--BUT HOW?
HMMM...
2

AND AFTER THE COPS FINALLY ARRIVED TO PICK UP THE PIECES...
REST IN PEACE, ARCHIE OL' PAL-- YOU'RE GONNA BE MISSED!
BY ALL OF US! ARCHIE EVERGREEN WAS ONE-OF-A-KIND!
YOU CAN SAY THAT AGAIN, SAILOR! I'D BE PUSHIN' UP DAISIES TODAY IF NOT FOR ARCHIE!
THERE ISN'T A PERSON HERE WHO DOESN'T OWE ARCHIE SOMETHING!
AND THE RANK IS CAPTAIN -- CAPTAIN MARK COMPASS -- CHIEF TROUBLE-SHOOTER FOR THE PENNY STEAM-SHIP LINES!
THIS SEEMS LIKE A GOOD TIME FOR INTRODUCTIONS ALL AROUND...
I'M JASON BARD, GOTHAM CITY'S BRIGHTEST YOUNG PRIVATE INVESTIGATOR --EVEN IF I SAY SO MYSELF!
MY PILOT'S LICENSE READS RICK CARTER, BUT ON STAGE-- I'M MYSTO, MAGICIAN-DETECTIVE, AT YOUR SERVICE!
AND MY NAME IS--!
HEY, NO NEED FOR YOU TO INTRODUCE YOURSELF --YOU'RE ROY RAYMOND, THE FAMOUS TV-DETECTIVE!
I'VE BEEN A FAN OF YOURS FOR YEARS!
TO MY BROTHERS OF THE SIOUX NATION, I AM OHIYESA THE WINNER--
--BUT THE WHITE MEN CALL ME POW-WOW SMITH, INDIAN LAWMAN!
THAT SEEMS TO LEAVE JUST TWO OF US! MY NAME IS CHRISTOPHER CHANCE!
THE PAPERS HAVE LABELED ME --THE HUMAN TARGET!
YEAH? WELL, MY HANDLE'S BRADLEY--SLAM BRADLEY-- AND I STOPPED READING THE PAPERS WHEN THEY RAISED THE PRICE FROM A NICKEL!
AN' NOW THAT WE'RE ALL THE BEST OF FRIENDS, YOU'LL HAVE TO EXCUSE ME--
--BUT ARCHIE EVERGREEN WENT TO HIS FINAL REWARD LEAVIN' A JOB HALF-DONE, AND I INTEND TO FINISH IT FOR HIM!
THOUGH I HAVE THE UNCOMFORTABLE FEELING I WON'T BE DOING IT ALONE!

IF THEY EVER GAVE THE ARMPIT OF THE UNIVERSE A NAME, IT WOULD HAVE TO BE McGONICKLE'S TAVERN, MEETING PLACE OF THE UNKNOWN, UNWASHED, AND UNWANTED --
--AND HABITUAL STOMPING GROUND OF ONE "SMOKEY" BAER, A TWO-BIT PUNK WITH A MILLION-DOLLAR MOUTH...
NEED A LIGHT, "SMOKEY"?
HUH-- ?!?
C-CRIPES, BRADLEY-- WH-WHADDAYA WANT WIT' ME?
JUST A LITTLE PLEASANT CONVERSATION, OL' BUDDY--AND THE ANSWERS TO A FEW POINTED QUESTIONS!
WHUMP
VICTOR DOMINION, "SMOKEY"--TELL ME ABOUT HIM!
TH-THERE AIN'T MUCH TA TELL! THE COPS FIGURE DOMINION'S BEHIND EVERY MAJOR RACKET IN THIS CITY...
TELL ME EVERYTHING ABOUT HIM!
THEY JUST AIN'T NEVER BEEN ABLE TA PROVE IT!
IF I WANTED TO FIND DOMINION, WHAT ROCK WOULD I LOOK UNDER?
H-HE'S GOT HIMSELF THIS BIG ESTATE OUT IN THE SUBURBS-- AN' A YACHT THE SIZE OF A BATTLE-SHIP!
YA CAN USUALLY FIND HIM AT ONE OR THE OTHER!
AN' THAT'S ALL I KNOW, SLAM--I SWEAR IT IS!
DON'T WORRY, "SMOKEY"-- I BELIEVE YOU!
YOU KNOW BETTER THAN TO LIE TO ME!
HERE--THIS OUGHT'A PAY FOR YOUR TROUBLE... AND YOUR SILENCE!
TRY NOT TO DRINK IT ALL IN ONE PLACE!
IT WASN'T MUCH INFORMATION, BUT IT WAS A START-- AND THAT WAS ALL THAT REALLY MATTERED...
4

DOMINION'S YACHT, THE JEZEBEL J, LAY ANCHORED IN THE BAY LIKE A SMALL ISLAND--ALIVE WITH THE MINDLESS CHATTERING OF THE PARTY-GOERS WHO CROWDED ITS DECKS...
WHILE, IN THE WATER BENEATH THE SHIP, ONE OF ARCHIE'S OTHER BUDDIES (CAPT. COMPASS) SOUGHT ANSWERS IN HIS OWN UNIQUE WAY...
ACCORDING TO MY INFORMANT, VICTOR DOMINION KEEPS ALL OF HIS ILLEGAL RECORDS HIDDEN IN A SAFE ABOARD THIS YACHT!
IF I CAN JUST MANAGE TO GET MY HANDS ON THEM, I'LL HAVE ENOUGH AMMUNITION TO PIN DOMINION TO THE DECK!
--AND THIS PARTY SHOULD PROVIDE JUST THE KIND OF COVER THAT I NEED!
AND, SURE ENOUGH, A FEW MINUTES LATER...
GREAT NEPTUNE! THIS MAN DOMINION IS A MONSTER! THESE DOCUMENTS CONNECT HIM TO HALF THE UNSOLVED CRIMES IN THIS CITY!
I'VE GOT TO GET THESE PAPERS INTO THE RIGHT HANDS BEFORE--
OKAY, FROGMAN-- FREEZE!!
EH-- ?!?
YOU'D BETTER LISTEN TO 'IM, FELLA-- OL' CHESTER HERE CAN SHOOT OUT THE EYE OF A GNAT AT 200 YARDS!
HEY, EASY NOW, FRIENDS --THERE MUST BE SOME MISTAKE HERE!
YOU BET THERE IS, BUSTER-- AN' YOU MADE IT!
YOU WANT I SHOULD WASTE 'IM NOW, CALVIN?
5

NAH, THE BOSS WILL WANNA TALK TO 'IM FIRST-- SO'S WE CAN FIND OUT WHO THIS CHUMP WAS WORKIN' FOR BEFORE WE...
...HUH?
?
PARDON ME, GENTLEMEN--BUT WOULD ANY OF YOU CARE FOR A COCKTAIL?
WHAT'RE YOU-- CRAZY, OLD MAN? CAN'T YOU SEE WE'RE BUSY HERE?
TAKE A HIKE, BUSTER--WHILE YOU STILL CAN!
VERY WELL, GENTLE-MEN--IF THAT'S THE WAY YOU FEEL ABOUT IT...
...I QUIT!
HUH-- ?!?
OOOWW
ANY TIME YOU'D CARE TO GIVE ME A HAND WITH THESE GOONS, COMPASS-- FEEL FREE!
NOW THAT'S THE BEST INVITATION I'VE HAD ALL DAY!
AARRG
I DON'T KNOW WHO YOU ARE, FRIEND-- OR WHAT YOU'RE DOING HERE--
HEY--!
--BUT I OWE YOU ONE FOR THIS!
WHUDD
UNNGGH
6

WELL, DON'T LET IT WORRY YOU, COMPASS. ONE THING YOU'LL SOON LEARN ABOUT ME IS--
--I ALWAYS COLLECT!
CHRISTOPHER CHANCE ?!?
WHAT IN THE DEEP ARE YOU DOING HERE?
APPARENTLY THE SAME THING AS YOU, CAPTAIN! I'D PLANNED TO SLIP AWAY IN THE THICK OF THE PARTY TO RIFLE DOMINION'S SAFE--
--BUT IT LOOKS LIKE YOU BEAT ME TO IT!
WELL, WHICHEVER OF US DID IT, THERE'S ENOUGH EVIDENCE IN THESE PAPERS TO PUT DOMINION AWAY PERMANENTLY!
AND, SPEAKING OF THE DEVIL-- WHAT SAY WE GRAB HIM?
DO YOU REALLY HAVE TO ASK?
BUT WHEN THE TWO OF 'EM HIT THE DECK...
DOMINION MUST'VE REALIZED SOMETHING WENT WRONG! HE'S MAKING A BREAK FOR IT!
AND THERE'S NO WAY WE CAN GET TO HIM THROUGH THIS HALF-CROCKED CROWD!
WE'RE TOO LATE--HE GOT AWAY CLEAN!
HE MAY HAVE GOTTEN AWAY, COMPASS--BUT IT WASN'T AT ALL CLEAN!
THE PAPERS WE'RE HOLDING SMEAR HIM AS DIRTY AS THEY COME!

IF VICTOR DOMINION'S COUNTRY ESTATE HAD BEEN ANY BIGGER, IT COULD'VE APPLIED FOR STATEHOOD...
AS IT WAS, THE JOINT WAS A FORTRESS THAT WOULD'VE MADE KING ARTHUR JEALOUS--HIGH STONE WALLS SURROUNDED THE SPRAWLING GROUNDS, PATROLLED BY BEETLE-BROWED GOONS ARMED TO THEIR YELLOWING TEETH--
--BUT THAT STILL DIDN'T MAKE THE JOINT IMPREGNABLE...
...NOT TO A GUY WHO WAS A BROTHER TO THE SHADOWS...
MMUUMPH
SAY WHAT, HARRY? I WISH YOU'D STOP MUMBLING LIKE A--HUH?!?
HEY, I DON'T KNOW HOW YOU GOT IN HERE, INJUN--BUT YOU'RE A DEAD--
WOK
UNNG!
ALWAYS KNEW THIS COCKAMAMIE CANE WOULD COME IN HANDY SOME DAY!
BARD?!? BY THE MANITOU, HOW DID YOU GET IN HERE? THIS ESTATE IS RINGED WITH ALARMS!
I ALMOST HATE TO ADMIT IT, SMITH--BUT I FOLLOWED YOU! YOU MOVE AS SMOOTHLY AS A CAT ON ICE--!
TO DO WHAT I CAME HERE TO DO--I'M GOING TO ARREST VICTOR DOMINION!
HEY--WHERE YOU GOING NOW?
WELL, FOR PETE'S SAKE--WAIT FOR ME!
8

YOU SURE THIS IS THE RIGHT PLACE? IT'S AS BLACK AS DOMINION'S SOUL IN THERE!
THIS IS NOT A JOKING MATTER, BARD!
A GOOD MAN--A GOOD FRIEND--IS DEAD BECAUSE OF VICTOR DOMINION...
...AND IN A VERY FEW MOMENTS, I'M AFRAID YOU'RE GOING TO JOIN HIM!
HUH--?!?
I BELIEVE YOU'VE BEEN LOOKING FOR ME, GENTLEMEN--
--AND, UNFORTUNATELY FOR YOU, YOUR SEARCH IS OVER!
VICTOR DOMINION!
AND FRIENDS... VERY UNHAPPY-LOOKING FRIENDS!
WE HAVEN'T BEEN FORMALLY INTRODUCED, GENTLEMEN, BUT THAT DOESN'T REALLY MATTER--SINCE OUR ACQUAINTANCESHIP IS GOING TO BE BRIEF!
ARNOLD, WOULD YOU KINDLY TAKE THESE TRESPASSERS OUT INTO THE GARDEN--
--AND PLANT THEM AMONG THE--
WHAT IN--?!?
NAH--IT COULDN'T BE...COULD IT?
THE NAME IS MYSTO, MAGICIAN-EXTRAORDINAIRE! KINDLY SAVE YOUR APPLAUSE UNTIL THE ACT IS OVER!
HOLY SMOKE--IT IS HIM!
WELL, DON'T JUST STAND THERE GAWKING, BARD! HE'S GIVEN US A SECOND CHANCE--
9

--SO LET'S NOT WASTE IT!
SORRY I COULDN'T GET HERE EARLIER, GUYS--BUT MY FLYING CARPET WAS RUNNING A LITTLE LATE!
AS FAR AS I'M CONCERNED, MYSTO--YOUR TIMING WAS PERFECT!
IN SECONDS, DOMINION'S LIVING ROOM HAD BECOME A BATTLEFIELD--AND THE BIG MAN HIMSELF HAD NO INTENTION OF WAITING AROUND TO SEE WHO CAME OUT THE WINNER...
GOT TO GET OUT OF HERE --WHILE I STILL CAN!
THIS SECRET TUNNEL I HAD BUILT LEADS OUTSIDE--TO MY PRIVATE HELIPAD!
ONCE I GET AIRBORNE, THERE ISN'T A COP IN THE WORLD WHO CAN STOP--
--ME!
GOING SOMEWHERE, DOMINION?
YOU BET I AM, MISTER--AS FAST AND AS FAR FROM HERE AS I CAN GET!
AND I WON'T HESITATE TO KILL ANYONE WHO GETS IN MY WAY!
JUST LIKE YOU KILLED ARCHIE EVERGREEN?
EVERGREEN WAS AN ANNOYANCE--JUST LIKE YOU! HE GOT WHAT HE DESERVED!
BLAM
BLAM
BLAM
10

AND SO WILL YOU, SLICK, AS SOON AS I GET MY HANDS ON--
KEEP AWAY FROM ME, BLAST YOU! WHY WON'T YOU LEAVE ME ALONE?
UUNNHH!!
WHY? BECAUSE A GOOD MAN LEFT THIS WORLD WITH A JOB HALF-DONE--
WHUP
WHUPWHUP
--AND HE HAS A LOT OF FRIENDS WHO INTEND TO FINISH THAT JOB FOR HIM!
NO! LET ME GO! I'LL PAY YOU--MAKE YOU RICH--!
MISTER, THERE AIN'T ENOUGH DIRTY MONEY IN THIS WORLD TO BUY YOUR FREEDOM--!
BESIDES, YOU AIN'T GOING ANYWHERE! THOSE SHOTS YOU PEGGED AT ME HAVE DAMAGED THIS COPTER'S--
HEY-- !?!
NO! YOU'RE LYING! THIS COPTER IS MY ONLY CHANCE--!
IN THAT CASE, MISTER--
UUNNGG!!
--YOU HAVE NO CHANCE AT ALL!
REST EASY NOW, ARCHIE--YOUR FINAL CASE IS CLOSED!
KWA-WHOOM
11

I LEFT THE COPS TO SCRAPE UP WHAT WAS LEFT OF VICTOR DOMINION, AND WENT WANDER-ING FOR A WHILE, LOST IN THOUGHT. EVENTUALLY I FOUND MYSELF BACK AT THE SKYTOP BALL-ROOM, THE SCENE OF THE CRIME--
--AND NOW THE SCENE OF A GRAND REUNION...
WELL, IF IT ISN'T THE HERO OF THE DAY! CARE TO JOIN US?
SEEMS I DON'T HAVE MUCH CHOICE!
YOU DON'T SEEM VERY HAPPY, BRADLEY-- FOR A MAN WHO JUST DID WHAT THE REST OF US WOULD'VE GIVEN OUR EYE-TEETH TO DO!
YEAH--YOU WASTED THE CREEP WHO MURDERED ARCHIE EVERGREEN!
ACE
DID I?
DO YOU DOUBT IT? PERHAPS DOMINION DID NOT PULL THE TRIGGER HIM-SELF--BUT HE CERTAINLY ORDERED IT DONE!
I FIGURE IT WAS DOMINION'S PET SHARPSHOOTER CHESTER WHO FIRED THE FATAL SHOT FROM DOMINION'S PRIVATE HELICOPTER!
THAT'S WHY WE COULDN'T FIND THE KILLER ON THE ROOFTOPS.
IT'S YOUR CLASSIC OPEN-AND-SHUT CASE! THE POLICE HAVE CHESTER DOWNTOWN RIGHT NOW--
--AND BY THE TIME THEY'RE THROUGH GRILLING HIM, I EXPECT THEY'LL HAVE A NICE FULL CONFESSION!
I HATE TO DIFFER WITH YOU, GENTLEMEN--BUT I'M AFRAID ARCHIE EVERGREEN'S DEATH WAS NOT MURDER...
IT WAS SUICIDE!
HUH--?!? TH-THAT'S IMPOSSIBLE--!
IMPOSSIBLE... BUT TRUE!
12

I KNEW IT! I SENSED ALL ALONG THAT THERE WAS SOMETHING NOT QUITE RIGHT ABOUT ALL THIS!
WOULD SOMEBODY HERE MIND EXPLAINING WHAT IN BLAZES YOU TWO ARE JABBERING ABOUT?
JASON, IT WOULD BE MY PLEASURE!
YOU SEE, WHILE YOU WERE ALL OUT CHASING DOWN SUSPECTS, I WAS BUSY SEEKING INFORMATION--AND WHAT I FOUND ASTONISHED ME!
ACCORDING TO HIS DOCTOR, ARCHIE EVERGREEN HAD TERMINAL CANCER--AND LESS THAN A MONTH TO LIVE!
B-BUT--IF HE WAS ALREADY DYING--WHY WOULD HE WANT TO KILL HIMSELF?
AND, MORE IMPORTANTLY--HOW DID HE KILL HIMSELF?
ACTUALLY, THE HOW OF IT IS RATHER EASY TO EXPLAIN...
"APPARENTLY, ARCHIE PLANTED A GUN ON THE LEDGE OUTSIDE THE WINDOW HERE--FITTED TO A HOMEMADE MECHANISM CAPABLE OF TRIGGERING THE WEAPON BY REMOTE-CONTROL...
"WHEN ARCHIE CAME OVER TO GREET YOU, BRADLEY--HE PURPOSEFULLY POSITIONED HIMSELF WITH HIS BACK TO THE WAITING WEAPON--
BLAM
"--AND, USING A SMALL TRANSMITTER HIDDEN IN HIS POCKET, HE SHOT HIMSELF TO DEATH!"
THE RECOIL OF THE SHOT SENT THE GUN AND THE MECHANISM BACK OFF THE LEDGE INTO THE RIVER BELOW--BUT I FOUND THE TRANSMITTER AMONG ARCHIE'S PERSONAL EFFECTS!
BUT WHAT DID HE HOPE TO ACCOMPLISH BY DOING SOMETHING LIKE THAT?
I THINK I CAN ANSWER THAT!
ARCHIE HAD BEEN ON VICTOR DOMINION'S CASE FOR MONTHS--AND WE'VE SAID HE WAS A GUY WHO NEVER LEFT A JOB HALF-FINISHED!
WHEN HE FOUND OUT HE WAS DYING, HE KNEW HE'D NEVER LIVE TO SEE DOMINION GET WHAT WAS COMING TO HIM--
--SO ARCHIE SET THIS WHOLE THING UP TO TRICK US INTO HANDLING DOMINION FOR HIM!
HE WAS TOO PROUD A GUY TO EVER ASK ANY OF US FOR A FAVOR--BUT HE WAS STILL EVERY INCH A PRO!
I MEAN--HOW MANY OTHER DETECTIVES CAN YOU NAME WHO SOLVED THEIR LAST CASE FROM BEYOND THE GRAVE?
13
THE END

THE WORLD'S GREATEST SUPERHEROES™

RELEASE WEEK OF OCTOBER 15, 1979

OLSEN! WHERE'S THE CRACKPOT INVENTOR PIECE? THE SUNDAY SUPPLEMENT CLOSES AT FIVE!
LEVITZ TUSKA Colletta
© DC COMICS INC. 1979 Distributed By C.T.N.Y.N.S.
AW, C'MON, CHIEF! YOU'RE NOT SERIOUS-- STICKING ME WITH THAT DULL ASSIGN-MENT?
YOU'RE BREAKING MY HEART. YOUR JOB IS TO MAKE IT A LIVELY STORY!
CLARK! YOU CAN TALK PERRY OUT OF THIS! HELP!
er--EXCUSE ME, JIMMY. I THINK I HEAR SOMEONE CALLING...
10/15

AT LEAST I'M NOT THE ONLY GUY WASTING MY TIME ON THIS "MAD SCIENTIST" STORY. LOOKS LIKE EVERY PAPER IN TOWN'S HERE!
LEVITZ TUSKA Colletta
IMAGINE A "JIMMY OLSEN" BYLINE BLOWN ON A TURKEY BACK-PAGE PIECE LIKE THIS! Sheesh!
© DC COMICS INC. 1979 Distributed By C.T.N.Y.N.S.
WELCOME, MISTER OLSEN-- Beep-- PLEASE FOLLOW ME...
Hmm...ON SECOND THOUGHT, MAYBE THIS IS WORTH THE MAGIC OLSEN TOUCH AFTER ALL--!
10/16

AH... IT'S OLDSON FROM THE DAILY TRIBUNE!
er...THAT'S OLSEN FROM THE DAILY PLANET!
ADVANCED RESEARCH LAB
FOLLOW ME...beep...
I'M...er...PROFESSOR PHINEAS POTTER...
PROFESSOR, YOUR ROBOT IS TERRIFIC! IT'LL MAKE A GREAT STORY!
10/17
THE ROBOT IS A MERE TOY! FORGET HIM!
OLDSON, YOU'RE ABOUT TO SEE AN INVENTION THAT WILL CHANGE THE WORLD!
LEVITZ TUSKA Colletta
© DC COMICS INC. 1979 Distributed By C.T.N.Y.N.S.

THE WORLD'S GREATEST SUPERHEROES™

RELEASE WEEK OF OCTOBER 15, 1979

SO YOU'RE OLSEN OF THE PLANET, huh!
MY FATHER'S BOY GENIUS JIMMY, THAT'S ME!
10/18
LEVITZ TUSKA Colletta
SID SHUMLEY FROM STEEL, STONE & MORTAR. I'M HERE FOR THE NUTTY PROFESSOR'S LATEST. BUT I DIDN'T THINK THE PLANET SENT YOU ON CRANK STORIES!
MY EDITOR HAS A WARPED SENSE OF HUMOR, SID. PERRY'LL BE SURPRISED, THOUGH--'CAUSE I THINK THE PROFESSOR'S ONTO SOMETHING!
GENTLEMEN, THIS WAY PLEASE!
© DC COMICS INC., 1979 Distributed By C.T.N.Y.N.S

IT'S MY MOST REMARKABLE INVENTION, GENTLEMEN--A "HIGH YIELD" CEMENT MIX FORMULA! NOW EVERYONE IN THE WORLD--NO MATTER HOW POOR--WILL BE ABLE TO AFFORD A HOME! JUST THREE DROPS OF WATER ADDED TO A BAG OF MY FORMULA CREATES
10/19
LEVITZ TUSKA Colletta
© DC COMICS INC., 1979 Distributed By C.T.N.Y.N.S
...A HUNDRED POUNDS OF CEMENT! IT MEANS THE END OF POVERTY, GENTLEMEN...
PROFESSOR POTTER--WHAT'S THE FOURTH DROP OF WATER GOING TO DO?
ULP...NOT AGAIN! GENTLEMEN--I SUGGEST AN ORDERLY PANIC!
GURGLE!
GURGLE!

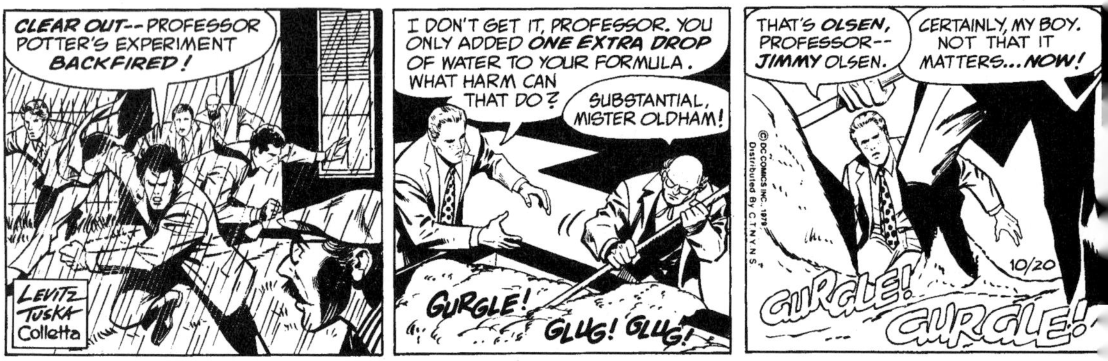
CLEAR OUT--PROFESSOR POTTER'S EXPERIMENT BACKFIRED!
LEVITZ TUSKA Colletta
I DON'T GET IT, PROFESSOR. YOU ONLY ADDED ONE EXTRA DROP OF WATER TO YOUR FORMULA. WHAT HARM CAN THAT DO?
SUBSTANTIAL, MISTER OLDHAM!
GURGLE!
GLUG! GLUG!
THAT'S OLSEN, PROFESSOR--JIMMY OLSEN.
CERTAINLY, MY BOY. NOT THAT IT MATTERS...NOW!
© DC COMICS INC., 1979 Distributed By C.T.N.Y.N.S.
10/20
GURGLE! GURGLE!

P-PROFESSOR! Y-YOUR FORMULA IS OUT OF CONTROL!
UNFORTUNATELY... JUST LIKE THE LAST TIME!
YOU MEAN THIS HAPPENED BEFORE?
er, YES. THAT WAS OUTDOORS, AND I WOUND UP WITH FORTY ACRES OF CEMENT!!
WHY, OH WHY DID I TEST MY NEW FORMULA INDOORS.
P-PROFESSOR POTTER! WE CAN'T GET OUT! WE'LL END UP DROWNING IN CONCRETE!
I'M AFRAID YOU'RE ENTIRELY CORRECT, MISTER OLSEN!
WE MIGHT HAVE TEN OR ELEVEN MINUTES LEFT... UNLESS, OF COURSE, I'VE MADE A MISCALCULATION.
FORGIVE ME IF I DON'T COUNT ON YOU MIS-CALCULATING, PROFESSOR... YOU MAY GOOF FREQUENTLY--
--BUT I'D RATHER COUNT ON SUPERMAN! HE ALWAYS COMES THROUGH!
ZEE ZEE ZEE
SUPPLY ROOM
THAT'S JIMMY'S SUPERSONIC SIGNAL! HE'S LANDED IN TROUBLE... AGAIN!
ZEE ZEE
DAILY PLANET EDITORIAL OFFICES
LEVITZ TUSKA Colletta
10/21
(C) DC COMICS INC 1979
Distributed By C T N Y N S
SUPERMAN!
AMAZING! PRECISELY WHEN NEEDED!
IN THE NAME OF SCIENCE YOU MUST LET ME RESEARCH YOUR REFLEXES, SUPERMAN!
SOME OTHER TIME, PROFESSOR...
THANKS FOR THE SAVE, SUPERMAN.
I KNOW A REPORTER IS ONLY INTERESTED IN CONCRETE FACTS, JIMMY, BUT ISN'T THIS GOING A LITTLE TOO FAR?

THE WORLD'S GREATEST SUPERHEROES™

RELEASE WEEK OF OCTOBER 22, 1979

SUPERMAN!
I GOT YOUR SUPERSONIC SIGNAL, JIMMY--AND I ASSUME THIS MESS IS THE PROBLEM?
I'M AFRAID MY EXPANDING CEMENT BACKFIRED, SUPERMAN!
NO TROUBLE, PROFESSOR--
LEVITZ TUSKA Colletta
--I'VE BEGUN TO THINK OF SAVING JIMMY AS ONE OF MY HOBBIES!
© DC COMICS INC. 1979 Distributed By C.T.N.Y.N.S.
10/22
SOME DAYS I JUST CAN'T WIN!

THERE HE IS, PROFESSOR POTTER!
YOU MAY HAVE NEARLY BEEN KILLED BY POTTER'S CRAZY EXPANDING CEMENT, JIMMY--BUT THAT DOESN'T MEAN IT CAN'T BE USEFUL!
NOT WHEN A TOUCH OF SUPER-PRESSURE CAN RESHAPE IT INTO A SUPER-THIN WATERTIGHT PATCH FOR PROFESSOR POTTER'S ROOF!
© DC COMICS INC. 1979 Distributed By C.T.N.Y.N.S.
10/23
LEVITZ TUSKA Colletta
AND A BURST OF HEAT VISION WILL SET IT SO IT STOPS EXPANDING!
AMAZING! SUPERMAN, I MUST HAVE THE CHANCE TO STUDY YOUR POWERS! I'M EVEN WILLING TO MAKE YOU MY PARTNER!

PLEASE, SUPERMAN-- CONSIDER MY OFFER! LET ME TEST YOUR POWERS AND WE CAN SHARE THE NOBEL PRIZE!
SORRY, PROFESSOR POTTER, THAT'S NOT MY STYLE!
© DC COMICS INC., 1979 Distributed By C.T.N.Y.N.S.
AND I HAVE THE FEELING YOUR EXPERIMENTS USUALLY END IN DISASTERS, ANYWAY!
LEVITZ TUSKA Colletta
AH, GENTLEMEN OF THE PRESS! YOU HAVE RETURNED! COME IN AND I'LL CONCLUDE MY DEMONSTRATION.
NO THANKS, PROF. WE'VE GOT THE STORY: "SUPERMAN SAVES MAD SCIENTIST FROM HIS OWN INVENTION!" HA HA HA HA
10/24

THE WORLD'S GREATEST SUPERHEROES™

RELEASE WEEK OF OCTOBER 22, 1979

WHY HAVEN'T YOU LEFT, OLSEN? ALL THE OTHER REPORTERS LAUGHED AT ME--THEY THINK MY DISCOVERIES ARE WORTHLESS!
YOUR METHODS ARE STRANGE, PROFESSOR POTTER--
LEVITZ TUSKA Colletta
10/25
© DC COMICS INC., 1979 Distributed By C.T.N.Y.N.S.
--BUT I CAME HERE FOR A STORY, AND I'M GOING TO GET ONE!
BRAVO, LAD! I SHALL REWARD YOUR FAITH IN ME!
YOU SHALL BE THE FIRST PERSON TO SEE MY INCREDIBLE MIRACLE RUBBERIZER!
OH, NO!
OLSEN WILL NEVER SEE THAT DEMONSTRATION--NOT IF I CAN HELP IT!

I'VE GOT TO STOP OLSEN FROM SEEING HOW THE PROFESSOR'S MIRACLE RUBBERIZER WORKS! WHEN I CAME HERE DISGUISED AS A REPORTER TO CASE THE JOINT, I WAS CONVINCED POTTER WAS A CRACKPOT!
LEVITZ TUSKA Colletta
BUT CRAZY OR NO, POTTER'S INVENTIONS WORK! WHICH MEANS I CAN CLEAN UP BY HEISTING THEM!
miracle vitamins
MIRACLE RUBBERIZER
THE FIRST STEP IS TO PULL THE OLD SWITCHEROO, SO OLSEN GETS CONVINCED THE RUBBERIZER DOESN'T WORK!
I CAN GET THE GIMMICKS OUT OF HERE EASIER IF OLSEN LEAVES PROFESSOR POTTER ALONE!
10/26
(C) DC COMICS INC. 1979 Distributed By C.T.N.Y.N.S.

OTHER REPORTERS MAY SCOFF, OLDMAN, BUT YOU'LL GET MY STORY INTO PRINT!
SURE, PRO-FESSOR--RIGHT OVER MY BYLINE--JIMMY OLSEN.
LEVITZ TUSKA Colletta
MY MIRACLE RUBBERIZER INSTANTLY MAKES ANYTHING ELASTIC! GIVE ME YOUR TIE, PLEASE.
MY TIE...?
© DC COMICS INC. 1979 Distributed By C.T.N.Y.N.S.
10/27
PROFESSOR, AFTER HOW YOUR LAST EXPERIMENT BACKFIRED, DO YOU THINK THIS IS A GOOD IDEA?
GOOD? IT'S WONDERFUL! I'M GOING TO MAKE RUBBER A THING OF THE PAST!

BLAST OLSEN! WHERE IS HE WITH THAT CRACKPOT INVENTOR STORY? HE KNOWS I NEED IT NOW!.
RELAX, PERRY!
WHAT-- SUPERMAN!
JIMMY'S NOT GOOFING OFF, PERRY... FOR A CHANGE!

JIMMY RAN INTO SOME TROUBLE ON THAT CRACKPOT INVENTOR STORY, PERRY. PROFESSOR POTTER MAY BE CRAZY-- BUT HIS INVENTIONS WORK-- SORT OF.
JUST THOUGHT I'D LET YOU KNOW.
THANKS, SUPERMAN. I WISH MY REPORTERS WERE HALF AS CONSIDERATE-- ESPECIALLY OLSEN! I'LL BREAK HIS NECK IF HE DOESN'T GET BACK SOON!

NO, PROFESSOR-- YOU CAN'T TEST YOUR MIRACLE RUBBERIZER ON MY TIE!
BUT I DON'T HAVE ANY OTHER TEST MATERIAL HERE, OLSEN.
OH, NEVER MIND! I'LL SHOW YOU MY MIRACLE VITAMINS INSTEAD. JUST TAKE SOME!
10/28

IT'S ONLY VITAMINS-- WHAT HARM CAN EVEN THE PROFESSOR'S VITAMINS DO?
LEVITZ
TUSKA
Colletta
HERE YOU AR-- PROFESSOR! WHAT'S HAPPENING TO ME?
OH NO. DON'T TELL ME I MIXED UP THE TEST TUBES AGAIN!

THE WORLD'S GREATEST SUPERHEROES™

RELEASE WEEK OF OCTOBER 29, 1979

PROFESSOR-- WHAT'S HAPPENING TO ME ?
OH NO! DON'T TELL ME I **MIXED UP** THE TEST TUBES **AGAIN** !
LEVITZ TUSKA Colletta
10/29
BLAST! MY SWITCH IS **BACKFIRING** ON ME! OLSEN DRANK THE MIRACLE RUBBERIZER!
CRASH!
SOMEONE'S IN HERE--TRYING TO STEAL MY SECRETS!
© DC COMICS INC. 1979 Distributed By C.T.N.Y.N.S.

PROFESSOR POTTER'S CRAZY FORMULA WORKS **TOO WELL**-- IT'S TURNED OLSEN INTO A RUBBER MAN!
STOP THIEF!!
10/30
LEVITZ TUSKA Colletta
DON'T WORRY, PROFESSOR-- I'LL GET HIM !
© DC COMICS INC., 1979 Distributed By C.T.N.Y.N.S.

SORRY I COULDN'T GRAB THE CROOK WHO WAS STEALING YOUR INVENTIONS, PROFESSOR, BUT I'M NOT USED TO BEING **ELASTIC**!
LEVITZ TUSKA Colletta
© DC COMICS INC., 1979 Distributed By C.T.N.Y.N.S.
I'M SORRY YOU ACCIDENTLY **DRANK** MY MIRACLE RUBBERIZER. I DIDN'T **DREAM** IT WOULD WORK ON HUMANS!
IS THE EFFECT PERMANENT ?
10/31
I **DOUBT** IT. THERE'S NO WAY TO REALLY **KNOW**, THOUGH... BUT TO SEE IF IT **WEARS OFF**!
GREAT! AND IF IT **DOESN'T** WEAR OFF--I GET TO SPEND EVERY HALLOWEEN AS A HUMAN RUBBER BAND.

THE WORLD'S GREATEST SUPERHEROES™

RELEASE WEEK OF OCTOBER 29, 197

IT'S EASY FOR PROFESSOR POTTER TO SAY, "DON'T WORRY, OLSEN!"
HE DOESN'T HAVE TO FACE THE REST OF HIS LIFE WITH A BODY THAT STRETCHES LIKE TAFFY!
DAILY PLANE
LEVITZ TUSKA Colletta
JIMMY--WATCH OUT! PERRY'S ON A RAMPAGE. HE'S BEEN YELLING FOR YOU FOR HOURS!
OH, THANKS, CLARK.
© DC COMICS INC. 1979 Distributed By C.T.N.Y.N.S.
11/1
BUT PERRY'S THE LEAST OF MY WORR--
OLSEN!!

OLSEN! THE SUPPLEMENT CLOSED TWO HOURS AGO! WHERE IS THAT CRACKPOT INVENTOR STORY?
UH, CHIEF...
DON'T CALL ME CHIEF! HAND OVER THAT PIECE OR PACK YOUR TYPEWRITER!
I'LL GET RIGHT ON IT, PERRY! JUST GIVE ME A SEC TO TYPE IT UP!
© DC COMICS INC. 1979 Distributed By C.T.N.Y.N.S.
JIMMY!
Uh... YEAH... YOU SEE, er... POTTER'S A CRACKPOT ALL RIGHT-- --BUT HE HAS AT LEAST ONE CRAZY INVENTION THAT WORKS!
LEVITZ TUSKA Colletta
11/2

I KNOW YOU THOUGHT IT WAS ONLY A ROUTINE STORY, PERRY--BUT THAT'S NOT HOW IT TURNED OUT!
THE PROFESSOR'S SERUM REALLY WORKS!
BUT I THOUGHT PROFESSOR POTTER HAD INVENTED AN AMAZING NEW CEMENT MIX, JIMMY--NOT SOME STRANGE BODY-CHANGING FORMULA!
YEAH, THAT'S TRUE, CLARK.
LEVITZ TUSKA Colletta
11/3
POTTER ALSO SHOWED OFF EXPANDING CEMENT, MIRACLE VITAMINS AND A KOOKY ROBOT BEFORE HE MIXED UP SOME TEST TUBES--
--AND I GOT A SWIG OF HIS MIRACLE RUBBERIZER!

SO THAT'S HOW I BEGAN IMPERSONATING A RUBBER BAND, GUYS. PROFESSOR POTTER'S FORMULA REALLY DID A NUMBER ON ME!
INCREDIBLE, JIMMY!
I WAS HOPING IT WOULD WEAR OFF BEFORE I HAD TO TELL YOU ABOUT IT, PERRY.
ANOTHER OF YOUR HAREBRAINED STUNTS, OLSEN!
IT'S NOT MY FAULT THE PROFESSOR'S MIRACLE RUBBERIZER CHANGED ME, PERRY!
BUT MEANWHILE, OLSEN, YOU'RE NO REPORTER-- NOT IF YOU CAN'T EVEN TYPE!
NOT THAT YOU WERE MUCH OF A REPORTER BEFORE, EITHER!
THAT'S IT, PERRY! I QUIT!
THE HECK WITH BEING A REPORTER ANYWAY--I DON'T NEED IT NOW! POTTER'S SERUM WILL GIVE ME A NEW CAREER!
BYE, PERRY-- CLARK! I'M OFF TO BE A SUPER HERO!
JIMMY-- WAIT!
SOMEHOW, PERRY, I THINK IT'S TOO LATE FOR THAT!
NO MORE PERRY WHITE-- NO MORE PLANET--AND NO MORE PROBLEMS! THAT'S MY NEW MOTTO!
LEVITZ
TUSKA
Colletta
11/4
ULP... I'M SLIPPING!
© DC COMICS INC. 1978
Distributed By C T N Y N S
SUPERMAN!

RELEASE WEEK OF NOVEMBER 5, 1979

THAT'S MY STORY, SUPERMAN: POTTER'S WHACKO FORMULA MADE ME STRETCHABLE, PERRY GOT ME MAD, AND I WALKED OUT!
OUT A SEVENTH-FLOOR WINDOW, JIMMY?
© DC COMICS INC. 1979 Distributed By C T N Y N S
YEAH, WELL --I FIGURED MY NEW POWERS WOULD HELP ME GET DOWN SAFELY.
BUT I'M GLAD YOU WERE THERE TO CATCH ME WHEN I FELL, SUPERMAN.
11/5
LEVITZ TUSKA Colletta
AND THAT GAVE ME THE IDEA FOR MY NEW CAREER! I'M GOING TO BECOME A SUPER-HERO --
ELASTIC LAD!
SIGH!

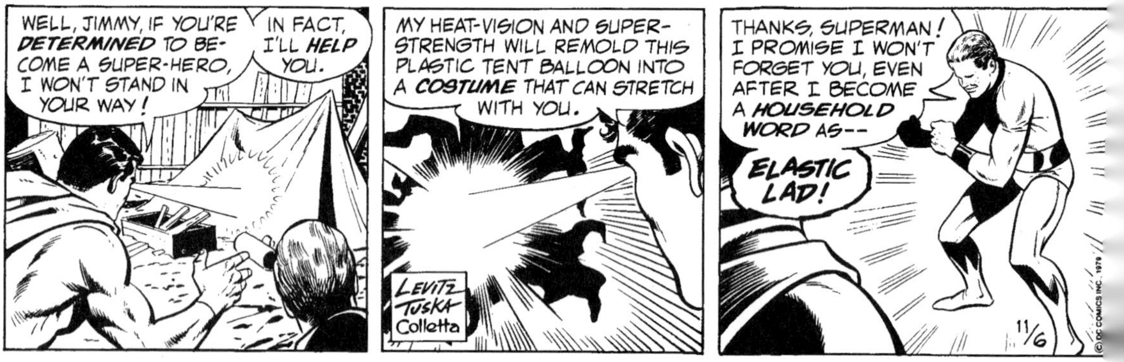

WELL, JIMMY, IF YOU'RE DETERMINED TO BECOME A SUPER-HERO, I WON'T STAND IN YOUR WAY!
IN FACT, I'LL HELP YOU.
MY HEAT-VISION AND SUPER-STRENGTH WILL REMOLD THIS PLASTIC TENT BALLOON INTO A COSTUME THAT CAN STRETCH WITH YOU.
LEVITZ TUSKA Colletta
THANKS, SUPERMAN! I PROMISE I WON'T FORGET YOU, EVEN AFTER I BECOME A HOUSEHOLD WORD AS--
ELASTIC LAD!
11/6

NOW THAT YOU'VE BECOME ELASTIC LAD, JIMMY, HOW DO YOU PLAN TO START YOUR SUPER-HERO CAREER?
ELASTIC LAD
I'M NOT SURE, SUPERMAN -- MAYBE I CAN STOP A DARING ROBBERY OR PULL OFF A HEROIC RESCUE!
11/7
YOU WOULDN'T KNOW OF ANY CRIMES ABOUT TO HAPPEN, WOULD YOU?
I'M AFRAID NOT, JIMMY.
LEVITZ TUSKA Colletta
JUST THOUGHT I'D ASK...

★★★SPECIAL MASTERS OF THE UNIVERSE PREVIEW★★★

DC
WHERE SCIENCE ENDS--MAGIC BEGINS...
MASTERS OF THE UNIVERSE†
A SPECIAL FREE GIFT TO YOU FROM THE NEW DC!
HE-MAN FIGHTS THE MYSTIC FORCES OF THE EVIL SKELETOR--WITH THE TIMELESS KINGDOM OF ETERNIA ITSELF AT STAKE!

★★★SPECIAL MASTERS OF THE UNIVERSE PREVIEW★★★

THE UNIVERSE IS A BIG PLACE.
THE MULTIVERSE IS EVEN BIGGER! FOR EVERY DECISION A MAN CAN MAKE, THERE ARE A MILLION DIMENSIONS WHERE EACH AND EVERY ALTERNATIVE TAKES PLACE AS WELL.
FOR EVERY POSSIBILITY OF EVOLUTION THERE LIKEWISE EXISTS A PLACE. MANY ARE SO ALIKE THAT AS SMALL A THING AS ONE PERSON MAY BE ALL THAT DIFFERENTIATES IT FROM THE UNIVERSE NEXT DOOR.
OTHERS ARE FAR FROM THE WORLD WE KNOW -- WORLDS WHERE THE PREDOMINANT LIFE FORMS ARE EXACTLY LIKE US... BUT CIVILIZATION HAS TAKEN A TOTALLY DIFFERENT TURN!
MASTERS OF THE UNIVERSE†
ETERNIA IS JUST SUCH A PLACE. FOR IN TRUTH, WHEN WAS THE LAST TIME YOU SAW A SIGHT SUCH AS THIS IN THE SKIES OVER EARTH--?
I'VE LONG TRANSVERSED THE MULTITUDE OF DIMENSIONAL PLANES WITH BUT THE STARS AS MY GUIDE AND INSPIRATION-- TOO LONG FOR ZODAC TO IGNORE THE SIGNS THEY GIVE ME THIS DAY!
THUS HAVE I RETURNED AGAIN TO ETERNIA, FOR THE STARS HAVE BIDDEN ME HENCE... TO SAVE THE LIFE OF A SINGLE MAN AND THUS INSURE THE FUTURE OF A WORLD!
FATE is the KILLER
PAUL KUPPERBERG WRITER / CURT SWAN & DAVE HUNT ARTISTS / BEN ODA LETTERER / ANTHONY TOLLIN COLORIST / PAUL CLEVELAND TALLEST / DAVE MANAK EDITOR

HOW VERY ODD THE QUIRKS OF FATE! MY MISSION IS TO SAVE ETERNIA... YET IN DOING SO, MY ACTIONS MAY WELL LEAD IT TO THE BRINK OF DESTRUCTION!
YET ONLY IN THIS WAY MAY THIS WORLD SURVIVE!
ZODAC FALLS SILENT THEN, FOR IT IS NOT EVEN TO THIS BEING FROM THE STARS TO FULLY UNDERSTAND THE WORKINGS OF FATE.--
--AND IT FALLS EVEN LESS TO THE PEOPLE OF ETERNIA FOR SUCH COSMIC AWARENESS! INSTEAD, THEY ARE LEFT TO REVEL IN THE SECURE WARMTH OF IGNORANCE.
WELCOME TO THE ROYAL COURT OF ETERNIA! DESPITE APPEARANCES TO THE CONTRARY, THESE ARE NOT A SIMPLE PEOPLE--FOR THOUGH THEIR CIVILIZATION IS BASED ON A MONARCHY UNLIKE ANY SEEN ON OUR WORLD OF CENTURIES--
--ETERNIA POSSESSES A STRANGE MIX OF FEUDALISM AND TECHNOLOGY. IT'S JUST THAT, EVERY NOW AND AGAIN, THE MORE PRIMITIVE SIDE OF ITS DUAL PERSONALITY TAKES HOLD--
--AND, AS IN ETERNIA'S ROYAL COURT, THEY WILL LET LOOSE FOR QUITE THE GOOD TIME!
BY THE PROPHETS--WHERE CAN THAT SON OF OURS BE, WOMAN! DOESN'T HE YET REALIZE THE HEIR TO THE THRONE MUST ATTEND THESE FEASTS?
WHAT MUST THE MEMBERS OF THE COURT BE THINKING?
CALM YOURSELF, MY HUSBAND! DIDN'T ADAM PROMISE HE WOULD BE HERE?
AYE! THAT HE DID, GOOD QUEEN--
--BUT YOU CERTAINLY DIDN'T EXPECT HIM TO SHOW UP WITHOUT SUITABLE COMPANIONSHIP, DID YOU?
HAIL, PRINCE ADAM?
AHHH... NOW THE REVELRY CAN BEGIN IN EARNEST!
ONLY TWO WENCHES, LAD--? YOU'RE LOSING YOUR CHARM!
2

★★★SPECIAL MASTERS OF THE UNIVERSE PREVIEW★★★

FORGIVE MY TARDINESS, MOTHER AND FATHER. AS YOU CAN SEE, I WAS, ER... UNAVOIDABLY DETAINED.
OUT WENCHING AGAIN, YOU MEAN, BOY!
I PREFER TO THINK OF IT AS TRAINING IN THE DELICATE ART OF NEGOTIATION, GOOD MAN-AT-ARMS!
REALLY--YOU TREAT ADAM AS IF HE WERE ALREADY KING... NOT JUST PRINCE OF THE REALM!
IF YOU PLEASE, MAJESTY--YOU INDULGE HIS TOMFOOLERY ENOUGH AS IS. I THINK THE LEAST HE COULD DO IS TO SOMETIMES FULFILL HIS PRINCELY DUTIES!
MAN-AT-ARMS--MOTHER! LET US NOT BICKER ON SUCH A MOMENTOUS OCCASION AS THIS--
--RATHER, ALLOW ME TO PROPOSE A TOAST! TO YOU, FATHER--THAT YOU MAY WEAR THE CROWN ROYALE FOR EONS TO COME IN HEALTH AND PROSPERITY...
...MAINLY THAT I'LL NEED NOT TAKE IT UP AND SPOIL MY FUN! HA HA!
THE ROYAL COURT ROARS WITH LAUGHTER. THERE'S NO DENYING THEY ALL LOVE THEIR PRINCE, TAKING VICARIOUS PLEASURE IN HIS RAUCOUS CAROUSING AND CHILD-LIKE SPIRIT.
BUT IN THE NEXT MOMENT, IT IS NOT THE IRRESPONSIBLE ADAM THEY WILL BE LOOKING TO AS THE BANQUET CHAMBER IS SWEPT SUDDENLY BY CHAOS--
ATTEND ME, PEOPLE OF ETERNIA! I AM ZODAC. I HAVE SPANNED THE COSMIC DISTANCES TO BRING YOU A WARNING!
YOU KNOW OF ME...AND YOU KNOW BETTER OF MY POWER! SUCH SHALL I UNLEASH UPON YOUR WORLD IF YOUR GREATEST CHAMPION IS NOT BROUGHT TO ME--TO BE TAKEN FOR ALL TIME FROM THIS WORLD!
BY MY CROWN! THE RIDER OF THE SPACE WINDS HAS GONE MAD! WHY WOULD HE MAKE SUCH A THREAT... AND WHY BRING IT HERE, TO THE ROYAL PALACE--?
I-I KNOW NOT, FATHER...
BUT THE TRUTH OF THE MATTER LIES DEEP WITHIN ADAM'S EYES--
3

★★★SPECIAL MASTERS OF THE UNIVERSE PREVIEW★★★
--AND THE SECRET THAT IS HIS ALONE TO KNOW OF ALL THE PEOPLE OF ETERNIA--
--BUT WHICH REMAINS AS AN OPEN BOOK TO THE RIDER OF THE SPACEWAYS!
MAJESTY! I THOUGHT I HEARD A COMMOTION IN... BY THE DARK GODS! TO ARMS, MY FAITHFUL TROOPS!
SWORD AND BLASTER WILL DO LITTLE AGAINST MIGHTY ZODAC, TEELA! I SUGGEST YOU...
AND I MOST "RESPECTFULLY" SUGGEST YOU STICK TO YOUR WENCHING AND CAROUSING, ADAM, AND LEAVE THE FIGHTING TO THOSE OF US VERSED IN SUCH THINGS!
ER... AS YOU SAY, GUARDSWOMAN...!
...IT'S ABOUT TIME FOR PRINCE ADAM TO TAKE HIS LEAVE AND A TRUE FIGHTER TO TAKE HIS PLACE!
AHH, THERE YOU ARE, GOOD CRINGER! COME, WE'VE TROUBLE THAT WARRANTS OUR RATHER SPECIAL TALENTS!
GROAN! I KNEW I SHOULD'VE FOUND INSTEAD SOME NICE, SAFE CORNER OF THE STABLES IN WHICH TO TAKE MY REST!
YOU COMPLAIN OVERLY MUCH, CAT! I WOULDN'T DREAM OF DISTURBING YOUR SLEEP WERE IT NOT IMPORTANT!
HA! A LIKELY STORY, MY PRINCE! SOMETIMES I THINK YOU TAKE PLEASURE IN BADGERING THIS POOR CAT WITH YOUR DANGEROUS ESCAPADES!
4

★★★SPECIAL MASTERS OF THE UNIVERSE PREVIEW★★★

SKREEEEEEE! SKREEEECHH!
AYE? THEN WHAT SAY YOU TO THAT, CRINGER... THE CALL TO ARMS OF THE FALCON?
-SIGH!- AS YOU SAY, ADAM... WE'RE NEEDED! THOUGH THE GODS KNOW WHY I WAS SO HONORED TO BE CHOSEN FOR SUCH HAZARDOUS DUTY!
THE AIR IS STILL IN THE COUNTRYSIDE BEYOND THE ROYAL CASTLE, SAVE FOR THE PLAINTIVE CRY OF A DARK BIRD OF PREY -- AND THE POUNDING FOOT-FALL OF THE PRINCE AND HIS CAT--
--AND IN THE NEXT INSTANT...
YE HAVE ANSWERED MY SUMMONS WITH HASTE, SWEET PRINCE--
--AS IT SHOULD BE, FOR THOU WOULD NOT BE SO CALLED DID NOT THE SORCERESS HAVE NEED OF THY POWERS!
I AM EVER AT YOUR COMMAND, GODDESS! SPEAK THEN AND SAY HOW MIGHTY HE-MAN AND FAITHFUL BATTLE CAT MAY BE OF SERVICE--
--THOUGH THIS ONCE I DO THINK I KNOW ALREADY OF THE MENACE THAT FACES ETERNIA!
YE SPEAK OF ZODAC, DO YE NOT, MY CHAMPION?
'TIS NOT HE OF WHICH I SPEAK! NAY, THE SAILOR OF THE SOLAR WINDS IS NO THREAT TO THIS WORLD'S WELL-BEING--
--NOT WHILST THE BEING OF EVIL INCARNATE IS YET LOOSE ON ETERNIA... NOT WHILST HE CALLED SKELETOR CONTINUES HIS SEARCH FOR THE POWER SWORD HE HOPES WILL MAKE HIM RULER SUPREME O'ER THY PEOPLE!
SKELETOR! MAY THE DARK GODS BURN HIS EVIL SOUL!
YE MAY RELY NOT UPON AID FROM BEYOND IN THY MISSION, HE-MAN... NOR MUST YE LET ANY STAND IN THE WAY OF COMPLETING THE TASK I HAVE SET TO THEE!
GO NOW, MY WARRIOR... AND MAY THE GODS BE WITH THEE!
MY THANKS, GODDESS! HE-MAN WILL NOT FAIL YOU... SKELETOR SHALL BE STOPPED!
5

AND SPEAKING OF THE DEVIL...
AS YOU COMMAND, SO HAS MER-MAN COME, MIGHTY SKELETOR! WHAT IS IT YOU WISH OF ME?
BESIDES YOUR UNDYING OBEDIENCE, FISH MAN?
SELDOM DOES THE DARK LORD HAVE NEED OF AID FROM SUCH AS YOU, BUT ON THIS DAY I FIND I MUST, FOR YOU HAVE KNOWLEDGE UNPARALLELED OF THE ETERNIAN SEAS, MER-MAN--
--AND 'TIS THERE I MAY FIND THE POWER I NEED TO AT LAST MAKE THIS WORLD MINE OWN! LONG HAVE I MEDITATED UPON THE LOCATION OF THAT POWER--
--WHICH RESTS IN THE TWIN HALVES OF THE AWESOME POWER SWORD JOINED TOGETHER AS ONE! I POSSESS BUT ONE HALF OF THE SWORD... AND MY MEDITATIONS HAVE SHOWN ME THE OTHER--
--LIES YONDER... BURIED IN THE DEEPEST TRENCH OF THE DARK SEA! 'TIS THERE YOU SHALL LEAD ME, MER-MAN!
BY THE WATER SPIRITS, SKELETOR... S-SURELY YOU KNOW THAT NONE HAVE CHALLENGED THE DEPTHS OF THE BLACK PIT AND EVER RETURNED TO TELL THE TALE!
GRRRR! LET YOUR HUMBLE BEAST-MAN HAVE AT THE IMPUDENT COWARD, MASTER!
NAY, BEAST-MAN. I DOUBT YOUR BRUTAL ANIMALISTIC MIGHT WILL BE NECESSARY HERE--
--WILL IT, FISH-MAN?
GAAK!
N-NO, MIGHTY DARK LORD! NO!
I THOUGHT NOT!
NOW, IF THERE ARE NO FURTHER DISCUSSIONS, SHALL WE BEGIN...?
6

★★★SPECIAL MASTERS OF THE UNIVERSE PREVIEW★★★

EARTH:
THERE ARE MANY SUCH WORLDS IN THE MULTIVERSE, MANY WITH CITIES CALLED METROPOLIS SET ON THE EASTERN SEA-BOARD OF A CONTINENT CALLED NORTH AMERICA. THIS EARTH, HOWEVER, IS UNIQUE--
--FOR IT IS THE ONLY ONE THAT IS HOME TO A MAN LIKE THIS... SUPERMAN!
ELLIS, INC.
ELLIS, INC
THIS IS THE LAST OF THEM!
IT'S A LUCKY THING FOR THE SHIPPING LINE'S INSURANCE COMPANY THAT I WAS IN THE NEIGHBOR-HOOD WHEN THAT CONTAINER BROKE UP IN HEAVY SEAS--
--OTHERWISE THEY'D BE PAYING OFF ON SEVERAL HUNDRED TONS OF VALUABLE ELECTRONICS!
NOW THAT THAT'S DONE, I'LL JUST TAKE ONE MORE FAST SPIN AROUND THE CITY AND HEAD ON HOME.
DON'T COUNT ON IT, SUPERMAN!
FOR EVEN AS THE MAN OF STEEL TAKES TO THE AIR, THE WATER IN METROPOLIS BAY BEGINS TO CHURN WILDLY--
--AND WHAT HAPPENS NEXT IS ENOUGH TO DRIVE ANY THOUGHTS OF REST FROM SUPERMAN'S HEAD!
GREAT KRYPTON!
I'M PRETTY FAMILIAR WITH JUST ABOUT EVERY FORM OF AQUATIC LIFE ON EARTH, BUT I'VE NEVER SEEN ANYTHING LIKE THIS ESCAPEE FROM A HORROR FILM!
WELL, IT LOOKS LIKE WE'RE BOTH SOMETHING NEW FOR EACH OTHER, HUH, UGLY? BECAUSE IT'S A SURE BET YOU'D PICK ON SOMEBODY ELSE FOR DINNER--
7

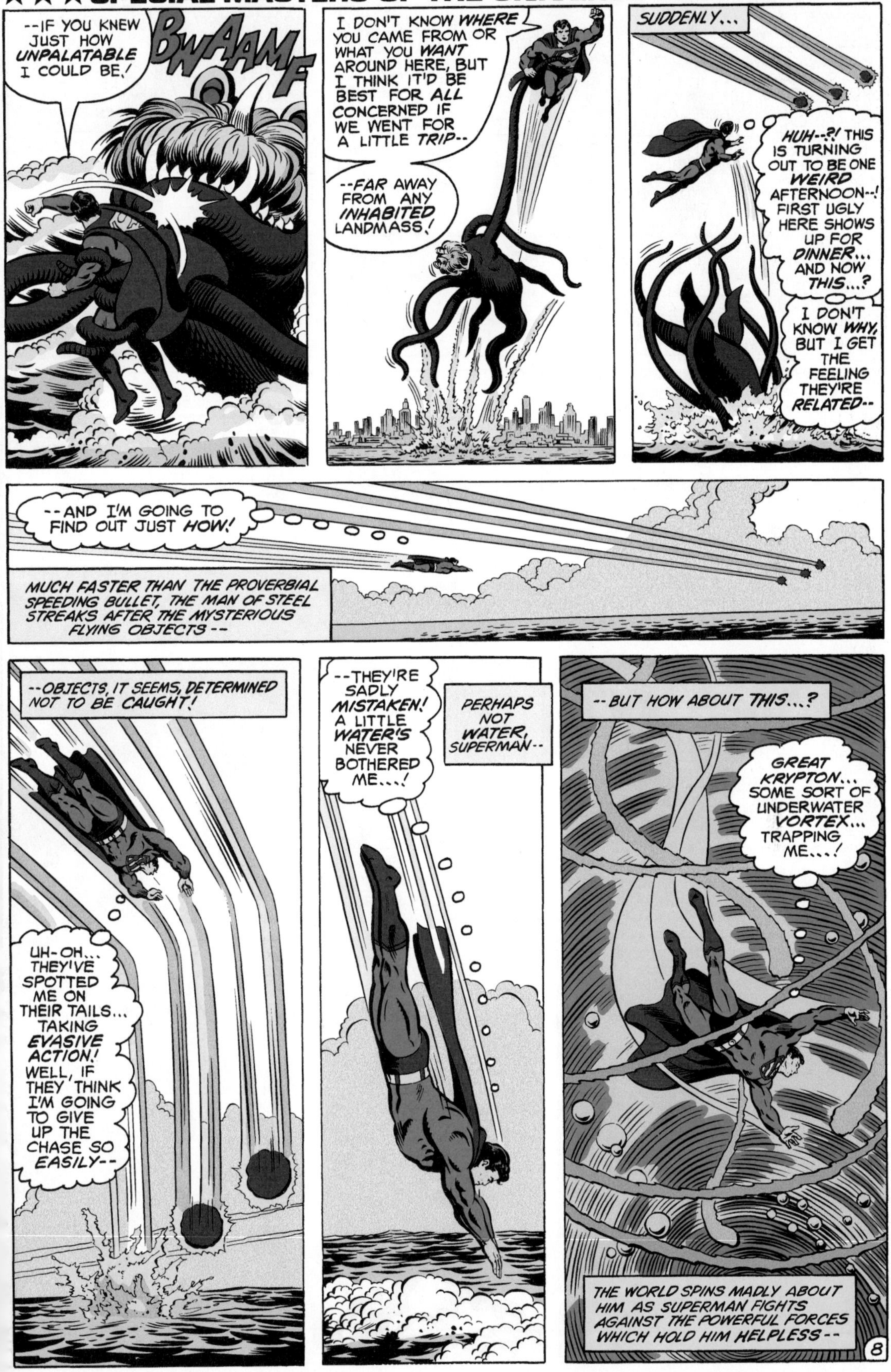
--IF YOU KNEW JUST HOW UNPALATABLE I COULD BE.!
BWAAMF
I DON'T KNOW WHERE YOU CAME FROM OR WHAT YOU WANT AROUND HERE, BUT I THINK IT'D BE BEST FOR ALL CONCERNED IF WE WENT FOR A LITTLE TRIP--
--FAR AWAY FROM ANY INHABITED LANDMASS.!
SUDDENLY...
HUH--?! THIS IS TURNING OUT TO BE ONE WEIRD AFTERNOON--! FIRST UGLY HERE SHOWS UP FOR DINNER... AND NOW THIS...?
I DON'T KNOW WHY, BUT I GET THE FEELING THEY'RE RELATED--
--AND I'M GOING TO FIND OUT JUST HOW!
MUCH FASTER THAN THE PROVERBIAL SPEEDING BULLET, THE MAN OF STEEL STREAKS AFTER THE MYSTERIOUS FLYING OBJECTS--
--OBJECTS, IT SEEMS, DETERMINED NOT TO BE CAUGHT!
UH-OH... THEY'VE SPOTTED ME ON THEIR TAILS... TAKING EVASIVE ACTION! WELL, IF THEY THINK I'M GOING TO GIVE UP THE CHASE SO EASILY--
--THEY'RE SADLY MISTAKEN! A LITTLE WATER'S NEVER BOTHERED ME...!
PERHAPS NOT WATER, SUPERMAN--
--BUT HOW ABOUT THIS...?
GREAT KRYPTON... SOME SORT OF UNDERWATER VORTEX... TRAPPING ME...!
THE WORLD SPINS MADLY ABOUT HIM AS SUPERMAN FIGHTS AGAINST THE POWERFUL FORCES WHICH HOLD HIM HELPLESS--
8

★★★SPECIAL MASTERS OF THE UNIVERSE PREVIEW★★★
--WHILE WE RETURN TO ETERNIA...
ONWARD, BRAVE BATTLE CAT! THE GODDESS WOULD NOT HAVE CALLED UPON US WERE NOT SKELETOR'S THREAT TO OUR WORLD IMMINENT!
AYE, HE-MAN... AS EVER! TRULY DO I LOOK FORWARD TO THE DAY WHEN THE MALEVOLENT SORCERER'S INFLUENCE UPON ETERNIA IS FOREVER ENDED!
AS DO I, CAT! ALL ETERNIA DOES RUE THE DAY THE EVIL FROM ANOTHER WORLD SET FOOT UPON OUR LAND!
GRRRR! THEN LET US FIND HIM, MAN ...SO I MAY AT LAST FASTEN MY JAWS ABOUT HIS FOUL FLESH!
YOU SHALL DO NO SUCH THING, CAT--ELSE IT CAN BE DONE WITHOUT YOUR MASTER'S AID!
ROAARRRR!
BY THE STARS! WE ARE ATTACKED! THEN EVIL SKELETOR HAS COME TO US--?
FAHTHHOOOM!
NAY, HE-MAN! 'TIS NOT THE DARK LORD YOU NEED CONCERN YOURSELF WITH THIS DAY... NOT WHEN YOU FACE THE RIDER OF THE SPACEWAYS--ZODAC!
STAND ASIDE, ZODAC! WHILE THE SHADOW OF SKELETOR LOOMS OMI-NOUS OVER THE LAND, I'VE NO QUARREL WITH THE LIKES OF YOU... SAVE SHOULD YOU DESIRE TO CREATE ONE!
I CARE NOT FOR YOUR PETTY WORLDLY CONCERNS, HE-MAN! YOU KNOW THAT ZODAC IS A BEING COSMIC... NEITHER GOOD NOR EVIL. THAT WHICH I COME TO TAKE YOU FOR IS OF FAR GREATER IMPORTANCE THAN THE FATE OF THIS WORLD!
ABANDON YOUR QUEST, MAN! COME WITH ME AND THE COSMOS SHALL BE YOUR HOME. STAY--AND YOU SHALL DIE!
YOU ARE BOLD, STAR SPAWN! THE GODDESS DID TELL ME I MAY LET NONE STAND IN THE WAY OF MY MISSION--
--YET SURELY DISPATCHING YOU TO WHENCE YOU CAME WILL DELAY ME NOT LONG!
THEN LET THE CONSEQUENCES BE ON YOUR HEAD, HE-MAN--
9

--SHOULD YOU BE FORTUNATE ENOUGH TO RETAIN IT ERE I AM DONE!
UHHHH!
GODDESS-- BUT ZODAC'S COSMIC MIGHT IS POTENT INDEED!
BWREEEET!
SURELY WOULD I BE MUCH MORE THAN STUNNED DID NOT MY POWER-VEST-CREATED FORCE-FIELD SHIELD ME FROM HIS ATTACK--
--AND GRANT ME THE STRENGTH TO STRIKE BACK!
WHAM!
I WOULD HAVE LET YOU BE, ZODAC... BUT YOUR ACTIONS HAVE LEFT ME NO CHOICE--
--BUT TO SEE TO IT YOU BOTHER ME NO FURTHER!
EH--?! THE STAR-MAN IS GONE...?
THONK!
NOT GONE, MORTAL--
--MERELY MOVED FROM BENEATH YOUR BLADE!
UGH! S-SO I DID UNDERESTIMATE YOUR POWER, ZODAC--
--YET TRUST I SHALL NOT DO SO AGAIN!
BOMMF!
HOLD, GOOD CAT! THIS BATTLE IS HE-MAN'S ALONE!
RRRRR! AS YOU WISH... YET KNOW YOU THAT BATTLE CAT MUST SOON TASTE COMBAT ERE HE GO MAD!
10

TASTE IT YOU SHALL, FELINE! FOR WITH ZODAC SO DISPATCHED, SKELETOR YET AWAITS--
--AND I CAN PROMISE YOU A VERITABLE FEAST!
DO NOT BE IN SUCH HASTE, MORTAL! THE BATTLE HERE HAS BUT BEGUN!
THE ETERNIAN HERO MAY ONLY GAPE IN AWE AT HIS FOE'S WORDS. NONE HAVE EVER WITHSTOOD SO EFFORTLESSLY HIS MIGHT AND HE-MAN KNOWS ZODAC SPEAKS TRUE!
AND THUS, DOES HE FEAR FOR THE SAFETY OF HIS WORLD--
--BELIEVING THERE IS NO ONE WHO CAN HELP!
HE-MAN IS WRONG... BUT NEITHER HE, NOR THE UNWITTING HELP, YET KNOW THIS!
THANK THE STARS-- WHATEVER IT IS THAT'S HOLDING ME IN THIS VORTEX IS WEAKENING EVER SO SLIGHTLY! I SHOULD BE ABLE TO GET FREE--
--WITH JUST A BIT OF EXTRA EFFORT!
DONE! AND IT LOOKS LIKE THE U.F.O.'S WERE SIMILARLY HELD UP BY THIS THING. I SUPPOSE I SHOULDN'T COMPLAIN--
--AS LONG AS THEY'RE STILL... HUH?! WHAT ON EARTH--?!
BUT EARTH, AS THE MAN OF STEEL SWIFTLY REALIZES, HAS NOTHING TO DO WITH HIS PRESENT SURROUNDINGS.
WAIT... I RECOGNIZE THIS PLACE! I'VE BEEN HERE BEFORE... ON ETERNIA! *
AND JUDGING FROM MY PAST EXPERIENCE, I CAN ONLY ASSUME THE CAUSE OF MY BEING HERE AGAIN WOULD HAVE TO BE--
*IN DC PRESENTS #47 -- Dave.
11

★★★SPECIAL MASTERS OF THE UNIVERSE PREVIEW★★★
"--SKELETOR!"
AT LAST--THE POWER SWORD IS MINE!
LONG HAVE I AWAITED THIS DAY WHEN THE ELUSIVE TWIN OF THE SWORD I DID HOLD WOULD BE MINE! LITTLE DID I SUSPECT THAT WHICH I SENSED AT THE OCEAN'S FLOOR WOULD BE BUT A DIMENSIONAL PORTAL TO WHERE THE SWORD TRULY LAY... UPON DISTANT EARTH!
'TWAS AS CHILD'S PLAY TO RELIEVE THE SWORD FROM WHENCE IT RESTED--
--WHILST DELAYING THAT WORLD'S MIGHTY SUPERMAN FROM INTERFERING IN MY THEFT BY CONJURING A SERPENT TO KEEP HIM OCCUPIED!
BUT NOW 'TIS DONE, AND ALL THAT REMAINS IS THE JOINING OF THE HALVES FOR THE SECRETS OF YON CASTLE GRAYSKULL TO BE REVEALED-- AND BY REVEALING THEM, MAKE ETERNIA MINE AS WELL! HA HA HA!
THEN DO IT, MASTER! YOUR HUMBLE SERVANT WOULD SEE IT DONE!
YIPE!
NOT YET, FOOLISH CUR! SUCH A GRANDIOSE EVENT MUST WAIT... FOR THE STARS ARE NOT YET IN PROPER ALIGNMENT FOR THE MAGICS TO WORK!
SWAK!
BUT SOON, LACKEY... VERY SOON THE TIME SHALL BE RIPE! AND WHEN THE DARK STAR DOES STAND POISED 'TWIXT THE ETERNIAN MOONS--
--THIS WORLD WILL FEEL MY MIGHT! HA HA HA HA!
I WOULDN'T COUNT ON THAT, SKELETOR--
--I WOULDN'T COUNT ON IT AT ALL!
SUPERMAN! CURSE YOU, ALIEN... I KNOW NOT HOW YOU FOUND ME, BUT YOU SHAN'T HALT MY SCHEME-- NOT AGAIN!
IT DOESN'T TAKE A GENIUS TO FIGURE YOU'RE STILL AFTER THE SAME THING AS WHEN WE LAST MET, SKULL-FACE, MAKING CASTLE GRAYSKULL THE FIRST PLACE I'D LOOK FOR YOU--
12

★★★SPECIAL MASTERS OF THE UNIVERSE PREVIEW★★★

--AS WELL AS A FITTING WATERLOO ... UGH!
T-THE PAIN... THE POWER SWORD... BURNING ME--!
AYE, EARTHLING! 'TIS WELL YOU SHOULD REMEMBER YOU ARE ON A WORLD WHERE MAGIC RULES... MAGIC THAT REMAINS YOUR WEAKNESS!
HAVE TO GET RID OF THESE... B-BEFORE SKELETOR CAN TURN THEIR POWER AGAINST ME!
NO! YOU MEDDLING BUFFOON... WHAT HAVE YOU DONE!
AFTER I HAVE SOUGHT SO LONG THE SWORD, YOU WOULD DARE SNATCH MY VICTORY FROM ME...?! YOU SHALL PAY FOR THIS, OFF WORLDER--YOU SHALL PAY DEARLY INDEED!
SUPERMAN CAN ONLY SHUDDER AT SKELETOR'S THREAT, BUT THE SWORD, AT LEAST, IS OUT OF HIS HANDS FOR THE NONCE --
--OFF TO A PLACE THAT IS HOPEFULLY, SAFER...
BAH! ALL YOU DO IS DELAY YOUR INEVITABLE FATE, HE-MAN! STAND STILL AND LET ZODAC HAVE DONE WITH YOU!
NEVER, STAR-RIDER! AS LONG AS THERE IS BREATH YET IN MY BODY, HE-MAN SHALL FIGHT--
--AND NEITHER VICTORY NOR DEFEAT SHALL COME EASILY... OOOFF!
WHAT MANNER OF ATTACK BE THIS...?
NAY... 'TIS ONE HALF OF THE POWER SWORD! YET... HOW--? UNLESS... AYE--THIS MUST THEN BE THE WORK OF EVIL SKELETOR! WHO ELSE WOULD BE SO BOLD!
TO ME, BATTLE CAT! THE GAUNTLET HAS BEEN THROWN DOWN AND I DO RISE TO THE CHALLENGE!
BUT WHAT OF ZODAC, HE-MAN--?
HE MUST WAIT! SKELETOR MENACES ALL OF ETERNIA ... AND MY LIFE IS ALL THAT IS THREATENED HERE! TRULY, DO I HAVE A CHOICE?
HE-MAN... NAY!
THIS MUST NOT BE! FOR DID NOT THE STARS TELL OF HE-MAN'S DEATH SHOULD HE THIS DAY MEET SKELETOR...?
MAYHAPS THEY DID, BUT THE ETERNIAN CHAMPION KNOWS NOT OF THE STARS--
--AND IN TRUTH, HE WOULD NOT CARE!
BY THE GODS! MADNESS SURELY REIGNS HERE! YONDER LIES AN ALLY FROM ANOTHER WORLD ... NEAR DEATH AT THE HANDS OF MY FOE! HALT, SKELETOR!
HE-MAN! BAH, BUT I DID EXPECT YOUR COMING--
13

★★★SPECIAL MASTERS OF THE UNIVERSE PREVIEW★★★

--THUS DID I PREPARE FOR YOU!
IT SEEMS THAT ALL THE FORCES OF THE COSMOS MOVE TO ACT AS ONE! A SPELL IS CAST--
--THE SWORD IS HURLED--
--AND WITHIN THE BLINK OF AN EYE, TWO BEINGS ARE STRUCK DOWN!
BY THE FATES! NAY! I-I AM TOO LATE--
--AND THE STARS HAVE CLAIMED THEIR VICTIM!
AAAK!-- I--CURSE YOU, MEDDLERS! I-I AM WOUNDED... THE POWER OF T-THE SWORD--
--CONSUMES MEEEEEE....
BUT BE IT MAGICAL OR PHYSICAL ENERGY, A SIMPLE LAW OF THE VERY NATURE OF THINGS HOLDS YET TRUE--
--AND THE ENERGY MUST BE MADE TO SEEK STILL ANOTHER FORM! SEEK IT IT DOES... INTO THE LIFE-FORCE OF THE MIGHTY HE MAN... AND AGAINST ALL REASON-- AGAINST EVEN THE VERY DICTATES OF FATE...
HE LIVES! HE-MAN RISES... ALIVE!
UHHHH... AYE... I - I LIVE, ZODAC--THOUGH MY EYES... DID THEY NOT JUST GLIMPSE A WORLD OF... DEATH--?
THAT THEY DID, MY FRIEND... BUT YOU NEED NOT FEAR IT AGAIN AT MY HANDS! WE SHALL FIGHT NO MORE, FOR ZODAC WILL EXPLAIN TO YOU A MYSTERY OF THE FATES--
--BUT FOR THE NONCE, BE SATISFIED THAT YOU HAVE MET THOSE FATES... AND CHEATED THEM OF THEIR VICTORY!
ER...THAT'S ALL WELL AND GOOD-- BUT WILL SOME-ONE PLEASE EXPLAIN WHAT I'M DOING HERE...?
14
END

WATCH FOR PART ONE OF THE MASTERS OF THE UNIVERSE MINI-SERIES ON SALE NEXT MONTH!

Printed in U.S.A. TM indicates Trademark of DC Comics Inc. © 1982 SM-11-B 1/82

Printed in U.S.A. ©DC Comics Inc. 1982 BM-7-B 1/82

Printed in U.S.A. BATMAN and BRUCE WAYNE are Trademarks of DC Comics Inc. © 1982 BM-5-B 1/82

Printed in U.S.A.

TM indicates Trademark of DC Comics Inc. © 1982

SM-1-C 1/82

Printed in U.S.A.

TM indicates Trademark of DC Comics Inc. © 1982

SM-2-C 1/82

Printed in U.S.A. TM indicates Trademark of DC Comics Inc. © 1982 WW-1-C 1/82

Printed in U.S.A. ©DC Comics Inc. 1982 WW-13-B 1/82

Printed in U.S.A.
TM indicates Trademark of DC Comics Inc. © 1982
JLA:F-5-B 1/82

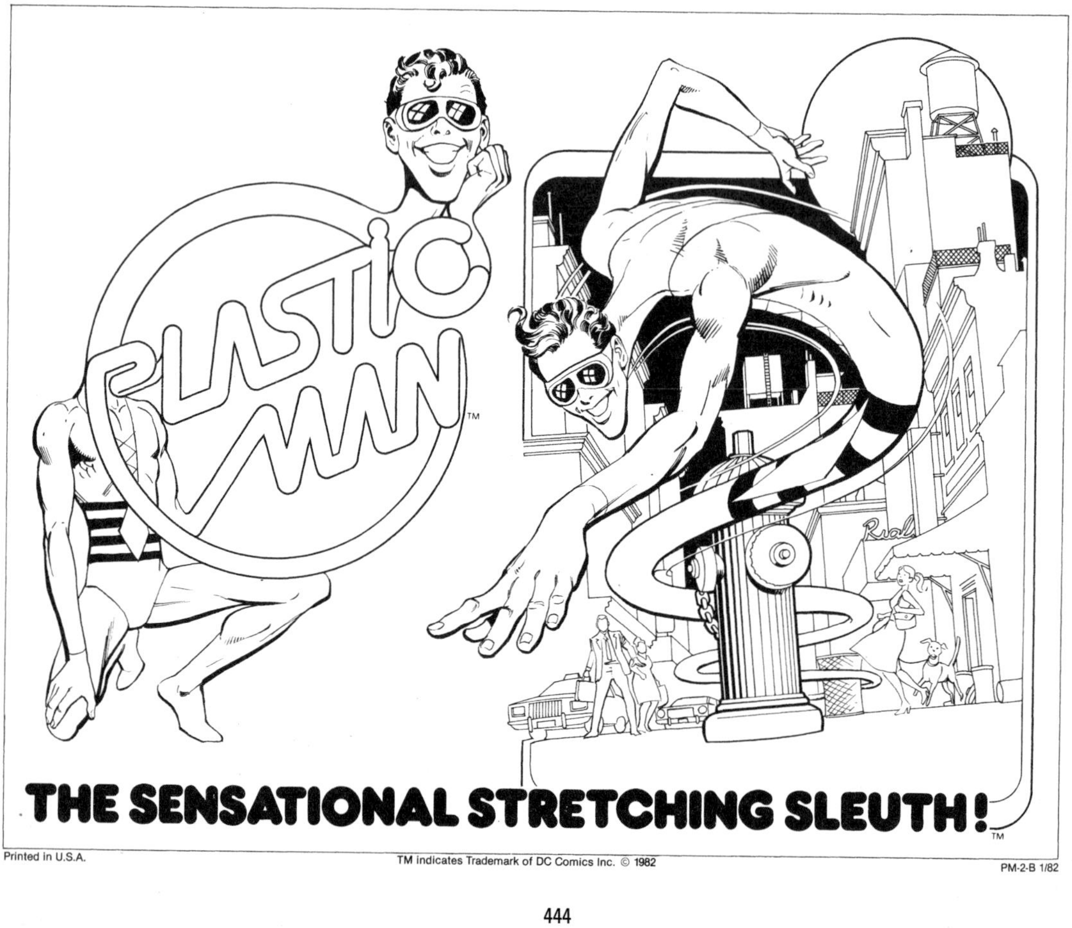

Printed in U.S.A.
TM indicates Trademark of DC Comics Inc. © 1982
PM-2-B 1/82

Printed in U.S.A. TM indicates Trademark of DC Comics Inc. © 1982 JLA:C-1-C 1/82

Printed in U.S.A. ©DC Comics Inc. 1982 JLA:C-3-B 1/82

Printed in U.S.A. TM indicates Trademark of DC Comics Inc. © 1982 SF-2-B 1/82

Printed in U.S.A. TM indicates Trademark of DC Comics Inc. © 1982 SJ-1-C 1/82

INTRODUCING HE-MAN

We were probably too old to be sitting on the conference room floor playing with action figures. It was all strictly professional, of course.

Honest.

Anyway, DC Comics editor Dave Manak and I weren't actually *playing* with action figures so much as we were familiarizing ourselves with a new product line that we had been assigned to turn into a comic book story—five comic book stories, when all was said and done, including two appearances with Superman.

The toy company was Mattel, makers of Barbie dolls and Hot Wheels cars (which had been a short-lived licensed DC Comics series in 1970), and the new product line was Masters of the Universe.

Mattel had a lot invested in MOTU. Launching a new toy line was an expensive proposition, costing as much as a million dollars in development, tooling, and inventory before a single toy left the warehouse. And ever since the success of Kenner's *Six Million Dollar Man* action figures changed the toy business from company-created originals to licensed properties, they could also face up to another half a million dollars in licensing fees.

According to Mark Ellis, then Mattel's Director of Marketing for Male Action Toys, Games, and Novelties in an interview with He-Man.org in 2013, "Mattel was having little success with its licensed products, like *MegaForce* [based on a 1982 Hal Needham action film that bombed at the box office and made more than one list of the year's worst movies] or *Clash of the Titans* [a 1981 heroic fantasy film featuring visual effects by Ray Harryhausen]. The solution [they] came up with was to develop our own characters and not be dependent on a license or its timing."

Ellis said, "To be clear, the task was not to develop He-Man and the Masters of the Universe. The idea was to develop a male action figure line." The exact form of that line would eventually be determined by research into "how the line would be played with, the composition of the line, and what elements made characters more popular with boys...Research was done to explore how and why children played with male action figures.

"What became clear was that for a five-year-old, power was a central issue because seemingly they were always being bossed around. Psychologically, they wanted to be the boss. They wanted the power. This was manifested in the figure by making him 'the strongest man in the universe.' The idea is...you are in charge of the most powerful man in the universe...As the line developed, the phrase 'I have the power' was born to emphasize that point."

By the time the Masters of the Universe figures arrived at DC for Dave and me to *familiarize* ourselves with them, all the research, development, design, innovation (like the "Battle Action Waist," whose mechanism dictated the figures' 5 1/4" height), and packaging had been done. The only thing He-Man and the MOTU didn't have was much of a history, or what we writer types call a backstory.

And, if not for Mark Ellis's snappy answer to a serious question from a buyer for the Child World toy store chain, DC might never have had the opportunity to provide one. Ellis recalled, "In the fall of 1982...at the end of the first presentation, they asked me, 'What marketing program do you have in conjunction with another company that is not just TV advertising?' I answered their question with a question, 'Did I tell you about the He-Man comic we are doing?'...but it left me with making good...I flew to New York to persuade [DC or Marvel Comics] to do a Masters of the Universe comic. When I showed DC the figures, they were excited about [it] and said yes...While it was a thought bred from necessity, it was a good marketing idea, which we eventually included with all of the figures in the form of a mini-comic inside the package."

He-Man and the Masters of the Universe made their mainstream comic book debut co-starring with Superman in the Man of Steel's monthly team-up title, *DC Comics Presents* #47 (July 1982). In a note in that issue's letters page, I wrote (in the third person), "Taking the idea of a line of action figures and turning them into a viable comic book required some work. Masters of the Universe project editor Dave Manak and writer Paul Kupperberg had to have several conferences with Mattel representative Mark Ellis to hammer out the characters and, effectively, create a whole new world on which to place them. There was some amount of fun to this, especially the opportunity to spend an entire morning playing with a million and a half dollars' worth of prototype action figures, accessories, and playsets."

Ellis recalled his role in crafting the backstory as largely advisory, saying, "We told DC about the research for the product line, the powers of each character, and the importance of power as a theme. The fact of the matter was that we were toy people, not comic people. All of the credit for the story lines in the comic goes to them."

But Dave and I *were* "comic people," and we saw immediately that what Mattel had bought with that extensive and expensive research was the basic formula for a comic book series. He-Man's personification of the power craved by their five-year-old research subjects was the same power fantasy superheroes have represented to readers since Superman defined the genre in 1938. Teela (and, later, She-Ra) was the tough, independent woman born in Lois Lane and given superheroic realization in Wonder Woman. Battle Cat was a bestial version of the loyal kid sidekick, like Robin or Bucky. Skeletor was the wannabe evil master of the world in the tradition of the Red Skull and Lex Luthor. As characters, they were still as much stereotypes as the action figures we played with were prototypes, but there was enough raw material there for us to work with.

He-Man's home world of Eternia was described as being a mix of medieval feudalism and high technology, ruled by Prince Adam's parents. Teela was the newly appointed captain of the Royal Guard. Man-at-Arms was the young prince's tutor (who also knew of Adam's double identity). Cringer, a giant talking green tiger, was his cowardly and lazy pet. Castle Grayskull was at the bottom of He-Man's power and was a sanctum sanctorum, your basic Batcave or Fortress of Solitude with a supernatural twist.

Ellis liked the idea of basing Prince Adam/He-Man on the Clark Kent/Superman dichotomy, i.e. Clark acts the coward to prevent anyone from suspecting he is really the heroic Man of Steel, which was then the standard model for the character. I countered by suggesting that Adam instead be a raucous, carousing womanizer to counterpoint his square-jawed and serious He-Man alter ego, using irresponsibility instead of meekness as his masquerade. While I wasn't a fan of the cowardly Clark conceit, the truth was I just thought it would be more fun to write a party boy character than a Clark-cloned party pooper.

The sword and sorcery genre in a medieval milieu made most of the choices for characterizations and speech patterns fairly easy: stern Man-at-Arms, tough-talking, impatient Teela, melodramatic Skeletor, and so on. The only one who gave me a little pause was Adam's giant green talking cowardly tiger; I knew how he would sound as the fearless Battle Cat ("Grrr! Then let us find him, man...so I may at last fasten my jaws about his foul flesh!"), but I couldn't nail down Cringer. What *does* a giant green talking, cowardly tiger sound like, anyway? Eventually, I found a role model in an earlier big cowardly cat, actor Bert Lahr's portrayal of the Cowardly Lion from 1939's *The Wizard of Oz*.

Four months after their debut in *DCCP #47*, the Masters of the Universe showed up in a self-titled insert running in most of DC's November 1982 titles. Under a cover blurb promising "Extra! Free 16-page comic preview MASTERS OF THE UNIVERSE," Superman once again found himself dragged from Earth to Eternia to help He-Man in his battle against Skeletor. Regular Superman artist Curt Swan pencilled the first two appearances (inked by Mike DeCarlo and Dave Hunt, respectively), but it was another veteran artist, George Tuska (inked by Alfredo Alcala and Rodin Rodriguez), who pencilled the three-issue *Masters of the Universe* miniseries that followed (December 1982-February 1983).

Masters of the Universe had been an interesting little side job, sort of a cross between my regular comic book gigs and the advertising/promotional "custom comics" projects I sometimes wrote. I certainly didn't expect it to take off the way that it did; most of these things, if they succeeded at all, usually had a fairly short shelf life. I also never expected that my contributions to the mythos would survive the decades along with it.

By the way, that day Dave and I were shown those Masters of the Universe prototypes? My He-Man beat his Skeletor *so bad*!

Paul Kupperberg
March 2020

Former DC Comics and fake news tabloid Weekly World News *editor and writer Paul Kupperberg has written more than 1,400 comic book stories, from 1979's* World of Krypton *(the first comic book miniseries) to the 2014 "Death of Archie" story line for Archie Comics. In between, he scripted (among others) the* Superman *syndicated newspaper strip,* Supergirl, Superboy, The Doom Patrol, Aquaman, Vigilante, Checkmate, Takion, *and* Arion, Lord of Atlantis. *He has also written books of fiction and nonfiction for readers of all ages, including 2013's GLAAD Award-nominated YA novel,* Kevin *(Grosset & Dunlap).*

HEROES REDUX

For the last word, how about the story that closed out Julie Schwartz's long run as editor of the Superman titles, as well as his four decades as a full-time DC staffer? The two-part tale "Whatever Happened to the Man of Tomorrow?" is an homage to all that was wonderful in both Schwartz's run and that of his predecessor, Mort Weisinger, who guided Superman for over a quarter of a century. And who better to deliver that last word than the undisputed best new comics

DC
SUPERMAN
75¢
423
SEPT. 86
APPROVED BY THE COMICS CODE AUTHORITY
in this
HISTORIC LAST ISSUE:
A Very Special Story by
ALAN MOORE, CURT SWAN & GEORGE PÉREZ
SEE
The RAMPAGE of BIZARRO!
MEET
The NEW BRAINIAC-LUTHOR TEAM!
EXPERIENCE
The RETURN OF THE FEARSOME FUNSTERS!
SURVIVE
The DAILY PLANET'S LAST STAND!
WITNESS
The KILLING of CLARK KENT!
ATTEND
The LEGION of SUPER-HEROES' LAST SALUTE!
IN MEMORIAM
"WHATEVER HAPPENED TO The MAN of TOMORROW?"
SWANDERSON

This is an IMAGINARY STORY (which may never happen, but then again may) about a perfect man who came from the sky and did only good. It tells of his twilight, when the great battles were over and the great miracles long since performed; of how his enemies conspired against him and of that final war in the snowblind wastes beneath the Northern Lights; of the women he loved and of the choice he made between them; of how he broke his most sacred oath, and how finally all the things he had were taken from him save for one. It ends with a wink. It begins in a quiet midwestern town, one summer afternoon in the quiet midwestern future. Away in the big city, people still sometimes glance up hopefully from the sidewalks, glimpsing a distant speck in the sky... but no: it's only a bird, only a plane. Superman died ten years ago. This is an IMAGINARY STORY...
Aren't they all?
"WHATEVER HAPPENED TO THE MAN OF TOMORROW?"
ALAN MOORE: WRITER
CURT SWAN & GEORGE PÉREZ ARTISTS
TODD KLEIN: LETTERER
GENE D'ANGELO: COLORIST
JULIUS SCHWARTZ: EDITOR
IN MEMORIAM

GENG-GLANG
ELLIOT
YES?
UH, EXCUSE ME... MS. LOIS LANE?
IT'S MRS. LOIS ELLIOT NOW. ANYWAY, COME IN... YOU MUST BE TIM CRANE, FROM THE PLANET.
UH, THAT'S RIGHT. IS IT STILL CONVENIENT TO DO THE INTERVIEW WITH YOU FOR OUR SUPERMAN MEMORIAL EDITION?
SURE. MY HUSBAND'S OUT AT WORK AND THE BABY'S ASLEEP, SO WE WON'T BE DISTURBED. WILL THIS ROOM BE OKAY?
FINE. JUST LET ME SET UP MY RECORDER...
OKAY, TESTING: AUGUST 16th, 1997. TIM CRANE INTERVIEWING LOIS LA...
...uh...LOIS ELLIOT FOR THE DAILY PLANET LEAD FEATURE. TITLE: "THE LAST DAYS OF SUPERMAN."

THERE...I THINK THAT SHOULD BE OKAY.
I...I FEEL KINDA NERVOUS INTERVIEWING YOU, MRS. ELLIOT. YOU'RE SORT OF A LEGEND AROUND THE DAILY PLANET. I'M PROBABLY DOING THIS ALL WRONG...
YOU'RE DOING FINE... AND IT'S LOIS.
LOIS. RIGHT.
UH, WELL, I SUPPOSE I SHOULD START BY ASKING ABOUT THE YEARS LEADING UP TO SUPERMAN'S DISAPPEARANCE AND PRESUMED DEATH.
WERE THOSE HAPPY TIMES?
HAPPY? I DON'T KNOW...THEY WERE A MIXTURE OF THINGS, LIKE MOST TIMES...
...BUT AT LEAST THEY WERE QUIET.
LUTHOR SEEMED TO BE LYING LOW, AND TWO YEARS EARLIER BRAINIAC'S LAST ORGANIC METAL BODY HAD BEEN POUNDED INTO A STATE BEYOND REPAIR.
AS I RECALL, SUPERMAN LATER RECOVERED EVERY FRAGMENT EXCEPT THE CREATURE'S HEAD.
THE PARASITE AND TERRA-MAN HAD DESTROYED EACH OTHER IN A LETHAL CLASH OF EGOS, AND IT SEEMED LIKE THERE WAS NOBODY LEFT TO FIGHT.
MOSTLY, SUPERMAN WORKED IN SPACE, DOING RESEARCH FOR THE GOVERNMENT.
IT WAS WHILE HE WAS STILL OUT IN SPACE RETURNING FROM SUCH A MISSION THAT WE GOT OUR FIRST TASTE OF THE CARNAGE THAT WAS TO FOLLOW...

GREAT SCOTT.
WHAT'S HAPPENED HERE?
SUPERMAN! THANK HEAVENS YOU'RE BACK!
YEAH! I TRIED USING MY SIGNAL-WATCH EARLIER, BUT I GUESS YOU WERE OUT OF RANGE...
BUT THIS DESTRUCTION... WHAT CAUSED IT? WAS IT A BOMB, OR...
WORSE THAN A BOMB. SUPERMAN, IT WAS BIZARRO!
BIZARRO DID THIS!
BIZARRO?
HE WAS COMPLETELY BERSERK, SMASHING THINGS, HURTING PEOPLE, PUSHING OVER BUILDINGS... IT WAS HORRIBLE. HE KEPT LAUGHING...
ABOUT TWENTY MINUTES AGO HE RETREATED INTO THAT DEPARTMENT STORE AND HASN'T COME OUT SINCE.
OKAY. I'M HERE NOW. I'LL HANDLE IT.
BIZARRO.
INCREDIBLE.

BIZARRO?
COME ON OUT AND SHOW YOURSELF! I WANT AN EXPLANATION FOR THIS!
HA! THAT EASY! IT AM PART OF GENIUS BIZARRO SELF-IMPROVEMENT PLAN!
KRUTTUNCH
BIZARRO--?
SEE, ME SUDDENLY REALIZE THAT ME AM NOT PERFECT IMPERFECT DUPLICATE! MAYBE ME NOT TRYING HARD ENOUGH.
EXAMPLE: WHEN YOUR PLANET KRYPTON BLOW UP BY ACCIDENT, YOU AM COMING TO EARTH AS BABY...
...SO ME DECIDE TO BLOW UP WHOLE BIZARRO WORLD ON PURPOSE AND COME TO EARTH AS ADULT!
THE BIZARRO WORLD? BLOWN UP?!
TH-THAT RIGHT! HA HA! PRETTY IMPERFECT, HUH?
BIZARRO
1/2 OFF

BIZARRO... WHAT'S HAPPENED TO YOU? I CAN'T BELIEVE YOU'VE REALLY DESTROYED YOUR HOMEWORLD!
HA! THAT AM ONLY BEGINNING! NEXT, ME REALIZE THAT SUPERMAN NEVER KILL, SO ME KILL LOTS OF PEOPLE! THEM VERY GRATEFUL! SCREAM WITH HAPPINESS!
KILLED PEOPLE? OH, MERCIFUL RAO...
...BUT THEN ME FINALLY UNDERSTAND WHAT ME NEED TO BE PERFECT IMPERFECT DUPLICATE:
IT AM LITTLE BLUE KRYPTONITE METEOR THAT ME CARRY IN LEAD CASE FOR GOOD LUCK!
BIZARRO!
SEE... YOU AM ALIVE, SUPERMAN... AND IF ME AM PERFECT IMPERFECT DUPLICATE, THEN ME HAVE TO BE...
H-HAVE TO BE...
KRETESSH
UH... EVERYTHING, HIM GO D-DARK...
HELLO, SUPERMAN.
HELLO.
"IT DIDN'T MAKE ANY SENSE AT ALL, EVEN BY BIZARRO STANDARDS..."
AFTER YEARS OF HARMLESS STUPIDITY THAT STRANGE, BACKWARDS CREATURE HAD SUDDENLY LAUNCHED HIMSELF ON A RAMPAGE OF GENOCIDE, HOMICIDE, AND FINALLY SUICIDE.
Y-YOU'RE TALKING ABOUT THE UNMASKING?
STILL, AFTER WHAT CAME NEXT, BIZARRO'S DEATH SEEMED TRIVIAL.

"YES. I'M TALKING ABOUT THE UNMASKING."
DELIVERY FOR MR. KENT...
UH, I'M CLARK KENT. WHAT IS IT?
TWO PARCELS, DELIVERED OUTSIDE JUST NOW. THE BIG ONE'S REAL HEAVY.
CLARK, WE'RE ON THE AIR IN THREE MINUTES!
OH, THIS WON'T TAKE A SECOND, LANA. I'LL JUST OPEN THE LITTLE ONE, AND...
HMM. THAT'S ODD.
WHAT IS IT?
IT'S A LOT OF LITTLE SUPERMAN ACTION FIGURES...
OH! I'VE SEEN THOSE AROUND! THEY'RE GREAT!
HAVE YOU SEEN HOW THEY WORK? YOU JUST PRESS THEIR LEGS TOGETHER LIKE THIS, AND...
AAAAAA!
WHOOMF
SSIIZZZZIIIK

CLARK? CLARK, IT'S MOVING!
TH-THEY'RE ALL MOVING...
SHAZZAAT
LOOK OUT!
CLARK! GET DOWN! YOU'RE IN THEIR LINE OF FIRE!
I...
OH, GOD. OH, MY GOD...
ZZZAAAZZAT
CLARK!
THEY... THEY'RE... ALL TURNING ON CLARK! THEY'RE SLICING HIM UP!
THIS IS HORRIBLE! YOU HAVE TO LET ME HELP HIM.
LANA, IT'S TOO LATE. WE CAN'T SAVE HIM. HE'S BEYOND...
...HELP--?!

OH.
CLARK...IT WAS YOU!
ALL THESE YEARS...IT WAS YOU ALL THE TIME!
HA HA! THAT'S RIGHT, MISS LANG...
...IT WAS HIM ALL THE TIME! HE JUST COMBED HIS HAIR AND STUCK ON A PAIR OF GLASSES! HA HA HA! WHAT A GREAT GAG!
CLARK... SUPERMAN... THOSE VOICES...
OH, COME ON! WE'VE TOYED WITH HIM ENOUGH!
YES. I RECOGNIZE THEM! THE TOYMAN AND THE PRANKSTER!
OKAY... HOW DID YOU KNOW THAT I WAS CLARK KENT?
HAH! WHAT A MORON! WHAT AN IMBECILE! WHY DON'T YOU LOOK IN THE BIG BOX AND FIND OUT?
...AND NO FAIR PEEKING! IT'S LEAD-LINED!
EVERYBODY STAND BACK! IF IT'S A BOMB, I'LL CONTAIN THE EXPLOSION.
ALL RIGHT... I'M OPENING IT NOW...
SPRONNNNNGGG

NO... NO!
OH, GOD... IT'S PETE, ISN'T IT? IT'S PETE ROSS, AND, AND HE'S DEAD...
RI-I-IGHT! BUT NOT BEFORE WE DRAGGED YOUR SECRET IDENTITY OUT OF HIM WITH A LITTLE BOFFO BRAINWASHING!
WE'D PLANNED TO WORK THROUGH YOUR FRIENDS, STARTING WITH THE FURTHEST AWAY, BUT WE HIT PAYDIRT FIRST TIME!
PRANKSTER... TOYMAN... LET ME ASK YOU ONE QUESTION:
DO YOU KNOW WHAT RADIO WAVES LOOK LIKE?
HUH? NO. WHY?
BECAUSE I DO!
YAAAGH!

"THEY GAVE IN ALMOST IMMEDIATELY, BUT DIDN'T SEEM ABLE TO TELL HIM WHY THEY'D SUDDENLY DECIDED TO START MURDERING HIS FRIENDS.
"WHEN HE ASKED, THEY JUST LOOKED DAZED AND CONFUSED.
"...AND, OF COURSE, PUTTING THEM BEHIND BARS DIDN'T MEND THE SENSELESS DAMAGE THEY'D CAUSED. PETE ROSS WAS STILL DEAD...
"...AND SO WAS CLARK KENT. ONCE PUBLICLY REVEALED, HIS SECRET IDENTITY WAS USELESS, SO HE DROPPED IT.
PLANET
CLARK KENT EXPOSED AS SUPERMAN
"I REMEMBER, AFTER PETE'S FUNERAL, HE TALKED TO US ALL. ABOUT HIS FEARS, HIS WORRIES..."
I HAVE BAD FEELINGS ABOUT THIS. BIZARRO, THE PRANKSTER, THE TOYMAN... THEY WERE ALL JUST NUISANCES BEFORE.
WHAT TURNED THEM INTO KILLERS?
ALL THESE YEARS, MY GREATEST NIGHTMARE HAS BEEN THAT SOMEONE WOULD STRIKE AT ME THROUGH MY FRIENDS. NOW IT'S COMING TRUE.
LISTEN, BIZARRO'S DEAD, THE OTHERS ARE BEHIND BARS. WHAT'S TO WORRY ABOUT?
I... I DON'T KNOW. IT ISN'T RATIONAL-- IT'S JUST... WELL, IF THE NUISANCES FROM MY PAST ARE COMING BACK AS KILLERS...
...WHAT HAPPENS WHEN THE KILLERS COME BACK?
HE DIDN'T HAVE TO MENTION ANY NAMES. WE ALL KNEW WHO HE WAS TALKING ABOUT. THE BIG GUNS: LUTHOR, BRAINIAC... WHAT IF THEY CAME BACK MORE VICIOUS THAN EVER?
UH, I THOUGHT BRAINIAC HAD BEEN DESTROYED?

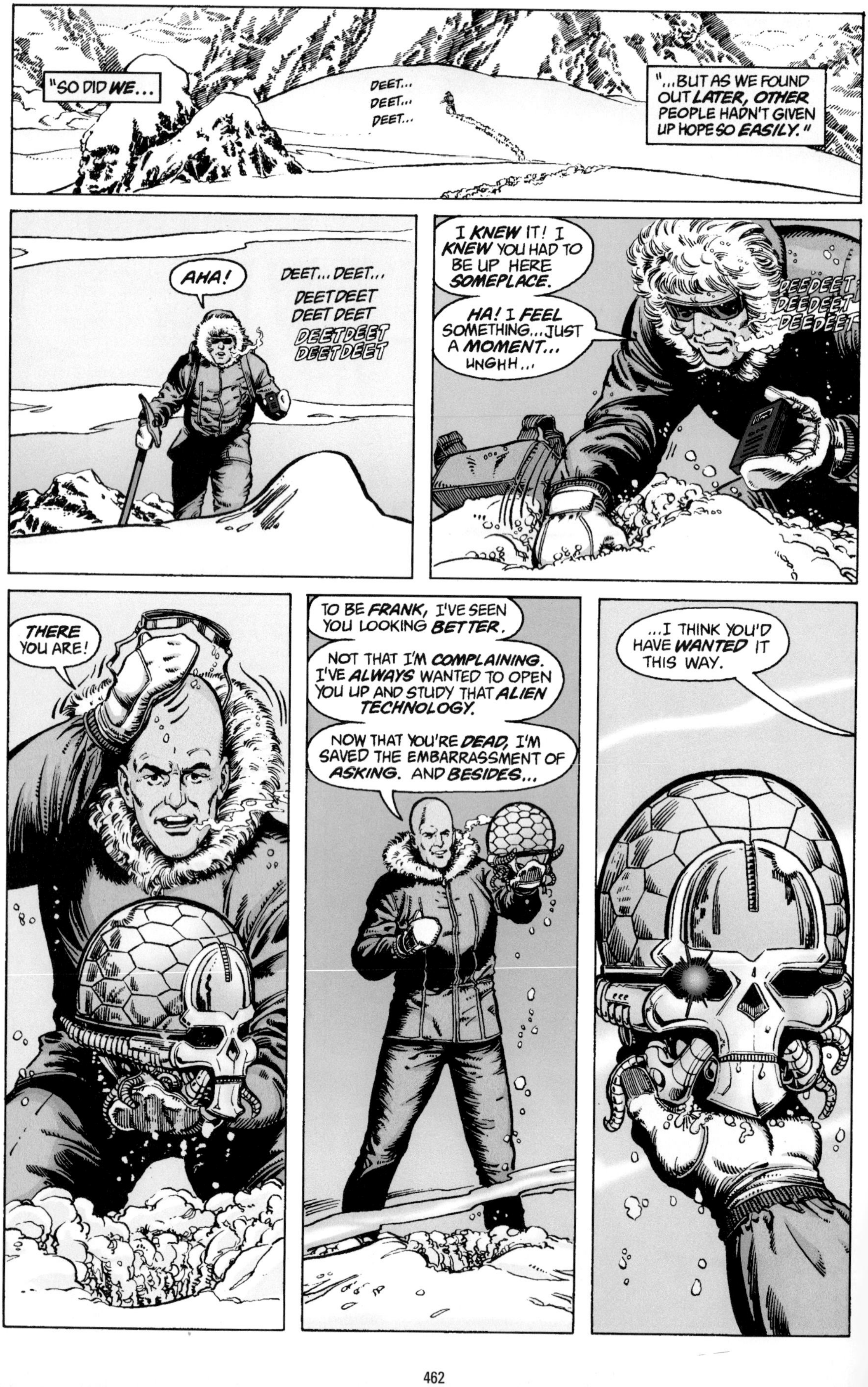
"SO DID WE...
DEET... DEET... DEET...
"...BUT AS WE FOUND OUT LATER, OTHER PEOPLE HADN'T GIVEN UP HOPE SO EASILY."
AHA!
DEET... DEET... DEETDEET DEET DEET DEETDEET DEETDEET
I KNEW IT! I KNEW YOU HAD TO BE UP HERE SOMEPLACE.
HA! I FEEL SOMETHING... JUST A MOMENT... UNGHH...
DEEDEET DEEDEET DEEDEET
THERE YOU ARE!
TO BE FRANK, I'VE SEEN YOU LOOKING BETTER.
NOT THAT I'M COMPLAINING. I'VE ALWAYS WANTED TO OPEN YOU UP AND STUDY THAT ALIEN TECHNOLOGY.
NOW THAT YOU'RE DEAD, I'M SAVED THE EMBARRASSMENT OF ASKING. AND BESIDES...
...I THINK YOU'D HAVE WANTED IT THIS WAY.

I MEAN, BACK WHEN YOU WERE STILL GREEN WITH A HEAD FULL OF LIGHT BULBS, WE WERE ALWAYS SUCH GREAT BUDDIES! REMEMBER THE BRAINIAC-LUTHOR TEAM? WE WERE...
UH...
TING PTING TLING GLING
WHAT THE HELL IS...
OH.
OH, NO...
PLITTING TING SKLING DRING
BRAINIAC...
BRAINIAC, STOP THIS! I DIDN'T KNOW YOU WERE ALIVE!
BRAINIAC, I'M WARNING YOU...
FLINGTING KTING PLING TING
ZING TING GLING KTING SKLITTING DRING TING BDING TINGLING KLING PRING QLING
NO! NO NO NO!
SLIDGE
SLIDGE
AAAAAAAAAAAA
GREETINGS, LEX LUTHOR.
YOUR BODY, MIND, AND VOCAL CORDS ALL NOW BELONG TO ME.
I WELCOME YOU TO THE NEW BRAINIAC-LUTHOR TEAM.

BY HUMAN STANDARDS, YOUR BRAIN IS SUPERB, ITS STORED DATA MASSIVELY USEFUL.
THE KRYPTONIAN HAS INTERRUPTED MY PROGRAMS AND CAUSED ME INDIGNITY. I SHALL TOLERATE HIM NO LONGER.
NOW: RAISE MY FACEPLATE TO YOUR HEAD.
THERE.
MY SHIP WAS DESTROYED BY THE SUPERMAN. OUR FIRST PRIORITY IS TO CONSTRUCT A REPLACEMENT. THE MATERIALS WILL ONLY BE FOUND IN POPULATED AREAS.
TAKE ONE STEP FORWARD.
I FEEL YOU RESISTING ME. IT IS USELESS.
I REPEAT MYSELF: TAKE ONE STEP FORWARD.
VERY GOOD.
NOW ANOTHER STEP.
AND ANOTHER.
AND ANOTHER.
AND ANOTHER...
DEET... DEET... DEET...

NATURALLY, WE WEREN'T AWARE OF BRAINIAC'S RETURN UNTIL LATER. OVER IN METROPOLIS, HOWEVER, WE HAD OUR OWN PROBLEMS.
I REMEMBER IT WAS JUST A COUPLE OF DAYS AFTER PETE'S FUNERAL...
DAILY PLANET
WGBS
"THE DAY WHEN SUPERMAN LOST A PLANET, FOR THE SECOND TIME IN HIS LIFE.
"WE WERE WORKING IN THE OFFICE. THE AIR-CONDITIONING WAS ON THE FRITZ AND THE SIDEWALKS OUT-SIDE WERE HOT, THRONGING WITH PEOPLE...
"ACCORDING TO LATER REPORTS, CERTAIN MEMBERS OF THE CROWD SUDDENLY STOPPED DEAD AND LOOKED UPWARDS.
"IT WAS AS IF SOME UNSEEN COMMUNICATION HAD PASSED BETWEEN THEM."
HEY! HEY, HONEY! YOU LOOK KINDA HOT 'N' BOTHERED. COULD YOU USE A DATE?
C'MON... WHAT'S TO LOSE?
FOR TWENTY BUCKS I COULD BREAK YOUR HEART.
I DOUBT IT.
EEEEEEEEEEE!
SHOOMF

"BY THE TIME WE HEARD THE SCREAMS FROM THE STREET, THE NIGHTMARE WAS ALREADY UNDER WAY...
SHOOMF
SHOOMF
SHOOMF
"THERE MUST HAVE BEEN HUNDREDS OF THEM...
"AND THEY ALL WANTED ONE THING: IN!"
KRITSSSSHH
GREAT CAESAR'S GHOST! WHAT'S HAPPENING?
CHIEF, THE BUILDING ...IT'S UNDER ATTACK!
WE'RE BEING BOARDED BY METALLOS!
WE'RE COMING, FRIENDS OF CLARK KENT! WE'RE COMING TO KILL YOU, THE WAY KENT KILLED MY BROTHER! PREPARE TO BE MASSACRED, FOR WE HAVE NO PITY!
WE HAVE NO HEARTS!
THERE'S TOO MANY OF THEM! JIMMY...USE THE WATCH!
UNNGH
I AM! YOU JUST CAN'T HEAR IT! NOBODY CAN...
ZEE ZEE ZEE ZEE ZEE
"...EXCEPT HIM."
ZEE ZEE
ZEE ZEE ZEE ZEE ZEE ZEE ZEE ZEE ZEE

UNGH
OUT OF MY WAY, KID. IT'S THE WOMAN I WANT TO KILL MOST, THE ALIEN-LOVING TRAMP...
AAA! LET ME GO! LET ME...
...GO...
"WHAT HAPPENED NEXT HAD ALL THE FAMILIARITY OF A RECURRING DREAM. I WAS FALLING, AND A VIOLET COMET WAS FALLING ALONGSIDE ME.
"THE REDS AND BLUES RAN TOGETHER, YOU SEE, SO THAT'S HOW HE LOOKED WHEN HE FLEW...
"...A VIOLET COMET."
HOLD ON, LOIS.
I DON'T KNOW HOW METALLO CONVERTED SO MANY HUMANS INTO CREATURES LIKE HIMSELF, BUT THERE'S A FAST WAY OF CONTAINING THEM.
WH-WHATEVER YOU SAY.
WHAT ARE YOU DOING...?
RUB ANY IRON ROD IN THE SAME DIRECTION FOR LONG ENOUGH AND YOU'LL ALIGN THE MAGNETIC POLES OF THE PARTICLES, TURNING IT INTO A MAGNET...

...OR IN THIS CASE, A SUPER-MAGNET.
RRRENNCH
"HE LIFTED THE MAGNETIZED GLOBE INTO THE SKY ABOVE THE GALAXY BUILDING.
"I REMEMBER HOPING HE HADN'T MADE IT STRONG ENOUGH TO LIFT THE CARS FROM THE STREET BELOW, BUT I NEEDN'T HAVE WORRIED.
"HE GOT EVERYTHING JUST RIGHT.
"AS ALWAYS!
"WHEN HE'D GATHERED UP ALL THE METALLOS... ALONG WITH MOST OTHER METAL FROM THE PLANET OFFICES... HE FLEW THE PARALYZED CYBORGS TO THE ST. THERESA PRISON COMPLEX.
"I GATHER MOST OF THEM WERE LATER SUCCESSFULLY RE-HUMANIZED.
"WHEN HE RETURNED, HE LOOKED AS DEVASTATED AS THE PLANET OFFICES.
"HE INSISTED ON TAKING ALL HIS CLOSEST FRIENDS TO THE FORTRESS OF SOLITUDE, WHERE HE COULD DEFEND THEM IF THE SITUATION CONTINUED TO WORSEN.
"HE FETCHED LANA, AND PERRY WHITE'S WIFE, ALICE. ALICE AND PERRY WERE NOT QUITE GETTING ON, AND SHE WAS VERY CONFUSED AND SCARED.
"I GUESS WE WERE ALL TENSE. EVERYTHING HAD SUCH AN AIR OF FINALITY...

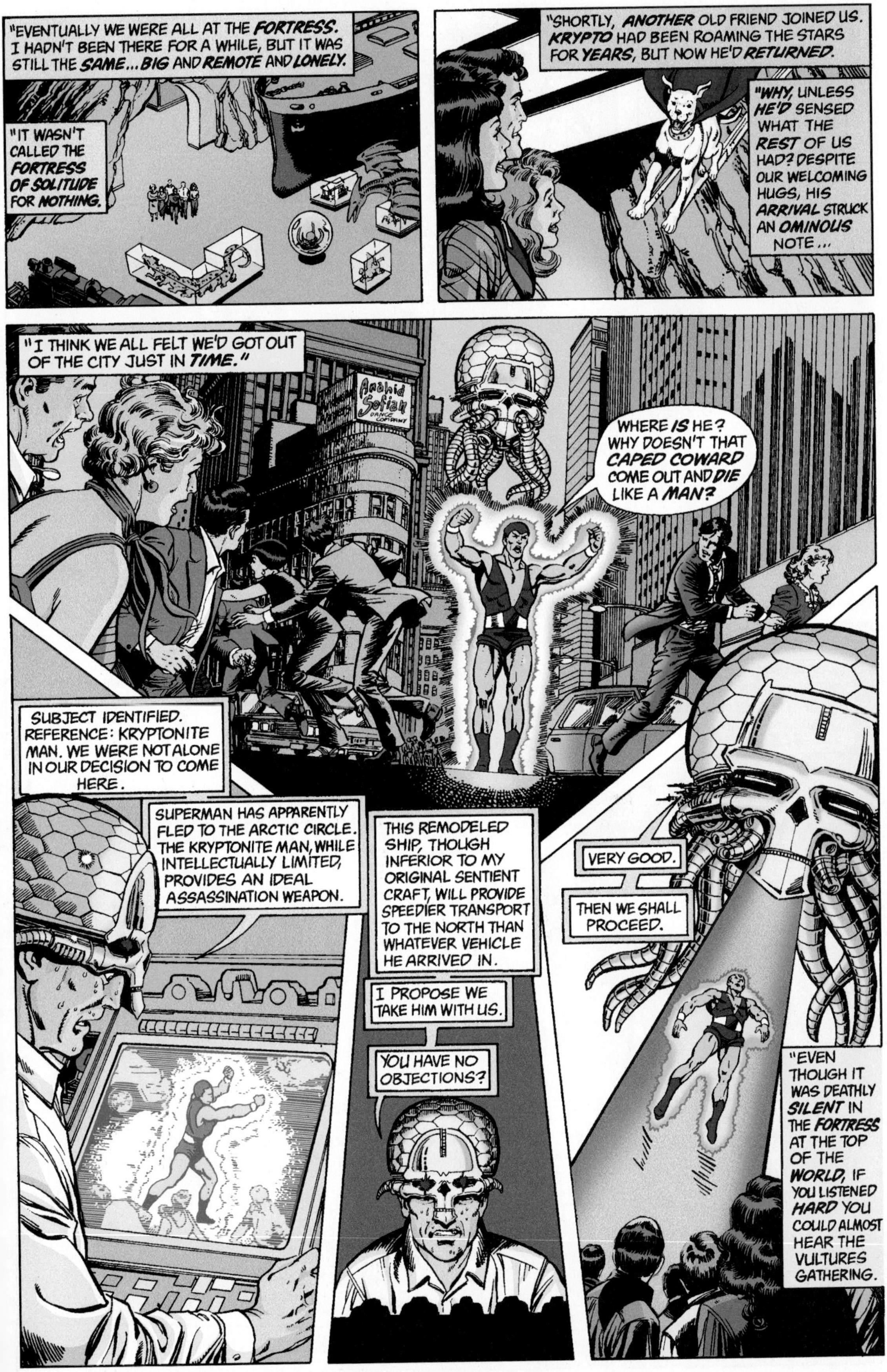
"EVENTUALLY WE WERE ALL AT THE FORTRESS. I HADN'T BEEN THERE FOR A WHILE, BUT IT WAS STILL THE SAME... BIG AND REMOTE AND LONELY.
"IT WASN'T CALLED THE FORTRESS OF SOLITUDE FOR NOTHING.
"SHORTLY, ANOTHER OLD FRIEND JOINED US. KRYPTO HAD BEEN ROAMING THE STARS FOR YEARS, BUT NOW HE'D RETURNED.
"WHY, UNLESS HE'D SENSED WHAT THE REST OF US HAD? DESPITE OUR WELCOMING HUGS, HIS ARRIVAL STRUCK AN OMINOUS NOTE...
"I THINK WE ALL FELT WE'D GOT OUT OF THE CITY JUST IN TIME."
Anahid Sofian DANCE COMPANY
WHERE IS HE? WHY DOESN'T THAT CAPED COWARD COME OUT AND DIE LIKE A MAN?
SUBJECT IDENTIFIED. REFERENCE: KRYPTONITE MAN. WE WERE NOT ALONE IN OUR DECISION TO COME HERE.
SUPERMAN HAS APPARENTLY FLED TO THE ARCTIC CIRCLE. THE KRYPTONITE MAN, WHILE INTELLECTUALLY LIMITED, PROVIDES AN IDEAL ASSASSINATION WEAPON.
THIS REMODELED SHIP, THOUGH INFERIOR TO MY ORIGINAL SENTIENT CRAFT, WILL PROVIDE SPEEDIER TRANSPORT TO THE NORTH THAN WHATEVER VEHICLE HE ARRIVED IN.
I PROPOSE WE TAKE HIM WITH US.
YOU HAVE NO OBJECTIONS?
VERY GOOD.
THEN WE SHALL PROCEED.
"EVEN THOUGH IT WAS DEATHLY SILENT IN THE FORTRESS AT THE TOP OF THE WORLD, IF YOU LISTENED HARD YOU COULD ALMOST HEAR THE VULTURES GATHERING.

"HE PREPARED A MEAL FOR US AND THEN IT WAS TIME FOR BED. HE SHOWED US ALL TO THE GUEST QUARTERS AND LOOKED SAD AS HE LED PERRY AND ALICE TO SEPARATE ROOMS.
"I COULDN'T SLEEP, SO I KNOCKED ON THE DOOR OF LANA'S ROOM, WHICH WAS NEXT TO MINE. OVER THE YEARS WE'D BEEN RIVALS, UNEASY FRIENDS, AND FINALLY STRANGERS.
"THAT NIGHT, NONE OF IT MATTERED.
"WE BOTH LOVED HIM, WE WERE BOTH SCARED THAT HE WAS GOING TO DIE, AND AFTER WE'D PUT THAT INTO WORDS, WE BOTH CRIED AND HELD EACH OTHER TILL WE FELL ASLEEP.
"AS FOR SUPERMAN...
"...WELL, I GUESS HE MUST HAVE FELT RESTLESS TOO, BUT IN A DIFFERENT WAY. I MEAN, WE ALL HAD TROUBLE GETTING TO SLEEP...
"...BUT HE DIDN'T NEED TO SLEEP AT ALL."
I'M GLAD YOU CAME BACK, KRYPTO. YOU'RE A PIECE OF MY LIFE, YOU KNOW THAT?
HAFF
I DON'T KNOW... I FEEL AS IF ALL THE PIECES OF MY LIFE ARE FINALLY COMING TOGETHER.
YOU KNOW WHAT I MEAN. ANIMALS GET THOSE FEELINGS TOO, WHEN THEY KNOW...
RRRRAFF! RAA-RAFF!
WHAT? WHAT'S THE MATTER? IS SOMETHING...

THE LEGION?
GREETINGS FROM THE 30TH CENTURY, SUPERMAN!
WE HOPE YOU DON'T MIND US DROPPING IN LIKE THIS...
...BUT WE THOUGHT YOU MIGHT APPRECIATE THE SIGHT OF A FEW FRIENDLY FACES.
K-KARA...?
HELLO, KAL. I WAS VISITING THE LEGION IN THE 30TH CENTURY WHEN THEY ANNOUNCED THEY WERE COMING BACK TO SEE YOU, HERE IN MY FUTURE.
WELL? HAVEN'T YOU GOT A HUG FOR YOUR COUSIN?
O-OF COURSE. IT...IT'S JUST SUCH A SURPRISE...
IT MUST BE. I BET I'M A GROWN-UP SUPERWOMAN IN THIS TIME ZONE. IS IT CHEATING IF YOU TELL ME WHETHER I GREW UP TO BE PRETTY?
YOU...YOU GREW UP BEAUTIFUL, KARA!
COME ON... LET'S GO THIS WAY, WHERE THE LIGHT'S BETTER.

HELLO, KRYPTO! HELLO, BOY! I HOPE YOU AND STREAKY AREN'T STILL SCRAPPING ALL THE TIME!
SUPERMAN? COULD I HAVE A WORD?
YES. YES, OF COURSE, BRAINIAC.
SUPERMAN, WE WANTED TO PRESENT YOU WITH THIS, ON BEHALF OF...
BRAINIAC, WHAT'S THE MEANING OF THIS?
YOU KNOW SUPERGIRL IS DEAD IN THIS ERA. YOU'RE FROM THE FUTURE! IT'S HISTORY TO YOU!
I--I'M SORRY. SHE INSISTED ON COMING. I REALIZE HOW DISTRESSING IT MUST BE...
I DOUBT IT! YOU TALK CALMLY TO US, ALL THE WHILE KNOWING OUR DEATH DATES AS ANCIENT HISTORY. HOW CAN YOU DO IT?
SUPERMAN, YOU ARE BEING UNFAIR.
IN YOUR PAST, AS SUPERBOY, YOU HAVE SEEN SOME OF OUR FUTURE. WOULD YOU TELL US IF YOU KNEW OF SOME UNAVOIDABLE DOOM AWAITING US?
NO. NO, YOU'RE RIGHT.
FORGIVE ME, BRAINIAC. I'M JUST UNDER PRESSURE AT THE MOMENT.
OF COURSE.
NOW, LET ME GIVE YOU THIS ON BEHALF OF THE LEGION. IT'S THE REASON WE CAME TO THIS PERIOD.
WELL, THANK YOU, BUT...
...WHY DID YOU CHOOSE THIS PARTICULAR DATE TO PRESENT IT TO ME?

W-WELL, BECAUSE OUR HISTORIES MARK THIS DATE AS A SPECIAL TIME IN YOUR LIFE. THEREFORE, WE CAME HERE TO MEET WITH YOU AGAIN, AND SALUTE YOU... AND...
...AND PAY YOUR LAST RESPECTS.
IS THAT IT?
COUSIN--?
I JUST THOUGHT OF SOMETHING...
AS THE SUPERGIRL OF THIS ERA, AM I AWAY VISITING ANOTHER TIME PERIOD OR SOMETHING? BECAUSE I THOUGHT YOU COULDN'T MATERIALIZE IN AN ERA WHERE YOU ALREADY EXISTED.
UH, YES. YES, YOU'RE RIGHT...
RIGHT NOW, SUPERGIRL... SUPERGIRL IS IN THE PAST.
UH, PERHAPS WE'D BEST RETURN YOU TO OUR 30TH CENTURY, TO PREVENT ANY PROBLEMS SHOULD THIS ERA'S SUPERGIRL RETURN, UH, UNEXPECTEDLY.
OH, WELL, I GUESS SO. GIVE ME MY REGARDS WHEN I RETURN FROM THE PAST.
GOOD-BYE, SUPERMAN. WE... WE ALWAYS MISS YOU.
BRAINIAC, CAN WE GO? M-MY EYES ARE WATERING. MUST BE SOME 20TH-CENTURY VIRUS...
"HE NEVER TOLD ME EXACTLY WHAT HAPPENED THAT NIGHT BEFORE THE SIEGE BEGAN, BUT AS SOON AS I SAW HIM THE NEXT MORNING, I KNEW SOMETHING HAD UPSET HIM.
"HE LOOKED FUNNY.

"HE LOOKED AS IF HE'D BEEN CRYING."

SUPERMAN
STARRING IN
ACTION COMICS
75¢
583
SEPT. 86
APPROVED BY THE COMICS CODE AUTHORITY
by ALAN MOORE, CURT SWAN and KURT SCHAFFENBERGER
DAILY PLANET
GOOD-BYE, SUPERMAN! WE'LL MISS YOU!
SWANDERSON

MORE COFFEE, TIM? INTERVIEWS ALWAYS MAKE ME SO DRY, WHAT WITH ME DOING ALL THE TALKING.
YOU MUST BE VERY BORED.
OH, NO! NO, IT'S JUST WHAT THE PLANET'S MEMORIAL EDITION NEEDS.
I'M JUST CHECKING WHERE WE'D GOT TO... SUPERMAN'S OLD ENEMIES HAD STARTED RETURNING WITH A VENGEANCE AND HE'D TAKEN EVERY-ONE TO HIS FORTRESS, FOR SAFETY.
THAT'S RIGHT. ME, LANA, JIMMY, PERRY AND ALICE WHITE... ALL HIS FRIENDS. WE WERE ALL...
SAY, IZZAT COFFEE I SMELL BREWIN' THROUGH HERE?
HA HA! BEST DARN NOSE FOR COFFEE IN THE WHOLE OF PITTSDALE. YOU'LL HAVE TO FIX IT YOURSELF, HON. I'M BUSY BEING A CELEBRITY.
TIM, THIS IS MY HUSBAND, JORDAN.
JORDY, THIS IS TIM CRANE, FROM THE PLANET.
OH. HI.
UHH... I HOPE YOU DON'T MIND ME INTERVIEWING YOUR WIFE ABOUT, WELL, ABOUT...
ABOUT HER EX? NAH! I CAN LIVE WITH IT. HE WEREN'T NOTHIN' SPECIAL. US ORDINARY WORKIN' SLOBS, SON... WE'RE THE REAL HEROES.
NOW, JORDY, DON'T YOU GET STARTED IN ON THAT! YOU JUST FIX YOUR COFFEE THEN GO AND CHECK THAT JONATHAN'S STILL ASLEEP.
WHERE HAD I GOT TO, TIM?
UH... YOU WERE ALL UP IN THE ARCTIC, WITH SUPERMAN...

"THAT'S RIGHT... WE STOOD ON A BALCONY AND WATCHED AS HE DESTROYED THE GOLDEN KEY. I THINK THAT'S WHEN WE FIRST REALIZED THAT HE WAS PREPARING FOR A SIEGE.
"THE SIEGE OF THE FORTRESS OF SOLITUDE...
"SUPERMAN'S LAST STAND.
"WHATEVER HAPPENED TO THE MAN OF TOMORROW?"
ALAN MOORE: WRITER
CURT SWAN & KURT SCHAFFENBERGER: ARTISTS
TODD KLEIN: LETTERER
GENE D'ANGELO: COLORIST
JULIUS SCHWARTZ: EDITOR

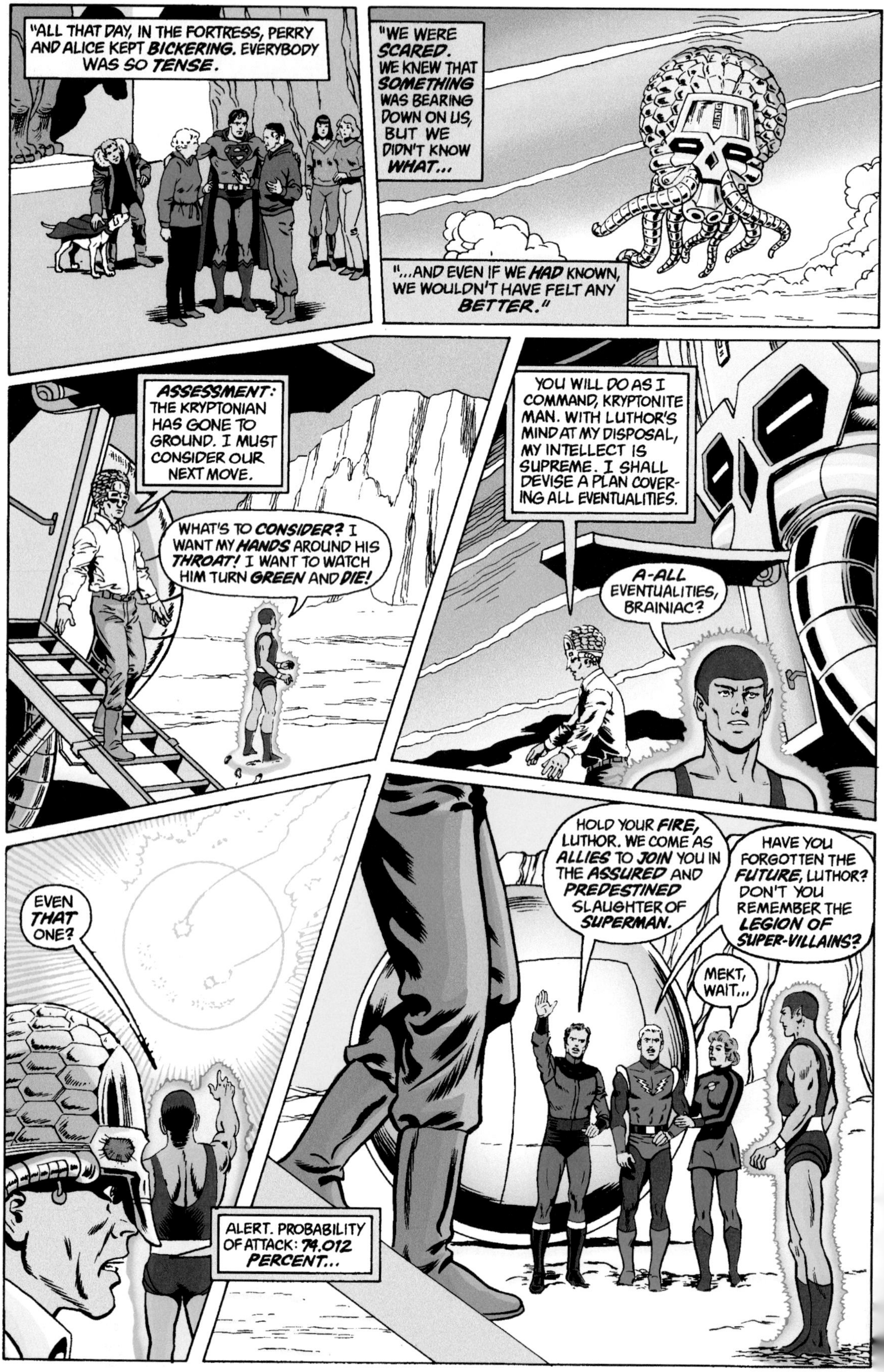
"ALL THAT DAY, IN THE FORTRESS, PERRY AND ALICE KEPT BICKERING. EVERYBODY WAS SO TENSE.
"WE WERE SCARED. WE KNEW THAT SOMETHING WAS BEARING DOWN ON US, BUT WE DIDN'T KNOW WHAT...
"...AND EVEN IF WE HAD KNOWN, WE WOULDN'T HAVE FELT ANY BETTER."
ASSESSMENT: THE KRYPTONIAN HAS GONE TO GROUND. I MUST CONSIDER OUR NEXT MOVE.
WHAT'S TO CONSIDER? I WANT MY HANDS AROUND HIS THROAT! I WANT TO WATCH HIM TURN GREEN AND DIE!
YOU WILL DO AS I COMMAND, KRYPTONITE MAN. WITH LUTHOR'S MIND AT MY DISPOSAL, MY INTELLECT IS SUPREME. I SHALL DEVISE A PLAN COVERING ALL EVENTUALITIES.
A-ALL EVENTUALITIES, BRAINIAC?
EVEN THAT ONE?
ALERT. PROBABILITY OF ATTACK: 74.012 PERCENT...
HOLD YOUR FIRE, LUTHOR. WE COME AS ALLIES TO JOIN YOU IN THE ASSURED AND PREDESTINED SLAUGHTER OF SUPERMAN.
HAVE YOU FORGOTTEN THE FUTURE, LUTHOR? DON'T YOU REMEMBER THE LEGION OF SUPER-VILLAINS?
MEKT, WAIT...

I--I'M SCANNING LUTHOR'S MIND... IT'S BEING DOMINATED BY SOMETHING COLD, EMOTIONLESS...
ON HIS HEAD... IS THAT SOME SORT OF HELMET, OR...?
LEX LUTHOR IS NOW MERELY THE VESSEL OF BRAINIAC.
QUERY: WHAT MANNER OF BEINGS ARE YOU?
W-WE ARE SATURN WOMAN, LIGHTNING LORD, AND COSMIC KING, FROM THE 30TH CENTURY...
ACCORDING TO LEGEND, DURING THESE DAYS, SUPERMAN MET HIS GREATEST FOE IN BATTLE AND WAS NO MORE.
CERTAIN OF VICTORY, WE'VE COME TO PARTIC-IPATE.
HIS GREATEST FOE? OF COURSE. I SHRUNK KANDOR. I WAS ALWAYS HIS GREATEST FOE.
QUERY: WHY SHOULD I PERMIT YOU TO SHARE MY VICTORY?
BECAUSE WE'RE FROM THE FUTURE. WE KNOW THINGS.
FOR EXAMPLE, IT'S SAID THAT DURING SUPERMAN'S LAST DAYS, ALL OF EARTH'S CHAMPIONS FLOCKED TO HELP HIM...
THAT IS LOGICAL. THIS WORLD'S OTHER SUPER-HUMANS ARE CERTAIN TO INTERFERE.
I SHALL ERECT AN IMPENETRABLE FORCE-SCREEN IMMEDIATELY.
FOR RESISTING MY WILL; FOR DESTROYING MY BODY; FOR THESE AFFRONTS SHALL THE KRYPTONIAN KNOW THE REVENGE OF BRAINIAC...
...AND NONE SHALL HELP HIM.
"WHEN THE FORTRESS' SENSORS REGISTERED BRAINIAC'S FORCE-SCREEN, WE KNEW IT HAD BEGUN.

"THE SCREEN TOOK THE FORM OF A GIANT BUBBLE, MORE THAN TWO MILES ACROSS. NOTHING COULD GET IN. NOTHING COULD GET OUT.
"AROUND NOON, THE VILLAINS BEGAN FIRING ON THE FORTRESS USING WEAPONS FROM BRAINIAC'S SHIP.
"SUPERMAN DESTROYED MOST OF THE DEVICES FROM LONG RANGE, USING HEAT VISION, BUT THE FORCE-SCREEN GENERATOR WAS TOO WELL SHIELDED.
"DURING THE AFTERNOON, HE TOOK KRYPTO AND ATTEMPTED A FRONTAL ASSAULT, BUT THEY WERE DRIVEN BACK BY THE KRYPTONITE MAN.
"HIS POWERS SEEMED TO HAVE INCREASED TENFOLD. THEY COULDN'T EVEN GET NEAR HIM.
"WITH TWILIGHT, OTHER HEROES BEGAN ARRIVING OUTSIDE THE BARRIER. THOSE THAT WERE HIS FRIENDS...
"THOSE THAT WERE ALMOST HIS RIVALS...
"...THOSE THAT MIGHT HAVE BEEN HIS LOVERS. IT DIDN'T MATTER. NONE OF THEM COULD PENETRATE IT.
"AS NIGHT FELL, IT SEEMED THAT A STANDOFF HAD BEEN DECLARED, AND THERE WAS A LULL IN THE BATTLE. WE ALL KNEW IT WOULDN'T LAST LONG.
"WE FIGURED WE HAD AT LEAST UNTIL MORNING, SO WE DECIDED TO GET SOME SLEEP...

"...OR AT LEAST, SOME OF US DID.
PERRY? ARE YOU AWAKE?
I WONDERED IF WE COULD TALK FOR A WHILE.
WELL, SURE. COME ON IN.
I COULD USE SOME CONVERSATION MYSELF. BEATS SITTING HERE THINKING ABOUT DOOM AND DIVORCE.
I'M SORRY. BEING COOPED UP HERE MUST BE A STRAIN FOR YOU AND ALICE.
YEAH, I GUESS SO. I DON'T KNOW... WE'VE BOTH GOT GOOD REASON TO BE AT LOGGERHEADS, BUT...
WELL, SITTING HERE WITH DEATH WAITING OUTSIDE MAKES ME SEE THINGS FROM A DIFFERENT PERSPECTIVE SOMEHOW...
ME, TOO.
YOU?
YES, ME. PERRY, I'M SCARED. I THINK I'M GOING TO DIE, AND THERE'S SO MUCH IN MY LIFE I HAVE TO GET STRAIGHT...
...LIKE ME AND LOIS. LIKE ME AND LANA.
YOU SEE, I'VE MESSED UP BOTH THEIR LIVES, HAVEN'T I?
THEY'VE WASTED THEIR LOVE ON ME, WHILE I COULDN'T LET MYSELF LOVE EITHER OF THEM THE WAY THEY DESERVED.
I WISH I'D EXPLAINED.
I WISH I HADN'T BEEN SUCH A COWARD.
S SUPREME HOUR
"WHY IS IT THAT THE NOBLEST PEOPLE ARE THE ONES MOST TROUBLED BY CONSCIENCE? I DON'T KNOW...

"...BUT SUPERMAN AND PERRY WEREN'T THE ONLY ONES WHO COULDN'T SLEEP THAT NIGHT."
LANA? WHAT ARE YOU DOING UP HERE?
WELL, IF THAT FLASK IN YOUR HAND'S WHAT I THINK IT IS, I'M DOING THE SAME THING AS YOU. I'M SICK OF SITTING AROUND. I WANT TO HELP HIM.
THAT'S THE ELASTIC LAD SERUM, ISN'T IT?
YES. I KNEW HE KEPT A SAMPLE IN HIS TROPHY ROOM ANNEX, SO I CAME TO FIND IT.
ALL THESE YEARS, THEY'VE CALLED ME "SUPERMAN'S FRIEND." I FIGURE HERE'S WHERE I START PAYING FOR THE PRIVILEGE.
HOW ABOUT YOU?
ELASTIC LAD SERUM
I HAD THE SAME IDEA. I REMEMBER YEARS AGO, THERE WERE TIMES WE GAINED SUPER-POWERS TEMPORARILY. I REMEMBER THERE WAS THIS LAKE THAT LOIS AND I BATHED IN...
ELASTIC LAD
"MAGIC" LAKE WATER (PROBABLE UNIDENTIFIED RADIATION SOURCE.)
HEY...LOOK! HERE'S A CASE OF SOUVENIR COSTUMES!
THEN WE'RE IN LUCK!
TURN YOUR BACK, RED, WHILE I TAKE A QUICK DIP.
OH.
OH, THE FEELING. I REMEMBER NOW... MY SKIN, TINGLING AS IT GETS HARDER... MY SENSES EXPANDING... X-RAY VISION... MICROSCOPIC VISION...

"...SUPER-HEARING..."
YOU SEE, BACK WHEN I WAS SUPERBOY, LANA WAS THE ONLY GIRL I LOVED.
SHE STILL REPRESENTS SMALLVILLE TO ME, THAT PART OF MY LIFE, AND BECAUSE OF THAT I COULD NEVER CAST HER ASIDE.
...BUT SINCE I'VE GROWN AND BECOME A MAN, THERE'S ONLY EVER BEEN ONE WOMAN FOR ME.
LOIS. BEAUTIFUL LOIS.
I LOVE HER, PERRY. DEAR GOD, I LOVE HER SO MUCH...
"...BUT I CAN'T TELL HER WITHOUT HURTING LANA. I'D NEVER HURT LANA, SO I JUST WALK AROUND WITH THIS SECRET, THIS WEIGHT IN MY HEART...
"...AND I'LL CARRY IT WITH ME TO MY GRAVE...
"...AND NEITHER OF THEM WILL EVER KNOW.
THERE. ARE YOU READY YET, LANA?
LANA? IS ANYTHING WRONG?
WRONG? NO. NO, WHY SHOULD ANYTHING BE WRONG?
I'M READY NOW. LET'S GET OUT THERE, WRECK THAT FORCE-SCREEN, AND GET HIM OUT OF THIS MESS. WE'RE ONLY SECOND STRINGERS, JIMMY, BUT WE'LL SHOW 'EM...
NOBODY LOVED HIM BETTER THAN US.
NOBODY!
ELASTIC LAD

"HAVING ASSUMED THAT THE KRYPTONITE MAN WOULD KEEP SUPERMAN AT A DISTANCE, WHAT HAPPENED NEXT TOOK EVEN BRAINIAC BY SURPRISE..."
SIZZZSSSSSSSS
AAOW! HE'S ATTACKING US! I'LL...
YOU'LL WHAT, YOU POISONOUS LITTLE CRUD?
WHAT ARE YOU GOING TO DO TO SOMEONE WHO DOESN'T GIVE A DAMN ABOUT KRYPTONITE?
BRAINIAC! HELP ME!
NOBODY'S GOING TO HELP YOU. NOBODY'S GOING TO HELP ANY OF YOU!
TAKE OUT THE GENERATOR, JIMMY, WHILE I DEAL WITH THEIR LEADER.
UNNGH
FOOLISH WOMAN. MY VICTORY IS PREDETERMINED. YOU SERVE ONLY TO HASTEN YOUR OWN DOOM.
LUTHOR? WHY ARE YOU TALKING LIKE THAT? AND...AND ON YOUR HEAD. WHAT'S...?
LUHH... LAA-NAA... BRUHH... BRAINIAC...HUHH HEEE'S... GOT...ME.
KUHH KILL MEE... LANA... PLEASE...
KILL ME.
LUTHOR. BE SILENT. I COMMAND YOU...
LEX?
LUH...LANA... DO IT NOW... PUH...PLEASE DO IT NOW...
CHRAK

SHE'S KILLED THE LUTHOR-BRAINIAC THING! HOW CAN WE STOP HER?
I'M SCANNING HER MIND...SHE RECEIVED HER POWER FROM BATHING IN SOME KIND OF RADIOACTIVE POOL...
THEN IT'S EASY...
I JUST USE MY TRANSMUTATION ABILITIES TO TURN THE RADIOACTIVE TRACES IN HER TISSUE TO NORMAL BODY SALTS...
OHH!
...AND SUDDENLY THERE'S NOTHING HOLDING HER UP!
TAKEN A FALL, MY DEAR?
HERE... LET ME GIVE YOU A HELPING HAND...
OH, NO.
ZZZZZZZAKK
LANA!
YOU MURDERING SCUM! YOU KILLED HER!
WELL, YOU'RE TOO LATE! YOUR FORCE-SCREEN'S WRECKED!
YOU'RE FINISHED!
NEVER.
AAAAAAAAP

HE'S DEAD.
BUT WHO...?
WHO...
...DO YOU...
...SUPPOSE...?
I... AM BRAINIAC... REDUCER OF KANDOR...AND HIS GREATEST FOE...
MY VICTORY... IS PREORDAINED. DO YOU THINK... THAT I WOULD LET... THE DEATH... OF THIS BODY... STAND IN ITS WAY?
OH MERCIFUL CREATOR...
LUTHOR'S NERVES... HIS MUSCLES... ARE INTACT. I CAN... MANIPULATE THEM...
...AT LEAST... FOR LONG ENOUGH... TO ENSURE... SUPERMAN'S DESTRUCTION.
BRAINIAC? SOMETHING'S WRONG. IF OLSEN WRECKED THE GENERATOR, WHY HASN'T THE FORCE-SCREEN COLLAPSED?
"ANALYSIS: YOU ARE CORRECT... EARTH'S CHAMPIONS REMAIN OUTSIDE... SOME UNKNOWN FORCE MAINTAINS THE SHIELD...
"PERHAPS... PERHAPS IT IS DESTINY. IN ANY EVENTUALITY... WE MUST MAKE USE OF IT... WHILE THIS FLUKE SITUATION ...ENDURES."
OUR FINAL ASSAULT... BEGINS...
PREPARE... FOR A NUCLEAR STRIKE...

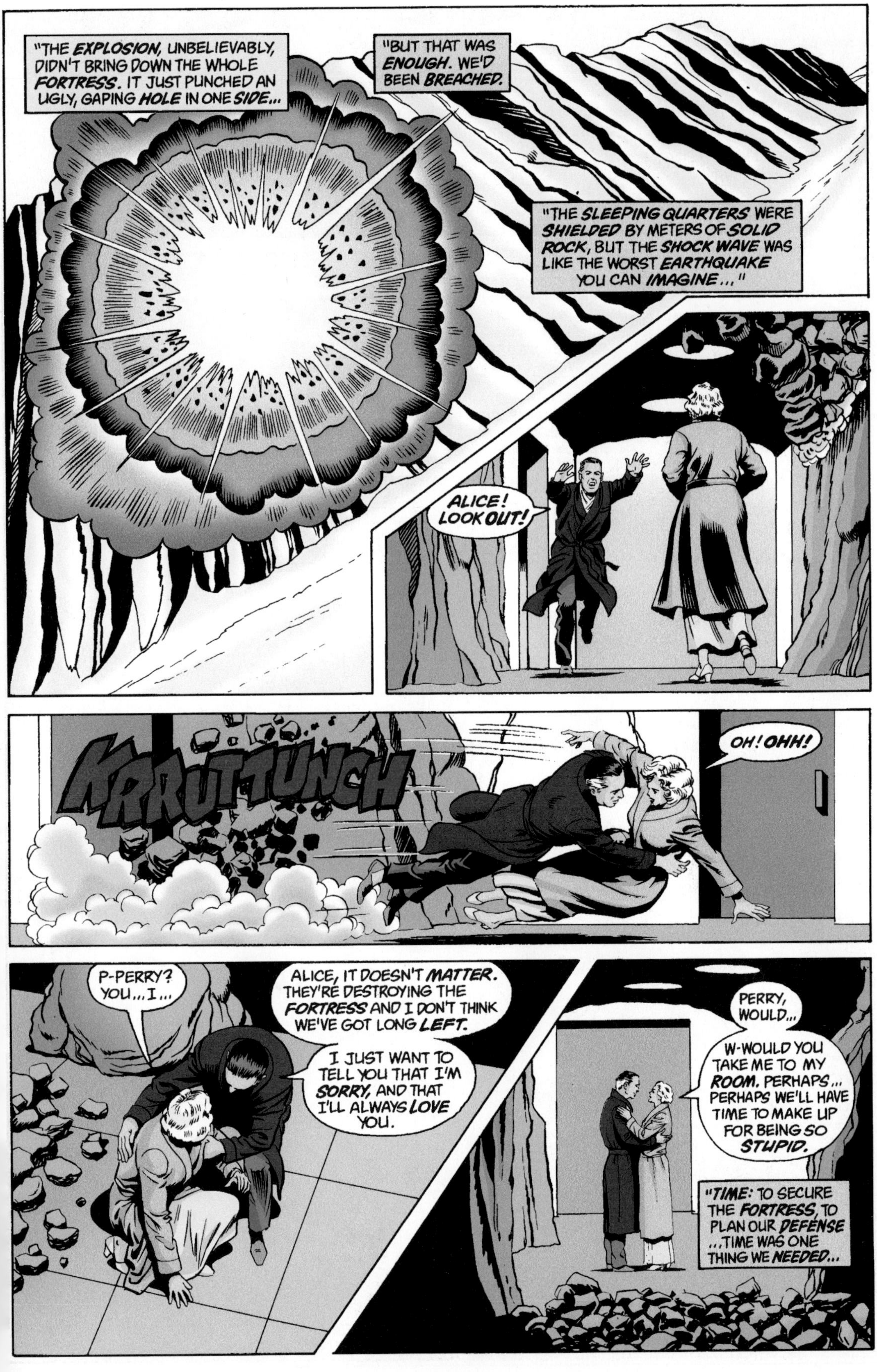
"THE EXPLOSION, UNBELIEVABLY, DIDN'T BRING DOWN THE WHOLE FORTRESS. IT JUST PUNCHED AN UGLY, GAPING HOLE IN ONE SIDE...
"BUT THAT WAS ENOUGH. WE'D BEEN BREACHED.
"THE SLEEPING QUARTERS WERE SHIELDED BY METERS OF SOLID ROCK, BUT THE SHOCK WAVE WAS LIKE THE WORST EARTHQUAKE YOU CAN IMAGINE..."
ALICE! LOOK OUT!
KRRUTTUNCH
OH! OHH!
P-PERRY? YOU... I...
ALICE, IT DOESN'T MATTER. THEY'RE DESTROYING THE FORTRESS AND I DON'T THINK WE'VE GOT LONG LEFT.
I JUST WANT TO TELL YOU THAT I'M SORRY, AND THAT I'LL ALWAYS LOVE YOU.
PERRY, WOULD...
W-WOULD YOU TAKE ME TO MY ROOM. PERHAPS... PERHAPS WE'LL HAVE TIME TO MAKE UP FOR BEING SO STUPID.
"TIME: TO SECURE THE FORTRESS, TO PLAN OUR DEFENSE ...TIME WAS ONE THING WE NEEDED...

"TIME WAS THE ONE THING WE DIDN'T HAVE."
WHERRRRE IS HE?
COME OUT, KRYPTONIAN. YOUR RAT-HOLE'S BEEN BREACHED. YOU CAN'T ESCAPE ME NOW.
THUDDUM THUDDUM
I'M ALMOST GLAD THAT I DIDN'T MANAGE TO KILL YOU WHEN WE WERE YOUNG. IT MAKES THIS MOMENT ALL THE SWEETER.
ARE YOU LISTENING, KRYPTONIAN? CAN YOU HEAR YOUR DEATH BEARING DOWN ON YOU?
THUDDUM THUDDUM
THUDDUM THUDDU
WELL? I'M WAITING FOR AN...
HM? WHAT'S...?
THRIDDUNCH
RRRRRAAAARRRRGH!

NO! NO!
AAAAEEEEARRGH! STOP IT! GET OFF GET OFF GET OFF!
I'M KILLING YOU, YOU STUPID ANIMAL! DON'T YOU UNDERSTAND? I'M KILLING YAAAAAAAAAA
AAAAF
SNOPF
AAAOOOOOOOOOooo
"PETE ROSS, LANA, JIMMY... NOW KRYPTO WAS GONE AS WELL.
"I WAS WITH SUPERMAN WHEN HE HEARD HIS PET'S DEATH-HOWL, BUT WE COULDN'T DO ANYTHING...

"...WE HAD OUR OWN PROBLEMS."
SUPERMAN... WHAT'S HAPPENING? WHERE ARE LANA AND THE OTHERS?
I...I DON'T KNOW. PERRY AND ALICE AREN'T HURT, BUT I CAN'T SEE LANA OR JIMMY ANYWHERE. MAYBE THEY FLED...
TITAN
LORI LEMARIS
...OR MAYBE THEY'RE DEAD!
AAA!
HA HA HA HA HA! WANT TO BUY YOURSELF SOME TIME, KRYPTONIAN?
WHY NOT THROW ME THE WOMAN, SO I CAN FRY HER THE WAY I FRIED YOUR OTHER GIRLFRIEND?
L-LANA?
YOU HURT LANA?
AAAAA! HE BURNED ME! HE BURNED ME!
HIS MIND... HE ISN'T BLUFFING... HE'S PREPARED TO KILL!
M-MAYBE THIS WASN'T SUCH A GOOD IDEA. FROM OUR LEGENDS, I'D EXPECTED A QUICK VICTORY...BUT THIS IS DANGEROUS!
LET'S GET OUT OF HERE. WE KNOW THAT BRAINIAC WILL WIN... THERE'S NO SENSE GETTING HURT IN THE PROCESS.
"BY THE TIME WE'D FOLLOWED THEM OUTSIDE, THEIR BUBBLE WAS ALREADY VANISHING BACK TO THE 30TH CENTURY...

"...AND THERE WAS ONLY ONE FOE LEFT TO FACE.
"OR MAYBE TWO."
ANALYSIS: STIFFENING... OF LIMBS... DIFFICULTY... IN MOVEMENT. ASSESSMENT: ONSET... OF RIGOR MORTIS... IN HOST BODY... IMMINENT.
OH, GOD, LOOK AT IT!
BUT... THE VILLAINS FROM THE FUTURE... THEY SAID YOU WOULD MEET... YOUR GREATEST FOE IN BATTLE... AND BE NO MORE. ME. BRAINIAC. YOUR GREATEST FOE...
I AM PREDESTINED... TO DESTROY YOU...
LOIS, GET BACK! HE'S FALLING!
NO! GET... UP! GET UP... LUTHOR. I... WILL NOT BE BETRAYED... BY YOUR... HUMAN WEAKNESS...
WHERE... IS MY KRYPTONITE MAN...? WHY... IS MY FORCE-SCREEN... STILL STANDING...? I DON'T KNOW... I DON'T CARE...
I... AM COMING FOR YOU... KRYPTONIAN... MY VICTORY... IS INEVITABLE...
SUPERMAN? IT'S CRAWLING OFF HIM...
CLINK RINK PLITTINK
IT'S OKAY, LOIS. I... I DON'T THINK HE'S IN ANY CONDITION TO HARM US.
SHRING CHLINK KINGLE TUNG
"THE DISINTEGRATING COLLECTION OF PLATES AND CIRCUITS CRAWLED A COUPLE OF INCHES, PROPELLED BY SHEER MALICE, THEN STOPPED MOVING.
"BRAINIAC WAS DEAD.
"IT WAS ALL OVER...

"...EXCEPT THAT IT COULDN'T BE."
LOIS... I DON'T LIKE THIS. THERE'S TOO MANY LOOSE ENDS.
WHY SHOULD ALL MY ENEMIES ATTACK AT ONCE? WHY IS BRAINIAC'S FORCE-SCREEN STILL KEEPING OUR FRIENDS OUT?
...AND THEN THERE'S THIS STATUETTE. THE LEGION VISITED LAST NIGHT AND GAVE IT TO ME, ALMOST AS IF THEY WERE GIVING ME MY OWN HEADSTONE AS A GIFT.
THE WHOLE 30TH CENTURY SEEMS CERTAIN I'M FINISHED.
"HE LAPSED INTO SILENCE WHILE I STUDIED THE STATUETTE, A GOLDEN FIGURE OF SUPERMAN, HOLDING SOMETHING FAMILIAR...
"EVERYTHING WAS STILL. THE KEENING ARCTIC WIND WAS BEING KEPT OUT BY THE FORCE-SCREEN.
"HE STOOD LIKE THAT FOR FOUR OR FIVE MINUTES, SILENT AND FROWNING, FIGURING SOMETHING OUT.
"WHEN HE SPOKE, EVER SO SOFTLY, IT STILL MADE ME JUMP."
OF COURSE.
BIZARRO, THE PRANKSTER, THE TOYMAN, METALLO, BRAINIAC, THE KRYPTONITE MAN, THE LEGION OF SUPER-VILLAINS... THERE'S ONLY ONE NAME MISSING, ISN'T THERE?
I KNOW YOU'RE THERE, MXYZPTLK!
COME ON OUT AND SHOW YOURSELF!
VWOOMF
EUUGH!

"WHEN THE SMOKE FINALLY CLEARED, HE WAS JUST SITTING THERE, IN THE AIR. HE LOOKED DIFFERENT SOMEHOW. HE DIDN'T LOOK FUNNY ANYMORE."
SO, YOU FINALLY GUESSED!
GREETINGS, SUPERMAN. GREETINGS FROM THE FIFTH DIMENSION.
YOU WERE GUIDING ALL THIS, FROM BEHIND THE SCENES? ALL THIS KILLING AND DESTRUCTION?
MXYZPTLK, IN RAO'S NAME, WHY?
DON'T BE NAIVE, SUPERMAN. I'M AN IMMORTAL, LIKE EVERYONE IN THE FIFTH DIMENSION.
THE BIG PROBLEM WITH BEING IMMORTAL IS FILLING YOUR TIME. FOR EXAMPLE, I SPENT THE FIRST TWO THOUSAND YEARS OF MY EXISTENCE DOING ABSOLUTELY NOTHING.
I DIDN'T MOVE... I DIDN'T EVEN BREATHE.
EVENTUALLY, SIMPLE INERTIA BECAME TIRESOME, SO I SPENT THE NEXT TWO THOUSAND YEARS BEING SAINTLY AND BENIGN, DOING ONLY GOOD DEEDS.
WHEN THAT NOVELTY BEGAN TO FADE, I DECIDED TO TRY BEING MISCHIEVOUS.
NOW, TWO THOUSAND YEARS LATER, I'M BORED AGAIN. I NEED A CHANGE. STARTING WITH YOUR DEATH, I SHALL SPEND THE NEXT TWO MILLENNIA BEING EVIL!
AFTER THAT, WHO KNOWS? PERHAPS I'LL TRY BEING GUILTY FOR A WHILE.
DID YOU HONESTLY BELIEVE A FIFTH-DIMENSIONAL SORCERER WOULD RESEMBLE A FUNNY LITTLE MAN IN A DERBY HAT? WOULD YOU LIKE TO SEE HOW I REALLY LOOK?
SUPERMAN... H-HE'S CHANGING!
WE'D BETTER GET INSIDE...

"I CAN'T DESCRIBE WHAT MXYZPTLK BECAME. IT HAD HEIGHT, LENGTH, BREADTH, AND A COUPLE OF OTHER THINGS.
"AS WE ENTERED THE FORTRESS I GLANCED BACK. IT WAS FOLLOWING US. LOOKING AT IT MADE MY HEAD HURT."
WHY STRUGGLE? YOU KNOW THERE'S NO ESCAPE. TODAY YOU MEET YOUR GREATEST FOE, AND SHALL BE NO MORE.
WHY, THE WHOLE 30TH CENTURY KNOWS IT!
"HE SHOULDN'T HAVE MENTIONED THE 30TH CENTURY! THAT WAS HIS MISTAKE.
"REMINDED, I LOOKED AT THE STATUETTE IN MY HANDS..."
LOIS, HE'S MAGICAL. I CAN'T BEAT HIM. RUN! I'LL HOLD HIM OFF AS LONG AS POSSIBLE...
NO! WAIT! THIS STATUETTE ...WHY DID THEY GIVE IT TO YOU?
AS A TRIBUTE... ALTHOUGH THEY MUST HAVE KNOWN HOW MUCH IT WOULD DISTURB ME.
EXACTLY! SO MAYBE THEY GAVE YOU IT FOR ANOTHER REASON...SOME KIND OF HINT, MAYBE?
TAKE ANOTHER LOOK AT IT, SUPERMAN!
LOOK AT WHAT IT'S HOLDING!
HIS SUPREME HOUR
"HE LOOKED AT THE GOLDEN FIGURINE, AT THE GOLDEN DEVICE IN ITS HANDS. HIS EYES NARROWED, EVER SO SLIGHTLY. HE KNEW.

"HE KNEW WHAT HAD TO BE DONE."
THIS WAY! IF WE CAN ONLY GET TO THE CHAMBER IN TIME!
WHUURP
"THE CHAMBER, WHEN WE REACHED IT, WAS AS EERIE AND UNPLEASANT AS I REMEMBERED. FROM A SCREEN AT ONE END, PALE MEN WITH MURDEROUS EYES MOUTHED OBSCENITIES AT US.
"TIME WAS RUNNING OUT...
"...AND THEN, SUDDENLY, IT WAS ALL GONE."
AHH. THERE YOU ARE.
TIME TO DIE, I THINK.
THAT'S RIGHT, MXYZPTLK.
TIME TO DIE.
"HE TURNED, THE PHANTOM ZONE PROJECTOR'S SINGLE CYCLOPS EYE STARING FROM BETWEEN HIS HANDS, FINGER MOVING TOWARDS ITS BLACK BUTTON. MXYZPTLK HAD NO MEANS OF ESCAPE...
"...EXCEPT ONE!"
KLTPZYXM!
"WITH THE UTTERANCE OF HIS REVERSED NAME, THE CREATURE'S MAGIC RETURNED HIM TO THE FIFTH DIMENSION...
"...WHILE AT THE SAME INSTANT THE RAY SENT HIM INTO THE PHANTOM ZONE."
UGGEAARRGH

THAT TERRIBLE SCREAM. IS HE...?
TORN IN HALF, BETWEEN DIMENSIONS. HE PANICKED WHEN HE SAW THE RAY AND MADE A FATAL ERROR. JUST AS I KNEW HE WOULD.
I KILLED HIM, LOIS! I INTENDED TO KILL HIM!
I JUST COULDN'T RISK LETTING ANYTHING THAT POWERFUL AND MALIGNANT SURVIVE, SO I MADE UP MY MIND, AND I DID IT.
I BROKE MY OATH. I KILLED HIM.
B-BUT YOU HAD TO! YOU HAVEN'T DONE ANYTHING WRONG...
YES, I HAVE.
NOBODY HAS THE RIGHT TO KILL. NOT MXYZPTLK, NOT YOU, NOT SUPERMAN...
ESPECIALLY NOT SUPERMAN!
"HE TURNED AND WALKED AWAY, IN COMPLETE SILENCE. I RAN AFTER HIM, CALLING HIS NAME.
"HE DIDN'T REPLY...
"...AND BY THE TIME I REALIZED WHERE HE WAS HEADING, IT WAS TOO LATE.
GOLD KRYPTONITE SAMPLE STORAGE CHAMBER KEEP OUT!
"AS HE WALKED INTO THE BLINDING GOLDEN LIGHT HE TURNED, AND LOOKED BACK OVER HIS SHOULDER. HE SMILED AT ME...
"I NEVER SAW SUPERMAN AGAIN.

"WITH MXYZPTLK'S DESTRUCTION, THE FORCE-SCREEN HIS MAGIC HAD BEEN MAINTAINING VANISHED, AND THE HEROES OUTSIDE WERE FREE TO ENTER.
"YOU PROBABLY READ ABOUT WHAT THEY FOUND...
"THE WRECKAGE IN AND AROUND THE FORTRESS SEEMED TO BE STREWN WITH BODIES. THOSE OF HIS MOST BITTER ENEMIES...
"...AND THOSE OF HIS MOST LOYAL FRIENDS. I REMEMBER THE BATMAN DESCRIBING IT AS 'LIKE WALKING AMONGST THE FRAGMENTS OF A LEGEND.'
"DEATH AND DESTRUCTION WERE EVERYWHERE...
"...ALMOST.
"ALMOST EVERYWHERE.
"THEY FOUND ME OUTSIDE THE LOCKED GOLD KRYPTONITE CHAMBER, WEEPING. WHEN SUPERWOMAN AND CAPTAIN MARVEL RIPPED THE VAULT OPEN, IT WAS EMPTY.
"HE WAS GONE."
THEY DISCOVERED A HIDDEN PASSAGEWAY, LEADING OUT OF THE FORTRESS, AND IT WAS FINALLY CONCLUDED THAT HE'D WALKED OUT POWERLESS INTO THE SUBZERO WASTES TO FREEZE.
THEY NEVER FOUND HIS BODY.
MORE COFFEE, TIM?

UH, NO, IT'S GETTING PRETTY LATE AND I THINK THE INTERVIEW'S ALMOST THROUGH.
TELL ME, MRS. ELLIOT, WHAT DO YOU THINK OF THE RUMORS THAT SUPERMAN IS STILL ALIVE SOMEWHERE?
WELL, I'M SURE A LOT OF PEOPLE WOULD LIKE TO BELIEVE THAT...
...BUT AS FAR AS I'M CONCERNED, SUPERMAN DIED IN THE ARCTIC.
I WAS THERE.
OF COURSE. I--I'M SORRY IF THAT LAST QUESTION WAS TACTLESS. YOU JUST HEAR A LOT OF TALK...
I GUESS IT'S THE SAME AS WITH JIM MORRISON OR BRUCE LEE, ALL THOSE OLD RUMORS...
HEEEEEERE'S JOHNNY!
WHAT...? OH! JONATHAN... YOU'RE AWAKE! HAVE YOU GOT A KISS FOR MOMMY?
A BAH!
UH, WELL, LISTEN, I OUGHT TO BE GOING. I'LL SEND YOU A COPY OF THE INTERVIEW TO CHECK ONCE I'VE TRANSCRIBED IT.
WELL, IF YOU GET TIME. I KNOW WHAT IT'S LIKE. GIVE MY LOVE TO THE PLANET.
I WILL. THANKS FOR EVERYTHING, MRS. ELLIOT. YOU TOO, MR. ELLIOT. I'LL BE IN TOUCH.
'BYE, FELLA. NICE MEETIN' YA.
DAH!

WELL, HE'S GONE. I GUESS THE MEDIA WON'T BE BOTHERING US FOR ANOTHER TEN YEARS NOW.
LET'S HOPE SO.
DOWN YOU GO, JONATHAN. YOU PLAY FOR A WHILE.
SO, HOW WAS WORK TODAY?
GREAT. OLD DAN HODGE BROUGHT IN SOME SNAPSHOTS OF HIS GRAND-CHILDREN, AND WE'RE WORKING ON THIS OLD '48 BUICK AT THE MOMENT, TRYING TO GET HER WORKING.
SHE'S BEAUTIFUL.
YOU REALLY LOVE IT, DON'T YOU? JUST GOING TO WORK EVERY DAY, TAKING OUT THE GARBAGE, CHANGING JONATHAN'S DIAPERS... ALL THIS NORMAL STUFF.
YUP. CAN'T BEAT IT... ALTHOUGH MAYBE I COULD LIVE WITHOUT THE DIAPERS.
HMMM. YOU KNOW, YOU WERE PRETTY HARD ON SUPERMAN EARLIER.
SUPERMAN? HE WAS OVERRATED, AND TOO WRAPPED UP IN HIMSELF. HE THOUGHT THE WORLD COULDN'T GET ALONG WITH-OUT HIM.
WHAT'S FOR DINNER?
PIZZA. AFTER THAT, IF JONATHAN'S QUIET, I THOUGHT MAYBE BED WITH A BOTTLE OF WINE. AND AFTER THAT, I FIGURE WE JUST LIVE HAPPILY EVER AFTER.
SOUND GOOD TO YOU?
LOIS, MY LOVE...
...WHAT DO YOU THINK?
The End...

TWILIGHT

BY ALAN MOORE

FIRST GLEAMINGS

Okay...I'm sure this is going to be an interminable ramble as these things usually are, but I first want to set down my thoughts on the whole idea of mass crossovers, partly in response to Paul's letter on the subject and partly just to clarify my thinking for myself. Hopefully, somewhere along the line you might catch a glimpse of some of the logic behind the story outline that follows and will thus be able to make a little more sense of my reasons for doing it that way.

Firstly, as I see the commercial side, taking into account what Paul was kind enough to pass on to me, the perfect mass crossover would be something like the following: It would have a sensible and logical reason for crossing over with other titles, so that the readers who were prompted to try a new title as a result of the crossover or vice versa didn't feel cheated by some tenuous linkage of story lines that was at best spurious and at worst nonexistent. It would provide a strong and resonant springboard from which to launch a number of new series or with which to revitalize old ones again in a manner that was not obviously crassly exploitative so as to insult the readers' intelligence. With an eye to the merchandising that Marvel managed to spin out of *Secret Wars*, I think it's safe to assume that if it were possible to credibly spin role-playing games, toys, "Waiting for *Twilight*" posters, and T-shirts and badges and all the rest of that stuff from the title, then that would be a good idea too. Ideally, it might even be possible, while appealing to the die-hard superhero junkie, to produce a central story idea simple, powerful, and resonant enough to bear translation to other media. I mean, I know that I'm probably still intoxicated by the *Watchmen* deal, but it never hurts to allow for these things as a possibility, does it?

Okay, so assuming that the above is an accurate summary of what, in heaven, DC would like to see happen with the title commercially, then I'll go on to tackle the other pertinent areas of concern with an eye to that and then hopefully tie the whole lot together at the end before moving on to the actual plot outline. If I don't manage that and just forget and wander off at a tangent or something then I'm afraid I'll have to ask you to bear with me. As long as I don't start free associating about my childhood then we should be okay.

The first of these other pertinent areas relates to the effect of the story line in question upon the DC Universe itself, and in response to this I figure that perhaps I ought to outline briefly my thoughts upon crossovers of this magnitude in general.

For one thing, they require some very hard thinking about in advance if they're not going to generate more problems than they solve, and in thinking about something which will affect every book that the company publishes, if only in subtle ways, then one obviously has to be very careful. I should say that as yet, although I saw the outlines, I haven't read any of the *Legends* series or its crossovers, mainly by reason of not having got out to a comic shop recently. The premise, if I understood it correctly, looked very good: it seemed to be attempting to give a sort of resonant mythic context to the DC pantheon while at the same time establishing a more vigorous social context for the assembled characters in terms of its story line, thus drawing the whole DC continuity together into an interesting whole, which is exactly what needs doing in the wake of the Crisis. The more we can reinforce the idea of the DC Universe as a magical and fascinating concept in itself, assuming that those are our aims, then the more successful we'll be in keeping readers hooked upon that universe and on the books that chronicle its various phenomena.

Of course, this approach isn't without its problems. If you don't do it right, if your assembled multitude of characters looks merely banal, which I personally believe happened with *Secret Wars* (although that may be mere personal prejudice on my part), then your entire continuity is cheapened in the long term along with its credibility, whatever the short-term benefits in terms of sales might be. When this happens, your only recourse is to greater acts of debasement in order to attract reader attention, more deaths to appease the arena crowd element in the fan marketplace, eventually degenerating into a geek show.

Then there are the unintentional injuries in internal logic that can be unwittingly inflicted upon the mass continuity by such a venture, whatever the individual merits of the creators or their efforts, purely by the vast organizational problems that a project of this size seems to encounter. To explain what I mean, I should perhaps look at a series that I *have* read, that being Marv and George's excellent *Crisis on Infinite Earths*.

Although the motive was pure and the aim true with regard to *Crisis*, I can't help feeling that somewhere along the line, in the attempt to consolidate and rationalize the DC cosmos, a situation even more potentially destabilizing and precarious was created. Instead of a parallel Earth cosmology that was, if the reader was sensible enough to overlook obvious discrepancies for what they were (i.e., simple mistakes), relatively easy to understand in the wake of *Crisis* and related seismic impacts upon the continuity such as John Byrne's new Superman books, we have a situation far less defined and precise. In the wake of the time altering at the end of the Crisis we are left with a universe where the entire past continuity of DC, for the most part, simply never happened. While I understand that Paul is attempting to sort out the Legion/Superboy problems over in *LSH* at the moment, and that other writers are tackling similar discrepancies, the fact remains that by far the larger part of DC's continuity will simply have to be scrapped and consigned to one of Orwell's memory holes along with a large amount of characters who, more than simply being dead, are now unpeople.

I believe this is dangerous for a couple of reasons. Firstly, by establishing the precedent of altering time, you are establishing an unconscious context for all stories that take place in the future, as well as for those which took place (or rather didn't take place) in the past. The readers of long standing, somewhere along the line, are going to have some slight feeling that all the stories that they followed avidly during their years of involvement with the hobby have been in some way invalidated, that all those countless plotlines weren't leading to anything more than what is in some respects an arbitrary cutoff point. By extension, the readers of today might well be left with the sensation that the stories they are currently reading are of less significance or moment because, after all, at some point 10 years in the future some comic book omnipotent, be it an editor or the Spectre, can go back in time and erase the whole slate, ready to start again. I myself felt something similar at the end of the first Superman film, when he turns time back to save Lois. It ruined the small but genuine enjoyment that I'd got from that first movie and destroyed all credibility for any of the following sequels as far as I was concerned.

I know that the average eight-year-old reader in the street is not thinking these things consciously while buying his monthly batch of titles. Probably the average 17- or 25-year-old reader isn't either, although that's more open to debate. My point is that the large and largely incomprehensible tides of public favor or dismissal that determine the success of a title are often influenced by very subtle things far below the waterline. I don't think it's too highfalutin to assume, for example, that the current success of the Teenage Superhero Group book has more than a little to do with the current massive sense of instability pervading our culture, especially with respect to instabilities in the family structure. I firmly believe that both this and the current seeming obsession with a strict formal continuity are some sort of broad response from an audience whose actual lives are spent living in a continuity far more uncertain and complex than anything ever envisaged by a comic book. I believe that one of the things that the comic fan is looking for in his multi-title crossover epics is some sense of a sanely ordered cosmos not offered to him or her by the news headlines or the arguments of their parents over breakfast.

That isn't to say that it's healthy or necessarily desirable to fulfill this fundamentally escapist sort of urge. I myself would feel uncomfortable if the imaginary reality I was offering my readers was intended as a pacifier rather than as something to make them think about their own reality. I'd cite *Watchmen* as an example of how it's possible to fulfill the requirements of a continuity much more strict and rigidly defined than is usual while still making some sort of relevant point, hopefully, about the real world that the book's readers are living in.

Attendant to this, there are a number of people in the industry (and in my opinion they have a good case even if I'm undecided about the right means to carry it off) who feel that it's time to break down the continuity and try to get rid of a lot of the rather anal and obsessive attitudes that have been allowed to dominate the marketplace and to some degree have hindered it in its periodic attempts to be taken seriously. I suppose a shining example of this would be Frank's *Dark Knight*, which, while it doesn't seem bothered about fitting into any graven-in-stone continuity, does service to the legend of Batman and brilliantly redefines the character for an eighties audience, and nobody really seems to care much how this all fits into the continuity because it's such a bloody good story. Will Jason Todd really die? Will all the superheroes leave Earth to Superman and his government pals? Will Oliver Queen really get his arm burned off at the elbow in a fight with Clark Kent and become an embittered urban terrorist? Who cares? The readers seem quite capable of accepting that this may or may not happen in the future, without getting worked up and starting to chew through their own arms over how the idea of alternate possible futures fits in with the *Crisis* idea that there is only one time stream with no possibility of alternate pasts, presents, or futures.

Okay...so on one hand we have an audience thirsty for the stability that an ordered continuity gives them, and on the other hand we have good creative reasons for throwing continuity to the winds altogether. Is there any way that these two apparently conflicting notions can both be accomplished at once? Yes, I believe there is. I think it is possible to create a limited-run series that would embrace both these attitudes comfortably and fulfill all the other requirements that we've gone over concerning crossovers of this type above. I think we could come up with a story that, like *Legends*, casts new light upon all the DC characters, and yet does no violence to however their creators and current creative teams are handling them in their own titles. Something that pulls together the threads of the DC Universe in an interesting and revealing way, while at the same time remaining simple enough in construction that the chances for any screwups in the crossover continuity are diminished or avoided altogether.

This last point is important. Looking at the practicalities of the situation with the hindsight that *Crisis* has afforded us, it is possible to see the various practical problems which have emerged and which are unlikely to be solved by vigorous debating between the parties or sides involved. Firstly, there will almost certainly be some writers or artists who do not really want to involve their stories with the crossover, whether they say so or not. Making them "toe the line" if they're vocal about it or taking comfort from the fact that most people, even if they don't like the idea, will go along with it for the sake of a quiet life clearly isn't practical when you're dealing with writers and artists. If they aren't motivated by an idea, while it is theoretically possible to force them to adapt to it, it isn't possible to ensure that you'll get better than a mediocre story out of them, thus cheapening the whole overall concept to some degree. It seems to me much more workable to come up with a concept by means of which whatever individual writers choose to do or not do in their own books will have relevance to the crossover, whether they necessarily intend it to or not. If they choose to involve themselves actively in the crossover, then that's fine. If they refuse to do so, then the very act of refusing to do anything about the crossover also becomes part of the overall story line, without doing any violence to the continuity of the books involved at all. If the mechanics of how all this is to be achieved seem a little farfetched at this stage then I'd ask you to bear with me until after the story outline, at which point I'll attempt to demonstrate how the outline fulfills the various criteria that I'm defining here, including the next pertinent area on our agenda after the demands of commerce and continuity have been covered, this being the purely creative opportunities and pitfalls involved.

Creatively, there is an immediate aesthetic problem in the multi-title crossover in that, baldly put, it is very easy to strain the credibility of the entire universe by putting certain characters next to each other. Swamp Thing and Blue Devil spring immediately to mind, or Sgt. Rock and the Legion of Super-Heroes. In such juxtapositions, the flawed seams of the illusion of unity that we're trying to create become most apparent, and some thought should be given to a way of avoiding this distracting effect. There is also the very real possibility that any story line involving so many characters in more than a superficial fashion is going to degenerate into incoherence and gibberish, becoming a sort of comic book Babel of difficult-to-explain powers and origins and characterizations topped off with a muddy cosmic conclusion, some of which I feel that I certainly fell prey to in my recent "Crisis in Heaven/American Gothic" conclusion in *Swamp Thing* and am anxious to avoid repeating here.

The creative plus side of the equation is more dependent upon the tastes and leanings of the creative people involved, in this instance myself and whomever we get to draw this thing and work with me on it. For my part, speaking purely subjectively for the moment, what I'd like to do creatively with the series, above and beyond the creative satisfaction to be had in fulfilling all the criteria above, is to create a story line that lends the whole superhero phenomenon, the whole cosmos and concept, a context that was intensely mythic, and we extract from the characters involved in it their last ounce of mythic potential, aiming at coming up with something that cements the link between superheroes and the gods of legend by attempting something as direct and resonant as the original legends themselves. One legend in particular will be the main thematic drift of the story line, this being the Norse legend of Ragnarok, Twilight of the Gods.

Okay...assuming that six pages is enough for preliminaries, we'll now move on to a discussion of the story line itself. Please bear in mind that firstly, since the story has time travel as one of its central motifs, it's often difficult to present events in a clear chronological sequence without getting muddled, for which I apologize in advance. Secondly, since I myself don't have all the fine details filled in yet... unless those details occur to me over the course of this writing, which often happens...then there are going to be a few areas where the plot is maybe fuzzy or the story line seems flatter and less inspiring than the areas surrounding it. I hope these don't detract too much from your enjoyment of the idea, since these will be things that will be polished up to their final shine in the actual scripting. I'd again cite *Watchmen* as an example of how much of this stuff only finds its way in at the final draft stage and ask your indulgence wherever necessary.

To kick off, I should perhaps explain the overall structure of the story, which, incidentally, I'm currently imagining as something in the *Watchmen* format, 12 issues long, 28 pages, no ads, although these are just working assumptions and are certainly open to alteration at this early stage.

The story is structured so that there is a central "core narrative" which in this case is the tale of the Twilight of the Superheroes, taking place at some point in the not-too-distant future, say 20 or 30 years. Around this there is a sort of framing narrative, a device which links these hypothetical future events with what is going on in the DC continuity at present. This device provides the sort of interface between the fairly self-contained story of *Twilight* and the numerous fairly self-contained story lines and continuities of the DC cosmos, and it is achieved as follows: We have agents in the future who have managed to send a message back to agents in the present-day DC continuity, urging them to warn the superhero community of the terrible future that is possibly waiting for them, and to avoid it if at all possible. (This is not without its own ambiguities, as we shall hopefully see, but it provides for the moment the easiest conceptual handle with which to grasp the mechanics of all this.) Thus, the agents in the present set about reaching various superheroes in the present and delivering the warning. Some of those who are warned heed the warning, and make decisions in their current doings and lifestyles that will hopefully avert what is to happen in the future, even though this is by no means definite. Others will ignore the warning and carry on with what they were doing, which of course has some relevance, even by default, to the outcome of this horrific Götterdämmerung waiting in the potential future. Some of the superheroes affected will perhaps not be reached at all, and thus remain ignorant of the whole thing, although this too obviously has relevance to the outcome of what will happen in the future. I hope this makes it comprehensible how I hope to solve the problem of writers/artists who don't really want to involve themselves in the story line: Even if they choose to have their characters remain oblivious to everything going on, or to ignore it, their actions are having an implied relevance upon what is going on in the crossover book while at the same time what happens in the crossover book down the line in the future will be seen as having a direct relevance to how those characters are perceived in their own books. Knowing the fate of characters in even a potential future lends them a sort of poignance which is very important and which I'll take a few moments to discuss.

As I mentioned in my introduction to Frank's *Dark Knight*, one of the things that prevents superhero stories from ever attaining the status of true modern myths or legends is that they are open-ended. An essential quality of a legend is that the events in it are clearly defined in time: Robin Hood is driven to become an outlaw by the injustices of King John and his minions. That is his origin. He meets Little John, Friar Tuck, and all the rest and forms the Merry Men. He wins the tournament in disguise. He falls in love with Maid Marian and thwarts the Sheriff of Nottingham. That is his career, including love interest, major villains, and the formation of a superhero group that he is part of. He lives to see the return of Good King Richard and is finally killed by a woman, firing a last arrow to mark the place where he shall be buried. That is his resolution. You can apply the same paradigm to King Arthur, Davy Crockett, or Sherlock Holmes with equal success. You cannot apply it to most comic book characters because, in order to meet the commercial demands of a continuing series, they can never have a resolution. Indeed, they find it difficult to embrace any of the changes in life that the passage of time brings about for these very same reasons, making them finally less than fully human as well as falling far short of true myth.

The reason this all came up in the *Dark Knight* intro was that I felt that Frank had managed to fulfill that requirement in terms of Superman and Batman, giving us an image which, while perhaps not of their actual deaths, showed us how they were at their endings, in their final years. Whether this story will actually ever happen in terms of "real" continuity is irrelevant: By providing a fitting and affective capstone to the Batman legend it makes it just that...a legend rather than an endlessly meandering continuity. It does no damage to the current stories of Batman in the present, and indeed it does the opposite by lending them a certain weight and power by implication and association. Every minor shift of attitude in the current Bruce Wayne's approach to life that might be seen in *Batman* or *Detective* over the next few years, whether intentionally or not, will provide twinges of excitement for the fans who can perceive their contemporary Batman inching ever closer to the intense and immortal giant portrayed in the *Dark Knight* chronicles. It also provides a special poignance...While I was doing some of the episodes of "Under the Hood" for the *Watchmen* text backups and especially upon seeing Dave's mockup photographs of the Minutemen in their early, innocent days, I felt as if I'd touched upon that sense of "Look at them all being happy. They didn't know then how it would turn out," that one sometimes gets when looking at old photographs. *Dark Knight* does this for the Batman to some degree, and I'd like to try to do the same for the whole DC cosmos in *Twilight*. I feel that by providing a capstone of the type mentioned above, but one which embraces the whole DC Universe rather than just a couple of its heroes, I can lend a coherence and emotional weight to the notion of a cohesive DC Universe, thus fulfilling the criteria set out in my ramblings about the effect of all this on the idea of DC continuity as mentioned above. Being set in a possible future, it does nothing that cannot be undone, and yet at the same time has a real and tangible effect upon the lives and activities of the various characters in their own books and their own current continuities. At the same time, by providing that capstone and setting the whole continuity into a framework of complete and whole legend, as Frank did in *Dark Knight*, we make the whole thing seem much more of a whole with a weight of circumstance and history that might help to cement over any shakiness left in the wake of *Crisis* and its ramifications. Even if we pull the threads of these various characters' circumstances together at some hypothetical point in the future, this does imply that there is a logical pattern or framework for the whole DC Universe, even if the resolution of the pattern is at a point 30 years in the hypothetical future.

This also fulfills the criteria that I outlined in my opening paragraphs concerning the commercial application of the idea. The framing device, which links the central story of *Twilight* to its possible crossover points with the mainstream DC Universe, is constructed so as to be detachable from the whole. While the whole story presented in the actual comic will have cutaways to what is going on in the present to show how the crossovers work, the main story line of *Twilight* will be working towards its resolution unimpeded. Thus, in order to make the central story line comprehensible to a wider audience than the trivia-mesmerized hordes of comic fandom, the link with the present can be ignored and effectively severed, leaving only a powerful and simple central story idea, that of an apocalypse for super-folk played out by warring factions against the fascinating backdrop of a drastically altered future, with all the plotting, romance, and intrigue of one of those stirring historical dramas about warring factions amongst the Medici or whatever. This central idea—that of a war and all its spectacular ramifications—makes it ideal material for a role-playing game...perhaps the ultimate superhero role-playing game. It also lends itself nicely to a wide range of other spinoff projects, including those in the toy soldier range. The apocalyptic mood of the series, tied in with current preoccupations and encapsulated in a phrase like the previously mentioned "Waiting for *Twilight*" could work nicely with regard to the advertising campaign as well as giving us a range of credible adult items such as badges, posters, and T-shirts. The story line would hopefully be resonant enough to provide a good springboard for new characters or revitalized old characters, and this again would work seamlessly when it came to actually orchestrating all this. A character who hasn't been seen yet...say, Barbara Randall's proposal for a female Flash...could be presented in *Twilight* as an old established character who's been in the Justice League for years. When the character appears on the newsstands in her own title some months later, this should strike a suitably ominous resonance back to the *Twilight* story line: Is it all coming true? Even if it doesn't all come true in every detail, even if, say, she never joins the Justice League, mightn't most of it come true? This is the sort of feedback effect that I want to foster. In addition to that, any changes that writers have planned for their characters in the future could be hinted at directly as having happened in the past, so that when they actually happen in the regular comic book, they have a meaning beyond that which they have on the surface. Even if plans change and certain things don't materialize as planned, then even *that* has its implications with regard to the Ragnarok proposed in *Twilight*, especially after certain key ambiguities that will be introduced in the final issues of this proposed crossover.

I should also point out (if only to start a new paragraph...I just noticed I didn't draw breath on the last page) that the fact that the meat of *Twilight*'s central story line is detachable from the crossover device means that *should* anyone see any potential in the ultimate superhero movie, bearing in mind that DC currently owns almost all of the really important superhero icons imprinted on the mass consciousness and could thus perhaps come up with something that legitimately laid claim to that title, then it will be simple to detach the central idea from the off-putting clutter of a massive continuity such as would almost certainly alienate the average non-comic-fan moviegoer. I'm talking about characters such as Superman, Batman, Wonder Woman, the Marvel Family, Blackhawk, Plastic Man, the Shadow, and all the other truly *classic* and publicly recognizable characters that DC is fortunate enough to have access to. Handled in the right way, with the inclusion of these classic figures, the *Twilight* story line could be presented as a spectacular and epic finale to the whole essential superhero dream. Like I say, anyway, it never hurts to consider these angles, just in case.

Okay, so now that the actual mechanics of this linking/framing device have been discussed, perhaps it would help if I told you what they actually are. Bear in mind that the details of this are subject to change, as long as the overall idea is sound, since I'm not absolutely sure about forthcoming events in the DC Universe that might invalidate some of this. I'm confident there'll be a way around any such problems anyway, so the following should still be fairly sound and useful.

The first thing we do is to solve the paradox mentioned earlier, concerning "Does *Dark Knight* really happen in the future?" and the attendant schism between those who want a concrete universe and those who want endless possibility free of the restrictions of a rigid cross-title continuity. At the same time, I'd also like to put right something that has bothered me since the resolution of *Crisis*, namely the fact that I actually *like* parallel world stories and that a lot of other creative people enjoy the freedom that gives them, too. Some of the better stories in DC's history have been those directly related to the idea of alternate Earths (including *Crisis* itself, paradoxically enough), and there are a lot of brilliant imaginary stories which display the same urges and the same ideas at work, albeit outside mainstream continuity. What I propose is something that would allow for the possibility of alternate world stories as well as the possibility of revisiting old, discarded continuities that still have charm without opening up the whole "Earth-One through 15" problem that prompted the Crisis in the first place. It will also be an idea central to the whole concept of this framing/linking device with which we connect the events of *Twilight* with the current continuity. What I propose, basically, is something like the following, subject to input by any creative people with prior claims on the characters I'm suggesting, of course...

Firstly, I understand that there is to be some restriction upon time travel in the revised post-*Crisis* continuity, which is all well and good by me. To consolidate the importance of these restrictions and their reverberations upon the various books that use time travel as a motif, I suggest that, as an example, some members of the Legion of Super-Heroes should volunteer for a reconnaissance mission exploring the time stream and testing its new limits with regard to their vehicles. Those Legionnaires might be selected for this that me and Paul have agreed between us are appropriate.

At the same time, in any other books that might have time travel problems, it could be mentioned in passing that from our own era, professor Rip Hunter was currently investigating the phenomenon in his time top.

Okay...now if Paul and Karen and everybody else involved are amenable to this, then I figure the next step is to introduce a scheme by the Time Trapper. The Time Trapper, living up to his name, intends to set up a sort of temporal fluke field in the time stream that will in effect make time travel in or out of this area all but impossible, thus trapping the Legionnaires who volunteered or were selected in the past unable to return. I suggest that the Legionnaires chosen should be some that Paul is able to do without for a few months, and maybe those that he'd like to see some changes made to. Like I say, these details can be sorted out later. The Time Trapper is maybe planning to trap these various Legionnaires in the past so that they cannot help prevent some plot he is planning to bedevil the Legion with in the future and might conceivably be useful as a plot springboard to Paul over in the Legion's own book. The important thing in terms of *Twilight* is that the Time Trapper successfully sets up his fluke field, which effectively distorts a whole stretch of the time stream from, say, 1990 to the year 2010. With very few exceptions, nothing can get in or out of this Time Tangle. Furthermore, as a result of an effect of the fluke field upon a continuum already sorely abused during the reality reordering of *Crisis on Infinite Earths*, within this bubble of fluke time, numerous alternate realities again become possible, if only for a limited 30-year stretch. Although we won't be exploring any of these realities save for one in *Twilight*, the possibilities there for story ideas in other books are limitless. Within the fluke, there are maybe worlds where the imaginary stories happened: What would the world of Superman Red/Superman Blue be like if you were to visit it 20 years on? Or the world in "The Death of Superman"? Is there a world perhaps like the old Earth-Two, or a world in which *Dark Knight* takes place? As well as opening up a wealth of story possibilities without opening up the attendant can of worms, it also provides a convenient trash bin for every story that DC ever published that didn't fit in with the continuity. Brother Power? It happened in the fluke. Prez? The fluke. The Rainbow Batman? In the fluke. Because travel by people in the mainstream continuities into the fluke zone of the time stream would be presented as all but impossible except in exceptional circumstances, the chance for the infinite number of maybe-worlds in the fluke to spill over and damage the mainstream continuity would be minimal.

Okay...so while the LSH volunteers are exploring the altered post-*Legends* time stream, the Time Trapper springs his ultimate time trap and the fluke comes into existence. The group of Legionnaires find themselves trapped upon an Earth circa the year 2000, albeit only one of the Earths A.D. 2000 that now exist in the fluke. As a result of the sudden moiré effect rippling across the time stream from the fluke, any time travelers in the time stream "at the time of the fluke coming into operation" (which, as we shall see later, poses an interesting little subparadox) are drawn to the same point, trapped within the enclosed multiple continuities of the fluke. These include Rip Hunter and some others who I'll detail later. They find themselves cut off from their own times on a world in which the superhero ideal seems to have gone badly awry, with events seeming to be leading to a terribly apocalyptic war between superheroes. As they struggle to find a way to return to their own times, they experience the terrible events which are going on in the world around them, these events making up the central core narrative of *Twilight*. Eventually, they find a way to escape, the Legionnaires and others returning to their respective times while Rip Hunter returns to the present, which is where our story proper "begins," if such a time-crossed tale can be said to have a real beginning. At some point during his unwanted stay in the future, Rip Hunter has met a 20-years-older version of John Constantine, who, as ever, seems to be a prime mover behind the scenes in the events going down in this world. Prior to Hunter's escape, Constantine circa A.D. 2000 has told Hunter that he must find and enlist the aid of John Constantine circa 1987, who will help him in alerting Earth's super-people to the possible danger waiting in their future and thus avert it. This Constantine and Hunter proceed to do, crossing over into a couple of current books in the process, or merely making phone calls and writing letters if a guest appearance was too much trouble for the various creative teams involved. They could also talk to a few people in the pages of *Twilight* itself, this narrative providing the stuff that makes up this linking/ framing device, as the two prophets of doom meet different reactions to their tale of a nightmare future waiting to claim the world. The mechanics of this as a crossover device, as explained above, allow all the creative people involved to do or not do whatever the hell they please while still directly or indirectly involving them in the concept of *Twilight* as a whole. Think how much mileage the *Thor* writers have got from the idea of the Norse gods trying to do something to prevent Ragnarok, or fearing that Ragnarok was about to come upon them, and I'm sure you'll get the possibilities.

Okay, so now that everybody is at least hopefully conversant with the concepts behind this framing/linking sequence, I'll go on to discuss the meat of the story, the terrible possible future that Constantine and Hunter are warning everybody about. To do this I'll start off with a brief description of the world and its background before moving on to give sketches of the main characters who make up the events which happen in this world.

The world of *Twilight* is not a world where the superheroes have deliberately taken over, but one where they have inherited the Earth almost by default as various social institutions started to crumble in the face of accelerating social change, leaving the superheroes in the often unwilling position of being a sort of new royalty. Even though government and civic authority has all but disintegrated, the various areas of America each have their own coteries of protecting super-folk to look after them, and the superheroes have thus tended to group into clans, each looking after a certain province. There are numerous "Houses" of this nature dividing America up into a kind of feudal barony system, effectively, in terms of politics if not in terms of technology, which is as advanced as one might expect by 2000 A.D.

The development of this future society is something which I intend to go into in detail, although not here. I want to avoid the sort of nuke-blighted future that has been a feature of *Dark Knight*, *Watchmen*, *Ronin*, and a lot of other futures presented in comic books and other media, like the Road Warrior films and their ilk, because I feel that is becoming something of a cliché, and, while it's gone some way towards serving its purpose and alerting people to the dangers of the present day by pointing out the possible effects waiting in the future, I personally feel that it's all but outlived its usefulness as a motif in 20th-century fiction and would prefer to come up with a different kind of holocaust. What I want to show is a world which, having lived through the terrors of the fifties through the early nineties with overhanging terror of a nuclear Armageddon that seemed inevitable at the time, has found itself faced with the equally inconceivable and terrifying notion that there might not *be* an apocalypse. That mankind might actually have a future, and might thus be faced with the terrifying prospect of having to deal with it rather than allowing himself the indulgence of getting rid of that responsibility with a convenient mushroom cloud or 900. Following the predictions made by Alvin Toffler and other eminent futurologists, I want to show a future in which everything from the family structure to the economy is decentralizing into an entirely new form that, while it might ultimately be better suited to survival in the changed conditions of life in the 21st century, is a constant and incomprehensible state of flux and chaos for those living through it, caught in one of those violent historical niches where one mode of society changes to another, such as the Industrial Revolution for example. The people of our world find themselves going through an upheaval more abstract and bizarre but every bit as violent, and as their institutions crumble in the face of the wave of social change, they find themselves clinging to the various superhero clans who represent their only anchor of stability in this rapidly altering world. At the time in which our central *Twilight* story line takes place, there are eight "Houses," each containing a different superhero clan, scattered across America, although as we shall see some of these are pretty well abandoned or nonfunctioning in any active sense. I'll deal with these one at a time, and introduce our main characters along the way, House by House.

THE HOUSE OF STEEL

This is one of the two most powerful clans, and it dominates the eastern seaboard around New York and environs. Alternatively, if I change my mind it could be outside America altogether and set in the Arctic Circle, based around a new Fortress of Solitude. This is because the House of Steel consists of the clan founded by Superman. We have Superman himself, a morally troubled figure who doesn't know what's best to do about the chaos he sees surrounding him, but who has come to accept

that the Houses provide the only real permanent structure in a destabilizing world and are thus important to maintain. Superman has married and raised a couple of kids, and the person that he has married is Wonder Woman, who has had an identity change to Superwoman to accommodate her new stature. We see the genuine and powerful love between these two in the face of the perils of the world surrounding them and the desire to do what's best. They are also troubled by their two offspring. One of these is a new Superboy, and he's about 18 when the story opens, and he's real bad news. The other child is a less delinquent Supergirl, a new one who, like Superboy, has been born of the union between Superman and Wonder Woman but who is much kinder and gentler, more her mother's child. Having three members in the Superman class and Wonder Woman (Superwoman) herself, they are obviously a clan to be reckoned with.

THE HOUSE OF THUNDER

The House of Thunder is the other major power, and it possesses members with power in the same class as that of the House of Steel. The House of Thunder is composed of the Marvel family, plus additions. Captain Marvel himself is the patriarch, and is if possible even more estranged and troubled by the state of the world than Superman is, perhaps because the Marvel family are having to come to terms with the difficulties of having human alter egos along with everything else, a point I'll return to when I outline the plot. Alongside Captain Marvel, there is Mary Marvel, who the Captain has married more to form a bona fide clan in opposition to that of Superman than for any other reason. There is also Captain Marvel Junior, now an adult superhero every bit as powerful and imposing as Captain Marvel in his prime, but forced to labor under the eternal shadow of a senior protégé. To complicate things, Captain Marvel Junior and Mary Marvel are having an affair behind the Captain's back, Guinevere and Lancelot style, which has every bit as dire consequences as in the Arthurian legends. The other member of the Marvel clan is Mary Marvel Junior, the daughter of Captain and Mary Marvel Senior. Mary Junior is fated to be part of a planned arranged marriage to the nasty delinquent Superboy during the course of our story, in order to form a powerful union between the two Houses. Peripheral to all this but perhaps interesting, somewhere in the House of Thunder (which rises up from the middle of Los Angeles over on the west coast, by the way) there are quarters occupied by those characters from the Fawcett universe who can no longer cope with life in an increasingly realistic and difficult outside world. These include a sad and aging Mr. Tawky Tawny and perhaps even Mr. Mind. Please don't laugh...I think I can make it work. The Houses of Steel and Thunder face each other across the country, with the various minor Houses and constellations gathered somewhere in between, vying for the power that's left over after the two major Houses have had their share.

THE HOUSE OF TITANS

One of the two foremost clans making up this collection of lesser Houses is a clan composed of the remains of the Teen Titans, now grown-up and a hell of a lot grimmer and more frightening than they ever were in the past. They are led by an adult Nightwing, who, trying to emulate and live up to the reputation of the Batman, has become every bit as driven and vicious as his mentor but who lacks the depth of compassion and understanding that separates the Batman from all the other grim vigilantes. As a result, Nightwing is not an altogether nice character. This isn't helped by the fact that Starfire has been killed some years earlier during a period when all the aliens were being forcibly expelled from Earth by the big powers, who feared alien influence moving in to take advantage of the disruption and uncertainty in society. Other Titans who have died include Jericho, while some, including Kid Flash and Wonder Girl, have left the Titans to take up with other clans, a cause of bitterness amongst the remaining Titans. These include an adult version of the Hawk (formerly of the Hawk and the Dove) who is maybe renamed Warhawk and who certainly lives up to his name...a sort of super-Rambo who Nightwing tends to use as a human weapon. There is also the Cyborg. Vic Stone has had some rejection problems with his bioelectronic parts in the time that's elapsed since our present day, and as a result more and more of his body has been replaced by mechanical parts, including one lobe of his brain. He is forced into considering the frightening question of when exactly something stops being a person and starts being a machine. How much do you have to take out and replace before there's just a robot left?

One thing that helps take Stone's mind off his own problems is that he must keep an eye on the Changeling, who has serious problems of his own. When the terrors of the world finally became too much for his jokey, lighthearted façade, the Changeling did what he always said he'd do: he went crazy. Not completely crazy, but more and more these days he stays in animal form, or worse, in some awful halfway form between the human and the animal. Worse still, increasingly these days he is starting to adopt the forms of animals that don't exist outside the increasingly tortured confines of his mind. Before the story is out he will have adopted a new identity, calling himself the Chimera. The only other Titan is Raven, who is now an aging, very dignified sorceress. She stays with the Titans out of loyalty for the way they stayed with her in the past when she had troubles, but increasingly she finds herself drawn to the tempting notion of leaving the House of Titans and moving into one of the other Houses, which is far more suited for her, this being the next House on our agenda for discussion. (The House of Titans, incidentally, can be constructed around the remains of the original Titans Tower, although I must confess I forget exactly where that's situated geographically.)

THE HOUSE OF MYSTERY

Nothing to do with the previous House of Mystery except in name, this House of Mystery is built around Baron Winter's Georgetown mansion and is the residence of a number of DC's supernatural characters. These include Jason Blood, a.k.a. the Demon, maybe the Spectre, Zatara, Doctor Fate, and a strange amalgam of Baron Winter and Deadman. Baron Winter has had his mind burned out in a psychic battle some years earlier and is now just an empty shell, except when he's inhabited by the spirit of Boston Brand, who uses the Baron's body as a kind of holiday home in the land of the living. The other person in residence at this new House of Mystery is a reformed Felix Faust. The supernatural presences at the House have very little to do with the outside world and have instead devoted their pooled knowledge and talents to plumbing the depths of the universe's many mysteries, being all but inactive in the world of men.

THE HOUSE OF SECRETS

Again, similar only to its predecessor in name, this House of Secrets is the residence of a rough conglomerate of the few surviving super-villains that haven't been wiped out in an earlier Justice League-headed purge on super-villains which makes up part of the historical background of our story. The villains, all considerably older than today, who make up this fraternity are roughly as follows, subject to revision: Luthor, the Joker, Gorilla Grodd, Captain Cold, Catwoman, Chronos, and Star Sapphire along with maybe Dr. Sivana and a couple of others. This House is powerful enough to defend itself against occasional attacks by the other hero-centered clans but isn't otherwise especially active and thus tends to get left alone, largely because the province that these villains protect, somewhere up in the reaches of Nevada, is just as well looked after as the places controlled by the heroes, whereby hangs some sort of moral.

THE HOUSE OF JUSTICE

The House of Justice, built around the remains of the JLA's old cavern headquarters, is the residence of the remains of the Justice League. This is the most important of the lesser Houses, along with the Titans. The lineup of the Justice League at the time of our story includes Captain Atom and the Blue Beetle, an Aqualad that has grown up to be the new Aquaman, and a Wonder Girl who has taken on the mantle of Wonder Woman after Wonder Woman herself opted to become Superwoman upon marrying Superman. In addition to this there is the Flash (Wally West) and the new female Flash, Slipstream (although I prefer the name Joannie Quick, but this is by the by). There is also Captain Comet and the new female Dr. Light.

THE HOUSE OF TOMORROW

This is the House built by all the various exiles from other eras who have been trapped in this world by the Time Trapper's fluke. These include Rip Hunter and some members of the Legion, but since anyone passing through that strip of time stream at any time in the "future" or "past" would be sucked into that time zone as well, there are a paradoxical number of past and future selves of the various time travelers also caught there, including two or three different Rip Hunters and two or three versions of the Legion at different stages in their development. Other time travelers might very well include Tommy Tomorrow and even maybe an earlier version of the Time Trapper himself, who might very well provide the help these stranded travelers need to return to their own times. It strikes me that amongst these travelers there might also be Space Ranger and Jonah Hex. This might even be an opportunity to return Jonah Hex to his original Western continuity, where we know he will eventually end up according to previous DC history. It would also be convenient to explain that the so far unassigned radioactive hellworld that Hex's adventures have been set on is one of the maybe-Earths that exist in the fluke. Another possibility that struck me for time travelers stuck at the House of Tomorrow would be past selves of those DC characters who've travelled through the time barrier in their past adventures. One that I'd like the limited use of is Barry Allen, the Flash. I understand that there might be reservations about this, but I think I could do it all lucidly enough to avoid any complications. Anyway, the people at the House of Tomorrow aren't terribly active since they are trying their best not to influence events going on around them too much with an eye to possible repercussions in the future if they mess around with the time stream in the past. Also, their energies are mainly directed towards finding a way out of their time trap...which, as I mentioned, is a problem that might be solved by a past self of the Time Trapper himself.

THE HOUSE OF LANTERNS

The House of Lanterns, at the time our story opens, is abandoned and shattered, since all the Green Lanterns, being self-confessed agents of an alien power (the Guardians) have been banished from Earth during the anti-alien purges mentioned earlier, which resulted in Starfire's death, and which also resulted in the banishment from Earth of the Martian Manhunter, the Hawks, and any other alien characters I may have forgotten. Superman, since his own alien culture no longer exists, and since he has lived on Earth since infancy, has been made a citizen of the United States and is thus exempt. Anyway, while the House of Lanterns no longer exists upon Earth, an emergency House of Lanterns has been set up upon one of the moons of Mars. (There's one that seems from radio telescope scans to be either hollow or riddled with caves, but I can't remember whether it's Phobos or Deimos.) Here, the exiled Green Lanterns conspire with the other space powers, including the Martians and Thanagarians, to restore their power on Earth. The space powers, knowing through their intelligence sources of the imminent joining of the House of Steel and the House of Thunder by marriage, are afraid that such a union will enable the Super/Marvel family to bring all the Houses under control and unify Earth as a resourceful planet ruled by a pantheon of invincible gods. The space people fear that such an empire might soon set its sights upon territories that are currently the provinces of the Hawks, Guardians, or Martians. The actual Green Lanterns residing in the House of Lanterns at this time are a reformed Sinestro; Carol Ferris and Guy Gardner, Green Lanterns of Earth; Sodam Yat, the Daxamite "Ultimate Green Lantern" whose existence I hinted at in the story Kevin and I did for the *Green Lantern Corps Annual*; and maybe an aging Tomar Re, just because I'd like to see what parrot-men look like when they get old.

Okay, so that's about it for the Houses. Not all the superheroes, however, are actually members of clans. Those who aren't in clans are almost totally inactive, and for the most part inhabit one of the rundown barrio areas of either Gotham or Metropolis, both cities transformed beyond anything we've seen previously by the passage of time and change. The way I see it, the scenes in the barrio will take up much of the book and will probably be some of the livelier ones. The barrio is a superhero slum where all the old heroes come to die. As I see it, almost every passerby, shopkeeper, and incidental background character there used to be some sort of super-character or other 20 years ago. A lot of them are drunks, some of them are hookers or panhandlers; the majority eke whatever living they can out of dead-end jobs, while there are a few who have actually adapted to their changed circumstances quite successfully, and certain others who still actively carry on their own personal vendettas against injustice, albeit secretly. I'll list these various characters one at a time, mainly because I have fairly specific ideas about all of them that I'd like to get across so that you'll know who we're talking about before I get on to the actual plot. Most of the following have been altered almost beyond recognition, so this is fairly necessary.

JOHN CONSTANTINE

Constantine is about 20 years older, but obviously hasn't changed a bit, except for the fact that he's living with a woman and has been for the past 15 years. This woman might even turn out to be the Fever character that I introduced in my two-part *Vigilante* story a while back. Anyway, she and Constantine are to all intents and purposes married, and are obviously loving it. Constantine is still into the same sort of scams and wheeler-dealing, and in the whole story of *Twilight* he seems to be the only character who has his finger upon all the pulses and knows exactly what's going on in this maze of plot and counterplot between the various factions involved. He thus becomes a central character in the story, and it strikes me that Constantine would probably be a logical choice to launch into his own title off the back of this crossover, if you're looking for characters to do that with.

SANDY'S PLACE

Sandy's Place is one of the pivotal settings in our story. It's the main barroom in the barrio, and thus acts as a meeting point for a lot of the characters involved. Its proprietress is Sandra Knight, formerly the Phantom Lady. I'll run through the main characters who hang out at her joint, starting with the Lady herself.

THE PHANTOM LADY

Sandra Knight is now somewhere approaching 50 and has a sort of ripe, down-at-the-heel Joan Collins sexuality to her still. She runs the bar and acts as sort of a den mother to all the regulars who drift in there, maybe occasionally sleeping with one of them for old times' sake, although never anything lasting or serious. She's a nice woman doing her best to get by in a difficult world who nevertheless seems to have a lot of care and affection to lavish on others, as evidenced by her care of the next member of our cast up for discussion.

THE DOLL MAN

Darrel Dane is probably the most unsettling and pitiful character in our cast, even though we don't see much of him. What has happened, basically, is that the constant shrinking and growing, plus the effects of the square-cube law with regard to size increase, have taken their toll upon him. As the years passed, his bones became brittle and would break easily if he stayed at normal size for too long. Eventually it became easier to stay at six inches tall all the time, but this itself was not the end to the problem. Remaining at a constant six inches, Dane's body and brain began to adapt to their new size, redistributing their mass and rearranging their neurons for greater comfort and effectiveness. As a result, Dane has slowly changed shape into a horrible elongated insect man, still six inches high, whose bone structure has altered dramatically into something barely recognizable as anything that used to be human, although just recognizable enough to be disturbing. His brain has also had to change to accommodate drastically reduced brain size and capacity. He's still intelligent, but it's a non-human intelligence and he can barely communicate coherently with normal humans anymore. Sandra Knight has taken him under her wing. She keeps him in a vivarium behind the bar (it brings in enough money to pay for his food, and he's too alien to mind being displayed like this, so what the hell, although she still feels bad about it), and Sandy is almost the only person that the former Doll Man can talk to and make himself understood. She's also the only person unselfish enough to be able to bear the creepy little bastard running up her arm to nestle on her shoulder and talk into her ear in his eerie, piping, almost inaudible voice. Darrel Dane, while he's the only person other than Sandy who lives at the bar full-time in his tank, is not the only lame duck that Sandy extends her sympathy to.

UNCLE SAM

Uncle Sam is the character I'm most looking forward to writing, taking my cue both from the character of Uncle Sam in Robert Coover's excellent book about the Rosenberg execution, *The Public Burning*, and from the portrayal of Richard Nixon in Robert Altman's *Secret Honor*. In Coover's book there is a sort of giant metaphorical narrator called Uncle Sam who is exactly like the old Quality character right down to his dialogue, which is a sort of breathless rush of manic cornball philosophy and darkly lyric jingoism. He talks endlessly about his exploits, boasting in Paul Bunyan fashion about how he strode across the sea, up to his red-and-white-striped thighs in the deepest waters of the Pacific and rooted out his archenemy, the Phantom, wherever he should strike. In the Altman film, there is a harrowing portrait of Richard Nixon putting himself through a solitary self-confessional, sitting in a lonely room and vomiting his history into a tape recorder, helplessly spilling out all the things that he'll never be able to tell another living soul for fear of his life. All the stuff about Watergate that nobody ever suspected, all the stuff about Kissinger and the Shah, all the places where the bodies are buried. As I see my Uncle Sam, he's a hopeless derelict with no power at all, and nobody is even entirely sure whether he actually is *the* Uncle Sam or some wino dressed up like him. He sprawls in a dark corner of the bar, drinking the last years of his life away and babbling to himself in a mixture of the two styles outlined above, his cornball jingoistic reminiscences occasionally leading his erratic memory up alleyways in the American past down which he'd rather not stray. Since his ramblings will have a kind of dark poetry to them, I see him as acting as a sort of surreal Greek chorus or something, his senile monologues having suggestive resonance within the main framework of the story. He is one of the other social cripples that Sandy can always find a free drink for, even though he is not an actual physical cripple yet, despite the fact that his liver is obviously deteriorating rapidly. The only actual physical cripple to regularly visit Sandy's Place is our next character for discussion.

BLACKHAWK

For a few issues it might not even be apparent that Blackhawk is a cripple. This is because he has a perfect pair of prosthetic legs to replace his own legs which, Douglas Bader style, are now missing. He is a sinister and obsessive figure, still fighting a private war inside his head which has never quite been the same since the mission in which all his teammates died and in which he lost his legs. He lives in a single room in the barrio, paid for out of the remains of the fortune that once funded Blackhawk Island. I figure at some point in the Second World War he got his hands on some Nazi gold and still has a reserve of it somewhere, albeit a dwindling one. Gold is more than ever a firm economic unit in the chaotic economic flux situation of this future world, so he could probably afford to live a less spartan existence. He just doesn't want to, rising at five every morning and strapping on his legs before working out in the gym and the flight simulator that he keeps at a secret location downtown. In the evenings he maybe calls in at Sandy's for a glass of Perrier before going on to cruise around the barrio's leather bars. At the bars, he singles out young men according to some system known only to him and offers them employment in some unspecified endeavor. We eventually find out that he is recruiting a new squadron of Blackhawks to replace his dead friends, and that he has seven F1-11 bombers hidden in a massive underground hangar that he has invested the remains of his gold into. He picks up boys and asks their names. Maybe one of them says, "My name's Charles." Blackhawk pats him on the shoulder and smiles and says, "I think I'll call you Chuck." A boy called Andrew becomes André and so on. Blackhawk is a sort of obsessive urban fascist with a survivalist mentality and a strong sociopathic streak. He is obviously building up his squadron of vicious leather-queen Blackhawks and equipping them to act out some terrible version of his own internal holocaust. You can take the boy out of the war, but you sometimes can't take the war out of the boy, and Blackhawk's new squadron will almost certainly figure prominently in the explosive climax to this series.

PLASTIC MAN

Like most of the old Quality characters, Plastic Man often calls by at Sandy's before moving on uptown to look for trade. Plastic Man is a male prostitute or gigolo or whatever the polite term might be. Thanks to his elastic consistency, he can keep himself looking young and attractive for a lot longer than many of his fellows, and it is this facet of his talent that he now exploits for a living. He is employed by the "Seductive Winks" escort agency, managed by one W. Winks. He is, in fact, the only employee of the agency. He is likable and kind despite his shady occupation, and everyone gets on with him. With traces of his past as Eel O'Brien finally starting to show through, he is a sort of attractive and romantic neighborhood hoodlum who always dresses well and buys flowers for old ladies and drinks for bums and apples for kids. There is a more somber side to him that he probably only reveals to old friends like Sandy, who is the only person whom he'll sleep with for nothing these days. Although he seems permanently youthful, he has started to notice a lessening of the elasticity in the skin around his lower back. It's becoming saggy and feels like crepe, like something that has been stretched once or twice too often and is becoming shapeless. Plastic Man has a sort of horrible half-formed vision in his head that he doesn't like to think about concerning how he might finally end up. He might end up as just a puddle. He often wakes up screaming in the dead of the night from dreams about this, and the shades that he habitually wears now are there to hide the tired and worried look around his eyes as much as anything else. Woozy Winks is a roguishly half-likable but mostly disgusting old pimp who will get a phone call from Kathy Kane (yeah, I know the Earth-One Batwoman died, but the one on Earth-Two didn't and has presumably been living in anonymous retirement on Earth-Composite ever since the Crisis) and notify Plas, who will go round to her mansion to keep Ms. Kane company for the evening, giving Woozy a cut of the subsequent monies. I see Plastic Man as being a sort of reluctant hero who'll come through in the end.

Okay...those are the main characters who hang out at Sandy's, although most of the other characters pass through from time to time. These include:

CONGORILLA

Another character that I'm looking forward to doing, and one of the nastier characters in our assembled cast. Basically, what has happened to Congo Bill is that he got old. His human body got older and older while at the rub of a ring he could transmit his body to that of a powerful and immortal sacred golden gorilla. Ask yourself, what would you do? Anyway, Bill eventually decided to stay in the body of the gorilla forever and now is quite a wealthy and successful local businessman, a golden gorilla wearing a business suit and even managing to talk just about recognizably, even if some of it has to be done in sign language. The sort of operation he runs is a sort of lucrative small-time criminal organization that services the bars and the gambling dens and the brothels and also supplies most of the barrio's drug traffic. His activities will bring him into contact with lots of the other characters...putting protection pressure on Sandy's bar, for example, or having Woozy Winks beaten up for non-union pimping, and assuming that the barrio is set in the remains of Gotham, which I'm starting to favor more and more, then effectively he becomes the new "Gorilla Boss of Gotham City." He has a dark secret in his closet, however...almost literally. The body of Congo Bill, now over 90 years old, refuses to die. The gorilla mind that has been trapped in it unfairly refuses to let go and is hanging on with a fierce and horrible willpower. Unable to bring himself to kill it outright, Congorilla keeps the shackled and naked old man in special rooms at his apartment, feeds it garbage, and hopes it will die soon, but it doesn't. It just lies in the corner and snarls weakly when he enters and fixes him with its ancient glaring eyes as he gives it its food.

GREEN ARROW AND BLACK CANARY

Oliver and Dinah have both retired from costumed crime-fighting and are now co-editors of a small but vital and thriving radical newspaper that serves the barrio and will be useful in getting over background information quickly and stylishly. Oliver and Dinah are two of the nicest and most normal people in the series, both fiercely committed and tireless in their efforts, both loving each other very much despite the violent rows that they have learned to weather and almost come to enjoy as part of their relationship. Their paper is called *Black Feathers*, and on its masthead there is a symbol of a drawn-back arrow about to be fired, fletched with black flight feathers.

THE QUESTION

The Question is a freelance investigator...a sort of masked Philip Marlowe who doesn't make very much money and who usually ends up taking cases just for the interest or the moral necessity. He's quite good friends with Oliver and Dinah and often gives them the inside dope on situations that he has knowledge of for reporting in *Black Feathers*. He and Oliver have strong political differences but are firm friends despite this. When our story opens, the Question is investigating an impossible locked-room murder mystery involving a midget and a six-foot-six-tall call girl into heavy bondage. Don't worry, I'll explain later. It's all vitally relevant.

THE BATMAN

Nobody's actually seen him for years. He's rumored to be around, he's rumored to be active, and he's rumored to be doing something, but nobody knows what or even really if. He might have died years ago.

THE SHADOW

See "The Batman."

In actual fact, these two crime-fighters have joined forces in a clandestine bid to rid the Earth of the oppressive and dominating superhero Houses forever, so that mankind can get on with its own destiny. We won't learn this until later in the series, although they play a big part in the ending. As an aside, are Tarzan and Doc Savage in the public domain yet? No big deal, but I'd really like a sort of secret council of the immortals: Batman, the Shadow, Doc Savage, and Tarzan, all planning to start the revolution that will rid Earth of the super-people forever. Being basically more elemental forces than people, these characters have remained exactly the same, except they got tougher.

THE METAL MEN

Very few of these survive. Platinum is working as a waitress in a sort of weird sci-fi autosex bar, while Iron is working as a construction worker, slowly corroding and losing his faculties as the rust claims his mind, no hope of a resurrection should he be damaged, since creator Will Magnus passed away years ago. Tin is destroyed, as is Mercury. Gold has gone into hiding, mainly because of the fact that, as mentioned earlier, gold is more in demand than ever, and there are a lot of people who would like to capture him and melt him down. We get to see Gold towards the end, but he isn't much in evidence throughout the rest of the series. The Metal Man with the strangest fate is Lead, who has become an animated part of the shielding surrounding a closed-down nuclear reactor that is still considered to be dangerous. As a result of his activities, Lead is radioactive and will not be able to go near anyone for about six million years. The Metal Men are not major characters, but I think we should be able to get some darkly comic stuff out of them, as well as a lot of genuine poignance.

ROBOTMAN

Still alive and clanking after all these years, this former Doom Patrol member is one of the few people hanging around the barrio who still has an ear amongst the superheroes in the Houses. He is friendly with Cyborg, of the Titans, whom he is maybe helping to adjust to his new, mostly robotic, state. He also has contact with the Justice League, since he was once close to the Teen Titans and since three ex-Titans—Wonder Girl, Kid Flash, and Aqualad—are now amongst the Justice League membership. Mostly, though, he just hangs around the barrio, maybe going out for an evening at the cinema with Platinum when she's finished work, or calling by at the construction site to talk to Iron. I figure a character who can cross the social boundaries will be useful, and it's nice to have someone from the Doom Patrol represented.

ADAM STRANGE

Adam Strange is trapped on Earth, but is still in contact with the alien alliance based around the new House of Lanterns on the moon of Mars. He is sort of a mole, and he will eventually figure largely in the aliens' plan to invade Earth and "liberate" it from superhero dominance. We see him around a lot, but don't realize who he is until near the end of the series.

OTHER CHARACTERS

There are maybe other characters that I don't have anything clear in mind for as yet but who I'll want to include when the time comes. I figure I ought to list them here, so that any real problems can be spotted in advance. I might want to use the Challengers of the Unknown, the Golden Age Flash, Roy Raymond, Bobo the Detective Chimp, Johnny Quick, the Black Condor, the Ray, Sarge Steel, and perhaps a few old villains from here and there. One thing that this series will enable us to do, if it should be called for, is to simply introduce a new and revamped group like the Challengers of the Unknown as an established fact, to try them out on the reader before launching them in a new title, which should be borne in mind.

Okay, I think that's about it as far as the character sketches go, so I'll get down to a sketchy outline of the central plot. This is the area I have the least worked out in detail, although I have the overall picture pretty clearly, so maybe I'll just trust to luck and hope it comes together as I go along. If not, I hope you'll bear with me, and I'll clarify and polish the weak points at some later date. As before, since the plot comes in two sections, with the central narrative and the framing/linking device, I'll discuss the plot in two parts for the sake of greater clarity, starting with a description of the events that make up the framing sequence. As before, since this is a time-travel story, telling things in a chronological sequence is sometimes difficult to do without getting muddled, but I'll give it my best shot:

THE PLOT (1)

The plot of the framing device is as follows: The story starts at its ending in a one-page prologue that takes place at the end of 1987 in a bar someplace in New York. John Constantine sits drinking alone, looking very bitter and pissed off at somebody or other. A striking and personable blonde enters the bar and, noticing Constantine, leans over and asks him for a light. Constantine, sitting there with a crumpled letter in one bunched fist and a glass in the other, glances up at her and then stares at her as if transfixed. We close up on his face and then move into flashback. Basically, the whole series is what passes through Constantine's mind in the two seconds it takes him to respond to the girl asking him for a light.

We flash back to the beginning of 1987, when Constantine is surprised by a visit from Rip Hunter, whom he doesn't know but who appears to know everything about Constantine, including some very personal details that Constantine has never told a living soul about. Intrigued, Constantine listens to Hunter's story. Hunter tells him about how he's been marooned in time for subjective months, stranded at the House of Tomorrow in the world of the Twilight. Hunter tells him about how, in this world, he had met up with an older version of John Constantine who was somehow instrumental in Hunter's escape back to his own time after the events to be chronicled in *Twilight* have concluded. This elder Constantine, explaining about the fluke that exists in the time stream, explains that there is a better-than-good chance that, of the potential future Earths waiting in the fluke down the time stream from our present, this future Earth is the one most likely to actually happen, with all of its chaos and carnage. It's a world of war, and it ends with all of the super-beings being either killed or exiled from Earth forever. Giving Hunter enough personal information to convince the younger Constantine and get him to aid Hunter in his mission to alert the people concerned and avert this nightmare future, the elder Constantine sends Hunter back in time with his dire story of horrors waiting in the future that must be averted. Hearing Hunter's tale (although the readers don't hear it all at first), Constantine the younger is convinced enough to help the time traveler contact some of the various personages affected and tell them the bits of the story that are relevant to them, maybe in their own books or maybe in *Twilight* itself. This framing device has its own resolution, but I'll leave that till later.

THE PLOT (2)

This is the main central plot of *Twilight*, being the story that Hunter tells Constantine and that Constantine passes on to the other parties involved, and it deals with the world of the Twilight. I don't have it broken down issue by issue or anything, but the rough shape is something like this: In the middle 1990s or earlier, when society was starting to break down, many of the villains on Earth tried to take advantage of this situation by exploiting the uncertainty and disaster. Incensed by this, the current Justice League decide to go on the offensive for the first time and plan a careful campaign that will remove all the super-villains forever. They enlist the aid of a lot of other superheroes in this, and they are mostly very effective. So effective, in fact, that they begin to be seen as the only effective force for reason and order in a fast-crumbling world.

This goes to the assembled heroes' heads a little, and in an attempt to secure their new power base they pass a majority motion outlawing aliens from Earth. While this is passed and is rigorously enforced, it is one of the decisions that causes the first serious rift in the ranks of the assembled super-doers, with some small groups like the Titans starting to drift away from the main group. This process continues until the state of the ruling Houses is pretty much as described above, with the House of Secrets containing the only super-villains to survive the purge other than those who reformed, and the House of Lanterns demolished upon Earth and temporarily relocated upon Mars pending the planned secret invasion.

At the start of our story proper, there is quite a lot of different activity going on in the various camps. The Houses of Steel and Thunder, each suffering their own internal stresses, are preparing for the marriage of the delinquent Superboy with Mary Marvel Junior, daughter of the Captain and Mary Senior. This is a development that causes considerable anxiety all over the place: previously, even the two most powerful Houses could not attempt to exert any pressure upon the others for fear that the other Houses would unite against them. Both Houses knew that individually they couldn't hope to take on the assembled might of the Titans, Justice League, and others. This preserved a status quo of sorts. However, with the prospect of an alliance in the offing, it seems quite possible that the assembled forces of three people with the power of Superman, four people with the power of Captain Marvel, and Wonder Woman into the bargain could easily smash the most firm resistance. This prospect worries both the Houses of Titans and Justice tremendously. It also worries the villains remaining at the House of Secrets, who remember back to the purges of the nineties and shudder. It certainly alarms the people living in the barrio, who, though downtrodden, still have a certain amount of liberty, impoverished though it be, and are not actually living under the absolute dictatorship that could result from a marriage between the Houses of Steel and Thunder. The other major party alarmed by the prospect are the assembled alien forces that are conspiring out on the moon of Mars. They don't like the thought of a planet ruled by an unstoppable superhuman elite purely because it might very quickly pose a threat to the aliens' own well-being. Their plan is cryptic, but we learn a bit of it at a time. The main thrust of their plan is that they intend to use Adam Strange's presence as their agent on Earth to set up a Zeta-Beam link through which an invading army of Hawkpeople, superpowered Green Martians, and members of the Green Lantern Corps could materialize in the center of Times Square or somewhere, this plan being linked to a Thanagarian plan that has to be abandoned in the current issues of *Swamp Thing*, resurrected here to much more spectacular purpose.

Okay, so that's the rough background. Down at Sandy's the bums are hanging out, Uncle Sam muttering in the corner, Plastic Man dropping by for a drink with Blackhawk before they both go to cruise the bars uptown, Doll Man scuttling around his vivarium, and so on. Oliver and Dinah are publishing their newspaper, with the Question occasionally dropping by for a political argument with Ollie or to pass on a bit of information. His current case is one that has him totally mystified: A midget turned up at a rough trade bar, was seen by witnesses, finally vanishing to an upstairs room with a very tall, very beautiful call girl that nobody had ever seen before. When the door was broken down, this after nobody had emerged from the room for some several hours, the body of the midget was found bound and gagged, with his neck broken by a single clean blow. The room was locked with no other possible exit. The call girl was gone. There was no murder weapon. This little conundrum will continue to puzzle them throughout the series until we get a few shocking revelations at the end.

In the Houses themselves, things are unsettled. At the House of Steel, both Superman and Super(Wonder)woman are worried about their delinquent son and his increasingly difficult-to-conceal tendencies towards sadism and sociopathic behavior. They are also worried about their daughter, whom they cannot find a suitable suitor for, since Captain Marvel Junior doesn't appear to be interested in her.

Captain Marvel Junior's disinterest is largely due to the fact that he is madly and passionately in love with Mary Marvel Senior, and is liaising with her behind Captain Marvel Senior's back. Their relationship has grown difficult of late, largely because the increasingly erratic and cranky behavior of the Captain seems to have taken a turn for the worse. All of the Marvel family have had problems with the fact that they have two sets of bodies, neither of which ever age in the slightest, but Mary and Junior have solved this by more or less giving up their human identities. This doesn't worry them, probably because they are a lot closer to the ages of their counterparts than, say, Billy Batson is to his alter ego. (I should point out that for reasons I've yet to find a good explanation for, the Marvel family seem to grow, in their superhuman forms, to an ideal age, and then stop. Thus, Mary and Junior are both around 25 in their superhuman forms, as is Captain Marvel himself, since he is already the ideal age and hasn't grown up any more in the intervening years.) All three are still children if they happen to say *Shazam*, but the only one who still uses the word is the Big Red Cheese himself, unable to give up his human self as Mary and Junior have done. Hanging on to his Billy Batson identity has caused a lot of problems for the Captain, as well as in his relationship with his wife, but these seem to have become a lot better recently. Now, however, there is a new element that is perhaps even more threatening. Whereas before Captain Marvel was wrapped up enough in his personal problems to leave Mary and Junior lots of time together, lately he has started to make more normal marital demands upon Mary's time. He's even being extra nice to her, which worries her like anything. There are other oddities of behavior...the Captain will no longer go down and sit and talk with Mr. Tawky Tawny as had been a regular habit of his. In the midst of all this, there are problems with Mary Junior, who really doesn't want to marry Superboy at all.

In the background of all this we see John Constantine moving around amongst the various characters, gathering a bit of information here and there, obviously conducting some plan that he has in mind. (Remember this is the older Constantine we are talking about here.) He seems to be paying particular attention to the areas of stress between the various Houses, and it becomes quickly apparent that although he's older he's still in the habit of manipulating people in various cryptic ways for reasons unclear to anyone but himself.

As things progress, we see the paranoia concerning the coming wedding between the Houses of Steel and Thunder amongst the lesser Houses start to come to a boiling point. The Titans, directed by a ruthless and embittered Nightwing, maybe approach the Justice League proposing that the two Houses should join forces, along with maybe the villains in the House of Secrets, to stand against the possible threat of being overrun by the Houses of Steel and Thunder. Maybe an uneasy alliance is formed between the three Houses, although the Houses of Mystery and Tomorrow are not at all interested in joining in. A plan starts to emerge for a massed attack upon the Houses of Steel and Thunder, perhaps even on the wedding day itself, in the hope that both Houses can be eliminated and the country divided up between the victors.

Meanwhile, we see Blackhawk continuing to recruit his new Blackhawks, and we see Constantine starting to step up his plan, making contact with more and more of the people he's going to need to accomplish it. For one thing, we see him finally manage to make contact with the elite council of the Shadow, the Batman, and maybe Doc Savage and Tarzan as well, and learn of their plan to oust all the superheroes from Earth. Constantine seems eager to help them with this, although we aren't sure about how much of a double game he's playing. He also makes contact with Adam Strange, and through gaining Strange's confidence learns of the aliens' planned attack upon Earth. Constantine seems eager to help with this plan as well. In fact, as Constantine brushes against the various groups involved, it becomes clear that he is promising his undivided assistance to all of them. It is maybe during this period that he calls at the House of Tomorrow and makes the acquaintance of Rip Hunter, who also figures in his plans. Beyond this, he also spends a lot of time hanging out with the Question and around the offices of *Black Feathers*, seeming to be everywhere at once as he works his dubious and incomprehensible scheme.

As the plot builds up in momentum, it is this ingenious and baffling juggling act of Constantine's that becomes the main attraction. We see him urging on the Justice League/Titans to their attack upon the Houses of Thunder and Steel, and yet we see him call at the House of Thunder and speak to Captain Marvel himself, telling him of the planned attack. This is a key scene: Constantine tells the Captain of the attack and asks him not to do anything to help the House of Steel in the thick of the battle. The Captain politely asks Constantine why he should do this when he is, after all, supposedly intent upon cementing the union between the Houses of Steel and Thunder. Lighting a cigarette, Constantine smiles and says that he thinks the Captain already knows what the reasons are. The Captain flinches back from the match as Constantine strikes it with a look of terror which passes, changing into a smile at Constantine's cleverness. He agrees to go along with Constantine so far as it suits his own plans.

While urging the Titans/Justice League to strike while the iron is hot and simultaneously urging Captain Marvel not to defend his allies, Constantine is at the same time urging the Batman/Shadow group to hold back in their attack upon the superpowers until a more advantageous time. After he has explained his plan to them, although not to the reader, they agree. On top of all this, Constantine is acting as a fifth columnist to the planned alien invasion through Adam Strange. He urges Strange to commence the alien invasion after the Titans/League and the Houses of Steel and Thunder have had a chance to weaken and decimate each other at the wedding. This sounds sensible, and they readily agree.

As if this wasn't thoroughly confusing enough, Constantine also has a number of other irons in the fire. In the barrio he is seen at various times searching for two people. One of these is the vanished Metal Man, Gold. The other is an old crippled man who is reputed to live somewhere in the barrio whom nobody knows the history of. Eventually, Constantine finds both of these. Gold, after leading him on with some story or other, he tricks cruelly and has melted down. The old man, when he finds him, he is much more careful with. I don't know when I'll reveal the information, but this old man is in fact Metron, formerly of the New Gods, banished to Earth for some treachery that he's committed in the past when the temptation to uncover new knowledge became too much for the feeble moral restraints that he places upon himself. What Constantine wants with Metron is fairly straightforward: he wants the Mobius Chair, although we don't find out why until later. I should point out that these various plot threads will be spread out dramatically, intercut with developments in the lives of the other characters, so it won't all be about John Constantine, endearing though I obviously find him.

For example, while planning their raid upon the Houses of Steel and Thunder, the assembled Houses of Titans, Justice, and Secrets will attempt to press-gang various heroes in the barrio into their army, with mixed results. Some of the barrio heroes either reluctantly or willingly go along with the revolutionary Houses, while some other people are enlisted by Constantine to aid in *his* master plan. When we finally have the various factions set up and defined, even if there are some ambiguous areas, we let the climactic fireworks commence.

On the wedding day, the planned attack by the Titans, Justice League, and villains upon the Houses of Steel and Thunder gets under way. The losses are heavy upon both sides. Wonder Woman (the former Wonder Girl) is killed in battle by Superwoman (formerly Wonder Woman), who is herself killed by Captain Atom. Superboy is also killed, along with most of the Justice League, Titans, and super-villains. Captain Marvel, who has been expecting the attack after being warned by Constantine, is unharmed, while Captain Marvel Junior and Mary Marvel decide to take advantage of the confusion to flee into space, where they hope to make a new home. Supergirl goes with them. This leaves only Captain Marvel and a badly battered Superman standing amongst the bruised and bloodied remnants of an army of beaten superheroes. The attempted coup by the Titans/League has been successfully repulsed, and three Houses lie shattered, but all that remain of the two most powerful Houses of all are the two archetypal superheroes, standing back to back, waiting for what's going to be thrown at them next.

This turns out to be the alien invasion. Arriving by Zeta-Beam, an army of Hawkmen, Lanterns, and Martians pour into Earth and quickly get rid of what remains of the armies recruited by the Houses of Titans, Justice, and Secrets in their failed attempt at a coup. They then advance upon the main palaces. Superman isn't worried, since with Captain Marvel by his side the two of them should still be just about powerful enough to send the invaders packing.

This is where the surprise card is played. Captain Marvel isn't Captain Marvel. Captain Marvel has been dead ever since the story opened.

It had all started with little Billy Batson and his problem. There he was, unwilling to give up being human, still spending a lot of time in a child's body. The unfortunate thing was that though little Billy's body didn't age, his mind did. Trapped in a child's body but afflicted with adult needs, Billy went quietly...well, bats, I suppose. A lot of the problems were sexual. Physically, Billy was not capable of normal sex and thus pretty soon began to experiment with more bizarre variations such as S&M, visiting the appropriate bars in clothing that made him look as grown-up as possible while he still had the face and body of a child. At a certain club on a certain night, Billy had met a strikingly tall call girl who seemed to meet his every fantasy requirement. They went to a room upstairs together and locked it from within. Billy was tied up, and then agreed to be gagged. At this point the call girl began to melt and change shape, shimmering as if through a heat haze before Billy's startled eyes. In the end, instead of a six-foot-six human woman, Billy is staring at a seven-and-a-half-foot tall Green Martian man. It is J'onn J'onzz, the Martian Manhunter, on Earth incognito using his power of disguise. Billy, being gagged, cannot say *Shazam* and turn into Captain Marvel. Nor can he prevent the Manhunter snapping his neck with one blow of his hand. The Manhunter then walks out invisibly through the walls and leaves a dead midget and an insoluble mystery. The Manhunter has assumed the Captain's identity, being able to convincingly duplicate his powers, in order to catch Superman by surprise when the alien invasion finally comes. This is why he flinched when Constantine struck a match and why he didn't mind letting the three rebel Houses and the House of Steel tear each other to bits.

Upon realizing how he has been set up, Superman fights with the Martian Manhunter, killing him with his heat vision. However, by this point it is too late, and the assembled Martians and Green Lanterns have arrived. We have a powerful and intense sequence where Superman manages to smash his way through a lot of the alien forces singlehanded while being ring-whipped by the Lanterns, only to finally be beaten to death in single combat by the massive and frighteningly powerful Sodam Yat. The alien invasion is a complete success, and the coalition forces of the Martians, Guardians, and Thanagarians will now govern Earth forever and keep it nice and peaceful. It seems that in his dealings, Constantine's plan has gone awry, unless he actually meant to impose an alien dictatorship upon the Earth.

It is at this point that the final pieces fall into place. The alien conquerors find themselves suddenly attacked by a small army of superheroes, these mostly being those recruited by Constantine as well as the forces of the council made up of Batman, the Shadow, etc. Most of these are wearing thin golden armor, made from the body of the unfortunate Gold, which renders the otherwise omnipotent power rings of the Green Lanterns useless. The aliens are driven back and contained by the surprise attack of the heroes, and the battle seems to come to a Mexican standoff when one of the Hawkpeople or Green Lanterns points out that however valiantly the heroes fight, there is a massive army of combined extraterrestrial warriors ready to keep pouring onto the Earth until all resistance is squashed. It is at this point that Constantine plays his trump card.

Using the Mobius Chair of Metron, Constantine has visited the antimatter universe of Qward. In return for a firm promise of immunity for the planet Earth and its immediate system, Constantine has then sold them the secret of the Boom Tube, which he has also managed to wheedle from Metron. Thus, while the assembled aliens are preparing to pour into Earth via Zeta-Beam, Thanagar, New Mars, Rann, and Oa are currently being overrun by a vast army of Qwardian weaponeers.

Stunned, the aliens are forced to return quickly to their respective homes to fight wars upon their own soil that may take them centuries to win, if they win them at all. For the most part, the only heroes left on Earth are the non-powered variety, and most of these are more than prepared to take off their masks and go public. Constantine explains to them that under the guidance of the Batman, the Shadow, and all the rest, American society, free of government or a super-dictatorship, will start to organize itself along different lines, so that it can deal with the future without fear or anxiety. The days of the big powers are over, and henceforth America will be built up from much smaller and more flexible units, both socially and economically. The story of *Twilight* ends with a delighted John Constantine standing at the verge of a new utopia, free from the interferences of power, all super-folk banished from Earth forever.

Of course, the story that he gives to Rip Hunter to take back to his past self, while it gives the gist of all this, doesn't give the whole story. This comes home to the younger Constantine right at the very end of the series, when we wrap up the framing device. Somewhere earlier on in the continuity, we'll have a scene where somebody says to Constantine that if he isn't careful, one day he'll run into somebody craftier than himself and get into a whole mess of trouble, to which Constantine replies confidently and with some justification that there isn't anybody smarter than him.

At the very end of the series, he finds out differently. Having contacted all the hero groups and people involved and met with varying responses, Constantine is disturbed. Has he failed? Some of the people he warned have taken his advice, some haven't. Some he hasn't been able to reach at all. He is still thinking of this event in the future as being a terrible thing, and he fears that he might not have averted it well enough. All he has for consolation is the knowledge that according to Hunter, at some point in this future, he's going to meet a woman whom he will love very much for the rest of his life and who will fill a big lonely hole in him. He even knows, thanks to Hunter, how he will meet her: she'll come up to him in a bar and ask him for a light, their eyes will meet, and that will be that.

While he is musing over the pros and cons of this, Hunter delivers the last part of his message from the future Constantine, which he has been instructed not to give to the younger Constantine until after he has warned as many people as he can. Surprised, Constantine reads what may turn out to be the ultimate "Dear John" letter.

Written by his future self, the letter apologizes for using his younger self so cynically, but assures John the younger that it's all for the best. The older Constantine, having the advantage of hindsight, can remember everything that happened to his younger self, including meeting with Rip Hunter, getting told a terrible story, and then launching on a mission to warn everybody affected of what waited in their future and how they might avert it. The elder Constantine can even remember how that all worked out: the world of the Twilight came about anyway, often *because* of people's actions in response to his warning. He can even remember getting a letter handed to him, exactly the same as this one. He muses briefly over the paradox of who really wrote the letter originally before apologizing to his younger self again and consoling him with the fact that a wonderful woman is waiting in his near future, and that she will be worth everything.

Reading the letter, the younger Constantine is furious. It has turned out that there *is* someone craftier than John Constantine...namely, John Constantine 20 years older and smarter. Constantine has been conned by himself. Worse, since the person who tricked him is 20 years away in an unreachable future, Constantine has no way of getting vengeance upon the person who did this to him. Angered and enraged, he goes into a bar and sits with the crumpled letter in his hand, getting drunk. This is the end of the story, and we only have a final one-page epilogue that takes us back to the beginning, now that we've come full circle. The woman enters the bar and notices John, asking him for a light. He looks up and their eyes meet. She is beautiful. He knows instantly that he could love this woman forever, knows who she is, knows how happy he and all his future selves are going to be with her... and finally, perversely, he understands how he can have his revenge against his future self, how he can avert the circumstances that lead to *Twilight* by throwing a small but important spanner into the workings of destiny.

"Excuse me, have you got a light?"

Constantine looks at her and blinks twice before replying.

"No. I'm sorry. I don't smoke."

The woman shrugs, and after a while leaves the bar without speaking to Constantine any further. After she's gone he sits, dead drunk at a dimly lit corner table, and cries his cold and cynical heart out.

And that's it. I hope you can see how it's meant to fulfill all the requirements mentioned earlier. There are opportunities for new characters to get a springboard, old characters to get a shot in the arm, and all the merchandising you can handle in terms of games and stuff, at least as I see it. The warring Houses idea sounds ideal for a role-playing game, or maybe even a video game. The overall continuity is hopefully enhanced without being damaged in any irreversible way, and I think we might get a damn good yarn out of it into the bargain. Anyway, I seem to have gone on far longer than I intended so I better wrap this up. I'll be looking forward with interest to hearing what any of you have to say about all this when you've had a chance to read it. If any sections are incomprehensible and need clarifying then please give me a call.